PUNISHMENT
WITHOUT CRIME

ALSO BY ALEXANDRA NATAPOFF

*Snitching: Criminal Informants
and the Erosion of American Justice*

The New Criminal Justice Thinking (coeditor)

PUNISHMENT WITHOUT CRIME

HOW OUR MASSIVE MISDEMEANOR SYSTEM TRAPS THE INNOCENT AND MAKES AMERICA MORE UNEQUAL

ALEXANDRA NATAPOFF

BASIC BOOKS

New York

Basic Books
Hachette Book Group
1290 Avenue of the Americas, New York, NY 10104
www.basicbooks.com

Printed in the United States of America

First Edition: December 2018

Published by Basic Books, an imprint of Perseus Books, LLC, a subsidiary of
Hachette Book Group, Inc. The Basic Books name and logo is a trademark of
the Hachette Book Group.

The Hachette Speakers Bureau provides a wide range of authors for speaking
events. To find out more, go to www.hachettespeakersbureau.com or call
(866) 376-6591.

The publisher is not responsible for websites (or their content) that are not
owned by the publisher.

Print book interior design by Linda Mark.

Library of Congress Cataloging-in-Publication Data
Names: Natapoff, Alexandra, author.
Title: Punishment without crime : how our massive misdemeanor system
    traps the innocent and makes America more unequal / Alexandra Natapoff.
Description: New York : Basic Books, 2018. | Includes bibliographical
    references and index.
Identifiers: LCCN 2018023630| ISBN 9780465093793 (hardcover) |
    ISBN 9780465093809 (ebook)
Subjects: LCSH: Crime—United States—Classification. | Criminal justice,
    Administration of—Social aspects—United States.
Classification: LCC KF9300 .N38 2018 | DDC 364.60973—dc23
LC record available at https://lccn.loc.gov/2018023630
ISBNs: 978-0-465-09379-3 (hardcover), 978-0-465-09380-9 (ebook)
LSC-C

10 9 8 7 6 5 4 3 2 1

For Raphael
no matter what

CONTENTS

INTRODUCTION

WHEN MAC WAS THREE YEARS OLD AND ANYA WAS FIVE, they watched their mother get arrested for a seatbelt violation. It was 1997, and the family was driving slowly, about fifteen miles per hour, around the park in their hometown of Lago Vista, Texas, because Mac had lost his special toy. The children had taken off their seat belts so they could look out the car windows for the toy. Officer Bart Turek pulled them over and began yelling and pointing his finger in Gail Atwater's face. "You're going to jail!" he hollered. Atwater asked if she could take her wailing children to a friend's house first, but Officer Turek said the children would go to the jail right along with her. Gail Atwater was handcuffed, taken to the police station, and locked in a cell. She was booked and fingerprinted for the misdemeanor seatbelt violation. Eventually she paid the maximum penalty for her offense, which was $50. Afterward, both children were terrified of police cars. If Mac saw a police officer, he would get down on the floor and curl up into ball. But the law permitted Officer Turek to do everything he

did. When the Supreme Court of the United States considered Gail Atwater's case, it decided that police may arrest and jail people for even
the most minor misdemeanors.[1]

A few years later across the country in New York, nineteen-year-
old Sharif Stinson had a different sort of encounter with the misdemeanor system. Stinson visited his aunt in the Bronx every week
to see how she was doing. One day, as he left his aunt's apartment
building, police ordered him up against the wall. They searched him,
and although they found nothing, they arrested him and took him to
jail. After four hours, he was released and charged with disorderly
conduct. Stinson hadn't actually committed any crime, and a judge
dismissed the charge, calling it "legally insufficient." Three weeks
later, Stinson was back checking on his aunt. Once again, he was
stopped, arrested, and jailed. This time he was charged with trespassing as well as disorderly conduct. Once again, he hadn't committed
any crimes, and a judge dismissed the charges. These sorts of arrest
practices have become controversial in New York. Some New York
police officers attribute them to informal quotas requiring that police
clock a certain number of arrests and citations or risk professional
discipline. The New York Police Department denies the quotas.[2]

Misdemeanors like Gail Atwater's traffic violation and Sharif Stinson's disorderly conduct charges are the chump change of the criminal
system. They are labeled "minor," "low-level," and "petty." Sometimes
they go by innocuous names like "infraction" or "violation." Because
the crimes are small and the punishments relatively light in comparison to felonies, this world of low-level offenses has not gotten much
attention. But it is enormous, powerful, and surprisingly harsh. Every
year, approximately 13 million people are charged with crimes as minor as littering or as serious as domestic violence.[3] Those 13 million
misdemeanors make up the vast majority, around 80 percent, of the
nation's criminal dockets. Most arrests in this country are for misdemeanors. Most convictions are misdemeanors. Most Americans will
experience the criminal system at the misdemeanor level. Through this
enormous process, millions of people are arrested, charged, booked,

perhaps jailed, convicted, and punished in ways that can haunt them and their families for the rest of their lives. While mass incarceration has become recognized as a multi-billion-dollar dehumanizing debacle, it turns out that the misdemeanor behemoth does quieter damage on an even grander scale.

Misdemeanors have slipped beneath the public radar largely because their impact and importance are so thoroughly underestimated. Punishments are usually deemed minor, but there is nothing petty about them. The misdemeanor process commonly strips the people who go through it of their liberty, money, health, jobs, housing, credit, immigration status, and government benefits. Even a brief stint in jail can be dangerous. People with misdemeanor arrests and convictions often lose their jobs and find it hard to get new ones. Fines and fees lead to incarceration for those who are too poor to pay them. Students, poor people, and the elderly can lose their government aid. For immigrants, a misdemeanor can trigger deportation. The petty-offense process does all this punishing quietly, often informally, without much fanfare, millions of times a year.

Sometimes misdemeanors don't even look much like *crimes*. In twenty-five states, speeding is a misdemeanor. Loitering, spitting, disorderly conduct, and jaywalking belong to a large group of crimes called "order-maintenance" or "quality-of-life" offenses, and they make it a crime to do unremarkable things that lots of people do all the time. By contrast, some misdemeanors are quite serious—drunk driving and domestic assault for example. The spectrum is wide: as we will see, some misdemeanors punish the same sorts of harms that felonies do, while many others go after common conduct that isn't particularly blameworthy or harmful at all. Because the law designates such a vast array of common behaviors as criminal, rendering a nearly unlimited number of people potentially subject to its reach, the misdemeanor system is enormous.

Because the petty-offense process is so large, it tends to move cases fast. This has earned it some choice nicknames like "cattle herding," "assembly-line justice," "meet 'em and plead 'em" lawyering, and

"McJustice." The Supreme Court has worried that the sheer volume of misdemeanors "create[s] an obsession for speedy dispositions, regardless of the fairness of the result."[4] In practice, this speedy volume means that people's rights and dignity often get trampled. In North Charleston, South Carolina, for example, a grandmother, whom we will call Grandma G, was on trial for shoplifting in 2014. She did not understand what was happening to her or the legal words that the judge was using, and she asked for a lawyer. This only seemed to make the judge angry. She couldn't afford an attorney, but the judge would not postpone the case to give her time to fill out the public defender form. But Grandma G could not represent herself. At first she tried to speak up. Then she spoke quietly. Then she just mumbled. Then she gave up and stopped talking. "How do you want to plead?" asked the judge. Grandma G said nothing. "Do you want a bench trial or a jury?" Grandma G said nothing. The judge went ahead anyway and swore in a witness from Walmart, who said Grandma G had taken meat and cake. "What's going on?" asked Grandma G. "Do you want a bench trial or a jury?" repeated the judge. Confused, Grandma G waved her hands around. "I don't care," she said. The Walmart witness said that Grandma G's two-year-old granddaughter had been with her in the store. This made the judge even madder. "There's not a lot I can do for you, ma'am." He pronounced her guilty and sentenced her to thirty days in jail. Grandma G was led out of the courtroom, sobbing and in handcuffs. The whole trial and sentencing took less than three minutes.[5]

Grandma G's experience was typical in a couple of ways. First, it was fast. In Florida, most misdemeanor cases are resolved by guilty plea in three minutes. Proceedings in the Hot Check Division of Sherwood District Court in Arkansas last less than two minutes. Some St. Louis municipal courts handle over five hundred cases in a single night court session, less than one minute per case.[6] Second, Grandma G's constitutional rights were violated. Defendants like her who face jail time have the right to counsel—the judge should have given her an attorney. But in practice misdemeanor defendants often don't get lawyers. In some lower courts, judges routinely instruct defendants to go work out their cases directly with the prosecutor. Sometimes there are no prosecutors; police officers prosecute the cases themselves. In yet other courts, the judge is not even a lawyer.[7]

Even when defendants do get lawyers, they still might not get proper representation. Many public defenders are burdened with hundreds and sometimes thousands of cases and therefore cannot give time or attention to any one of them. In cities like Chicago, Atlanta, and Miami, misdemeanor public defenders carry over 2,000 cases a year—over five times the caseload recommended by the American Bar Association.[8] Such overburdened attorneys may simply inform their clients about the deal offered by the prosecutor and get them to sign. Hence the nickname "meet 'em and plead 'em."

In this sense Grandma G's experience was unusual: she did not plead guilty. Misdemeanor trials like hers are rare—around 97 percent of misdemeanor convictions are the result of a guilty plea.[9] Because the misdemeanor system speeds cases along, defendants often take a deal without being fully informed of their rights and options or without fully understanding the consequences of their choice. Many will plead guilty without anyone checking the evidence to see whether they actually committed a crime. This dynamic not only contradicts numerous fundamental legal rules, it also invites wrongful conviction: innocent people arrested for low-level offenses routinely plead guilty to crimes they did not commit. They might do so because they do not have a lawyer, or their court-appointed attorney might lack the resources to investigate the case. Innocent people might also plead because they are too poor to pay bail—a financial deposit required by the court—meaning that they will remain in jail for weeks or even months until their cases are over. Pleading guilty, on the other hand, typically lets them go home. Because the pressures to plead guilty are omnipresent and the petty-offense process is huge, wrongful convictions probably occur hundreds of thousands of times a year.

In short, the American misdemeanor system often violates basic legal principles of justice and fairness. Here are a few examples, detailed later in this book, that show how troubling the low-level criminal process can get:

- In a Maryland misdemeanor court, a judge made up an imaginary rule of evidence to help the prosecution. When the defense attorney complained, he threatened to hold her in contempt.[10]
- A junior public defender in Washington carried a caseload of over 250 misdemeanor cases every month. She was expected to get her clients to plead guilty immediately so she could move on to the next case. When she asked for more time to address a client's legal issue, she was fired.[11]
- In the lower court in Florence, South Carolina, there are no prosecutors. Instead, police act simultaneously as the prosecuting official and the witness. People must defend themselves against, or work out a plea deal with, the same officer who arrested them.[12]
- Kawana Young, a single mother of two in Washtenaw County, Michigan, was sent to jail because she could not afford to pay $300 in misdemeanor traffic fines. The jail then charged her a booking fee and, for each day she spent in jail, an additional daily pay-to-stay fee.[13]
- Baltimore police use a form to record trespassing arrests. It has a blank space for the name of the arrestee, but race and gender are already filled in as "BLACK MALE."[14]

As such examples show, the petty-offense process can be gravely unfair, inaccurate, and disrespectful. But it isn't always. In some places and for some people, the process works more like it should. In federal courts, for instance, which have smaller caseloads and more resources, indigent defendants charged with shoplifting or DUI get skilled counsel, and courts routinely hold hearings and proper trials. In some cities, senior prosecutors carefully screen the misdemeanor docket to make sure that only the right cases go forward. There are top-notch public defender offices around the country that provide representation as good or better than any expensive law firm.

Wealthy defendants with time and resources can ensure that their minor cases are treated seriously. This kind of care and attention is the legal gold standard. Rules matter. Evidence makes a difference. Prosecutors honor their obligation to do justice. Defendants have lawyers who have the resources to do their jobs. If the criminal system is a pyramid, this is the top, where the criminal process works as well as it can—for misdemeanors and serious felonies alike.[15]

Of course even the best legal process cannot make up for fundamentally unjust rules. No amount of good lawyering will ever make it fair to criminalize people based on their race or religion or for being sick or poor.[16] But the better the process, the more likely it is that unfair rules will be challenged, that officials will exercise their discretion carefully, and that punishment will be balanced. Sometimes, at its best, the US criminal process lives up to these important values.

Unfortunately, the top of the pyramid is small. Most of the misdemeanor system, and quite a bit of the felony system too, falls far short of the gold standard. It is often said that we have two justice systems, one for the rich and one for the poor, but in practice there is no bright line. Rather, there is a gradual erosion. As offenses get pettier and defendants get poorer, a host of pressures and resource constraints diminish basic commitments to rules, evidence, fairness, and the presumption of innocence, slowly and quietly changing how the system does its work. By the time we hit the bottom of the pyramid, the criminal process has become an enormous, sloppy, shadowy world through which millions of Americans get rushed every year. There are felony cases down here—low-level drug felonies are often handled in speedy, sloppy ways, and even the most serious felony defendants are sometimes treated with shocking indifference. But the bottom is mostly misdemeanors.

As a result of such dynamics, our misdemeanor system does something that criminal justice is not supposed to do: it punishes people who have not actually committed a crime or done anything to deserve punishment. Hence the title of this book. The petty-offense process punishes people while they wait for their cases to be handled and are still presumed innocent. It punishes innocent people for crimes they didn't commit. It punishes people for harmless or common minor behavior that should never have been treated as a crime in the first place. And it keeps punishing people long after they have served their sentences. In each of these scenarios innocent people are unfairly trapped: punished before they have been convicted, punished although they did nothing wrong, or punished after they have already paid their debt to society. It turns out that the court-imposed formal penalty of a fine or probation or jail is only part of what actually happens to people; the sentence is neither the beginning nor the end of the misdemeanor punishment story. Rather, individuals caught up in the misdemeanor process live through layers of punitive treatment that can outweigh and outlast any legal sentence. The experiences of being arrested, jailed, fined, and supervised, telling your family, fearing to tell your employer, getting a criminal record, and potentially losing your job, credit, welfare benefits, immigration status, or housing—all of these taken together amount to an enormous burden. Unlike with most felonies, that burden can be far worse than the legal sentence itself. And it can kick in regardless of whether the person deserves it or has committed anything resembling a blameworthy or dangerous offense. This is punishment without crime.

Misdemeanor convictions, moreover, don't always mean what they say. A conviction is a weighty thing. It is supposed to represent the justice system's studied conclusion that the defendant engaged in blameworthy conduct worthy of censure and punishment. A solid murder or rape conviction tells us something meaningful about that person's conduct and by extension his or her moral choices. But convictions are only as meaningful as we make them. The quality of the decisions, evidence, and processes that underlie a criminal conviction determine its true significance. Because the misdemeanor system consistently generates convictions in sloppy and biased ways, it distorts the meaning of those millions of convictions, divesting them of their factual and moral content. Being convicted of a misdemeanor, in other words, might mean that you did something bad and deserve to be labeled a criminal. But it very well might not.

Like mass incarceration, the misdemeanor phenomenon reflects deep and abiding flaws in the US justice system. But its significance does not end there. Misdemeanors influence vital aspects of the public sphere; they shape race relations; they regulate employment; they affect immigration. The process is also an economic behemoth, quietly redistributing billions of public and private dollars. Misdemeanors thus fuel some of America's most infamous inequalities, especially the gap between rich and poor and the disparate treatment of people of color.

The misdemeanor system widens the rich-poor gap by punishing low-income and working people on a grand scale. It makes it a crime to do lots of things that poor people can't help doing, like failing to pay fines, fees, speeding tickets, or car registrations. It strips working people of crucial resources like driver's licenses, housing, and credit, which hurts their ability to earn a living and thrive. It pushes the poor back into poverty even as civil welfare programs struggle to lift them out. US jails are filled with working, poor, and homeless individuals who are there solely because they could not pay a fine or a fee—a new kind of debtors' prison.[17]

Many of these regressive practices can be traced back to the economic incentives of key institutions in the misdemeanor system. Courts, municipalities, and police departments around the country rely on misdemeanor revenues to fund their own operations. Some judges' salaries depend on collecting fines and fees from the people they convict. Small cities and local courts raise millions of dollars from misdemeanor and traffic offenses. Port Arthur, one of the poorest cities in Texas, created a special infraction unit that brings in $1.5 million a year. In Sherwood, Arkansas, the county imposes a $25 prosecution fee, a $50 warrant fee, and two $20 jail fees for each bounced-check case; Sherwood police collect fines on the spot from those they arrest.[18] Meanwhile, private probation companies derive all their revenue from user fees charged to defendants, as does the powerful bail bond industry.

And so, in effect, the petty-offense process has quietly become a regressive feature of American tax policy. It actively extracts revenue from an ever-widening pool of mostly low-income people in order to fund the operations of private as well as public criminal justice institutions. This is not how the criminal system is supposed to work—generating revenue is not a good reason to punish people—but it is a core characteristic of the misdemeanor institution.

This is not an entirely new problem: the American criminal system has an ignominious history of punishing the poor. It is equally if not more infamous for punishing people of color, especially African Americans, and misdemeanors have long been central players in that shameful drama. After the Civil War, southern states used misdemeanors to effectively re-enslave hundreds of thousands of African Americans, rounding them up to convict them of petty offenses and selling them to plantations and factories to work off their sentences.[19] In many of those same states, modern jails are now debtors' prisons filled with poor people of color who have been arrested and convicted in order to generate revenue.

Today, the misdemeanor system is the frontline mechanism through which many people of color are drawn into the criminal system in the first place, arrested, marked, and convicted for minor offenses, or sometimes for no crimes at all. We have come to understand mass incarceration as an engine of race discrimination that unfairly and disproportionately criminalizes black and Latino Americans. But the trouble actually starts earlier with racial inequities in misdemeanor policing and processing. Chicago police arrest African Americans for marijuana possession seven times more often than they arrest whites, even though whites and blacks use marijuana at the same rates. In North Sacramento, California, half of all 2016 jaywalking tickets were issued to black residents, who make up just 15 percent of the population. It is here at the bottom of the pyramid that the criminal process first aims broadly at people of color, mostly black men, arresting them for disorderly conduct, trespassing, drug possession, and other minor order-maintenance offenses. Once arrested and funneled into the legal system, the majority plead guilty. Because the system is sloppy and fast, moreover, many of these convictions are wrongful—the risks are especially high that black men are pleading guilty to petty offenses that they did not actually commit.[20]

This is how the petty-offense process actively marks thousands of African Americans as "criminal," a corrosive dynamic with both immediate and historic effects. The criminal marking prevents people from getting jobs, housing, education, and loans, derailing major aspects of their lives. It sets some people up for the more serious felony convictions that have created our current mass incarceration crisis. And it insidiously fuels the racist stereotype that black men are criminals. Although it has not received its fair share of blame, the misdemeanor process has long been centrally responsible for forging that pernicious link between blackness and criminality that has haunted American culture and politics for centuries. Arrest by arrest and case by case, the misdemeanor process forcibly connects black people to the criminal system, arresting them, convicting them, and labeling them criminals for minor conduct, and sometimes for no good reason at all.

In these ways, the misdemeanor experience has become an integral feature of what it means to be socially disadvantaged in the United States. Most misdemeanor enforcement impacts the disadvantaged: the poor and working-class, African Americans and Latinos, immigrants, the young, the homeless, the mentally ill, and the addicted. It is a *feature* of disadvantage—poor people and people of color are more likely to encounter the petty-offense process in the first place. But it also *generates* disadvantage by impoverishing the already poor, stigmatizing people of color as criminal, and generally making vulnerable people worse off. The petty-offense process is an omnipresent aspect of growing up in disadvantaged neighborhoods, of being a young black male, increasingly of being an immigrant, and generally of being poor. As a result, the misdemeanor apparatus is powerfully stratifying. Like low-quality public schools and segregated housing, misdemeanors are an integral part of the downward social cycle that creates and perpetuates inequality.

It is time to recognize that the misdemeanor process is more than just a criminal system. In practice and effect it is also an influential economic and social welfare institution. The misdemeanor process has become a tool for cities to regulate residents of public housing and enforce gentrification boundaries. Police departments use minor offenses to measure productivity and to generate salary increases and promotions. Courts, jails, and cities rely on misdemeanors to raise revenue. In other words, we have authorized the misdemeanor system do all sorts of social, political, and economic work that has little or nothing to do with crime, public safety, or justice.[21] Like education, housing, and welfare policy, the petty-offense process is one of those central collective institutions through which we make big decisions about our democracy, how to allocate and redistribute resources, and how to manage poverty, crime, and community. Although it is not traditionally understood in this way, the misdemeanor process belongs in the pantheon of social institutions that shape the basic contours of organized society.

This book examines the entire misdemeanor process, from arrest through prosecution and punishment, what happens to people in the system and afterward, and its implications for the US economy, society, and democracy. Until now no one has tried to write a book of this scope, and there are some good reasons for that. The misdemeanor system is enormous, decentralized, and complicated. It isn't even really a "system" at all—it is actually thousands of interlocking offices, players, and practices. It encompasses police, prosecutors, public defenders, judges, jurors, attorneys, arrestees, sheriffs, probation officers, clerks, defendants, victims, families, and members of the public. It also includes powerful private entities like bail bondsmen, probation companies, drug-testing companies, and data aggregators. Each institution plays a different role. Sometimes they align and cooperate; sometimes they compete and conflict. Jurisdictions vary wildly from state to state, county to county, even city to city. Massachusetts has little in common with Mississippi. I use words like "system" and "institution" for convenience and clarity, but it would be just as accurate to refer to the whole misdemeanor apparatus metaphorically as a machine or an ecosystem or a behemoth. Indeed, the difficulty in finding a good word is part of the problem—what the hell is this thing, anyway? It is challenging to draw strong general conclusions about something that is so tough to pin down.

Another reason that this book hasn't been written before is that it is very hard to get national information about the petty-offense process. Many jurisdictions do not even count all their minor offenses. A 2009 report estimated, based on the limited data available at the time, an annual docket of 10.5 million cases. Until then no one had even tried to figure out how many misdemeanors were filed nationally. As I prepared to write this book, I collected extensive new data from every state around the country. That information, summarized in the appendix, now provides the most accurate picture of the national landscape to date—the data show that approximately 13 million misdemeanors were filed in this country in 2015. This is an astounding number—the system is 25 percent bigger than we thought it was, and four times the size of the felony system.[22] And even that 13 million number doesn't tell the whole story. Jurisdictions do not keep records in the same ways or sometimes at all. Although I provide caseload estimates for every state, comparisons should be made cautiously. Labels mean different things in different courts, so totals are not always comparable. Moreover, 2015 is just a snapshot: the system could well have been even bigger ten years ago. Nevertheless, my data compendium offers an unprecedented window into the size, specifics, and variations of an institution that has long resisted scrutiny and oversight. I hope it will inspire future research.

Perhaps the real reason no one has tried to write a book like this is that the misdemeanor process has not traditionally been conceptualized as a whole, from start to finish, as a single thing. Rather, it is chopped up into components. Many people have written about stop-and-frisk policing and low-level drug arrests. Others analyze the overwhelmed and underfunded misdemeanor defense bar. Since the 1920s sociologists have been studying the peculiar operations of low-level courts.[23] More recently, misdemeanor bail has moved into the spotlight. The US Department of Justice's 2015 investigation of the Ferguson Police Department exposed the importance of misdemeanor fines and fees. I spent the last seven years researching and writing about many of these components myself.[24] But they are parts of a larger whole. This book offers a unifying framework that reveals the connections between all sorts of seemingly disparate criminal justice phenomena, from order-maintenance policing and "driving while black" to bail, fines, and fees, debtors' prison, the underfunded public defense bar, and the impact of criminal records. This bird's-eye view reveals a massive criminal institution that stops, arrests, fines, incarcerates, labels, and otherwise punishes millions of people for all sorts of reasons that are often tenuously connected to public safety, in ways that baldly contradict principles of fairness, accuracy, and due process.

All of this has profound implications for our democracy. The criminal system performs a unique and vital governance function. It goes after people who have done bad and harmful things, it labels them so we know who they are, and it punishes them. We give the state enormous coercive and punitive power to do this work, including the authority to forcibly stop us on the street or search our houses, to seize our personal information, and even to shoot at us. Only the government can accuse us of crimes and then punish us, often harshly, if we are found guilty. Indeed, when the government fails to investigate or punish crime it can be cause for public outcry. We confer these awesome powers on government because the challenge of identifying and stopping wrongdoers is so important and because, on a basic moral level, we think someone shown to have committed a crime rightfully deserves to be punished.

Thirteen million times a year, the state performs this vital task through the misdemeanor process. It needs to do a good job. Millions of people suffer the harms of drunk driving, domestic violence, minor thefts, and simple assaults. Good low-level policing can help make the difference between a desirable neighborhood and one in which parents are reluctant to let their children play outside. Too much law enforcement is a kind of state failure, and so is too little.[25] But the excesses of the misdemeanor system suggest that we are getting that all-important balance wrong. When the government treats so much minor common conduct as *crime*, it overburdens our criminal institutions and overpunishes millions of Americans. The sprawling reach of the misdemeanor system has imbued it with vast social and economic authority that all too often it exercises in unfair and unaccountable ways. By permitting this state of affairs, we erode the efficacy and integrity of one of our most important democratic institutions.

Put differently, a fair and just misdemeanor system requires the right balance between crime control, liberty, and equality. Achieving that balance is a political challenge of the highest order, and big political questions often play out on the misdemeanor stage. Sometimes those debates result in stronger crime controls. This is where Mothers Against Drunk Driving famously won the argument that driving while intoxicated should be treated as a serious crime. This is where domestic violence advocates spent decades convincing the state to respond more forcefully to violence within families. Conversely, sometimes those debates make the criminal system less intrusive. Today, the state cannot punish married couples for using birth control, or punish same-sex partners for engaging in intimacy, or punish men for using indecent language in the presence of women, even though at various points in American history all of those behaviors were once misdemeanors.[26] More recently, the push for marijuana legalization and decriminalization is a political counterpunch to decades of harsh and racially disparate drug enforcement. Such developments are about crime, of course, but they are also conversations about privacy, gender, family, race, and wealth. Getting misdemeanors right is a way for government to get the balance right on these fundamental issues as well.

For the first time in decades, the American public appears interested in rolling back a criminal system that many people see as ineffective, expensive, and unfair. That system, however, is largely studied and judged on the basis of its most serious cases—violent felonies, long drug sentences, federal indictments—about which there is the most information and the most scholarship and which are familiar subjects in the news media and popular culture. To truly improve the system and make it fairer and more effective, that worldview needs to be turned on its head so as to begin at the bottom, with the least important, smallest, pettiest cases in state, county, and municipal courts. This upside-down view, in turn, offers many new, fruitful, and often startling insights that can help us think differently about systemic problems. In that vein, at the end of this book I propose a series of disruptive interventions at key junctures in the misdemeanor process. They involve, first and foremost, shrinking the enormous pipeline that fills the system at the front end. They also involve reducing our overreliance on arrest and incarceration and easing the many punitive consequences of minor convictions. They resist the habit of using misdemeanors as a method of taxation. And they would strengthen basic commitments to justice, equality, and public transparency. Such interventions are specifically designed to respond to the dysfunctions of the petty-offense process. But they would also improve many aspects of the low-level felony apparatus, which often behaves in similarly cavalier and punitive ways.

The approach of this book has been shaped by my own background. Fifteen years ago, before I became a law professor, I worked as a federal public defender in Baltimore, Maryland, where I represented many misdemeanor defendants. They taught me an enormous amount. In particular, they showed me that conventional legal analysis and the rules as they appear on paper rarely capture the true significance of criminal law and punishment. A full understanding requires information about the experiences of individuals who pass through the system—how it really works and what really happens. Accordingly, this book includes dozens of stories, examples, and quotations from and about ordinary people. Some of them come from my own conversations and interviews. I asked people who had gone through the misdemeanor process about their experiences, and I have talked to numerous police, prosecutors, public defenders, and judges over the years. Other stories come from legal cases and from reports by government agencies, journalists, and nonprofit organizations. They include the voices of single mothers incarcerated for failing to pay their traffic fines and African American men arrested for order-maintenance offenses. They offer glimpses of how public defenders struggle with thousands of low-level cases and how prosecutors and judges cope with pressure to clear enormous dockets. They draw from large urban areas and small rural towns, from North and South, from black as well as white and Latino communities.

There are limits to what individual anecdotes can tell us. No one story—no one jurisdiction—is fully representative of the system as a whole. Just because a terrible thing happened to someone in Mississippi does not mean that everyone in Mississippi experiences the same thing, and it certainly doesn't tell us what is happening in Minnesota. Moreover, the state of play is often changing, so the fact that a problematic example is included here does not mean that the situation is still as it was, and by including it I do not mean to imply that things have not gotten better since then.[27] At the same time, stories from numerous states and localities reveal egregious cases of injustice, often affecting hundreds or even thousands of people. Indeed, observers are often shocked that such things can happen in a wealthy, developed democracy like ours. While individual examples should not be mistaken for the whole picture, they can tell us how far the misdemeanor system sometimes careens off course, even if we don't know exactly how widespread the problem is. They are thus warning signs that the petty-offense process—itself the lion's share of our criminal system—contains serious structural flaws. Just as importantly, the voices of real people in actual cases remind us of the misdemeanor system's deep human consequences. These voices can help us reevaluate the moral and democratic implications of running so much of our criminal system in this way.

This book is highly critical of how the misdemeanor system currently works. It spends the bulk of its time uncovering what is amiss and less on the system's strengths. This seeming imbalance is designed to compensate for the fact that, for the most part, the misdemeanor world has not had to explain or justify itself, proceeding largely under the radar without scrutiny, data collection, or oversight. Although there are many skilled, committed public servants who labor every day in its service, the misdemeanor institution is rife with dysfunctional incentives and practices. When the institution is challenged, the public lacks information about its full costs and inequities. As with many criminal justice debates, the obvious need for law and order tends to overshadow other values, including the substantial inefficiencies, harms, and injustices that the process inflicts. This book is an effort to remedy that long-standing imbalance by filling in the other, neglected half of the conversation.

The misdemeanor system remains one of our most profoundly important public institutions. At its best, it offers ordinary people protection against common minor crimes in their homes, neighborhoods, and workplaces. At its best, it does so carefully and fairly, in accord with basic principles of law and democracy. At its worst, it makes our entire country less safe, less fair, and less equal. This is where American justice succeeds or fails, 13 million times every year. It is time that it was held to account.

IMPACT

ONE OF THE GREAT MYTHS OF OUR CRIMINAL SYSTEM IS that minor arrests and convictions are not especially terrible for the people who experience them. It is a highly influential myth. It helps justify the speed and sloppiness of misdemeanor processing. It supports the assignment of the least-experienced prosecutors and public defenders to misdemeanor dockets. It makes pleading guilty seem sensible so as to avoid the difficult and expensive process of contesting a case. It even explains the Supreme Court's habit of withholding constitutional rights from misdemeanor defendants. The Court has held that people who face less than six months' imprisonment have no right to a jury trial. If they are not incarcerated for a misdemeanor, they have no right to a lawyer.[1] In effect, when the law deems *punishment* not particularly burdensome, it makes it easier to *convict* people in the first place.

But misdemeanor punishments are not petty at all. People with minor arrests and convictions are jailed, fined, supervised, tracked, marked, and stigmatized. They can lose their jobs, driver's licenses, welfare benefits, child custody, immigration status, and housing. They may be disqualified for loans and professional licenses or sink into debt and ruin their credit. Sometimes these things happen even when their cases are dismissed and they are never convicted at all.

Current US law barely acknowledges the broad punitive impact of the misdemeanor experience. Criminal law draws a line between formal legal "punishment"—the jail time, probation, and fines imposed by a judge when someone is convicted—and all the other "collateral consequences" of that conviction. But in the misdemeanor arena such legal distinctions obscure the sprawling reality of the punishment experience. The full impact of a misdemeanor begins long before people are convicted and ends long after they have served their sentences. It can amount to a crushing burden, heavier than the punishment ordered by the court and often wildly disproportionate to the seriousness of the offense.

A misdemeanor's impact can flow from many different sources. We'll look at the main categories that make up the punishment experience: jail, probation, fines and fees, warrants, criminal records, the loss of public benefits, immigration consequences, future encounters with the criminal system, and, finally, the fear and stigma that go with it all.

JAIL

Tyrone Tomlin was a fifty-three-year-old construction worker in Brooklyn, New York. One afternoon in late November 2014, chatting with friends, he popped into the corner store to buy a soda. When he came out, two undercover police officers were frisking his friends. An officer took Tomlin's soda. "What you got in the other hand?" the officer asked. "I got a straw that I'm about to use for the soda," said Tomlin. The office searched Tomlin and arrested him for the straw. "Drug paraphernalia," the officer explained.

When Tomlin got to court, the prosecutor offered him a thirty-day sentence if he pled guilty. He wouldn't, but Tomlin couldn't afford the

$1,500 bail set by the judge, so he was sent to Riker's Island, New York's infamously violent jail complex. He went back to court on November 25, two days before Thanksgiving. There was still no drug evidence, but the government continued to insist on a plea; Tomlin continued to insist that he was innocent, but since he still couldn't make bail, back to Riker's he went. Days later, he was jumped by a group of inmates in the shower who punched, kicked, and stomped him in his head and his eyes. When Tomlin went to court two weeks later, his eye was still swollen shut. At that hearing, however, the prosecution produced a report from the police lab confirming that the straw was just a straw: "No Controlled Substance Identified" was written at the top of the report in bold. The report had been faxed to the district attorney on November 25, the very same day that Tomlin was in court before the beating, but no one had picked it up. Now the government dismissed the case. At the time, Tomlin was relieved. "It feels great to go home," he said.

Six months later, Tomlin's eye remained askew, and his sight was blurry. "I still feel the aftereffects," he said. "Pain my eye, in my head." Now that the threat of Riker's had passed, he was thinking about the fact that he got locked up and beaten up, lost three weeks of salary, and missed Thanksgiving with his family, all because he could not afford to pay bail. "I got a raw deal," he concluded, but he was philosophical. "I'm not Johnny Rich-Kid with a silver spoon. Sure, yeah, I'm mad about it. But that's the way it is. I've got to accept it. It's not right, but that's the way it is." He shrugged. "What are you going to do?"[2]

Jail is one of the most damaging aspects of the misdemeanor experience, and it looms large throughout. It is where you go when you are arrested, where you stay if you can't make bail, where you will serve your sentence if convicted, and where you might end up if you can't pay your fine. Jails are different from prisons. Prison is where people serve felony sentences, and the US prison population of 1.5 million has made this country internationally infamous. But there are 11 million admissions to 3,000 American jails every year—on any given day, approximately 730,000 people are in jail. On average, approximately one-third of them are there for misdemeanors, but in some cities it is as many as 50 percent. Sixty percent—nearly half a million people—are incarcerated pretrial; like Tyrone Tomlin they have not been convicted of anything and are thus presumptively innocent.[3]

Jails stays can be short or long. Some people spend a single night after an arrest, but 18 percent of the jail population will remain over six months. Over half of all unconvicted inmates will spend more than a month in jail; one-quarter will spend two to six months. The average pretrial detainee can expect to be incarcerated for at least a month whether or not he or she is ever convicted of anything.[4]

While a great deal of litigation has focused on the dangerous and unhealthy conditions in prisons, state and county jails have received less attention. But they can be just as hazardous. Many are overcrowded, and inmates endure violence, rape, and crime. Disease is widespread: even a brief stint in jail can expose an inmate to tuberculosis, staph infections, and hepatitis. In Florida, for example, Dorothy Palinchik was jailed for stealing a $9 Philly cheesesteak sandwich. Within days, the forty-two-year old waitress contracted a staph infection and pneumonia, sending her into a fatal coma. On average, nearly 1,000 people die in jails every year, 30 percent within the first few days of incarceration.[5]

As Tyrone Tomlin's story illustrates, jail is intimately connected to the phenomenon of bail. Bail is supposed to be a kind of good faith down payment—an amount of money set by the court to ensure that defendants show up for future court appearances. Defendants who can afford to pay it get released. When their case is over, they get it back. (Chapter 3 examines the rules and operations of misdemeanor bail in greater detail.) For people who don't have the money, however, the cost of bail creates pressure to plead guilty. Most misdemeanor defendants who are set bail cannot pay it, so they either plead out or stay in jail until their cases are over.

The impact of going to jail is substantial, both for individuals and their families. Studies have shown that as few as twenty-four hours of pretrial detention can have negative effects. Longer stays are highly disruptive and can lead to evictions, towed cars, and the loss of food stamps and other resources. More than 5 million children have seen a parent go to jail or prison. In 2009, over 400,000 parents were in local jails. Incarcerated parents can lose custody or visitation rights or face further incarceration for failing to pay child support that accrued while they were in jail.[6] In sum, whether incarceration occurs before or after conviction, going to jail is an enormously costly aspect of the misdemeanor experience.

PROBATION

Sometimes people are sentenced not to jail but to probation, a period of court-ordered supervision. While it can be a way of avoiding in-carceration, probation carries its own unique burdens. In 2014, for example, Donyelle and Roland Hall threw a Christmas Day party for friends and family. Afterward, Hall drove two of her guests home and was stopped for driving thirty-eight in a twenty-five-mph zone. A breathalyzer test showed a blood alcohol content of .09, just over the Maryland legal limit of .07, the difference of about one glass of wine.

Although Hall had no criminal record and no history of alcohol abuse, she was sentenced to eighteen months' probation—if she com-pleted it successfully, the case would be dismissed, and she would avoid a criminal record. The conditions of that probation included $105 a month in supervision fees, twenty-six weeks of alcohol education at $280 a month, $252 in court costs, and three Alcoholics Anonymous (AA) meetings a week. If Hall wanted to change addresses, she would need the judge's permission. Hall also owed $2,000 to the bail bonds-man and $1,500 to her lawyer. Because her license was suspended for two weeks, she lost her job as a nurse's aide, making it difficult for her and her husband to pay those costs.

After she had been in compliance for several months, Hall's apart-ment developed a mouse infestation. She wrote to the court explaining her intention to move, but the court issued a summons stating that she did not have permission to change her address. When Hall lost the paperwork proving her attendance at the AA meetings, the judge issued a warrant for her arrest. Hall went to jail for a month, and the judge entered the conviction onto her record. As a result, her driver's license was suspended for six months. Because she couldn't drive to work, she lost her new job.[7]

Probation, sometimes referred to as community supervision, is the most common misdemeanor sentence other than fines. The federal Bureau of Justice Statistics (BJS) reports that approximately 4 million Americans are on some form of probationary supervision, nearly half of them for misdemeanors, but this is an undercount since many low-level probations are not reported to BJS at all.[8]

Probation is often seen as a lenient sentence because it permits people to avoid jail time, but as Donyelle Hall's story reveals, it can be expensive, burdensome, and intrusive. Probationers lose their privacy rights: probation officers can search them and their homes at any time. Probation usually requires periodic drug tests, visits to the probation office, electronic monitoring, counseling, fines, or other conditions that can be difficult to meet, especially for low-income and working-class probationers. A typical misdemeanor probation term can last from six months to a year or more. During that time, violation of any condition, including failure to pay fines and fees, can subject the defendant to incarceration; only about two-thirds of probationers successfully complete their terms.[9]

FINES, FEES, AND THE NEW DEBTORS' PRISON

Most misdemeanor defendants have to pay fines and fees of some kind, and they can have a devastating impact. Patricia Parker, for example, was a cook at a Methodist conference center. To make the breakfast shift, she had to leave home before 6 a.m. and drive her boyfriend's pickup truck through the neighboring town of Woodworth, Louisiana. One morning, Parker was driving to work when a Woodworth police officer named David Godwin began following her. Parker was not speeding or violating any traffic laws, but Officer Godwin pulled her over anyway, "just to check and see," he said. Ultimately Godwin issued Parker four citations. The first was because the computer said her license was suspended. Parker said she had the paperwork to show that it was valid, but Godwin issued the citation anyway. He also issued citations for driving without registration and insurance, although Parker showed him her insurance card. The total fines for the citations came to $1,060. Godwin then had the truck towed for a fee of $193.61.

The judge for the magistrate court in Woodworth also happened to be its mayor, David Butler, who had held that office for over thirty years. Parker showed Butler papers proving that she had registration and insurance and that her license was valid. In other words, all of the citations were incorrect. Butler asked her "how much money she had with her." She said $300, and the mayor/judge told her to pay the license citation fine of $215, which she did. The city of Woodworth then pursued Parker for the entire amount of all four citations, issuing a warrant for her arrest stating that she now owed the city $1,580. Months later she was arrested at her home, in front of her children, and spent twenty-five days in jail.

The National Motorists Association lists the worst speed traps around the country: Woodworth has ranked number one in the state. In 2007, the Louisiana legislature issued a report titled "Excessive Fine Enforcement," driven by concerns that municipalities were engaging in revenue-driven law enforcement. That report concluded that traffic fines supplied Woodworth with 61 percent of its entire municipal budget.[10]

Woodworth may look like an extreme case, but fines are a widely used form of punishment that imposes hundreds and sometimes thousands of dollars of debt on misdemeanor offenders. California alone has $10 billion in outstanding unpaid traffic debt. The practice can have far-reaching consequences because so many people cannot afford to pay.[11] Low-income defendants are punished not only with their original fine but with long-term debt, loss of credit, or pressure to forgo rent payments or other necessities such as food, health care, and education. If people do not pay, they may be jailed.

In contrast to fines, fees are technically not punishment: they are instead financial charges imposed on defendants by courts, jails, cities, public defenders, prosecutors, probation officers, and clerks to pay for the operations of the criminal process itself. They can include court costs, fees for using the public defender, supervision or "tether" fees, drug testing fees, electronic monitoring fees, warrant fees, jail fees, and late fees. Total fees can far exceed any fine. In California, for example, failing to carry proof of auto insurance carries a $100 fine. In addition, a person will be charged a $100 penalty assessment, a $20 criminal surcharge, a $40 court operations assessment, a $50 court construction fee, a $70 county fund fee, a $50 DNA fund fee, a $4 emergency medical air transportation fee, a $20 EMS fund fee, a $35 conviction assessment, and a $1 night court assessment, for a total of $490. If the payment deadline is missed, there will be an additional $10 DMV warrant fee, a $15 failure-to-appear fee, and a $300 civil assessment, for a total of $815.[12]

Thousands of people like Patricia Parker end up incarcerated every year because they cannot afford to pay fines and fees. Often their incarceration becomes a way of paying off their debt: some states offer a $50 or $100 credit for every day spent in jail. Because this kind of debt-based incarceration only occurs when people are too poor to pay, the phenomenon is commonly referred to as the new debtors' prison.

WARRANTS

The failure to pay a misdemeanor fine or to show up in court for a minor offense can also trigger the issuance of a warrant, which is a court order authorizing the person's arrest at any time by any police officer. There are millions of such outstanding warrants in the United States, and they have wide legal and practical ramifications. When Woodworth issued its warrant for Patricia Parker, for instance, it meant that she could be arrested in her own home in front of her children. An outstanding warrant also has constitutional significance—it inoculates the police against the usual consequences of stopping that person illegally.

This was the case for Edward Strieff. In 2006, Utah police had been watching a house in Salt Lake City for a week or so after an anonymous tip suggested that there might be drug activity going on inside. One day, Strieff walked out of the house, and police stopped and searched him. The stop was clearly illegal—the police didn't have nearly enough evidence to stop him in the first place—but it turned out that Strieff had an outstanding minor traffic warrant. In 2016, the Supreme Court held that the existence of that warrant rendered the drug evidence found on Strieff admissible, even though the stop itself was illegal.

US Supreme Court justice Sonia Sotomayor dissented from the decision in the *Strieff* case, in part because of how many misdemeanor warrants exist nationwide. "Outstanding warrants are surprisingly common," she wrote. "When a person with a traffic ticket misses a fine payment or court appearance, a court will issue a warrant. When a person on probation drinks alcohol or breaks curfew, a court will issue a warrant. The States and Federal Government maintain databases with over 7.8 million outstanding warrants, the vast majority of which appear to be for minor offenses. Even these sources may not track the 'staggering' numbers of warrants, 'drawers and drawers' full, that many cities issue for traffic violations and ordinance infractions."[13]

Some places use warrants more than others. In Texas, the city of El Paso issues 87,000 warrants per year in a city of 680,000 residents. In New York City alone, there are over 1.2 million outstanding warrants; in Pennsylvania, 1.4 million; in California, 2.5 million. Pine Lawn, a small town in St. Louis County near Ferguson, had 23,457 outstanding warrants pending in 2013—more than seven per resident.[14] These warrants subject people to being stopped and arrested at any time.

Not only do warrants create an enormous cloud hanging over the lives of millions of people, but all too often the databases that contain warrant information are inaccurate. The US Department of Justice's investigation of the Ferguson Police Department reported a lack of basic record-keeping processes. "Correctional officers have at times tried to find a warrant in the court's files to determine the bond amount owed, but have been unable to do so. . . . Court staff reported that they typically take weeks, if not months, to enter warrants into the system." Justice Ruth Bader Ginsburg has warned that "law enforcement databases are insufficiently monitored and often out of date," that "the risk of error stemming from these [warrant] databases is not slim," and that "inaccuracies in expansive, interconnected collections of electronic information raise grave concerns for individual liberty."[15] Because warrant databases are unreliable, many people will not know whether a misdemeanor warrant has been issued for their arrest or be able to correct it—and thus avoid arrest—if it is inaccurate.

CRIMINAL RECORDS AND EMPLOYMENT

Perhaps the best-known informal consequence of a criminal conviction is its impact on employment. Job listings on Craigslist often warn people with misdemeanors not to bother applying: "No Exceptions! . . . No Misdemeanors and/or Felonies of any type ever in background"; "Do Not Apply with Any Misdemeanors/Felonies"; and "You must not have any felony or misdemeanor convictions on your record. Period."[16]

Such barriers can last a long time. Johnny Magee was forty years old when he picked up a package for his uncle. Unbeknownst to Magee, who is developmentally disabled, the package contained drugs. Magee was convicted of misdemeanor conspiracy—the only contact with drugs or the criminal system he ever had. But nine years later, a Lowe's home improvement store still wouldn't give him a job in its garden center. "Lowe's policy is unfair to me and lots of other good people," says Magee. "It's unfair because they only see something that happened to me many years ago, even though I've never been in trouble since."[17]

Over 65 million Americans have a criminal record, the majority for misdemeanors. These low-level convictions increasingly inhibit employment. Most employers now use criminal background checks. Indeed, some insurance companies require employers to conduct checks as a condition of their coverage.[18] And online searches and commercial databases make access to criminal records easy.

"I've come to expect being turned down," said Justin Gannon. Despite eight years of Army National Guard service and numerous medals, he routinely received job offers that were rescinded after a background check. Gannon pled guilty to misdemeanor assault in 2003 after a bar fight. He was scared of going to jail, he said, and they "told [me] the misdemeanor wouldn't be that big of a deal on my record."[19]

Contrary to the advice that Gannon received, the National Taskforce on the Commercial Sale of Criminal Justice Record Information concludes that criminal records are indeed a big deal. "Today, background checking—for employment purposes, for eligibility to serve as a volunteer, for tenant screening, and for so many other purposes—has become a necessary, even if not always a welcome, rite of passage for almost every adult American. Like a medical record, a bank record, or a credit record, a background check record is increasingly a part of every American's information footprint." As the book *The Eternal Criminal Record* emphasizes, "A criminal record is for life."[20]

The growing reliance on criminal records means that even very low-level conduct can trigger widespread employment disqualifications. After September 11, 2001, for example, the pharmaceutical company Eli Lilly expanded its background check procedures to include misdemeanors. This resulted in the banning of a number of employees from Eli Lilly facilities, including a woman whose only offense was a misdemeanor conviction for a $60 bounced check to a refrigerator rental company, which she said occurred because she closed the account without realizing that the check had not yet cleared.[21]

Criminal records include arrest records, rap sheets, court documents, and case files. Increasingly they include DNA. Most states collect DNA from people arrested for as well as convicted of felonies, but the practice is expanding to misdemeanors. New York requires the collection of DNA samples from every person convicted of a state misdemeanor. Two-thirds of all states require DNA collection after certain misdemeanor convictions, usually sex offenses; seven states permit DNA collection from some misdemeanor arrestees who have not been convicted. Federal law authorizes the collection of DNA samples from any federal arrestee, including misdemeanor arrestees. Orange County, California, is actively building up its local law enforcement DNA database—it runs a "spit and acquit" program in which misdemeanor arrestees can get their charges dropped if they agree to give a DNA sample. DNA samples can expose a person and their relatives to future criminal investigations, but they can also potentially reveal genetic traits, diseases, and family genealogies to anyone with access to the genetic material. Landing in a DNA database because of a misdemeanor could eventually have far-reaching consequences that we cannot yet imagine.[22]

LOSING PUBLIC BENEFITS

A misdemeanor conviction or probation violation disqualifies a person from a wide range of benefits and opportunities. Under federal law, any probation violation for any type of misdemeanor disqualifies an individual from welfare benefits, including Temporary Assistance to Needy Families, food stamps, low-income housing, and Supplemental Security Income for the elderly and disabled. The consequences of a drug misdemeanor conviction are particularly harsh and can include the loss of health-care coverage, welfare, and student financial aid.[23]

Marisa Garcia, for instance, was a month away from starting her freshman year of college. It was also her nineteenth birthday, and she and her friends were out celebrating. But when they stopped for gas, police parked behind their van. "Eventually they started searching the car," Garcia remembers. "There was a little coin purse, with a small pipe with ash in it." It was hers.

Garcia had never been in trouble before and did not want to tell her mother, so she went to court alone, without a lawyer, and pled guilty immediately. She paid a $400 fine. Two months later, a letter from the federal financial aid office arrived, asking whether she had a drug conviction. "My heart kind of stopped," she says. Garcia lost her financial aid for a year. Her mother, already supporting four children, took out a loan to pay Garcia's tuition.

Garcia feels that she was punished twice: first with the fine and then again, far more severely, with the loss of her financial aid. If she had been richer, she could have paid for a drug-treatment program, which would have let her get her aid back sooner. "I still would have been arrested for marijuana," she muses, "but if I was wealthier, I could go out and do whatever I wanted and just be punished once."[24]

The Council of State Governments maintains a database of the collateral legal consequences of a criminal conviction; that database counts 8,958 different statutory provisions across the country that disqualify people with various misdemeanor convictions from professional occupations, housing opportunities, educational programs, and other benefits. For example, a misdemeanor could disqualify a person from being an athletic trainer or a midwife in Alabama, an optician in Alaska, a teacher in Colorado, joining a witness protection program in Delaware, visiting an inmate in Florida, being a veterinarian in Idaho or a real estate appraiser in Iowa, a geologist in Kentucky, getting a license to use cats and dogs for research in Michigan, obtaining securities licenses in Rhode Island, receiving unemployment benefits in Vermont, or, in West Virginia, obtaining a whitewater outfitter's license.[25]

One of the most devastating consequences of a low-level conviction can be the loss of housing, both private and public. Like employers, private landlords have easy access to criminal records; criminal background checks are a routine aspect of lease applications. For public housing, a conviction can cut off access by law. A conviction for disorderly conduct makes a person presumptively ineligible for New York City public housing for two years. In Baltimore, a misdemeanor conviction disqualifies a person from public housing for eighteen months.[26]

IMMIGRATION

The misdemeanor net puts immigrants at an especially heightened risk because it touches so many people and imposes criminal convictions for such low-level conduct. Hundreds of thousands of noncitizens are deported every year, the majority of them triggered by an arrest or conviction for minor offenses.

One of those people was Elizabeth Perez's husband. "We were supposed to do this together," said Perez, as her three-year-old son tugged on her long hair and her four-year-old daughter screamed for attention. "Raise the kids, I mean." Perez was thirty-five years old, an American-born former marine who served in Afghanistan. She lived in Painesville, Ohio. Her husband was deported to Mexico in 2010 after the police detained him during a traffic stop. He had fourteen-year-old misdemeanor charges for assault and marijuana possession. "It's been hard without my husband here," said Perez.[27]

Legal residents can lose their immigration status if they sustain a misdemeanor conviction. As one scholar describes it, deportable offenses include "misdemeanor drug possession[,] . . . theft of a ten-dollar video game, shoplifting fifteen dollars worth of baby clothes, . . . forging a check for less than twenty dollars . . . , theft of services offenses like turnstile jumping, misdemeanor indecent exposure, [and] petty shoplifting offenses." Undocumented immigrants, meanwhile, can face deportation if they are taken into government custody for something as minor as speeding. From 2009 to 2014, nearly 200,000 people were deported a result of being arrested solely for a traffic offense.[28]

Anabel Barron had lived in the United States for nearly twenty years and had four American-born children. In 2014, however, she faced deportation after being stopped for speeding and driving without a license. "I am afraid of being deported," she said at the time. "But for my children it's worse. They don't sleep the same. They don't eat. They don't want to go to school because they are afraid I am not going to be there when they get home."[29]

In places like Nashville, Tennessee, which deported nearly 10,000 people between 2007 and 2012, parents and college students interviewed during that period said that they were afraid to drive to school, to the hospital, and to their jobs for fear of being pulled over and deported.[30]

A misdemeanor arrest or conviction can completely alter an individual's immigration outlook. For undocumented defendants who are jailed on minor offenses but who have not yet come to the attention of immigration authorities, there is massive pressure to plead guilty immediately in the hope of avoiding an immigration warrant, called a detainer. Small plea bargain details, moreover, can have big immigration consequences for legal residents. Subtracting a single day from a 365-day sentence can transform a deportable offense into a nondeportable one. Attorneys can bargain a minor marijuana-possession charge into a disorderly conduct charge to spare the defendant automatic deportation.[31]

The main constitutional protections for misdemeanor defendants with immigration issues come in connection with the right to counsel. In *Padilla v. Kentucky*, the Supreme Court recognized that immigration law generates some of the most important penalties associated with a criminal conviction. Accordingly, a lawyer who fails to advise her client that he or she might be deportable as a result of a conviction is deemed "ineffective," that is, not acting as the kind of advocate guaranteed by the Sixth Amendment. Nevertheless, many immigrants still plead guilty to low-level offenses without knowing the full repercussions—in part because many of them never get a lawyer in the first place. Misdemeanor defendants have no constitutional right to a lawyer if they are not sentenced to incarceration, and many defendants who do have the right to counsel never get a lawyer even though they should. Many immigrants thus face the complicated consequences of a misdemeanor, including civil detention and deportation, on their own and without legal advice.[32]

FUTURE ENCOUNTERS

After a misdemeanor conviction, a person's interactions with the criminal process will never be the same. Police are more likely to arrest individuals who have prior low-level convictions rather than letting them walk away or merely issuing a ticket. Prosecutors are more likely to seek bail or to charge them with more serious crimes.[33] Judges typically impose longer sentences on people who have prior convictions, even minor convictions not involving a lawyer.

That is what happened to Kenneth Nichols. In 1983, driving under the influence was considered a relatively minor offense. When Nichols called a lawyer about it, the attorney was blunt, telling him not to bother paying a lawyer if he was pleading guilty. Nichols pled nolo contendere (no contest) with no lawyer and was fined $250. Seven years later, he was convicted of another offense. This time around, however, that old DUI did not seem so minor to the sentencing judge. Under the federal sentencing guidelines, Nichol's 1983 uncounseled misdemeanor conviction added over two years to his prison sentence for the new offense.[34]

Because a prior misdemeanor turns a person into a "recidivist," all sort of new rules and restrictions kick into place. A prior misdemeanor may disqualify a person from a drug or diversion program. Statutory penalties are usually higher for second-time offenders. For fine-only offenses, a prior conviction can double or triple the fine imposed or even convert the offense into a jailable crime.[35] The legal system's generally dismissive attitude toward misdemeanors exacerbates the problem, giving people the impression that racking up numerous low-level convictions will not haunt them later. By the time they learn the truth, it is too late.

These ratcheting dynamics are particularly destructive where people and neighborhoods are heavily policed. In places like Baltimore and Brooklyn, where African American men are stopped more often than average, their chances of getting an initial low-level conviction rise accordingly. The next time they are stopped, they have already been marked by the process and will be treated more harshly. The more times this happens, the harsher the system will act. For example, the New York City Transit Police Department operates on a recidivism policy. The first time people are stopped in the subway for a fare violation, they will be given a ticket. If they have a prior transit violation or arrest, however, they will be arrested. Because the New York Police Department has a history of racially disproportionate stops and arrests—92 percent of turnstile-jumping tickets are issued to people of color, who comprise 66 percent of city residents—this recidivism policy ensures that people of color will continue to be arrested at higher rates. This type of negative feedback loop imposes long records and increasingly harsh sentences not because people have become more dangerous or worse offenders but because the system is responding to its own cues and criminalizing and recriminalizing the same people over and over.[36]

FEAR, STIGMA, AND CIVIC DISRESPECT

By now it should be clear how many concrete burdens and disabilities are triggered by the misdemeanor experience. Being labeled a criminal, however, inflicts its own special psychological and social wounds.

Legal scholar Paul Butler has shared his own experiences. As law professors go, Butler is indisputably prominent. Educated at Yale and Harvard, a former federal prosecutor, and now an eminent scholar at Georgetown Law School, he appears routinely on national television and in national newspapers. Back in 1993, however, an unsavory neighbor falsely accused him of misdemeanor assault. After being arrested and released on his own recognizance, Butler went home and cried. "If I get convicted of this crime—this stupid little misdemeanor," he thought, "life as I know it is over." He hired one of the best criminal defense attorneys in Washington, DC, and a private investigator. Even so, he stayed frightened and uncertain right up until the moment of his acquittal. He later wrote that he knew that his innocence was "beside the point." Afterward, despite his acquittal and stellar background, he never quite recovered. "I'm not as innocent as I was before," he concluded. "I have a record."[37]

Even for highly educated, well-resourced professionals like Butler, the misdemeanor process can be painful and alienating. For the less educated, less wealthy people who are even more likely to encounter the system, it is often confusing, frightening, and disrespectful. Recall the story at the beginning of this book of Grandma G, who was led sobbing and in handcuffs out of the courtroom after a proceeding she did not understand and no one bothered to explain to her. For those with criminal records who have been through the process before, repeated exposure to the criminal system is a special trauma all its own. As legal scholar Jonathan Simon puts it, "The whole structure of misdemeanor justice . . . seems intended to subject the urban poor to a series of petty but cumulative blows to their dignity as citizens of equal standing."[38]

A misdemeanor arrest or conviction can undermine a person's relationships with friends and family, colleagues, and places of worship. Cindy Rodriguez, for example, could not afford her fines and fees while on probation in Rutherford County, Tennessee. The court decided that she had violated her probation by failing to pay, issued an arrest warrant, and put her mug shot on Facebook.

Her attorneys described what happened next: "Ms. Rodriguez . . . immediately received calls from her preacher and nearly ten people in the community, telling her that they saw that she had violated her probation. [She] was humiliated because she had to tell numerous people in her church and her community that she was destitute and disabled and had been 'violated' for not being able to pay. . . . It was deeply embarrassing for her to tell people in her community that she was too poor to pay."[39]

Contact with the criminal system also changes people's relationship to government; indeed, it can taint their very understanding of democratic society and their place in it. People who have been arrested and convicted may avoid institutions that keep formal records, such as banks, hospitals, and schools, exhibiting what one scholar calls "system avoidance." Studies show that people who have gone through the criminal system, even for minor offenses, distrust the government more and participate less in politics. As one interviewee explained, the unresponsive, heavy-handed criminal system is "the only government I know." Others are even more pessimistic: "All we know about government is bad. We don't know the good aspects."[40] The petty-offense process teaches this cynical, destructive lesson in civics to 13 million Americans every year.

It is a lesson that has been taught in lower courts for a long time. In 1979, sociologist Malcolm Feeley wrote a famous book about the misdemeanor court in New Haven, Connecticut, called *The Process Is the Punishment*.[41] His title captured the fact that merely being hauled into court and going through the judicial process was often more punitive than any formal sentence the judge might impose. Even when their cases were dismissed, people had already been punished simply by being forced to show up and account for themselves. Feeley argued that the judicial process itself—not the formal conviction or punishment—was in many ways the point of the exercise, a way of managing poor, disadvantaged, or disorderly people regardless of whether they were legally guilty.

Feeley's aphorism is even truer today. The petty-offense process starts "punishing" people long before they get to court, and it keeps punishing them long after they have completed their court-imposed sentences. It can even punish those who are never convicted of anything. Being stopped, arrested, cited, jailed, posting bail, telling your family and employer—these experiences take a heavy personal and social toll. The damaging consequences of a brush with the criminal system kick in from the very beginning. Indeed, for people of color, immigrants, and others who fully expect to be touched by the criminal system, fear of the inevitable encounter can haunt them long before it ever takes place. Afterward, the repercussions continue long after the legal punishment is over. The formal mark of an arrest or conviction record lasts a lifetime; the psychological and economic burdens of being convicted can last just as long. The total impact of these burdens and exclusions can be so great as to amount to what some call a "new civil death," a permanent barrier to full civic and economic participation.[42]

Technically speaking, the law does not recognize all these different hardships as punishment; nor does it acknowledge the many ways that we punish without crime. From the law's formal perspective, Tyrone Tomlin's eye injury doesn't count. Donyelle Hall losing her job doesn't count. Neither does Marisa Garcia losing her financial aid. The impact on their families doesn't count either.[43] But as these stories reveal, a legalistic approach misses the true punitive weight and extent of the misdemeanor experience for those who actually go through it. An encounter with the misdemeanor system for even the pettiest conduct can derail a person's life.

Conversely, avoiding that misdemeanor can keep all sorts of doors open. In his memoir *Dreams from My Father*, former president Barack Obama acknowledges that like many young people in high school and college, he experimented with drugs. He was never arrested and therefore never sustained the lasting damage that a low-level drug offense would have entailed. Many years later, speaking to journalists outside a federal prison, Obama compared himself to the prisoners inside. "These are young people who made mistakes that aren't that different from the mistakes I made. . . . The difference is that they did not have the kind of support structures, the second chances, the resources that would allow them to survive those mistakes."[44] Had the young Barack Obama been forced to survive the impact of a misdemeanor conviction, American history might have been very different indeed.

| 2 |

SIZE

WHEN I DECIDED TO WRITE THIS BOOK A FEW YEARS
ago, there was almost no public information about the national misdemeanor landscape, how many cases there were, or what kinds of
crimes were being prosecuted. There is still very little. There are two
main reasons for this lack of information. First, misdemeanors have
long been deemed unimportant by government officials, scholars, and
the media and therefore have not gotten the attention and resources
needed to keep track of them. Second, counting them is difficult. The
petty-offense process is enormous and decentralized, comprised of
thousands of courts and judicial institutions. States vary wildly in how
they keep track of their misdemeanor data, or even whether they do so
at all. Some states have unified court systems in which all misdemeanors are filed and counted in one type of court, while other states maintain a dizzying array of local institutions that process misdemeanors,
including municipal courts, summary courts, magistrate courts, justice
courts, and mayor courts, each maintained by a different jurisdiction,

often with its own separate municipal code. Some of those lower courts report their caseloads to a statewide authority; some don't. Indeed, some states may not even know how many *courts* they have because cities have the power to create and abolish municipal courts at will.[1]

In 2009, a report titled *Minor Crimes, Massive Waste: The Terrible Toll of America's Broken Misdemeanor Courts* concluded that 10.5 million misdemeanors were filed nationally every year. The report did not actually count all those misdemeanors—the numbers were simply not available. Rather, the researchers extrapolated a national figure from the filing rates for twelve states that had reported their caseloads to the National Center for State Courts (NCSC). At the time, that 10 million number was shocking. By comparison, between 3 million and 4 million felony cases are filed annually in state and federal courts, generating approximately 1 million new convictions each year. The federal system is even smaller, with around 80,000 criminal filings and approximately 70,000 convictions per year. Homicide and rape—the most serious state crimes—comprise less than 4 percent of felonies. Mass incarceration and the oversized prison population are largely the result of felony convictions: most of America's 2.2 million prisoners are serving felony sentences. But the 2009 report made clear that the bottom of the pyramid was much larger than anyone had realized.[2]

In 2016, I decided to take a closer look. Every state has an Administrative Office of the Court (AOC), an agency responsible for collecting information about the state's court systems and caseloads. I sent a letter to every AOC asking how many misdemeanors its state had filed the year before, in 2015, for what kinds of crimes, and what happened to those cases. As far as I know, no one had ever tried this before. In addition, since 2009 the NCSC had begun collecting information from more states about their misdemeanor dockets, so new data for thirty-five states were now available. I also gathered all the other sources I could find: judicial annual reports, governmental investigations, studies by nonprofits and journalists. Eventually, I had the largest collection of data on the size and composition of the US misdemeanor system ever assembled.

This research leads me to conclude that over 13 million misdemeanor cases were filed in the United States in 2015. (Again, you can look at the appendix to see where I got the information for each state.) Thirteen million annual misdemeanors is an astounding number. It means that getting charged with a low-level crime is a normal part of American life, about as common as going the doctor when you get the flu, buying a truck or SUV, or attending a four-year college.[3]

This new information not only tells us the size of the national docket, it lets us see how different states vary in their reliance on misdemeanors. The national average filing rate is 4,124 per 100,000 people, approximately four times the rate for felonies. At the low end, Wisconsin, Oregon, and Kansas each file fewer than 1,300 misdemeanors per 100,000 residents (Table 2.1). At the high end, Delaware, Arkansas, and West Virginia file over 12,000 misdemeanors per 100,000—one case or more for every ten people in the state.[4] It's hard to know what high filing rates mean all by themselves. They might, for example, signify overcriminalization—sweeping too many people into the system. But they could also reflect a decision to treat potential felony offenses as misdemeanors more often. Either way, the extent to which a state relies on misdemeanors is an important part of its criminal justice fingerprint.

The size of the misdemeanor system, however, cannot be measured in numbers alone. The ultimate point of the exercise is to map out the scale and nature of a crucial aspect of our democracy. How broad is the state apparatus that creates and manages low-level offenses? Which misdemeanors does it rely on the most, and what kinds of conduct do they punish? A system that targeted mostly DUIs, for example, would be very different from a system that largely went after jaywalking. Where are misdemeanors used and against whom? And what really happens to those millions of people in the system? Knowing the total number of misdemeanors is important, but it is just a step toward understanding the true scale of the phenomenon.

Measuring the size of the misdemeanor system, however, is tricky in a number of ways. First, as we have just seen, misdemeanor punishment

TABLE 2.1. 2015 STATE MISDEMEANOR FILING RATES

RANK	STATE	FILING RATE PER 100,000
1	Delaware	15,557
2	Arkansas	12,997
3	West Virginia	12,489
4	Mississippi	10,841
5	Texas	9,637
6	Arizona	7,130
7	Virginia	6,930
8	Montana	6,738
9	Kentucky	5,751
10	North Dakota	5,549
11	New Jersey	5,312
12	Nebraska	5,241
13	Ohio	5,201
14	Michigan	4,960
15	Alabama	4,926
16	Hawaii	4,770
17	South Carolina	4,637
18	Nevada	4,536
19	Idaho	4,457
20	Maryland	4,197
21	North Carolina	3,856
22	Wyoming	3,609
23	Alaska	3,325
24	Iowa	3,299
25	District of Columbia	3,158
26	Maine	3,088
27	Utah	3,054
28	Georgia	2,933
29	California	2,932
30	Florida	2,810
31	Minnesota	2,767
32	Washington	2,698
33	Connecticut	2,556
34	South Dakota	2,445
35	Massachusetts	2,325

RANK	STATE	FILING RATE PER 100,000
36	New Hampshire	2,315
37	Rhode Island	2,288
38	New Mexico	2,251
39	Pennsylvania	2,232
40	Indiana	2,211
41	Vermont	2,050
42	Illinois	1,918
43	Missouri	1,830
44	New York	1,684
45	Colorado	1,340
46	Wisconsin	1,277
47	Oregon	1,250
48	Kansas	891
49	Louisiana	Unknown
50	Oklahoma	Unknown
51	Tennessee	Unknown

Note: Filing rates based on data compiled by the author. See the appendix and Table A.1.

is far-reaching and amorphous. The full impact of a misdemeanor—and thus the full influence of the misdemeanor system—turns on all the ways that an encounter with the petty-offense process can affect a person's life. It's hard to measure that. But the problem tells us where to look. For example, it makes the initial filing of a case just as important, if not more so, as its eventual outcome. Many petty cases are diverted—put on hold for months while the person is monitored and supervised—and then eventually dismissed, which means that people may endure the grueling misdemeanor process without sustaining a permanent conviction. One study estimates that approximately one-third of all misdemeanor cases are diverted or dismissed. In New York, nearly half are. In Connecticut, almost 60 percent of misdemeanor cases get diverted. It might look as if those people escaped the system, but it's not that simple. They may have spent time in jail, lost jobs and housing, or paid out hundreds of dollars in fines and fees. Diversion programs permit people to avoid formal convictions but can involve long periods of expensive, intrusive supervision. People in such situations may never be formally convicted of a crime but can still be punished in a wide variety of ways.[5] Convictions are thus an imperfect measure of just how big and influential the petty-offense process really is.

Evaluating the size of the misdemeanor system is also difficult for logistical reasons. Some states denied my data request altogether. Others gave me only some of the information I asked for. Some told me they didn't keep such data. For some states, there were significant disparities between the totals reported to the NCSC and the data I collected from other sources. In addition, the misdemeanor system includes many small independent courts that do not report their caseloads to the state AOC or otherwise make that data public, even though they generate many thousands of criminal cases. I looked for filing statistics from those courts, but whether or not I found them was often a matter of luck. South Carolina, for example, has a huge summary court system. Over four hundred magistrate and municipal courts handle over 200,000 criminal misdemeanor cases per year, not including nearly 1 million additional traffic cases. I didn't unearth that information myself—the South Carolina judiciary denied my records request and does not report its lower-court data to the NCSC or on its public website. We only have these figures because of a 2014 public records request made by the National Association of Criminal Defense Lawyers and the American Civil Liberties Union. In 2014, Mississippi began to require its hundreds of municipal and justice courts to report their caseload data to the state for the first time. Accordingly, we now know that those courts generated approximately 300,000 misdemeanors and another 400,000 traffic cases in 2015. But if I had tried gathering this data just a year earlier, I couldn't have learned that.[6]

These kinds of counting challenges make it hard to talk about the system over time. Thirteen million cases in 2015 is more than the 10 million cases estimated in 2009, but that doesn't necessarily mean that the system is growing. Indeed, there are some indications that it might be shrinking. Misdemeanor arrests, like all arrests, have been falling since 2008. Misdemeanor filing rates may also have been going down.[7] It could well be that the system was even bigger a decade ago—we just didn't know it.

Even if we had perfect information from police, prosecutors, and courts, it would still be tricky to say just how big the misdemeanor system is because the term "misdemeanor" itself is both over- and underinclusive.[8] On the one hand, it is a legal label: states have criminal codes that officially designate certain crimes as "misdemeanors." But sometimes that label is applied to behaviors that we don't think of as crimes at all, like speeding or spitting. Should we count them? Conversely, there are other legal categories—violations, infractions, summonses—that technically are not misdemeanors, or sometimes not even crimes at all, but function just like misdemeanors and impose the same sorts of punishments and burdens. Should we include those? Throughout this book I use the term "misdemeanor" broadly to refer to all forms of low-level criminal offenses, but that category contains all sorts of variations.

Traffic misdemeanors are particularly challenging. Twenty-five states designate various kinds of speeding as a criminal misdemeanor carrying a potential jail sentence. In Mississippi, speeding can trigger a ten-day jail term, and courts routinely impose suspended sentences for speeding tickets to enforce compliance. In Georgia, all traffic violations are criminal misdemeanors. This creates a counting dilemma. If we included all those criminal speeding cases, the national misdemeanor total would be closer to 33 million, swamped by the speeding cases.[9] For this reason I decided to leave them out; state judiciaries do not count speeding cases in their misdemeanor totals either, even when they are technically crimes. But leaving them out admittedly understates the scope of the criminal misdemeanor system and its potential impact on an additional 20 million lives.

Conversely, serious motor vehicle offenses such as driving under the influence and driving on a suspended license are usually labeled misdemeanors, and most states count them—or at least they count DUIs—in their misdemeanor totals. But not always. And traffic is not the only challenge. There are civil or noncriminal charges that are not technically crimes but can result in incarceration and other substantial punishments. For example, thousands of civil citations for offenses like disorderly conduct are filed in the Milwaukee Municipal Court every year. They are not misdemeanors or even crimes, but failure to pay the fines—for disorderly conduct up to $500—carries a twenty-day jail sentence, and thousands of Milwaukee residents are incarcerated every year as a result.[10]

It turns out that counting misdemeanors requires a number of judgment calls. In arriving at a national total, I did not include speeding, civil violations, and other offenses that are not technically crimes, even though many such cases impose misdemeanor-like punishments. As a result, 13 million understates the size of the misdemeanor apparatus and the full national impact of low-level offense prosecutions.

The misdemeanor category is further complicated because "minor" and "serious" are relative concepts. In 1769, eminent English legal commentator Sir William Blackstone explained the difference between felony crimes and misdemeanors like this. "In common usage," he wrote, "the word, 'crimes,' is made to denote such offenses as are of a deeper and more atrocious dye; while smaller faults, and omissions of less consequence, are comprized under the gentler name of 'misdemeanors' only." But that felony-misdemeanor distinction used to have a very different meaning. In Blackstone's England, and in the early decades of the American states, which borrowed English law, felonies referred to heinous crimes that could be punished by death. All lesser crimes were misdemeanors, punishable by fine or imprisonment, a class that included many serious offenses. An 1842 British treatise lists dozens of grave offenses deemed misdemeanors, including stealing dead bodies, perjury, extortion, and witchcraft.[11]

When it comes to punishment, moreover, misdemeanors can be punished as seriously as felonies and vice versa. As one government official complained in a report to the US Senate in 1900, "The distinction between felonies and misdemeanors is ill-defined and arbitrary. The relation between the two is constantly shifting in the laws of the different States; misdemeanors become felonies and felonies become misdemeanors. . . . So far as the duration of the punishment is concerned, the sentence for a misdemeanor may last longer than that for a felony. . . . It was formerly assumed that a sentence to a penitentiary or State prison was a much severer punishment than a sentence to a county jail. This is no longer really true."[12]

Today, the modern legal approach is to define a misdemeanor as an offense for which a person cannot be sentenced to more than one year of incarceration. But that one-year maximum is not hard and fast. Some states have misdemeanors that carry two- or three-year sentences. Federal law defines "petty offense" as a crime that carries no more than a six-month sentence, a "Class B misdemeanor" in federal parlance.[13] Offenses such as criminal violations and infractions all have different definitions in different jurisdictions: some carry jail time, some don't.

Because the misdemeanor label is so broad and flexible, it does not reveal how serious the underlying crime is. Some quite serious crimes are misdemeanors, such as domestic violence or drunk driving. Misdemeanor theft can involve hundreds of dollars of stolen merchandise or stealing a pack of gum. A felony theft in one state might well be treated as misdemeanor larceny in another. Drug-possession crimes are especially malleable. In some jurisdictions, possessing even a trace amount of cocaine is a felony, while other states treat that very same conduct as a minor offense. Paraphernalia possession can be either a felony or a misdemeanor. "I don't make a clear distinction between misdemeanors and felonies," says Milwaukee district attorney John Chisholm. "There can be really, really serious misdemeanors, and some felonies are not all that serious."[14]

The misdemeanor-felony distinction is further eroded by the fact that many low-level felonies are handled a lot like misdemeanors even though, as a matter of law, they carry longer potential sentences. The average felony sentence in this country is just over four years, but that average masks wide variation. At least a quarter of felony offenders are released the same year they are incarcerated: in effect they serve misdemeanor-sized sentences. Anywhere from a sixth to a third of fel-onies end up being pled down to misdemeanors.[15] Less serious felonies, moreover, are often processed in the same ways as misdemeanors—in bulk, quickly, with heavy pressure on defendants to plead guilty.

In sum, there are few bright lines between different types of misde-meanors or even between misdemeanors and low-level felonies. This further complicates the task of evaluating the size of the misdemeanor system, since it is hard to say precisely where it begins and where it ends. Instead of relying on legal labels, we need to ask substantive questions about the purposes of these low-level crimes, what sorts of conduct they go after, how they are generated, and what they signify for the individuals who go through the process. These can be some of the most complex and socially significant questions that we collec-tively ask about our criminal justice system.

For example, the most serious misdemeanors such as domestic violence and DUI are "serious" in two senses. First, the conduct that they prohibit is harmful and wrong: society has come to the (rela-tively recent) consensus that intimate violence is a serious matter, that driving drunk is a grave threat to others, and that engaging in either type of conduct is blameworthy and deserving of public cen-sure and punishment. This is the classic model of criminal culpabil-ity. Criminal laws define bad and dangerous behavior; people who engage in that behavior must be deterred and deserve to be punished. Such misdemeanors are like miniature felonies.

Domestic violence and DUI are also "serious" in a second sense: the criminal system devotes significant time and resources to think-ing about, deciding, and managing such cases. Domestic violence en-forcement has come to include a complex and often highly intrusive array of arrest and prosecution policies, injunctions, specialized courts, and social welfare institutions.[16] Convictions sometimes carry special penalties—including the prohibition against carrying a firearm. Simi-larly, DUI arrests and prosecutions typically rely on specialized breath-alyzer technologies, while drunk-driving litigation is animated by a robust and sophisticated defense bar that serves a relatively wealthy defendant population. Penalties can include ignition locks, mandatory Alcoholics Anonymous meetings, and a wide array of monitoring strategies. Many jurisdictions collect specialized data on DUI and domestic violence cases. To be sure, these offenses raise their own thorny questions of fairness and accuracy, but they do not suffer from obscurity or neglect. They may be misdemeanors, but no one thinks they are petty, and the system as a whole does not treat them lightly.

At the other end of the spectrum are the least serious misdemeanors: order-maintenance or so-called quality-of-life offenses such as trespassing, jaywalking, and disorderly conduct. These offenses are "minor" for the reverse reasons. The conduct they prohibit is not particularly harmful or wrong. The New York disorderly conduct statute, for example, includes the offense of making "unreasonable noise." The jaywalking ordinance in Ferguson, Missouri, titled "Manner of walking along roadway," made it a crime to walk in the street. The decision to criminalize such conduct does not flow from fear or moral outrage. Instead, order-maintenance offenses are designed to regulate unwanted conduct, to move disfavored people in and out of certain places, and to give the police flexibility. Sometimes they are seen as ways of preventing more serious crime later on down the road. Such strategies take aim not so much at individual criminals as at classes of people and types of places. These crimes are not miniature felonies— they are doing something different. They target unpopular people and groups who are deemed unpleasant or inherently risky, not individuals who have harmed someone else or done something morally wrong.[17]

Order offenses are also "minor" in the sense that the system handles them cavalierly. Arrests can be shaky, often lacking in probable cause, and made in bulk aimed at groups, neighborhoods, or classes of people. There are no special courts, advocates, or technologies— defendants are swept through the system in speedy and routine ways. Some jurisdictions do not even keep track of how many such cases pass through their courts.

When I asked the various state AOCs for their misdemeanor information, I asked what kinds of cases were being filed. Few states gave me that information. As a result, we still do not know precisely what percentage of the national docket is made up of more serious misdemeanors like assault, what percentage consists of order-maintenance offenses, and how many are suspended-license cases. But I did find partial answers. Some states gave me data on individual offense categories as described below, and sometimes state-level information was available from other sources. FBI data, while incomplete, indicate that theft, assault, and DUI are probably the most common misdemeanors—the meat and potatoes of low-level dockets.[18] Domestic violence is sometimes included in the assault category, while some states keep track of it separately.

I specifically asked the state AOCs for statistics on suspended-license, marijuana-possession, and order-maintenance cases because these three categories exert outsized social and economic influence. Although we can't always calculate how common they are, we know that they sweep up hundreds of thousands of people in ways that turn heavily on wealth and race. For example, suspended-license cases comprise as much as 30 percent of certain local dockets, in some places reaching 60 percent. In both Washington and Florida, they constitute one-third of all state misdemeanors. Connecticut told me that 28,000 such cases are filed each year—over 16 percent of all misdemeanors. The offense is problematic because it is largely a crime of poverty: most licenses are suspended because people cannot afford to pay a traffic fine. Sometimes enforcement is immigration related. In 2012, the top charge triggering deportation in Davidson County, Tennessee, was driving without a license. License suspensions, and the threat of criminal charges for driving while suspended, are a major source of job loss and impoverishment.[19] It would be great to know how many of these cases there are in the United States as a whole.

Marijuana possession is another enormously influential misdemeanor, the most common US drug offense. According to the FBI, there were 574,640 marijuana-possession arrests in 2015—nearly half of all drug arrests nationwide. While national data do not reveal what happened after those arrests, local data show a wide range of outcomes. In New York City, the majority of possession arrests resulted in a diversionary disposition called an adjournment in contemplation of dismissal, which might or might not become a conviction. In Texas county courts, by contrast, 40 percent of marijuana-possession filings result in immediate conviction, and less than 20 percent are diverted. In Kentucky, 62 percent of possession cases result in immediate convictions.[20]

Drug misdemeanor totals are underinclusive because they do not include the millions of citations and summonses issued every year for marijuana possession that do not involve arrest. This is an increasingly large and important category as more and more localities decriminalize. But even decriminalized citations can mark people's records and can still translate into incarceration when people fail to pay their fines. For example, Illinois makes approximately 41,000 marijuana arrests every year, but over one hundred municipalities also have ticketing ordinances, and local police in those jurisdictions issue hundreds of additional citations for possession. New York City alone issued over 13,000 marijuana summonses in 2014.[21] Because it is heavily skewed by both race and class, marijuana enforcement drives some of the most problematic aspects of the war on drugs as well as the misdemeanor process.

Order-maintenance crimes are another crucial category of misdemeanor, sitting at the heart of urban policing and the criminal system's social control function. It's hard to know how many cases there are—I asked every state AOC, but only a few responded. Here's what we know. For 2015 the FBI reported 386,078 arrests for disorderly conduct, 405,880 for drunkenness, 25,151 for vagrancy, 44,802 for curfew and loitering offenses, and, oddly enough, 1,389 for "suspicion," which by definition is not a crime at all. As with many misdemeanor statistics, however, these numbers are incomplete. The FBI's catch-all category of "all other offenses" includes over 3 million additional arrests, many of them likely for order-maintenance crimes. Where available, local data reveal thousands of additional order-maintenance cases. The FBI does not provide national data on trespassing arrests, but in 2016 approximately 1,000 criminal trespassing charges were filed in Seattle Municipal Court alone, while Baltimore arrests over 1,000 people for trespassing every year. In 2015, Kentucky prosecuted over 7,000 trespassing cases; Connecticut filed nearly 5,000 trespassing cases, as well as another 15,000 disorderly conduct cases. In Wisconsin, over 20 percent of the entire misdemeanor docket in state circuit courts consists of disorderly conduct and resisting-arrest cases.[22]

Order-maintenance crimes raise thorny questions of accuracy as well as fairness: they have long served as a way of managing disfavored and vulnerable populations.[23] The fact that counting them is so hard reminds us just how informal and discretionary the practice has been. Keeping better track of these offenses is a first step toward recognizing their influence. Likewise, driving on a suspended license and marijuana possession fuel deep inegalitarian aspects of the misdemeanor process. While they may not constitute the majority of cases, they generate some of the institution's most important challenges and thus deserve sustained scrutiny.

What about the people? I asked the state AOCs for the gender, race, and ethnicity of the people in their misdemeanor case filings, but few gave me that information. Nationally, approximately half of all misdemeanor arrests are of white men: between one-quarter and one-third are of women, depending on the offense; one-third are of African Americans, and one-fifth are of Hispanics.[24] We don't know if these statistics hold true for particular states or whether the demographics are the same for arrests as they are for case filings. Moreover, these kinds of general statistics don't reveal the income, education, health, or other characteristics of the individuals who populate the misdemeanor system. So we have to think about those questions in additional ways.

On the one hand, anybody can get a misdemeanor. Recall law professor Paul Butler, the Harvard- and Yale-educated federal prosecutor charged with and acquitted of minor assault. Celebrities as famous as Justin Bieber (resisting arrest), Kiefer Sutherland (drunk driving), and Hugh Grant (lewd conduct) have been convicted of misdemeanors. Victoria's Secret model Jessica White was sentenced to community service, anger management classes, and a fine in exchange for the dismissal of a 2010 misdemeanor assault charge.[25]

Sometimes misdemeanors are used proactively against political activists and dissidents. Hundreds of participants in the 2011 Occupy movement were charged with offenses such as disorderly conduct and trespassing. In May 1960, Dr. Martin Luther King Jr.—who went to jail thirty times—was convicted of driving without a Georgia license (at the time he apparently had an Alabama license). He was sentenced to a $25 fine and a twelve-month suspended sentence. Seven months later, he was arrested for trespassing during a sit-in demonstration at an Atlanta department store, which violated his misdemeanor probation. He was sentenced to four months in prison.[26]

But most of the time, misdemeanor defendants are not so high profile. Thousands of poor, homeless, or addicted individuals fill municipal and other lower courts, cycling in and out of jail and accruing fines and fees that they will never be able to pay. Generally speaking, the average criminal defendant is poorer, less educated, less employed, and less healthy than the average American. As many as 80 percent of male arrestees may have a recent history of substance abuse or test positive for drugs at the time of arrest; in many jurisdictions fewer than half are employed. More than half of prison inmates lack basic literacy and information-processing skills. Forty percent have trouble using a menu to calculate the cost of a sandwich and salad. Thirty-seven percent are high school dropouts, more than half of jail inmates have mental health problems, and 80 percent of felony defendants are too poor to afford a lawyer.[27]

Most of these statistics are drawn from felony populations. Even as the misdemeanor system reaches more broadly and affects a wider array of people than the felony machinery, it keeps less data on its 13 million subjects, and so, ironically, we know less about who those individuals are, where they live, and their economic and educational status. It is clear, nevertheless, that the vulnerable—the poor, homeless, young, and addicted—are particularly likely to get caught up by the petty-offense process. The Honorable Andra Sparks, for example,

is presiding judge for the City of Birmingham Municipal Court in Alabama. When judges tell people to go fix their licenses, he says, people
often come back to court without having done so. He explains why.
In his courtroom, "it turns out that the single biggest problem with
people getting their licenses fixed is that they can't read."[28]

The misdemeanor population is complicated. Poverty is not the
entire story since the misdemeanor system reaches above and beyond the truly disadvantaged. Working people who can't afford to
pay a speeding ticket can get trapped in the misdemeanor net; so
can homeowners saddled with municipal citations or urban residents
subject to order-maintenance policing on their way home from work.
Different crimes, moreover, have different profiles. Drunk-driving
defendants tend to have higher education and income levels, while
order-maintenance crimes disproportionately sweep up people of
color.[29] Because it is so large and does so many different kinds of
work for the state, the misdemeanor process touches the employed,
the educated, the middle- and working-class, the destitute, and the
homeless; people of all races, ages, and ethnicities; those living in the
largest cities and in the smallest rural communities. This reach makes
the petty-offense process an extraordinarily influential American institution. The next chapter explains how it works.

PROCESS

ON PAPER, THE MISDEMEANOR LEGAL PROCESS LOOKS A lot like the criminal process that we use to handle serious felonies such as murder or rape. Most of the constitutional and evidentiary rules are the same. Police, prosecutors, defense attorneys, and judges have more or less the same job descriptions. There are courtrooms, occasional trials, and a lot of plea bargains. But as we have already begun to see, the misdemeanor and felony worlds can differ greatly in practice. Enormous, sloppy, and fast, much of the misdemeanor process takes place on the fly, in bulk, without public scrutiny or even a public record. In courtrooms across the country, defendants are rushed through en masse in minutes, routinely without lawyers, under heavy pressure to plead guilty. Police, prosecutors, defense attorneys, and judges often behave differently when dealing with misdemeanors than they do when handling serious cases.

Because the petty-offense process marches to the beat of its own peculiar drum, the convictions that it produces do not convey the same meaning as serious felony convictions. Of course, misdemeanors differ from felonies in the sense that felony crimes usually involve more dangerous or blameworthy criminal behavior. But misdemeanor convictions are also different because they are made differently. Remember that a criminal conviction is a weighty pronouncement. It conveys negative information about its bearer—most importantly the idea that he or she *did something bad*. When the process of making that conviction is flawed, unreliable, or unfair, the conviction itself may become misleading.

To be sure, the line between the misdemeanor and felony process is not always a bright one. Sometimes felony conduct is indistinguishable from misdemeanor conduct. Sometimes the felony world also rushes through its low-level cases in ways that undermine fairness and accuracy.[1] But the misdemeanor machinery is uniquely cavalier about following rules, checking the evidence, and honoring the rule of law. Understanding how that machinery actually works forces us to reconsider the significance of the millions of convictions that it generates every year. Accordingly, this chapter examines each step of the misdemeanor process, the major players, the decisions they make, and the rules governing those decisions. Starting with the police.

STOPS AND ARRESTS

The misdemeanor process begins on the street. Police make that all-important initial decision—who will get swept up into the petty offense process in the first place? Those policing decisions fill the system at the front end, shaping its entire character and exercising enormous influence over what happens later on.

When a police officer stops or arrests someone, constitutional law refers to the encounter as a "seizure." Seizures are governed by the Fourth Amendment: a person is deemed to have been seized when he or she is no longer free to walk away or decline the encounter with the police. Constitutional law regulates the kinds of seizures police can make depending on how much evidence they have. If police have no evidence that a person has committed a crime, they cannot stop him or her at all. If police have "reasonable suspicion" that a crime has been committed, they can engage in a brief "investigative detention," which can only last as long as it takes to confirm or deny police suspicions. This type of seizure is commonly referred to as a "Terry stop," named for the Supreme Court case *Terry v. Ohio*. Stops occurring on the street are typically accompanied by a body search for weapons—a "frisk"—so the whole encounter is referred to as a "stop-and-frisk."[2]

Reasonable suspicion does not require a lot of evidence. The Court has said that it must be "more than an inchoate and unparticularized suspicion or hunch," which means that police cannot seize people based merely on their intuitions about who looks suspicious. And it has to be "grounded in specific and articulable facts" that suggest that a crime is being committed. But police can rely on common or innocent facts if they could be taken to imply that criminal activity might be afoot. Running away from police in a high-crime neighborhood is legally sufficient to give police reasonable suspicion to stop you. Conversely, courts have held that, by themselves, "furtive movements," "time of day," and "looking out of place" are not enough to establish reasonable suspicion, although in practice people are often stopped on those bases. Car stops are also Terry stops, and violation of any provision of the traffic code is legally sufficient to permit them. Typically such seizures are made for speeding and other routine traffic violations, but they also have a problematic history of being used as a pretext to stop and search African American and Latino drivers.[3]

To arrest someone police need more evidence, so-called probable cause. By definition, probable cause is more than reasonable suspicion. This explains why police stop more people than they arrest. In New York City, for example, which for decades had a very high stop-and-frisk rate, only about 12 percent of stops resulted in an arrest or summons. Everyone else walked away, meaning that most of the time police did not find probable cause to arrest them.

But probable cause is still not very much evidence. It is less than a fifty-fifty chance that the person is guilty, and it requires far less evidence than guilt beyond a reasonable doubt. The Court defines it as a fair probability, given all the circumstances, that a crime has been committed. It "requires only a probability or substantial chance of criminal activity, not an actual showing of such activity." There is no need to show that a crime is actually being committed: innocent behavior can be enough. For example, being a passenger in a car in which drugs are found is sufficient to establish probable cause and justify arrest. Playing video games in a bar where the bartender is a known heroin dealer is not.[4]

An arrest is far more intrusive than a Terry stop. It involves being taken into custody and can include booking, fingerprinting, mug shots, and a strip search at the police station or jail. It generates a permanent arrest record. Once arrested, a person can be jailed for up to two days before a judge must review the evidence to determine whether the police had probable cause to make the arrest in the first place. If you are arrested in your car, police can search it. If you are arrested in your home, police can search the area of your residence in which you are arrested.[5]

Although the legal standards for misdemeanor and felony seizures are technically the same, in practice they shake out very differently. Basically it is easier to articulate probable cause that a person has been disorderly than it is to state a fair probability that he or she has killed someone. The ease with which police can legally make a stop or an arrest thus depends in part on the seriousness of the underlying crime.[6] Getting arrested for murder is hard; getting arrested for an order-maintenance crime or, like Gail Atwater, a fine-only traffic violation is relatively easy.

Gail Atwater's seatbelt arrest was important for another reason. Even as the Supreme Court decided that her arrest was constitutional, the justices admitted that it probably wasn't a good idea. They called her arrest a "pointless indignity" and "gratuitous humiliation . . . imposed by a police officer who was (at best) exercising extremely poor judgment." The Court even recognized the irony of arresting and jailing a person who could not be sentenced to jail for the actual offense. Nevertheless, the Court permitted it. In so doing, it authorized a wide range of intrusions on anyone arrested for a minor violation, even if the maximum punishment for the violation itself is only a fine.[7]

An arrest is the beginning of the formal criminal process, the doorway to a possible prosecution. But arrests are not the only way to initiate a case. Alternatively, a summons or a citation can inform people of the charges against them and instruct them to show up in court. The most familiar version of this model is the traffic ticket, which lets people skip court by admitting guilt and paying a fixed amount. In many cities, police can issue tickets for everything from littering to marijuana possession to disorderly conduct; some ticketable offenses are fine only, but many carry potential jail time. Low-level courts process millions of such citations each year.[8]

Arrests are an enormously complex arena of interaction between police and citizens. While the legal purpose of an arrest is to identify people who may have committed a crime, in practice police use their arrest power for many reasons: to maintain neighborhood order, clear a corner, send a message in a high-crime neighborhood, stop a fight, or gather information. Sometimes arrests are a response to community demands: in interviews police and prosecutors report that they face heavy political pressure to "do something" to address disorder.[9]

Police officers may also be under pressure to make arrests in order to demonstrate productivity or meet a departmental quota. Some police departments use misdemeanor arrests as performance indicators, instructing officers like the ones who arrested Sharif Stinson to make arrests and issue summonses regardless of whether a crime has been committed. In Baltimore, the US Department of Justice discovered a long-standing policy whereby, as the 2016 report put it, "[police] leadership pressured officers to increase the number of arrests and to 'clear corners,' whether or not the officers observed criminal activity." In Ferguson, Missouri, police made high numbers of arrests under pressure to raise revenue.[10]

Sometimes police make arrests because their supervisors want to send a message. The following statements were tape recorded in 2008 in Brooklyn's 81st Precinct, where Deputy Inspector Steven Mauriello ordered his officers to arrest virtually everybody at 120 Chauncey Street: "Everybody goes. I don't care. You're on 120 Chauncey and they're popping champagne? Yoke 'em. Put them through the system. They got bandannas on, arrest them. Everybody goes tonight. They're underage? Fuck it." Similar orders were given by a sergeant. "If they're on a corner, make 'em move. If they don't want to move, lock 'em up. Done deal."[11]

Back in 1967, the Supreme Court recognized that low-level policing can be as much about asserting police clout as it is about catching criminals. The Court worried about "situations where the 'stop and frisk' of youths or minority group members is motivated by the officers' perceived need to maintain the power image of the beat officer, an aim sometimes accomplished by humiliating anyone who attempts to undermine police control of the streets.'" Forty years later, former Baltimore police officer Peter Moskos described the modern practice as follows: "On street corners in Baltimore's Eastern District, people—usually young black males involved with drugs—are arrested when they talk back to police or refuse to obey a police officer's orders to move. . . . These lockups are used by the police to assert authority or get criminals off the street."[12]

Offenses like disorderly conduct and resisting arrest are sometimes referred to as "contempt-of-cop" crimes because they give police the opportunity to arrest people who challenge police authority. Such offenses pose a unique problem in misdemeanor policing because they give police the ability to *generate* probable cause during a stop by asserting that the stopped person has engaged in disruptive behavior. According to one study, "There is abundant evidence that police overuse disorderly conduct and similar statutes to arrest people who 'disrespect' them or express disagreement with their actions." In Seattle, for example, a 2008 investigation uncovered the police's heavy use of resisting-arrest and obstruction charges against African American men. The six-year investigation found that nearly 2 percent of Seattle's black male population had been arrested solely for obstructing their own arrest and that African Americans were eight times as likely as whites to be arrested for obstruction or resisting. Most of the charges were later dismissed.[13]

In New York, high rates of stop-and-frisk invited a similar dynamic. Tyquan Brehon was eighteen years old and lived in Brooklyn. In a 2012 interview, he estimated that since he was fifteen years old, New York police had stopped him between sixty and seventy times. In his experience, if he asked a question or complained about the stop, police converted the stop into an arrest: "I've been taken in a lot of times because if you're stopping me, I'm going to want to know why. And that's when you can hear a change in their tone, they start to get a little more aggressive, and you feel threatened. They were like 'If you're going to talk back, we're going to take you in. If you're going to ask questions, we're going to take you in.'"[14]

Of course it's not supposed to work this way—"talking back" and "asking questions" are not crimes. Indeed, as the Supreme Court has declared, "The freedom of individuals verbally to oppose or challenge police action without thereby risking arrest is one of the principal characteristics by which we distinguish a free nation from a police state."[15] But because offenses like disorderly conduct, obstruction, and resisting arrest are easily alleged, they effectively give police the power to arrest based on violations of their own sense of authority.

"Contempt of cop" is not only a civil liberties challenge—it is an evidentiary problem. In 1974, the Supreme Court struck down a disorderly conduct ordinance that made it a crime for a person to curse at a police officer, holding that the statute infringed on constitutionally protected free speech. Justice Lewis Powell noted the additional danger, inherent in all such statutes, in giving police officers the power to establish probable cause based solely on their own say-so: "This ordinance . . . confers on police a virtually unrestrained power to arrest and charge persons with a violation. Many arrests are made in 'one-on-one' situations where the only witnesses are the arresting officer and the person charged. All that is required for conviction is that the court accept the testimony of the officer that obscene or opprobrious language had been used toward him while in performance of his duties."[16]

In these ways, the internal dynamics of petty-offense policing can literally create criminals. The reasonable suspicion standard broadly permits police to stop thousands of individuals based on very little evidence of very minor misconduct. Those initial encounters open the door to arrests that flow not necessarily from evidence of any separate crime but from the conflictual nature of the encounters themselves. Those new crimes can be real: people may actually resist arrest or become disorderly in response to police. Or they may not. Either way, the mere fact of arrest—with or without probable cause—sets the misdemeanor process in motion in ways that are then difficult to halt.

Low-level arrests like these sweep millions of Americans into the criminal system every single year. In 2015, police arrested approximately 11 million people; the year before that, another 11 million people. One in three Americans can expect to be arrested for a nontraffic offense before the age of twenty-three. For men and people of color, rates are even higher: by age twenty-three, 38 percent of white, 44 percent of Latino, and 50 percent of black males have been arrested. The majority of these arrests are for misdemeanors.[17] The misdemeanor process thus casts an enormous initial net.

BAIL

Once a person is arrested and in custody, the court process kicks into gear. Specifically, a judge will decide whether and under what conditions the person might be released. In violent felony cases, defendants often have no choice—they will remain incarcerated for the duration of their cases. In low-level cases, however, defendants may be released on their own recognizance with orders to come back to court for future hearings. Sometimes conditions accompany that release—reporting back to the court, electronic monitoring, drug testing—and are enforced by an office of pretrial services. For hundreds of thousands of others, however, their release will depend on whether they can pay bail, sometimes referred to as "money bond," "cash bond," or a "surety." This is an amount of money that the defendant—or someone on his or her behalf—puts up as a guarantee that he or she will show up later. If defendants can't "make bail," like Tyrone Tomlin in Chapter 1, they stay in jail until their cases are resolved.[18]

The Eighth Amendment prohibits the imposition of "excessive bail." But several courts have held that the mere fact that a defendant cannot afford bail does not make it unconstitutionally "excessive." The Supreme Court has also decided that pretrial detention is not "punishment" but rather "regulatory." This is an important point. People can't legally be punished before they have been convicted. Because pretrial detention is not technically punishment, people can thus legally be incarcerated prior to trial, either because they can't make bail or because the court decides that they should not be released under any circumstances.[19]

Bail and pretrial detention thus create a paradox. Although pretrial detention is not supposed to be punishment, defendants typically receive credit for their pretrial incarceration against any jail or prison sentence they eventually receive. In other words, their pretrial detention retroactively becomes punishment. If they are acquitted or the case is dismissed, however, that time counts for nothing. A person who is incarcerated pretrial and cannot afford bail can often plead guilty and accept a sentence of "time served"—the amount of time he or she has already been incarcerated—and thereby obtain immediate release. For many people, this common arrangement confirms their intuition that they were, in effect, being punished for being poor, since if they could have afforded bail, they never would have been locked up in the first place and might have escaped incarceration or even conviction altogether. A 2015 Vera Institute of Justice report points out that "these cases . . . turn our ideals about justice upside down. Sentenced to 'time served' and released, the system punishes these individuals while they are presumed to be innocent, and then releases them once they are found guilty."[20]

There is wide variation in how bail is administered. In federal court, indigent defendants are given an attorney for bail hearings, and judges consider a wide range of factors, including the nature of the offense, the defendant's ties to the community, the defendant's financial situation, and whether he or she poses a risk of flight. By contrast, many low-level courts rely on bail schedules, which automatically set bail at certain amounts depending on the nature of the offense. In Los Angeles, the default bail for a misdemeanor is $500. In Chicago, the default for a Class A or B misdemeanor is $1,500. In these courts defendants typically do not get lawyers: it remains an open constitutional question whether defendants are entitled to counsel at bail hearings. Bail is set quickly, often in minutes and without consideration of the defendant's particular circumstances or ability to pay. In one South Carolina municipal court, for example, observers witnessed the judge set bail amounts for twenty-three defendants in approximately thirty minutes—less than two minutes per defendant. In Harris County, Texas, bail hearings used to be conducted in under a minute by videoconference. Most of the time, bail is set by judges or bail commissioners, but in some jurisdictions clerks or police have the power to set bail.[21]

Many misdemeanor defendants who are set bail cannot afford to pay it and thus remain incarcerated. In 2016, 40 percent of all misdemeanor defendants in Harris County were detained largely because they could not afford bail. In 2017 a judge found this state of affairs unconstitutional. In New York, 87 percent of nonfelony defendants set bail in 2010 couldn't pay.[22] When people cannot afford bail, they often plead guilty in order to get out of jail. This is a key difference between misdemeanors and felonies. In serious felony cases, when defendants plead guilty they typically remain incarcerated and start serving a prison sentence. Pleading guilty does not set them free any earlier. But many low-level defendants are incarcerated only pretrial and only because they can't make bail. Pleading guilty thus lets them go home and avoid further incarceration.

Unless the court specifies a cash bond, in which case the defendant must put up the full amount themselves, bail can also be met by paying a private bail bondsman. Every state except Illinois, Kentucky, Oregon, and Wisconsin permits commercial bail, where bondsmen act as sureties, putting money up on behalf of defendants and guaranteeing their appearance in court.[23] Bondsmen typically charge a nonrefundable 10 percent fee, so a $5,000 bail amount would require a $500 payment. Misdemeanor bail bonds are widely available, although some bondsmen will not provide them because the payments and profits are too low. But even these lesser amounts remain out of reach for many misdemeanor defendants, and so they remain in jail.

The impact of pretrial detention is powerful. Most obviously, it pressures defendants to plead guilty, thereby increasing the likelihood of their conviction. But pretrial detention also does other damage. The most recent study of the effects of pretrial detention, conducted in Harris County, Texas, evaluated over 300,000 misdemeanor cases filed over five years. It concluded that detained defendants were more likely to be sentenced to jail than probation and found that they were more likely to be charged with new crimes later on.[24] These results mean that defendants who cannot afford bail are being further disadvantaged in all sorts of additional ways.

The bail problem gained new national prominence in 2015 after Sandra Bland died in a Texas jail; she was incarcerated for a traffic incident after she could not post a $515 bail bond. Lawsuits have been filed around the country, and dozens of jurisdictions no longer require money bail for low-level offenses.[25]

Bail originally arose as a mechanism to ensure that people appeared in court when they were supposed to. It has nothing to do with guilt or innocence. Indeed, by definition everyone subject to bail has not been convicted and is therefore presumed innocent. Bail has morphed, however, into a practice that offers release to those who can afford it while increasing the likelihood of conviction for those who cannot.[26] Think back to Tyrone Tomlin, who was beaten up in Riker's because he couldn't make bail and refused to plead guilty. Bail exerts enormous influence over whether people get convicted, the length of their sentences, and their future well-being.

PROSECUTORS

I asked Ron Paschal, a senior prosecutor in Sedgwick County, Kansas, what he thought about misdemeanors. He said,

> Look, I'm a prosecutor. I'm not afraid to lock people up. Some people need to be hammered, but that's a short list of people. And I think we're all getting smarter about it. Money drives a lot of stuff, most of our states are hurting, the costs of incarceration are high. Bottom line is, we're here to protect the public—the question is how am I really protecting the public? Somebody shoots or stabs someone, frankly that's pretty easy. But with petty crimes, you have to ask, am I really enhancing public safety by going about it in a particular manner?[27]

The prosecutor is often said to be the most powerful player in the American criminal system. Imbued with complete, unreviewable discretion over whether to bring charges and what charges to bring, prosecutors define the contours of criminal cases, how much pressure to exert on defendants to plead, and what the eventual sentence is likely to be. Prosecutorial decisions are both judicially unreviewable—courts cannot order prosecutors either to bring or drop charges—and immune from lawsuit: prosecutors cannot be sued either for failing to bring a charge or for bringing one, even if the decision is malicious or dishonest.[28]

Freed of most external constraints, prosecutors' charging decisions are largely regulated by ethical rules and their obligation to "do justice." Prosecutors have this freedom precisely because their role is so important. As the Supreme Court put it in 1935, "The [prosecutor] is the representative not of an ordinary party to a controversy, but of a sovereignty whose . . . interest, therefore, in a criminal prosecution is not that it shall win a case, but that justice shall be done."[29]

In the misdemeanor world, prosecutors have the power to decide whether an arrest will become a criminal charge, what the formal charges will be, whether to seek bail, whether to offer diversion, what plea deal to offer, if any, and what sentence to recommend to the judge. That's a lot of leverage—and another reason that defendants typically plead guilty. The sheer number of misdemeanors on the books—what we sometimes call overcriminalization—also confers enormous power on prosecutors. So many behaviors have been defined as unlawful, from spitting to speeding to walking in the middle of the street, that almost everyone can be charged with something.[30]

In the felony world, defendants are under heavy pressure to plead guilty because they can face years of additional incarceration if they lose at trial. With misdemeanors, the pressures to plead guilty stem from additional sources—for example, pretrial incarceration and the inability to make bail, as we just saw. Pressure can also flow from a lack of defense resources or, for pro se defendants who have no lawyer, from ignorance and fear. Each of these standard features of the misdemeanor process enhances the prosecutor's ability to get defendants to take a deal rather than contest their guilt. As a result, misdemeanor trials are rare, often just 1 or 2 percent of cases.[31]

One of the most important relationships in the misdemeanor criminal process is the one between prosecutors and police. At the very beginning of the pipeline, police bring people into the system by arresting them. Prosecutors then screen those arrests, making the critical decision about whether to "decline" a case and let the arrested individual go home. If the prosecutor decides instead to convert the arrest into a full-fledged criminal case, the "arrestee" becomes a "defendant" enmeshed in the criminal process and facing the possibility of conviction. The decision to charge, in turn, is a momentous constitutional turning point. It triggers the defendant's right to counsel and a wide array of other procedural protections and marks the formal beginning of the adversarial process.[32]

Prosecutors can also screen further and dismiss cases later in the process once they get to court. Dismissals differ from declinations: they can take time, sometimes months, and defendants must still go through the court process and withstand the pressures to plead guilty along the way. Sometimes prosecutors require people to submit to supervision and various conditions for months or even a year before they will dismiss a case. These deals are referred to as diversions because they divert defendants out of the process before they are formally convicted.

The whole criminal system relies on prosecutorial screening—declinations, dismissals, and diversions—for its overall fairness and legitimacy. Declinations are a particularly crucial mechanism for ensuring that criminal cases are only brought when they are well founded, fair, and in the public interest. They are the reason why getting arrested is not the same thing as being charged with a crime, and they give meaning to the all-important boundary between the policing function and the adversarial legal system.

Screening is complex. In felony cases, prosecutors typically have both the time and incentives to consider a wide range of issues when deciding whether to charge a person, including the seriousness of the case, the weight of the evidence, the public interests at stake, and the rigor of the investigation that gave rise to the arrest. One study found that state prosecutors spend approximately forty hours deciding whether or not to charge a homicide case. The more serious the case, the more prosecutors know that the defense will test their decisions in a public adversarial process. Felony declination decisions are thus a robust screening opportunity. Approximately one-third of all federal cases get declined.[33]

Misdemeanor prosecutors screen in a very different environment. Enormous caseloads filled with minor offenses and pressure to clear dockets quickly mean that prosecutors may have only minutes to decide whether to decline or proceed. Misdemeanor policing often produces little in the way of reviewable evidence, so prosecutors must rely heavily on allegations in police reports. For example, in one county that handled over 100,000 cases a year, researchers found that misdemeanor prosecutors decided whether to screen, bring charges, and plead cases all at the same time, based only on the information in the police citation and the defendant's record. The researchers also concluded that "while the screening decision may be the most important, it is also the decision which prosecutors have the least time to make."[34]

It is also a decision often made by the least experienced attorneys in the office. In the county study, misdemeanor cases were handled by the least experienced junior prosecutors. A Missouri study found that misdemeanor units were typically operated by inexperienced attorneys who made charging decisions and recommendations that were not reviewed by more experienced trial attorneys.[35]

By contrast, in Riverside, California, and Wichita, Kansas, senior prosecutors do the initial screening. A study by the American Prosecutors Research Institute found that experienced prosecutors spent an average of 35 percent more time screening cases than less experienced attorneys.[36] As a senior prosecutor in North Carolina explains,

> When you first start on the Misdemeanor Team, those DWIs [driving while intoxicated] are serious stuff. And then you move on to the Drug Team, and all of a sudden, the DWIs don't seem so serious anymore. And all of a sudden, a couple of ounces of weed seems like the biggest crime on the planet. Then you do Drug Team for a while, and you realize that there's kilos of cocaine out there, and weed doesn't seem like a big deal anymore. And then you do the Persons Team, and you see people actually getting robbed at gunpoint. Then drugs don't seem like a big deal anymore. So as you kind of go up the ladder, everything gets put in perspective. . . . Over time, you learn what the real priorities are.[37]

The effect of letting junior prosecutors screen can mean that too many weak, unfair, or otherwise inappropriate cases are permitted to go forward. Sometimes this is because inexperienced prosecutors may be reluctant to challenge the police. In one study, junior prosecutors accepted and relied on police accounts more often than their senior colleagues did. A mid-level prosecutor told interviewers that "when she was a young attorney, she 'didn't have the words' to challenge a police officer."[38]

The combination of enormous caseloads and inexperienced prosecutors creates institutional barriers to robust misdemeanor screening. Data on this aspect of prosecutorial decision-making is scarce, but there are telling examples. When the Vera Institute collaborated with the prosecutor's office in Mecklenburg, North Carolina, to collect data on declination rates, they discovered that the office was declining only 3 to 4 percent of drug cases and that prosecutors mostly adopted all police charges. In Iowa, the declination rate for simple misdemeanors in 2008 was less than 2 percent. In Alaska in 2015, it was 3.7 percent.[39]

In some jurisdictions, by contrast, declination rates are relatively high. In Baltimore, arrests are screened at the jail, and approximately 16 percent are immediately declined—the figure climbs as high as 25 percent for some order-maintenance crimes. Florida prosecutors appear to decline over 16 percent of cases. Moreover, subsequent dismissals and diversions are common. In Baltimore, 50 percent of cases may eventually be "nolle prossed," or dismissed. In Connecticut, up to 60 percent of misdemeanors may be diverted. In other states, as many as a third of cases may eventually be dismissed or diverted.[40]

Declinations are important because they determine who will immediately be set free and who will instead be charged with a crime. But they are structurally significant as well because they regulate the institutional relationship between prosecutors and police. Robust initial screening means that prosecutors are performing the gatekeeping role that the Supreme Court and everyone else assumes they do, checking policing decisions and making sure that only appropriate cases go forward. As one Los Angeles district attorney put it, prosecutors are "an important bulwark against overreaching by police."[41] By contrast, where prosecutors do not screen rigorously, where declination rates are routinely low and arrests convert easily into formal criminal charges, police will effectively have made that all-important charging decision, even if they didn't intend to. When police become accidental prosecutors, a vital check on the integrity of our criminal legal process is eliminated.

This quasi-prosecutorial power of police is endemic to the misdemeanor world. In some lower courts it is not even accidental: there are no prosecutors at all, and police directly charge and prosecute their own cases. In a recent investigation of South Carolina lower courts, observers documented numerous courtrooms in which there were no prosecuting attorneys and arresting officers prosecuted hundreds of cases. The report noted that since most defendants did not have lawyers, "it was not uncommon for court observers to overhear defendants asking the officers who charged them, 'What should I do?'"[42]

Similarly, in New Mexico's municipal courts the arresting police officer acts as prosecutor as well as witness. New Hampshire permits police officers to directly prosecute violations and some misdemeanors. In courts like these, there is no independent screening: individuals must defend themselves against (or work out a plea bargain with) a police officer, typically the same one who arrested them in the first place.[43]

This is a very different atmosphere from the world of felonies in which the prosecutorial role is understood to be special and distinct from the role of the police. That specialness is embodied in key rules: prosecutors have absolute immunity from suit when they decide to file criminal charges, for example, whereas police have only limited immunity when they decide to make an arrest. Prosecutors actually lose their absolute immunity if they behave too much like police during investigations.[44] But in the misdemeanor world, the roles of police and prosecutor blur. This happens formally in those courts where police file charges directly and informally in courts where prosecutors lack the time and incentives to screen thoroughly. Despite the common understanding that prosecutors are the system's most powerful players, in the misdemeanor world police often wield de facto prosecutorial authority.

DEFENSE COUNSEL

In America's adversarial judicial system, police and prosecutors sit on one side of the courtroom; the defendant sits on the other. To make that a fair fight, the Constitution guarantees the defendant his or her own lawyer. In the landmark case of *Gideon v. Wainwright*, the Supreme Court wrote that "any person haled into court, who is too poor to hire a lawyer, cannot be assured a fair trial unless counsel is provided for him. This seems to us to be an obvious truth." The job of defense counsel is to zealously ensure that their clients' rights are observed, that the government's case is rigorously challenged, and that the government plays by the rules. The Sixth Amendment right to a lawyer is thus more than just a benefit for individual defendants: the fairness, accuracy, and integrity of the entire system rely on it. Indeed, when asked the perennial question "How can you represent those people," public defenders often point out that their job is to enforce the Constitution.[45]

Gideon v. Wainwright established the formal right to counsel in 1963. But the principle has been around for much longer. Back in 1932, when the American criminal system was much smaller and less complex than it is today, the Supreme Court recognized that people without law degrees would have a tough time navigating it alone. As Justice George Sutherland wrote, "Even the intelligent and educated layman has small and sometimes no skill in the science of law. . . . He is unfamiliar with the rules of evidence. Left without the aid of counsel he may be put on trial without a proper charge, and convicted upon incompetent evidence, or evidence irrelevant to the issue or otherwise inadmissible."[46]

What is true for trials is also true for misdemeanor guilty pleas. The Court has recognized that when a misdemeanor defendant pleads guilty, "counsel is needed so that the accused may know precisely what he is doing, so that he is fully aware of the prospect of going to jail or prison, and so that he is treated fairly by the prosecution."[47]

The constitutional rules for misdemeanors are a bit different than for felonies. In its *Gideon* decision, the Court declared broadly that "lawyers in criminal courts are necessities, not luxuries." This means that if a person cannot afford to hire a lawyer, the state must provide them with one—a public defender. In 1972, the Court clarified that this is true for minor offenses as well as felonies. But the Court subsequently retreated from these general principles when people are not ultimately sentenced to incarceration. In 1979, the Court decided that people convicted of minor offenses but not sentenced to jail do not have the right to counsel. A defendant punished only through a fine is not entitled to a lawyer to defend him or her against the initial misdemeanor conviction. In 2002, in *Alabama v. Shelton*, the Court clarified that this no-lawyer rule applies only when the person could *never* be sentenced to jail for that offense. If a person receives a suspended sentence, or so-called jailable probation, where a violation could send them to jail, they still must be given a lawyer. The *Shelton* Court reasoned that "actual imprisonment is a penalty different in kind" from other criminal penalties and that no one should be punished with jail time—actual or conditional—unless they have been represented by counsel.[48] The *Shelton* constitutional rule is important because so many misdemeanor defendants are sentenced to jailable probation. By contrast, other common punishments and burdens stemming from misdemeanor convictions, such as fines, fees, supervision, drug testing, and the loss of jobs, housing, or immigration status, do not trigger the right to counsel at all.

Defense attorneys are not just legal machines. At their best, they support their clients' humanity, dignity, and personal needs. Public defenders often serve as informal social workers, finding their clients jobs, social services, and housing.[49] Harvard law professor and former public defender Charles Ogletree described the importance of empathy in representing clients: "My relationships with clients were rarely limited to the provision of conventional legal services. . . . I took phone calls at all hours, helped clients find jobs, and even interceded in domestic conflicts. I attended my clients' weddings and their funerals. When clients were sent to prison, I maintained contact with their families."[50]

Robin Steinberg founded The Bronx Defenders, one of the top public defender offices in the country. She once had a client who seemed like she might not show up for trial. So Steinberg did something that, in her words, "only a young public defender would do": she brought her heroin-addicted client home with her to keep an eye on her.[51]

Misdemeanors can involve complicated legal issues that require sophisticated lawyering. In 2013, for example, Haneef Ross was charged with disorderly conduct after he was stopped by military police outside the National Security Agency at Fort Meade, Maryland. His federal public defender, a twenty-five-year veteran attorney, challenged the constitutionality of the federal regulation under which Ross was charged. The case took eighteen months and involved over two hundred pages of legal filings. In the end, a federal judge threw out the case.[52]

Public defenders are often devoted, highly skilled attorneys, and in many places misdemeanor representation can be as rigorous as the best felony representation. Prestigious public defender offices from San Francisco to Washington, DC, and New York attract Supreme Court clerks and other top lawyers, who litigate misdemeanors with sophistication.[53] In federal court, misdemeanor defendants like Ross can receive top-notch representation. And public defenders are not the only zealous defense attorneys in lower courts. Wealthy DUI defendants, for example, have at their disposal a large and aggressive private defense bar.

But more often the right to counsel fizzles out in misdemeanor court. Public defense is commonly disparaged as "meet 'em and plead 'em" lawyering, a reflection of the widespread reality that many public defenders spend little or no time talking to their misdemeanor clients, investigating their cases, or litigating legal issues. Instead, they meet their clients briefly in the courthouse or jail, explain the government's plea offer, and get their clients to accept it that day, sometimes that very hour. This reality contradicts core values of the adversarial system and the right to counsel. Indeed, one federal court in Washington State found it unconstitutional, concluding that the misdemeanor defense system of two municipalities "amounted to little more than a 'meet and plead' system. . . . [T]he indigent defendants had virtually no relationship with their assigned counsel and could not fairly be said to have been 'represented' by them at all."[54]

Much of the problem stems from a lack of time and resources. Public defense is notoriously underfunded: average spending in the United States on indigent defense is $11.86 per capita, less than 2 percent of the $265 billion spent on criminal justice every year. The American Bar Association recommends that no lawyer maintain a caseload of more than three hundred misdemeanor cases per year. But in Dallas, public defenders juggle 1,200 misdemeanors a year; in Chicago, Atlanta, and Miami, annual caseloads exceed 2,000. Public defense offices typically have limited resources to investigate the facts in any sort of case; misdemeanors get even less investigative attention. A supervising attorney from Chicago admitted that their lawyers "don't have time to do research and investigation." Eleven percent of public defenders in a national survey stated that they have no investigative services at all; 2 percent said they could only obtain investigative services if they paid for them out of their own pockets.[55]

In jurisdictions without public defender offices, low-level cases are sometimes contracted out to private firms, typically going to the lowest bidder. This creates even more pressure to plead cases quickly, since contract attorneys lose money the more time they spend on each case. In one rural California county, the senior lawyer who won the low-bid defense contract assigned his misdemeanor cases to a single junior attorney. She carried a caseload of between 250 and 300 cases per month and was expected to get defendants to plead guilty immediately the first time they came to court so that she could move on to the next case. When she asked for more time to address a legal issue, the senior lawyer fired her. In the Washington State litigation noted above, the court found almost no evidence that the attorneys investigated any of their thousands of cases, that they engaged in legal analysis, or that they even discussed issues with their clients.[56]

Like prosecutors, new public defenders typically train in misdemeanor court. That means that misdemeanor clients are represented by the least experienced attorneys in the office. A 2009 report from the National Association of Criminal Defense Lawyers describes the troubling phenomenon: "Many public defenders start in misdemeanor courts after being hired right out of law school. They are handed a stack of case files and told their courtroom assignment. No supervisor accompanies them and there is no training before they begin. On their first day, they will talk to clients, negotiate plea deals, appear before a judge and, frequently, advise clients to plead guilty."[57]

"We can't pay a competitive salary," explained former Miami-Dade chief defender Bennett Brummer as to why his office was forced to hire inexperienced lawyers straight from law school. "We need to train them." Misdemeanors are those training grounds, the little league before attorneys move up to felonies.[58]

Public defense is not an easy job. For many, the pressures and grueling pace can lead to burnout. Law professor and veteran public defender Abbe Smith notes that "defenders [may] buckle under the pressures of the job, the prevailing atmosphere of disrespect and contempt for the accused, the relentless cycle of poverty, inequality, and crime." Professor Eve Brensike Primus studies public defense and puts it bluntly: "It is easy for judges, prosecutors, and court personnel to make the life of a defender miserable. Imagine what life is like when no one in your working environment is willing to cut you a break or help you out, when everyone is waiting (and hoping) for you to screw up, and when the environment is, by definition, adversarial."[59]

Because they lack time and resources, defense attorneys may resist going to trial and instead pressure their clients to take a plea. If they do go to trial, they are likely to be unprepared.[60] As one senior Kentucky public defender admitted, "Without time to properly prepare and gather facts and information, I cannot ethically perform my responsibilities. When I settle a case on the courthouse steps because both the prosecutor and myself are overworked (not because we know the facts and are prepared to get the best possible compromise) I do not believe I have fulfilled my ethical obligations to my client."[61]

Defendants may be well aware that their public defenders are over-worked and do not have time to do a thorough job. As a result, they do not trust their lawyers. One Baltimore resident offers this analysis: "People want to go home, and they can't afford proper representation. So they get the public defender. How does he represent you? You probably never met him until your court date. Probably didn't review your file until that morning. He doesn't know your name, and then you go to court, and he's asking you what you are going to do. You're saying, 'I'm innocent. I'm fighting this to the end. I really didn't do this.' And he's like, 'This is the state's offer.'"[62]

Even when misdemeanor attorneys have the resources and ability to provide robust representation, they face structural barriers. Prose-cutors often threaten to withdraw favorable plea offers if defendants do not accept them immediately, leaving attorneys no time to inves-tigate or develop a defense. Judges are often in a hurry to move their dockets along and penalize attorneys who try to litigate. Primus, for-merly a misdemeanor public defender in Maryland, recalls that some judges rejected her efforts to raise constitutional issues on behalf of her clients. "I routinely had misdemeanor court judges refuse to ad-dress legal issues and tell me to save my legal arguments for appeal."[63]

Other public defenders are affirmatively punished for trying to do their jobs. Brian Jones, for example, was a young public defender in Portage, Ohio, assigned to represent Jordan Scott, a man charged with misdemeanor assault. The case was set for trial the very next day, but Jones had six other clients he had to meet with before he could even look at Scott's case. The next day at trial, Jones told the judge that he needed more time to interview witnesses and prepare. The judge told him to prepare over lunch. After lunch, Jones told the judge that he could not proceed to trial because he was insufficiently prepared to represent Scott properly. The judge held Jones in contempt and put him in jail, reasoning that defenders plead cases and take cases to trial with minimal preparation all the time.[64]

One of the most powerful structural impediments to zealous repre-sentation is the pressure on clients to plead in order to obtain release from jail or to end the grueling process of repeated court appearances. Even when attorneys know that a case has viable issues or even that a client is innocent, they must honor the client's wish to plead guilty in order to go home or cut their losses. For example, between 2011 and 2012, The Bronx Defenders identified fifty-four marijuana misdemeanor cases—"Fighter" cases—in which clients wanted to fight their misdemeanor charges. The Fighters were represented by lawyers at The Bronx Defenders and by attorneys at the elite law firm Cleary Gottlieb Steen & Hamilton. But because of court delays, numerous postponements, and the requirement that defendants be physically present at every court date, few Fighters actually managed to contest their cases, and in the end the majority pled guilty. Thirty percent of the Fighter cases were dismissed outright, but only after an average of nine months. Many Fighters reluctantly accepted plea deals because the costs of fighting their cases were too high.[65]

Sometimes the right to counsel dies in misdemeanor court altogether. Many courts appoint counsel late or not at all. One Mississippi woman, accused of shoplifting $72 worth of merchandise, was detained for eleven months before counsel was appointed. She spent two more months in jail before the lawyer came to see her and then another month before they went to court; she pled guilty to time served. A Georgia defendant arrested for loitering spent thirteen months in jail before seeing a lawyer. Edward Monahan is a deputy public advocate in Kentucky. "The dirty little secret of the criminal justice system," he says, "is that most eligible people do not get defenders."[66]

Some judges baldly require misdemeanor defendants to work out their cases directly with police or prosecutors. In one courtroom in northeastern Pennsylvania, for example, misdemeanor defendants were told to go to the basement. When observers went down there, they discovered a prosecutor in a conference room. The prosecutor was negotiating plea deals directly with defendants, who then went back up to the courtroom to plead guilty and be sentenced. In Georgia, observers watched a judge inform a large group of misdemeanor defendants of their rights. Then the judge left the bench. Three prosecutors then instructed the defendants to line up and follow them one by one into a private room. When the judge returned to the courtroom, each defendant came forward with the prosecutor, who informed the judge that the defendant intended to give up his or her right to a defense attorney and plead guilty.[67]

Remember Grandma G at the beginning of this book? She wanted a public defender, but the judge would not postpone the trial in order to give her time to get one.

It is blatantly unconstitutional to withhold counsel from a defendant who faces incarceration. The fact that the Constitution and other legal authorities are so openly flouted is itself a deep characteristic of the misdemeanor system. Indeed, it is hard to think of many other places in American governance where constitutional rights are so routinely trampled. In study after study, researchers have documented courts where judges commonly and unapologetically do not appoint counsel. In 2007, Jean Hoefer Toal was chief justice of the South Carolina Supreme Court, the highest-ranking judicial official in the state. At a public meeting, she candidly admitted that the South Carolina court system does not provide counsel even when required by the US Constitution. As she explained, "*Alabama v. Shelton* [is] one of the more misguided decisions of the United States Supreme Court, I must say. If we adhered to it in South Carolina we would have the right to counsel probably . . . by dragooning lawyers out of their law offices to take these cases in every magistrate's court in South Carolina, and I have simply told my magistrates that we just don't have the resources to do that. So I will tell you straight up we [are] not adhering to *Alabama v. Shelton* in every situation."[68]

In sum, one of the primary guarantors of fairness and accuracy—a robust defense—is largely missing in action from misdemeanor court. Sometimes there are no defense attorneys at all. Even when there are, massive caseloads, a lack of resources, and pressures from prosecutors and judges mean that defense attorneys may not be able to perform their appointed role. The routine failure to honor the constitutional right to counsel thus explains much of the broader lawlessness and dysfunction of the misdemeanor process. It also means that many misdemeanor defendants must effectively face the court on their own.

JUDGES AND COURTS

Judges are the highest-ranking officials in the criminal system. They preside over cases, resolve legal disputes, determine facts, create records, enter judgments and final dispositions, and set sentences. Criminal convictions cannot occur without a judge's approval, and judges ultimately decide the punishment. The court is the venue in which these activities take place—both in the courtroom itself, presided over by individual judges, and in the courthouse with its community of clerks, bailiffs, administrators, and supervisors who together create the culture of the judicial system in each jurisdiction.

The US government is built on the idea of separation of powers: the legislature makes the law, the executive enforces it, and the judiciary interprets and applies it in individual cases.[69] Judges have the unique job of preserving legal principles even when those principles, such as defendants' rights, may be unpopular or expensive. As Supreme Court justice John Paul Stevens wrote, "There is a critical difference between the work of the judge and the work of other public officials. In a democracy, issues of policy are properly decided by majority vote; it is the business of legislators and executives to be popular. But in litigation, issues of law or fact should not be determined by popular vote; it is the business of judges to be indifferent to unpopularity."[70] Justice Ruth Bader Ginsburg adds, "A[n] [independent] judiciary . . . is a longstanding Anglo-American tradition, an essential bulwark of constitutional government, a constant guardian of the rule of law."[71]

The authoritative role of judges and the courts over which they preside is reflected in numerous ways, from the judge's black robe to the tradition of standing when the judge ascends the bench. Courtrooms are traditionally solemn places in which hats are taken off, quiet is required, and cameras are forbidden. These gestures reflect the understanding that decisions made by judges in courtrooms are of deep and lasting significance to the individual parties as well as to a democratic society and that these exercises in law deserve respect.

Much of the time, however, misdemeanor courts do not work in this considered, solemn fashion. Instead, their quick-and-dirty resolution of a high volume of cases has prompted nicknames like "assembly-line processing" and "McJustice," derogatory terms that reflect not only the speed and size of the docket but a lack of decorum and various forms of disrespect for the individuals who come to court. "If you turn off the sound," says one lawyer, "and watch Manhattan criminal court, there is no way you don't think it is a cattle auction." A bankruptcy judge, accustomed to the formalities at the top of the pyramid, spent an eye-opening day in Bronx criminal court, exclaiming afterward, "I was shocked by the casual racism emanating from the bench." In Harris County, Texas, people sat for hours in long lines outside one of the misdemeanor courtrooms; some days the judge never showed up. Other judges are appalled by this state of affairs. "It is time to end the wasteful and harmful practices that have turned our misdemeanor courts into mindless conviction mills," says Florida Supreme Court chief justice Gerald Kogan.[72]

To be sure, misdemeanor courts are not the only culprits; sometimes felonies are handled in slipshod and lawless ways too. Chicago felony court can be an undignified affair, with two-minute attorney meetings, one-minute bond hearings, and fifteen-minute dispositions. In her book *Ordinary Injustice: How America Holds Court*, Amy Bach describes felony courtrooms so loud, crowded, and disorganized that no one, not even the judge, can tell what is happening. But low-level courts are especially fast and informal and have been so for a long time. In 1883, the busy police court in Alameda County, California, disposed of twenty cases "in ten minutes—two cases per minute." In his 1954 study, Professor Caleb Foote described a typical day in Philadelphia misdemeanor courts. "Four . . . defendants were tried, found guilty and sentenced in the elapsed time of *seventeen seconds*. . . . In each of these cases the magistrate merely read off the name of the defendant, took one look at him and said, 'Three months in the House of Correction.' As the third man was being led out he objected, stating, 'But I'm working . . . ,' to which the magistrate replied, 'Aw, go on.'"[73]

In 1979, Malcolm Feeley described the low-level criminal court in New Haven, Connecticut, as a speedy "supermarket" filled with "casualness and confusion":

> Not one defendant in a sample of 1,640 cases insisted upon [trial by jury]. . . . [O]nly one-half of all defendants journeyed through the criminal process with an attorney at their side. . . . Even in those cases in which counsel was present, his contribution was questionable. "Interviews" with clients were often little more than quick, whispered exchanges in the corridor. . . . There was little independent investigation of facts. . . . Arrestees were arraigned in groups and informed of their rights en masse. At times the arrestees were not even aware that they are being addressed. Judges did not always look at them, and even if a judge made an effort to be heard, he could not always be understood over the constant din of the courtroom. . . . While a few cases took up as much as a minute or two of the court's time . . . the overwhelming majority of cases took just a few seconds.[74]

Thirty-two years later, a 2011 report titled *Three Minute Justice: Haste and Waste in Florida's Misdemeanor Courts* described the operations of that state's misdemeanor courts in much the same vein. Most proceedings lasted less than three minutes; nearly 70 percent of defendants pleaded guilty, 66 percent of whom did not have lawyers.[75]

In such courtrooms, law itself often falls by the wayside. Motions are rarely filed, legal arguments rarely heard. Sometimes the law is just wrong. Primus recalls "misdemeanor judges who regularly made up state rules of evidence to aid the prosecution. For example, one judge told me that anything one officer said to another officer was admissible under the 'teamwork exception' to the prohibition against hearsay evidence. When I pointed out that no such exception existed in the state evidentiary rules, the judge angrily told me to stand down and threatened to hold me in contempt." In some municipal courts, judges are not lawyers and may not know what the law requires at all.[76]

Because municipal courts are highly local institutions, conflicts of interest are a special risk. Court officials and law enforcement know and depend on each other. Police and prosecutors may share office space. Prosecutors may sit next to the judge in the courtroom. Some judges in lower courts work as prosecutors in other courthouses. Others may depend on municipal officials for their judgeships. One New Jersey attorney, who subsequently became a judge, concluded that because of these close relationships between courts and law enforcement, "many people believe somewhat cynically that it is nearly impossible to win a municipal court case involving an officer's word against a private citizen's word, no matter how many other credible witnesses testify in the defendant's favor."[77]

Misdemeanor courts are characterized not only by their great speed but also, ironically, by their chronic delay: speed for people who plead guilty immediately, delay for those who want a public defender or who seek to contest their cases. Courts often take a long time not only to appoint counsel but to set trial dates; even when set, trial dates are often postponed. This means that defendants unwilling to plead guilty must often wait months to resolve their cases, months during which they may remain incarcerated. In Atlanta, for example, Tony Humphries was charged with jumping a subway turnstile. He sat in jail for fifty-four days before a lawyer was appointed, far longer than any sentence he might have received if convicted. In Allegheny County, Pennsylvania, up to ten weeks can pass after an arraignment before an attorney begins working on the case. In the Bronx, it took an average of eight months for the Fighter defendants contesting marijuana-possession charges to resolve their cases.[78]

Not all misdemeanor courtrooms are so dismissive of defendants' rights and needs. A special kind of low-level court referred to as "problem-solving court" or "community court" takes a different approach altogether. There are approximately 4,500 such courts around the country, and they handle a relatively small number of cases, mostly misdemeanors. These increasingly popular courts are designed to manage and serve populations with special needs such as drug addicts, people with mental health issues, veterans, or prostitutes, routing them out of the conventional criminal system. These courts do not merely adjudicate guilt but may provide social services, health care, jobs, training, and therapy. Moreover, they are not adversarial in the conventional sense. Judges take a hands-on approach, engaging defendants personally, acting as coach or cheerleader when they succeed and as disciplinarian when they don't. In Newark's community court, Judge Victoria Pratt applauds—and makes the whole room clap with her—when defendants pay their fines, complete their programs, or just make an effort to do better. She is also creative, sentencing a particularly unmotivated young man to film himself doing twenty-five pushups. In Red Hook Community Court in Brooklyn, Judge Alex Calabrese became known for actually going into public housing buildings when handling housing cases.[79]

Such problem-solving courts are both popular and controversial. Some applaud them as a much-needed and less punitive response to the chronic welfare and health needs of the criminal justice population. Others worry about deregulating legal proceedings and turning them into social interventions, especially where they intrude deeply into the lives of disadvantaged defendants or where people end up incarcerated for more time than they would have gotten in a conventional court. Under either view, judges in these courts—as well as prosecutors and defense attorneys—have very different roles than they do in the classic adversarial model.[80]

Because problem-solving courts are small and labor intensive, they do not solve the problems of scale that plague the misdemeanor system. Red Hook is unusual—it handles thousands of cases—but most courts admit fewer than fifty people a year.[81] By contrast, the challenges of traditional misdemeanor courts flow in large part from their enormous dockets. Like prosecutors and defense attorneys, misdemeanor judges are under pressure to clear cases. Judges around the country complain that they are forced by judicial administrators to move cases more and more quickly. Slower judges may see their funding cut. Some judges need to clear dockets not only for efficiency's sake but to raise revenue, since many courts depend on the fines and fees generated by misdemeanor cases for funding. In effect, judges who process high volumes of guilty pleas are raising money for themselves and the courthouse.

Gayle Williams-Byers is presiding judge for the South Euclid Municipal Court in Ohio. She is especially worried about the influence of money on the lower court system. "Municipal court is the court of first impression for most citizens," she says. "What happens to them informs their whole impression of the judicial system. The perception is that municipal court serves a different function than other courts, that it's more about profit than justice. It takes a lot of courage to reject that, to insist that as an independent judiciary we can do better."[82]

These kinds of judicial pressures are not limited to misdemeanors. An increasing number of felony judges get directly involved in resolving cases, and many labor under pressure to clear their dockets quickly. In Chicago felony court, judge disposition rates are monitored by the week. When judges are up for retention, their disposition totals are published and disseminated, leading one Chicago judge to admit that his job is "'to keep things moving as fast as I can.'" What some scholars call "managerial judging" appears to have become firmly ensconced as a feature not only of misdemeanor courts but of large modern criminal dockets. It is a consequence of overcriminalization and the resulting enormity of the criminal system, its lack of time and resources, and the pressure on official decision-makers to prioritize efficiency.[83] The pathologies of low-level courts thus offer a cautionary tale for the rest of the system.

Police, prosecutors, defense attorneys, and judges are the main official actors in the misdemeanor drama. Other players include sheriffs, bail bondsmen, probation officers, and court clerks, to name just a few. All together, these decision-makers and their respective institutions determine how the process works at each step along the way.

As we have now seen, it is a complicated drama. Each institution has its own requirements; every player has multiple goals and incentives. Sometimes there are "bad apples," officials who flout basic rules, but just as often the hydraulic forces of the system produce dysfunctional results that no one fully intends. With too many cases and not enough resources, the institution as a whole does not work as it should. Millions of people from all walks of life pass through it every year, sometimes alone, often without meaningful legal assistance. Under heavy pressure to plead guilty, they may receive far heavier punishments than they deserve or than anyone thinks they should get. The consequences of the encounter can be lifelong.

The remainder of this book explores the profound legal, social, and democratic implications of running the great bulk of our criminal system in this way—beginning with the fact that the petty-offense process convicts thousands of innocent people each year.

| 4 |

INNOCENCE

JACK FORD'S GIRLFRIEND SAID THE TWO OF THEM COULD crash at the house, so he wasn't worried when they walked in. That is, until the irate owner called the police. Ford was charged with misdemeanor fourth-degree burglary for entering a house uninvited. But Ford wasn't guilty. In order to be guilty of burglary, a person has to know that the entry was unauthorized. Ford was assigned an experienced public defender, Sarah Elkins, who said they had an excellent chance at trial: Ford's ignorance made him innocent. But to prove it, he was going to have to wait.[1]

It takes a month to get a misdemeanor trial in Baltimore. Because Ford couldn't afford bail, he spent that month in jail at Central Booking. The Baltimore City detention complex is so filthy and dangerous that a few years later, in 2015, the governor of Maryland personally intervened and shut part of it down, calling it "deplorable," "horrendous," and "a disgrace."[2] When Ford finally got to court, the government had an offer ready: plead to time served and he could go home.

Ford had already been locked up for an entire month; the prosecutor thought that was enough. Ford, however, wanted to prove his innocence and turned down the plea. "We're ready for trial," Elkins told the judge.

After a while, it became clear that the homeowner—the government's only witness—was never going to show up. The government asked for more time to try to find its witness, and the judge granted the postponement. Elkins objected. "At least reconsider his bail and release him pending trial," she argued. Otherwise, Ford would languish in jail for many more weeks. The judge refused.

Crushed, Ford looked at his lawyer. "Okay, well, I'll just take the time served," he told her. Elkins had seen this before—innocent clients for whom a guilty plea was the only way to get out of jail. "I've practiced all over the country, and Baltimore City jail is the worst place I've ever seen," Elkins now says. "I have clients plead all the time to get out of that jail. They don't care what the deal is, they just want to leave."

The judge nudged her along. "You can advise your client," she told Elkins. And so Ford pled to the burglary that he did not actually commit, glad at least to escape more jail time. But Elkins can't forget the case.

"I was so offended," she says. "The government got what it wanted—they weren't asking for any more jail time. The judge could have released him and let him have his trial. The judge knew he had a defense, that he might have won. She deliberately extended his incarceration, basically forced him to take the plea just to get out of jail. And it didn't even seem to faze her."

Having now charted the speed, sloppiness, and institutional pressures of the petty-offense process, it is easy to see how they invite wrongful convictions. Arrests don't require much evidence, but most misdemeanor arrests nevertheless lead to formal criminal charges. Once they do, the petty-offense process puts heavy pressure on defendants to plead guilty, usually very quickly. The legal players who are supposed to screen for innocence—prosecutors, defense attorneys, judges—are typically in too much of a hurry or juggling too many other demands to do so. Ford was unusual in that he and his lawyer resisted that pressure for a while, but even he eventually gave in. Law professor Albert Alschuler calls this process "a nearly perfect system for convicting the innocent."[3]

How many innocent people are convicted of minor crimes in this way? The basic answer is that we don't know and can't know. Wrongful convictions are inherently invisible because they represent a breakdown of the very process that is supposed to reveal whether a person is guilty or not. But some types of cases are more problematic than others. Sometimes arrests and guilty pleas are based on especially unreliable kinds of evidence such as dubious field drug tests. People who plead guilty to order-maintenance crimes such as loitering and trespassing will often be innocent too: this is because people are frequently arrested for such crimes even when they have not actually loitered or trespassed as a matter of law.

Conversely, other types of misdemeanors do not raise these sorts of systemic risks, at least no more than any other type of crime. Driving on a suspended license is an offense triggered by DMV records of suspension, which are readily accessible to police when they arrest a motorist. To the extent that DMV databases are accurate, that person's license was probably actually suspended. Most DUI arrests now rely on breathalyzer tests, which typically provide solid evidence of intoxication. Even where the accuracy of those tests is questionable, most states have statutes that define DUI in terms of breathalyzer test results. If the test result is .10 or higher, you are guilty by definition, regardless of the machine's accuracy.[4] This is not to say that everyone arrested for such offenses is necessarily guilty, that DMV databases contain no errors (as we will see below, they do) or that breathalyzer tests are perfect (they aren't). But in these kinds of cases, there is no particular reason why the evidence that leads to arrest couldn't also support the higher standard of proof necessary for conviction. In short, these arrestees are probably guilty.

But much of the misdemeanor system does not offer this level of certainty. Many people are convicted based on types of evidence that we already know to be unreliable. For millions of others, we will never know whether they were innocent or not because the system is so sloppy and opaque that no one can tell. This gets criminal law exactly backward. The presumption of innocence means that if we don't know whether someone is guilty, they are not supposed to get convicted. But the misdemeanor system reverses those presumptions so that uncertainty all too often leads to conviction.

Over the past twenty-five years, the innocence movement has revealed that our criminal system regularly produces wrongful convictions in the most serious cases.[5] With over 2,000 exonerations documented in the National Registry of Exonerations and more than 150 death row inmates found to be innocent, it has become clear to lawyers, judges, legislators, and the public that some of the basic investigative techniques used to convict people are highly inaccurate: lineups, eye witness identifications, criminal informants, confessions, bite-mark evidence, and many other forensic methods. These wrongful convictions have spawned important debates and reforms. But misdemeanors have mostly been left out of that national innocence conversation. The founder of the National Registry of Exonerations once noted that "we rarely even think about wrongful convictions for misdemeanors."[6]

This chapter explores the largely ignored world of misdemeanor wrongful convictions. Or rather, a specific kind of wrongful conviction. Convictions can be wrongful for lots of reasons, including bad evidence, legal mistakes by lawyers and judges, or unconstitutional behavior on the part of the government. Many misdemeanor convictions are wrong in the fundamental sense that they are unfair or discriminatory or punish behavior that never should have been a crime in the first place. But the term of art "wrongful conviction" conventionally refers to factual innocence: the defendant did not actually commit the crime for which he or she was convicted. This chapter is about this kind of miscarriage of justice, which probably occurs thousands of times every year. Such convictions, in turn, have large, underappreciated implications for the criminal system as a whole. African American men, for example, face especially high risks of wrongful conviction for low-level order-maintenance crimes. More broadly, the phenomenon reveals an uncomfortable reality about the petty-offense process—namely, that it doesn't actually care that much about accuracy or guilt.

GARBAGE IN, GARBAGE OUT

Criminal convictions are only as reliable as the ingredients that go into them. There is no magic mirror to tell the truth at the end of the day: we have to rely on evidence, the people who collect it, the processes of plea bargaining and trial, and all those who make pivotal decisions along the way. We have already seen that the misdemeanor process can be sloppy and generally unreliable. But the threat of wrongful conviction is heightened in cases that rest on inherently problematic evidence. For example, unreliable forensic tests.

Amy Albritton knew she didn't have any cocaine, but she wasn't so sure about her new boyfriend sitting beside her in the car. Pulled over to the side of the road, she had consented to a search of her vehicle by the Houston police, and now Officer David Helms was holding up a small white crumb of something he found on the floor. She told him it wasn't drugs, but he handcuffed her anyway. Helms pulled out a vial of pink liquid—a roadside chemical drug test—and dropped in a bit of the crumb. If the liquid stayed pink, Albritton was good to go. But it turned blue. Helms waved the vial in front of her face. "You're busted."

After Albritton spent a night in jail, her court-appointed lawyer told her that the prosecutor was offering a deal: forty-five days in jail if she pled guilty. Albritton told him she was innocent, but the maximum for cocaine possession was two years, and her sixteen-year-old son, Landon, had cerebral palsy. So Albritton took the deal. She cried through the whole court proceeding, barely managing to stammer out the word "guilty."

Albritton served twenty-one days in jail. During those three weeks, she lost her job as an apartment manager and got evicted from her home—all her furniture and belongings were put out on the street. "So I lost all that," she says. The new conviction made it impossible to get a good job, so she moved Landon to Baton Rouge and tried to start a new life. It was 2010.

Five months after Albritton got out of jail, a lab technician named Ahtavea Barker tested the white crumb at Houston's crime lab. It wasn't cocaine—or any other drug. "N.C.S.," Barker wrote on the form: "No Controlled Substance." The field test was wrong, and Albritton was innocent, but there was no mechanism to fix the error. Another four years went by. Finally, the Houston District Attorney's Office sent Albritton a form letter telling her that she had been wrongfully convicted. "I knew it!" she shouted when she heard the news. "I told them!"[7]

Since mid-2014, 134 people who pled guilty to low-level drug-possession crimes of which they were innocent have been exonerated in Houston. Eighty-six of those convictions were based on roadside field drug tests. Although approximately two-thirds were felonies, not misdemeanors, the exonerations provide a revealing window into the wrongful guilty plea phenomenon for both classes of offense. It is a relatively unique window because Houston did two unusual things. First, it hung onto drug samples and tested them even when the individual legal cases were over. This definitively established that dozens of innocent people were pleading guilty, something that many people previously had a hard time believing. Second, in 2014 Houston created a Conviction Integrity Unit to go back over cases and exonerate the innocent. It sent letters to people like Albritton telling them that they had been wrongfully convicted. This publicized just how easily wrongful guilty pleas could occur. The city eventually decided to stop using the tests altogether.[8]

In 2016, *ProPublica* and the *New York Times* teamed up to investigate the validity of these widely used field drug tests. The investigation revealed how often the tests can go wrong. The chemical in the test tube used in Amy Albritton's case reacts not only to cocaine but to eighty additional compounds, including common household cleaners.

Some tests require very specific procedures—performing the steps in the wrong order can invalidate the results. Heat, cold, and even lighting can interfere with the tests' accuracy.[9]

Essentially, field drug tests were never designed to provide definitive evidence of guilt, only probable cause, just enough for arrest. The Safariland Group, the largest manufacturer of the test kits, said in a statement that "field tests are specifically not intended to be used as a factor in the decision to prosecute or convict a suspect."[10] They are inadmissible in court—judges have decided that they are too unreliable—but a positive result can exert enough pressure on defendants to get them to plead guilty, even when, like Albritton, they know they are innocent. This is a classic example of a broader misdemeanor dysfunction: evidence that was only supposed to be good enough for arrest becomes enough to generate a conviction.

Despite their flaws, field drug tests are used in hundreds of thousands of cases and in jurisdictions all over the country. In Las Vegas, Nevada, three-quarters of drug cases—nearly 3,500 convictions in 2015 in that one city—relied on field drug tests. By one estimate, at least 100,000 Americans plead guilty every year based on field drug test results.[11] The drug test industry has not disclosed error rates for its product. But even a small error rate would yield hundreds of wrongful convictions every year.

Low-level drug cases like these reveal the blurry line that separates misdemeanors from minor felonies. In Texas, Nevada, and many other states, non-marijuana-drug possession cases are often charged as felonies; elsewhere—for example, in California and Oregon and under federal law—small amounts of drugs are treated as misdemeanors. While drug felonies carry longer sentences and heavier stigma, the processes by which they are generated are often indistinguishable from petty-offense handling—at high speed, with little scrutiny and almost no trials. Sentences are sometimes comparable too. Nationwide, 30 percent of felony drug possession defendants receive probation, while others receive short, misdemeanor-like jail sentences.[12] Bail in such cases can induce guilty pleas just as it does in misdemeanor cases.

Also like in many misdemeanor court systems, defense counsel in some of these jurisdictions failed to intervene. For years, Las Vegas public defenders did not challenge the field tests even though there was ample evidence of their unreliability. A series of reports from 2000 to 2008 documented heavy caseloads and lack of aggression in the public defender office. One report concluded that few lawyers filed motions to suppress evidence at all, and some hadn't done so in years.[13] Such a lack of defense intervention and absence of investigation is typical of misdemeanor dockets but can bleed into low-level felony practice as well, permitting both misdemeanor and felony wrongful convictions.

Field drug tests are not an isolated phenomenon. The criminal system is full of similarly unreliable tests and processes. Several courts have found, for example, that standard roadside field sobriety tests— walking and turning, standing on one leg, touching a finger to the nose—lack scientific validity when used to establish blood alcohol content. Likewise, determining whether a person is driving under the influence of marijuana is still an evolving science. For years, federal courts relied on a sweat patch to monitor defendants on probation to see if they were using drugs, even though the patch reacted not only to the wearer's sweat but to environmental factors.[14] Such common tests and processes are designed for limited purposes, but they can morph—especially in the misdemeanor context—into more influential roles, most importantly by inducing guilty pleas. This gives them the potential to generate wrongful convictions and other injustices on a large scale, even as they fly beneath the radar because the tests seem unimportant.

Wrongful convictions can also flow from inaccurate database records. Walter Rothgery, for example, a former West Point cadet, was not a felon. In fact, he had no criminal convictions at all. He was the manager at the Oakwood RV Park in Fredericksburg, Texas, where sometimes there was trouble, so he wore a security guard belt with a holstered gun during his rounds. One day, a tenant called the police to report that Rothgery was carrying a gun. The Fredericksburg police ran a background check on him, and a six-year-old California felony conviction came up. The computer was wrong: Rothgery had been charged with a felony in California, but the case had been dismissed after he completed a diversion program. Nevertheless, Rothgery was arrested and charged with being a felon in possession of a firearm, itself a felony. He lost his job and could not find another. With no income, Rothgery asked repeatedly for a lawyer, but the court didn't give him one, and he spent three weeks in jail. "I grew up kind of being an idealist American," said Rothgery. "I never thought anything like this could happen to me." Finally, an attorney was appointed who assembled the paperwork to show that Rothgery was not a felon. The case was dismissed. "I guess everybody who gets arrested says they're innocent," he mused afterward. "Sometimes they are."[15]

The American criminal system depends heavily on databases. Criminal records, warrants, DNA, fingerprints, gang databases, and driving records are all increasingly accessible to police officers at a moment's notice while they are deciding whether or not to make an arrest. "Electronic databases form the nervous system of contemporary criminal justice operations," wrote Justice Ruth Bader Ginsburg. That nervous system includes national crime records databases, terrorist watchlists, DNA databases, and a wide variety of commercial databases. And it is expanding.[16]

Typically, database records are just one part of a criminal case, and especially when the case is serious, the information will ultimately be checked after an arrest. If the database turns out to be inaccurate, as it was for Rothgery, a wrongful arrest will probably not lead to a wrongful conviction. But as we have seen, the misdemeanor system often fails to check its evidence, relying instead on the mere fact of arrest to induce a guilty plea. In such cases, inaccurate databases can generate convictions.

There are two main types of databases on which the misdemeanor system routinely relies: driving records and criminal records. The first is more reliable than the second. Driver's records are contained in databases maintained by state motor vehicle departments. Offenses such as driving on a suspended license or without valid registration or insurance account for hundreds of thousands of convictions every year. In effect, the law presumes that DMV records are accurate: the certified DMV record of a license suspension constitutes definitive proof of that suspension. When a person is arrested, moreover, police have direct access to DMV records, so there is low risk of error in transmission. Nevertheless, even DMV records are not infallible. A 2000 Florida legislative study of DMV insurance records found error rates as high as 35 percent, leading to thousands of wrongful seizures. Anecdotes reveal other breakdowns. In New Jersey, Brian Pitcher's license was incorrectly recorded as suspended due to a child support order that had in fact been withdrawn. In Oregon, DMV records incorrectly indicated that Kyle Petterson's registration was expired; the arresting officer admitted that he knew DMV records were sometimes inaccurate due to delays in reporting. In Massachusetts, DMV records wrongly indicated that Ron Wilkerson's license was revoked, even though it had been reinstated years before.[17] Other than the Florida study, I was unable to find a single systematic study of DMV error rates, surprising given the importance of these records to millions of drivers. Because so many cases are generated using DMV records, however, even a very low rate of error could produce thousands of wrongful convictions.

In contrast to the relatively accessible and centralized DMV system, criminal record databases are widely known to be unreliable. The FBI criminal background check is considered the gold standard, but roughly 50 percent of its records are incomplete or otherwise inaccurate. Rap sheets—compilations of arrest and prosecution records—often reflect old or partial information: the time it takes to update an individual's felony status varies enormously, from one day in Delaware to a year and half in Kansas. Sometimes crucial information, like whether the person was acquitted or convicted, is never recorded at all. Identity theft makes errors even more common. Expungement and sealing processes are not always effective, which means that even when a person's record should have been expunged or corrected, old convictions and errors may still show up.[18] Such widespread inaccuracies explain how Walter Rothgery's record came up wrong.

A person mistakenly identified as having a prior criminal record may be subject to a number of different criminal charges. All fifty states make it a crime to possess a gun or other weapon if a person has a prior conviction, usually a prior felony or violent offense but sometimes also a prior misdemeanor. Being a felon in possession of a restricted weapon is a Class A misdemeanor in Oregon, and possession of a firearm by a felon can be a misdemeanor in Minnesota, New York, and West Virginia.[19]

Once a person is arrested and charged with one of these misdemeanors based on an erroneous criminal record, they face the standard pressure to plead guilty, particularly if they have trouble making bail or getting a lawyer. Walter Rothgery, facing a felony, made numerous requests for an attorney that were ignored or denied even while he languished in jail. A different person might well have given up and pled to a lesser charge. An arrestee might not even know whether the record is wrong: dismissals and diversionary programs are technical legal proceedings that can leave nonlawyers uncertain about their own legal status. Under such circumstances, given the offer to plead to a misdemeanor, many people might take that deal even though they are legally innocent.

The role of electronic data collection in criminal law enforcement is growing, and as Justice Ginsburg warned, "the risk of error stemming from these databases is not slim." Young people of color are often improperly labeled as gang members and included in gang databases, making them subject to wrongful arrest and prosecution for gang-related misdemeanors. Mistaken criminal records can threaten noncitizens with deportation. Warrant databases are routinely incorrect, leading to wrongful arrests, illegal searches, and unsupported incarcerations.[20] Such errors, when combined with the general sloppiness of the misdemeanor process, pose growing risks of wrongful conviction.

Unreliable forensic tests and inaccurate databases generate wrong-ful convictions because they offer up evidence to police that is factually wrong. Order-maintenance policing creates its own kind of unreliable evidence generated by police themselves. Typically, the evidence in such cases consists of an assertion by a police officer that a person engaged in criminal behavior such as disorderly conduct, trespassing, loitering, or other offenses sometimes referred to as quality-of-life crimes. Un-like with drug possession or driving on a suspended license, there is usually no physical evidence or written record that can be objectively verified or disproved after the fact. Often there are no witnesses, or at least no witnesses legally sophisticated enough to know whether the arrestee actually loitered or trespassed. The evidence is therefore only as reliable as the police officer. No more, no less.

The new ubiquity of phone and body cameras has thrust part of this phenomenon into the spotlight. Numerous videos now show arrests during which the arrested person was neither disorderly nor resistant but was later falsely charged with disorderly conduct or resisting arrest.[21] People arrested in such circumstances are clearly innocent. But the forces producing baseless arrests for these kinds of minor crimes are broader and deeper than individual police miscon-duct. Many police officers are under professional pressure to make large numbers of order-maintenance arrests. Some police depart-ments impose arrest quotas on their officers; others train police to use arrests to "clear the corner." Such policies generate a high volume of arrests that lack probable cause—evidence that those arrested actu-ally committed a crime. When such arrests lead to convictions, those convictions are wrongful.

For example, New York City engaged for years in practices that generated hundreds of wrongful trespassing convictions until they were halted in 2013 by a civil rights lawsuit. Under a policy called Operation Clean Halls, New York police saturated housing projects and arrested people for trespassing, mostly African American and Latino men. Many of the individuals arrested were not in fact trespassing: they were visiting friends or even lived in the buildings but failed to produce identification. Once arrested, many pled guilty. Chris Fabricant, a public defender in the Bronx who handled these cases, lamented that he had "a disgraceful number of innocent clients."[22]

New York law defines trespassing as when a person "knowingly enters or remains unlawfully in a dwelling . . . when he is not licensed or privileged to do so. In general, a person is 'licensed or privileged' to enter private premises when he has obtained the consent of the owner or another whose relationship to the premises gives him authority to issue such consent."[23] As part of Operation Clean Halls, however, police routinely arrested individuals who were visiting friends or family and therefore were not trespassing.

One of those individuals was Charles Bradley, a fifty-one-year old security guard. It was 2011, and he had just gotten off the subway to visit his fiancée, Lisa Michelle Rappa. Bradley was waiting on the sidewalk in front of Rappa's apartment building when an unmarked green van approached him. "What are you doing here?" asked Officer Miguel Santiago. Bradley explained that he was visiting Rappa, but Santiago searched Bradley's pockets, handcuffed him, and put him in the van with two other officers. "When was the last time you saw a gun?" they asked him. "When was the last time you got high? When was the last time you bought some drugs?" In the jail, Bradley was strip-searched, fingerprinted, and charged with trespassing. Bradley got a lawyer from The Bronx Defenders who obtained a notarized letter from Rappa saying that Bradley was visiting her. The trespassing charge was eventually dismissed.

"It was a nightmare for me," said Bradley afterward. "I'm coming to see my fiancée, I'm coming to see my loved one." He was seething and sad at the same time. The arrest nearly cost him his security job. "I could have lost everything in my life because of this arrest." He knew it could happen again. "The psychological and mental damage that can be caused by their tactics to good hardworking human beings like myself can last a lifetime."[24]

Between 2007 and 2012, when Operation Clean Halls was in effect, the New York Police Department made at least 16,000 trespass arrests every year, making it one of the highest-volume crimes charged in the city. Thirty-seven percent of trespass cases were resolved in favor of defendants, usually because prosecutors declined to prosecute or because, like Charles Bradley's, the case was dismissed. In New York there are few misdemeanor trials and almost no acquittals, and this holds for trespassing cases as well. As Fabricant explained, "I have handled more trespassing cases than any other single criminal charge, and I've never had one actually go to trial. That was unheard of." The remaining 63 percent of those 16,000 annual trespass arrests—over 10,000 cases—thus translated into criminal dispositions of some kind. As a general matter, around 30 percent of New York misdemeanor defendants get their cases diverted. The rest, which would include as many as 7,000 trespassing defendants, plead guilty.[25]

At the end of the day, we will never know exactly how many of those 7,000 people each year were wrongfully convicted of trespassing. But some clearly were. Fabricant said at the time that "virtually all of my clients [are] worn down by the methodical torture of Bronx Criminal Justice and tak[e] a guilty plea." Judge Shira Scheindlin, the federal judge who ultimately held Operation Clean Halls unconstitutional, also recognized the danger that innocent people could easily be convicted under this scenario. "If an unjustified stop happens to lead to an unjustified arrest for trespassing, as it did in Charles Bradley's case, not every overburdened public defender will have the wherewithal to obtain a notarized letter from the defendant's host explaining that the defendant was invited."[26] In other words, without the scarce resource of a zealous defense attorney, innocent people charged with trespass are likely to succumb to the heavy pressure to plead.

The New York misdemeanor arrest landscape has changed enormously over the past few years. In 2012, the Bronx district attorney unilaterally stopped prosecuting trespass arrests based solely on police reports, recognizing that many arrestees were innocent.[27] Multiple lawsuits have generated new rules and police practices. But other cities maintain comparable policies.

Baltimore police, for example, are locally notorious for wrongfully arresting black men for loitering. Former Baltimore police officer Peter Moskos, writing in 2008, called loitering "the most widely used minor criminal charge in Baltimore," levied against young black men when they talk back to police or refuse a police officer's order to move.[28]

In 2006, the National Association for the Advancement of Colored People (NAACP) and the American Civil Liberties Union sued the Baltimore Police Department (BPD) for its racially discriminatory mass-arrest practices, especially the overuse of baseless loitering arrests. The complaint proffered a representative scenario: "At approximately 5:45 p.m. on July 23, 2006, Tavis Crockett and approximately six other young men from his neighborhood were sitting on the front steps of a friend's building, getting ready to watch a neighborhood game of basketball. As the group began to get up and move toward the basketball courts, a number of police cruisers pulled up and Officer Grey exited his cruiser. Officer Grey asked the group where [a suspected drug dealer] Brandon was. . . . Upon learning that Brandon was not present, Officer Grey told all seven young men that they were being arrested for loitering."[29] The young men were taken to jail, booked, strip-searched, and held for fourteen hours.

Baltimore also maintained a quota policy under which police officers were required to make large numbers of arrests regardless of their quality. "Each patrol officer is required to tally his enforcement statistics, including citations and arrests," the NAACP lawsuit alleged. "These numbers are then compared to averages from that officer's squad and shift. The three officers in each district with the lowest scores are subject to reassignment to other districts."[30]

In 2010, Baltimore City entered into a consent decree under which it agreed to roll back these arrest and quota practices, and a court-appointed monitor was installed. Six years later, the US Department of Justice released the results of its investigation of the city's police force, which concluded that although overall arrest rates had fallen,

BPD had nevertheless continued its unlawful practices, including departmental pressure on police to make large numbers of arrests. As the 2016 report stated, "The legacy of zero tolerance persists in many aspects of the Department's enforcement. Many supervisors who were inculcated in the era of zero tolerance continue to focus on the raw number of officers' stops and arrests, rather than more nuanced measures of performance. As one example of this approach, supervisors frequently encourage officers to 'clear corners'—an instruction many officers understand to stop, disperse, or arrest groups of individuals standing on public sidewalks."[31]

For example, during the investigation, a Justice Department observer watched a Baltimore police supervisor order a subordinate officer to stop, question, and disperse a group of men on the street. The lower-ranking officer protested that he had no reason to stop them because they weren't doing anything wrong. "Then make something up," responded the supervisor.[32]

Loitering is one of a suite of common quality-of-life crimes. From 2010 to 2015, BPD made more than 25,000 arrests for nonviolent misdemeanor offenses, which included approximately 6,500 arrests for disorderly conduct, 4,000 for failing to obey a police officer, 6,500 for trespassing, 1,000 for hindering or impeding, 3,200 for interference, 760 for being rogue and vagabond, and 650 for playing cards or dice.[33]

As a matter of Maryland law and constitutional doctrine, many of the people arrested under such circumstances are innocent: they are not actually loitering, trespassing, or otherwise violating the law. For example, the Baltimore loitering statute reads in part as follows:

Prohibited loitering.

(b)(1) It shall be unlawful for any person to loiter at, on, or in a public place or place open to the public in such manner . . . to interfere with, impede, or hinder the free passage of pedestrian or vehicular traffic;

(c)(1) No person shall be charged with a violation of this section unless and until the arresting officer has first warned the person of the violation and the person has failed or refused to stop the violation.[34]

The warning requirement is a crucial piece of statutes like these because it preserves their constitutionality against the charge that they are too vague. Police must tell people that they are violating the law and give them an opportunity to desist before they can be prosecuted.[35]

Because of these legal constraints, it turns out that it's not that easy to loiter in Baltimore. A person must "impede" traffic—either people or cars—and *then* be warned to desist, and *then* fail to stop. In 2001, the Maryland Court of Appeals held that because of this relatively high threshold of proof, much of the conduct for which Baltimore police typically arrest people does not actually amount to loitering. Nevertheless, the 2016 Department of Justice investigation found that many loitering arrests still violate these statutory and con-stitutional warning requirements.[36] In other words, BPD is still arrest-ing innocent people.

Similarly, Baltimore police often charge people with trespassing when they are not actually trespassing, much as the police did in New York. The Department of Justice reported that "[Baltimore] officers often arrest individuals for 'trespassing' where the person arrested was standing on a public street that bordered property owned by the City or a private party. Such conduct is not criminal." For example, "officers . . . approached a man who was 'standing in front of 1524 Mount Mor Ct looking around' and who walked away when he saw officers. Officers stopped the man and arrested him when he 'could not provide a valid explanation for being in front of 1524 Mount Mor Ct.'" Because this conduct is not trespassing, this man was in-nocent. People have a constitutionally protected interest in standing and walking on public sidewalks—these activities are expressions of individual liberty—and they are not obligated to explain why they do so.[37]

How often do unfounded arrests like these lead to wrongful con-victions? "It happens all the time," says Natalie Finegar, deputy district public defender for the city of Baltimore. "We might want to go to trial, but clients are locked up, they want to get out, they want time-served. Or we [ask for] a jury trial and go downtown to Circuit Court, and clients get scared and want to take the deal."[38]

Not all arrests convert to criminal cases. Although we don't have exact data, the overall dismissal rate for Baltimore quality-of-life charges is high, probably somewhere between 50 and 65 percent. After arrest, a person is taken to Central Booking, where supervisors and prosecutors review the arrest documents. As of 2016, "this initial review resulted in dismissal of 1 in 6 of these [low-level] charges. Over 20 percent of all disorderly conduct charges and 25 percent of failure to obey charges were dismissed." Similarly, according to the Department of Justice, "officials rejected 24 percent of disturbing the peace charges, 23 percent of failure to obey charges, and 24 percent of hindering charges. Officials likewise rejected 156 trespassing charges, comprising roughly 5 percent of the total."[39]

These initial declinations—approximately 16 percent of all cases—eliminate low-hanging fruit, arrests whose paperwork alone reveals that police lacked probable cause. The second opportunity for dismissal comes in court. Quality-of-life crimes in Baltimore are handled in district court, a court of limited jurisdiction that handles mostly misdemeanors. This is where Jack Ford took that burglary plea. Once cases get to court, prosecutors decide not to prosecute about half of all cases—what is called "nolle prosequi." The data do not distinguish between types of cases, so we do not know whether this rate holds true for all types of misdemeanors.[40]

Of the approximately 10,000 criminal cases in 2015 that survived dismissal and went on to resolution in district court, 53 percent—around 5,300—resulted in convictions. This allows a rough estimate of the number of order-maintenance convictions that the process would have produced. Baltimore police made over 25,000 quality-of-life arrests between 2010 and 2015, around 5,000 per year. Approximately 84 percent—4,200 per year—would have survived initial declination and made it into the court system. Assuming that the overall "nolle prosequi" rate of 50 percent held for quality-of-life misdemeanors, 2,100 such cases would remain. Given a 53 percent conviction rate, that would translate into approximately 1,100 convictions for those original quality-of-life cases. That's about one-fifth of all convictions that occur in Baltimore City District Court each year.[41]

How much faith should we have in those 1,100 convictions? On the one hand, they are the result of two levels of prosecutorial screening, which suggests that prosecutors considered them valid. On the other hand, legally speaking, it is pretty difficult to loiter in Baltimore. The Baltimore statute and the Maryland Court of Appeals' interpretation of it are very specific: police cannot simply order people to move along, and the warning must adequately state the nature of the offense. According to a multiyear high-profile lawsuit and a separate federal investigation, Baltimore police routinely omit such warnings. Accordingly, it is likely that this widely used offense generates a substantial number of wrongful convictions, even if we will never know exactly how many.

Similarly, Baltimore police made 6,500 trespassing arrests between 2010 and 2015, or about 1,300 per year. The Department of Justice concluded that BPD trespassing enforcement practices commonly involved the arrest of innocent people. Since only 5 percent of trespass cases were initially screened out, this suggests that a large number of weak cases make it through the system, generating further risks of wrongful conviction.

Of course prosecutors are not the only screeners; public defenders are supposed to challenge cases where the evidence is suspect. Baltimore has a relatively aggressive public defender office—"we try a fair amount of cases," says Finegar. But even where defense attorneys are ready to contest cases, their clients may not want to stay in jail or risk the chance of worse punishment if they lose at trial. "Our clients want to get out as quickly as possible," Finegar explains. "Time-served is frequently offered, even by judges. . . . People want that, they want to go home." Or as one Baltimore resident mourned, "It's normal for guys to accept convictions for things that they didn't do."[42]

Baltimore is a good example of the inherent danger of wrongful conviction because it has a strong adversarial process. Prosecutors dismiss a high percentage of cases. Public defenders are prepared to try them. And yet, even here, the high volume of low-quality arrests, combined with the pressure to plead guilty, produces a significant risk of wrongful conviction. In jurisdictions with lower declination and dismissal rates and less aggressive public defender offices, the risks are even greater.

Baltimore and New York are high-profile examples, made infamous by lawsuits and federal investigations, but they reveal the basic anatomy of an innocence problem that pervades the US misdemeanor system. The first and most important systemic weakness lies with bulk arrests for low-level order-maintenance offenses that lack probable cause. This primes the pump, filling the system with unreliable cases. The next weakness occurs in the failure of the adversarial process—a lack of prosecutorial and defense attorney screening. Finally, defendants under strong pressure to plead guilty will tolerate convictions for things they didn't do. All three of these factors are commonplace around the country. Cities as diverse as Newark and Seattle overrely on order-maintenance arrests.[43] Prosecutorial offices vary greatly in their screening practices: some, like Baltimore's, screen heavily, but many others have declination rates on the order of 1 or 2 percent. Public defender's offices are glaringly overburdened. And finally, the misdemeanor process exerts enormous, across-the-board pressure on people to plead guilty, particularly when they cannot afford to make bail. In sum, the scenarios under which order-maintenance policing is likely to generate wrongful convictions turn out to be standard operating procedure throughout much of the petty-offense universe.

RACIAL IMPLICATIONS

Wrongful convictions like these can happen to anyone. But certain features of the misdemeanor process are racially skewed, making it more likely that poor African Americans will be wrongfully convicted of low-level crimes.

First and foremost, the types of order-maintenance offenses that are likely to produce wrongful convictions disproportionately target people of color. In Baltimore, the Department of Justice's investigation found racial disparities throughout BPD's arrest practices: "Although they make up only 63 percent of Baltimore's population, African Americans accounted for: 87 percent of the 3,400 charges for resisting arrest; 89 percent of 1,350 charges for making a false statement to an officer; 84 percent of the 4,000 charges for failing to obey an order; 86 percent of the more than 1,000 charges for hindering or obstruction; 83 percent of the roughly 6,500 arrests for disorderly conduct; and 88 percent of the nearly 3,500 arrests for trespassing on posted property."[44]

Other cities exhibit similar tendencies. Half of all "contempt-of-cop" arrests in Seattle are of African Americans, even though Seattle is largely white, making black people eight times more likely to be arrested for the offenses of obstructing or resisting arrest. In San Jose, California, a newspaper investigation found that 70 percent of arrests for disturbing the peace, 57 percent of arrests for resisting, and 57 percent of arrests for public intoxication were of Latinos, even though the group comprises only approximately 30 percent of San Jose residents. In New York at the time of its trespassing litigation, 80 percent of people stopped and frisked by police were African American or Latino: most of those unconstitutional trespassing arrests were imposed on people of color.[45]

Low-level drug arrests are also disproportionately aimed at people of color. In Houston where Amy Albritton was convicted, the *New York Times* found that "the racial disparity is stark. Blacks made up 59 percent of those wrongfully convicted in a city where they are 24 percent of the population." Nationally, Africans Americans make up 31 percent of drug arrests, although they represent only 12 percent of the population and use drugs at the same rate as whites.[46]

Such statistics translate into a higher likelihood that people of color will be arrested for precisely the sorts of misdemeanors that can easily lead to wrongful conviction. Innocent African Americans in particular are overexposed to wrongful conviction because they are more likely to be arrested for order-maintenance crimes, for drug possession, and for resisting police authority. Risks are especially high for black men because they are disproportionately arrested for such offenses.[47] These offenses often rest on weak evidence—forensically flawed in the case of roadside drug tests, legally insufficient in the case of order maintenance and resisting arrest. In combination with the strong pressure on people to plead guilty, this is a recipe for the wrongful conviction of people of color, black men in particular.

The racial implications of misdemeanor wrongful conviction go deeper than the numbers. The American criminal system is infamous for criminalizing African Americans—we'll come back to this in Chapter 6. That bias has leaked into society's collective consciousness, casting black men and women as criminals in the news, politics, and popular culture. The petty-offense process is a major engine of that criminalization, conferring arrest and conviction records and providing grist for the stereotype, especially for men who make up the majority of the criminal justice population. It turns out that the very people most often presumed to be guilty and disproportionately convicted may very well be factually and legally innocent.

ACCURACY AND INNOCENCE IN THE AGE OF THE PLEA BARGAIN

The misdemeanor threat to innocence is racially skewed, but it is not only about race. The petty-offense process has a generally cavalier attitude toward accuracy that poses a threat to everyone who passes through the system. This attitude is built into standard institutional habits and individual decisions made thousands of times every day. By relying too heavily on the fact of arrest, by failing to check the evidence, by shortchanging the screening and adversarial processes that are supposed to ensure factual accuracy, the misdemeanor process effectively announces that it does not care all that much whether anyone is guilty or innocent.

This negligent attitude has many sources, but one of the most important is plea bargaining. Facts and charges in low-level cases are highly negotiable. Over 95 percent of misdemeanor convictions are the product of a plea, which means nobody ever *demonstrated* that the defendant was guilty.[48] Everyone just *agreed* to it. In such negotiations, as we have seen many times already in this book, evidence is only one factor, often not the most important one. Deals are worked out in the shadow of prosecutorial charging policies, defender caseloads, the defendant's bail status, prior record, immigration status, and financial situation, and the habits of the judge. Outcomes depend on lots of things that have nothing to do with guilt. The guilty plea is thus the central, structural mechanism through which the institutional commitment to accuracy is eroded.

Even when people are well represented and not incarcerated prior to trial, the process can deter them from asserting their innocence. Angel Cardona and his New York high school friends, for example, were waiting for the bus. A police car pulled up, and the officers began frisking the teenagers. They found a small amount of marijuana in Cardona's pocket, arrested him, and gave him a ticket for the noncriminal violation. Three months later, Cardona and his mother went to court for his arraignment, his first formal court hearing. There, they learned that the officer had falsely accused Cardona of smoking marijuana in public—a misdemeanor that would mark him with a criminal record and potential jail time. Cardona got a lawyer from The Bronx Defenders to fight the wrongful charge and to challenge the illegal search. Cardona and his mother went to court four times over ten months, missing school and work and using up his mother's vacation days. When those ran out, with no prospect of an actual trial date, Cardona reluctantly accepted the prosecution's offer. Over a year after his arrest, he pled guilty to disorderly conduct—not the crime he was arrested for—and went home.[49]

As Cardona's case illustrates, almost everything in plea bargaining—including the facts and the nature of the crime—is up for negotiation. The plea bargaining process can also be factually misleading in another way: it obscures the question of whether the government is obeying the Constitution. Notice that Cardona not only wanted to establish his innocence but also sought to challenge the constitutionality of the stop-and-frisk for which the police did not have enough evidence. The pressures of the process, however, persuaded him to forgo that challenge and the public information that it would have produced. His was one of fifty-four similar marijuana cases brought in New York between 2011 and 2012 involving potentially illegal police conduct. Because of delay, cost, and other challenges, not a single suppression hearing was held in any of them, and the majority of defendants, like Cardona, negotiated a deal.[50]

Plea bargaining's loosey-goosey attitude toward accuracy is not limited to misdemeanors. As the Supreme Court acknowledged in 2015, "Criminal justice today is for the most part a system of pleas, not a system of trials. Ninety-seven percent of federal convictions and ninety-four percent of state convictions are the result of guilty pleas." Facts and charges are negotiated and altered in felony cases all the time. Accordingly, the entire US criminal process revolves around a kind of deal-making in which accuracy—the question of whether the defendant actually did it—is inherently at risk. The misdemeanor system is especially prone to producing wrongful convictions because it is enormous, fast, and sloppy. But even if it were small, slow, and careful like the top of the criminal justice pyramid, wrongful convictions would still occur because the ultimate question of guilt remains negotiable. Indeed, the National Registry of Exonerations contains over three hundred cases in which innocent defendants pled guilty to felonies, seventy-two of them for homicide.[51]

The felony world, however, mitigates the omnipresent risk of wrongful guilty pleas through a more robust adversarial process. Serious cases involve more evidence. More people are arguing about it. Negotiations take a while. The incentives for defendants are also different. Sentences are longer, so the cost of pleading guilty is higher, as is the potential benefit of fighting it out. Bail, too, works differently. Because pleading guilty to a serious felony will generally not let anyone go home right away, there is less immediate pressure on innocent people to do it.

Most importantly, questions of guilt and innocence matter in serious cases even when they are being negotiated. This is the lesson of the innocence movement—once people understood that wrongful convictions were occurring regularly in homicide and rape cases, a widespread consensus developed that innocent people should not be convicted of serious crimes. Dozens of innocence projects sprang up around the country, while some prosecutors' offices established conviction integrity units to identify and prevent wrongful convictions. But that consensus does not yet extend to petty offenses. Many individual judges and lawyers already realize that innocent people are routinely pleading guilty to petty crimes, but the system nevertheless proceeds apace. Innocence projects almost never take misdemeanor cases, and there are scarcely any exonerations.[52] All this even though the risks to accuracy are obvious and extreme. We know that innocent people are being convicted. It is an essential and defining aspect of misdemeanor culture that almost no one cares.

The phenomenon of wrongful misdemeanor conviction is exacerbated by the fact that it is nearly invisible to the public. The legal process is supposed to provide information about the strengths and weaknesses of convictions: assemble the facts, create a record, and let the lawyers fight it out. Because this so rarely happens for misdemeanors, the truth may never come to light. Incredibly, even the people pleading guilty may not know whether they are innocent. Unlike, say, a bank robbery, where the defendant probably knows whether or not he "did it," many people will have no idea whether they were actually loitering or engaging in disorderly conduct. Others, like Amy Albritton, will not know whether a field drug test is accurate. At the end of the day, if no one knows the convictions were wrongful, there is no one to complain. The threat of wrongful conviction thus lurks quietly behind the entire petty-offense process, enormous, indeterminate, and deeply problematic.

| 5 |

MONEY

Q IANA W ILLIAMS IS A SINGLE MOTHER IN HER THIRTIES.
Her voice is clear and musical, but she is not accustomed to speaking
in front of others and hides behind her hair while she tells her story.
When Williams was nineteen years old, she got a ticket in St. Louis
County for driving without a license. Because she couldn't afford to
pay that ticket, she was charged additional fines and fees. After that,
her life was never the same.

My story spans the course of about twenty years. I received my first
traffic tickets as a young adult. I made a bad choice of driving without a license. I was unable to pay the fines and fees associated with
those first traffic tickets that I received. Upon going to court I was
asked to pay what I could, and I did that, every month, twenty dollars or whatever I could pay, until you eventually miss a court date,
or you just don't have the money to pay, and you get a warrant.
So I have warrants for unpaid traffic tickets, that, um [embarrassed

pause], prevent you from getting a job. It affects getting a job, nobody wants to hire a person who has a warrant out for their arrest. It doesn't say that it's for a traffic ticket, it only says I'm a fugitive, I'm a wanted person. And so I was forced to do odd jobs. For twenty years, I've done odd jobs all of my life.[1]

Her voice quavers. This was not the life she was hoping for. "It affects housing, it affects housing twofold because you can't get a job to pay rent, and property owners don't want to rent to someone who has a warrant out for their arrest. Which leads to homelessness, that I was for so many years, off and on. Not having anything but my car to live in, myself and my child. I was forced to drive. You know school buses are not going to come to wherever I'm at on a particular night to pick up my daughter, so I was forced to get her to school."

Williams speaks just a little louder. This is the part she is sure of. "I would never want her to miss school because of my inability to pay these fines and fees that I incurred over these twenty years, so I made sure that she didn't miss a day."

It is 2015, and Williams is speaking at a White House conference on criminal justice debt, bail, and incarceration. The US Department of Justice (DOJ) has just released a scathing report on the Ferguson lower-court system, triggering a new national conversation about misdemeanor fines and fees. Williams is now part of that conversation, explaining to the White House audience how her debt impacted every part of her life.

"Not only was I unable to get a job, get adequate housing, I didn't see a way out, I didn't see a way to pay for these fines and fees. I thought maybe if I just got an education, that I would be able to be in an earning income bracket that would help me to pay these fines and fees. And so I went to school. Many times I went to school. I even made the dean's list." You can almost hear a smile in her voice. But then it's gone. "And twelve credits away from getting my degree I was arrested for traffic tickets. I've spent over four months in jail. Not all at once. Maybe three weeks, I spent three weeks in Pine Lawn jail for unpaid traffic tickets. I spent two weeks in Arnold for unpaid traffic tickets. This has been my life for the past twenty or so years."

It takes a second for her to share the next part. She is determined not to cry. "I suffered not being able to be the best member of society that I wanted to be, but my daughter suffered the most by having her parent taken away from her, at any given day, Christmas, New Year's, all of the nights that I spent in jail because I didn't have the resources to pay the traffic tickets that I incurred over my life."

Deep breath. That was the worst part. The rest she can handle. "The conditions in the jail were deplorable. Just imagine being in an eight-by-five cell, shoulder to shoulder with about eight other women, no toilet, no water, you have to beg to use the bathroom. However," her musical voice hardens, "they do put a phone in the cell, they pass the cell phone into the cell because if you don't like it, you have to bond out, you have bail out. That's what the control officers always said, 'If you don't like it, bail out.' And for a person who couldn't bail out, staying there until they decided to let me out was what I had to do, every time that I was picked up for these unpaid traffic fees and fines."

It is hard to overstate the pervasive influence of money and wealth in shaping, motivating, and expanding nearly every aspect of the misdemeanor system. In the first instance, many low-level crimes are crimes of poverty: they punish people for being unable to afford car insurance, housing, or child care by making it a crime to drive without insurance, sleep in a public place, or leave a child briefly unattended. Misdemeanors also make people poorer in a variety of ways. Fines and fees strip them of their wealth. Driver's license suspensions—a common result of failing to pay traffic fines—get people fired and cause them to miss school, doctor's visits, and job interviews. Being jailed for failure to pay fines and fees drives people deeper into poverty. Since nearly half of all Americans have trouble coming up with an extra $400 in an emergency, standard misdemeanor fines and fees threaten devastation for a broad swath of the population.[2]

These regressive policies, in turn, help pay for the misdemeanor process itself. In effect, the petty-offense process is a method of taxation. It rounds up low-level offenders and charges them fines and fees, which are then plowed back into the system to fund those very same courts, jails, probation offices, and the local governments that oversee them. Thomas Edsall of the *New York Times* called this phenomenon "poverty capitalism," a "unique sector of the economy [where the] costs of essential government services are shifted to the poor."[3] Often the misdemeanor process indirectly transfers wealth away from the poor behind the scenes; sometimes it does it overtly.

Judge Marilyn Lambert, for example, was the only judge on the Ascension Parish Court bench, a Louisiana municipal court handling misdemeanors and traffic infractions. If Judge Lambert convicted an individual, that person paid a $15 conviction fee, which went into a judicial expense fund. If Judge Lambert found them not guilty, they paid nothing. Judge Lambert controlled the Judicial Expense Fund. In 2015, the Judicial Expense Fund paid a portion of Judge Lambert's salary—$35,684—as well as $9,670 in retirement, $6,000 for a car, and $5,894 for travel and conference expenses, for a total of over $57,000—the equivalent of 3,800 convictions.[4]

Sherwood, Arkansas, operates a "hot check court" every Thursday, which handles misdemeanors involving bounced checks. For each bounced check, regardless of the amount of the check, defendants are assessed fines and fees of at least $400. In 2011, Nikki Rachelle Petree wrote a check for $28.93 that was returned for insufficient funds. As a result of that one bounced check, the city of Sherwood arrested her seven times, charged her over $2,600, and jailed her for over twenty-five days. The court collects so many fines and fees from its mostly low-income defendants that the court staff nicknamed it "Million-Dollar Thursday." The city advertises the hot check court on its website as a "service . . . available to merchants . . . free of charge as part of our many efforts to create and maintain a business friendly environment here in Sherwood." The website also boasts of its 85 percent collection rate.[5]

The misdemeanor system regulates the poor and the low-wage workers in ways that make it an enormously influential socioeconomic institution, redistributing wealth and recasting people's lives while shaping the practices and economic viability of local governmental entities. The system is regressive—it takes largely from those with the lowest incomes. Like the rest of the criminal system, it is racially skewed, aimed disproportionately at poor people of color. Perhaps most fundamentally, it alters the very meaning of criminal justice because its arrests, convictions, and punishments can no longer be said to be motivated primarily by wrongdoing, public safety, or justice. Instead, they are heavily incentivized by money.

It is, of course, fundamentally wrong to punish people for profit. But that does not mean that fines are always bad. Sometimes monetary sanctions represent an enlightened alternative to incarceration or other harsh penalties. Fines, as Supreme Court justice Sandra Day O'Connor once noted, date back to "the early days of English justice" before the Norman conquest, serving as a substitute for vengeance by private parties.[6] Some people deserve to be fined. In our modern penal system, especially in theft and fraud cases, fines enable restitution and vindication for victims. But the misdemeanor world has invested fines and fees with new and sometimes dysfunctional significance, skewing the entire criminal process against the less wealthy. They make punishments longer and harsher for people who cannot afford to pay. They strip poor and working people of their life resources, often in order to fund the system itself. And because the system is so large, its aggregate effect on millions of people every year amounts to a kind of accidental anti-welfare policy, exacerbating economic inequalities on a massive scale.

PUNISHING POVERTY

Most criminal defendants are assessed fines. But fines are worst for the people who can afford them least. After two back surgeries, Cindy

Rodriguez was in constant pain and couldn't work. Her federal disability check wasn't much; she had no bank account and could not always pay her water and electric bills. At age fifty, she had no criminal record until she was arrested for shoplifting. Her punishment: fines and court fees totaling $578. Because Cindy couldn't pay that much right away, she was placed on probation for a year with Providence Community Corrections, Inc. (PCC), a private probation company hired by the Rutherford County Court in Tennessee to supervise all misdemeanor defendants and collect their payments. As soon as Cindy began her supervision, PCC began charging her fees. First, PCC charged her $40 per month for supervision. It also required that she take numerous drug tests, although she had no drug history and her offense was not drug related. For each drug test, PCC charged $20. When Cindy told her probation officer that she did not have enough money to pay that month, the officer threatened to have her arrested and put in jail. When Cindy appealed to a supervisor, the supervisor told her, "One more time of this bullshit, and I'm gonna violate you. You'll spend seven days in jail."

Over the course of that year, to avoid jail, Cindy Rodriguez channeled all her resources to PCC. She signed over to PCC her disability benefits, her sole source of income. She paid PCC instead of paying her car loan; as a result, she lost her car and had to walk. She fainted in public three times and broke her arm. She broke her tooth but had no money to fix it. By the end of her probation year, Cindy had paid PCC over $500, nearly enough to meet her court debts. But PCC took all but $66 for itself to pay off its own fees. The company told Cindy that she still owed the court $512 and that if she did not pay, she would be in violation of her probation and go to jail. Because Cindy could not come up with $512, PCC had a warrant issued for her arrest—for which it charged her a fee—and asked the court to extend her probation with PCC for an extra year.[7]

It is often said that the American criminal system as a whole "punishes the poor" and that we "criminalize poverty." This is true in a number of ways. Most criminal defendants start out poor. Over half of all inmates lived in poverty prior to their incarceration, and more than one-third were jobless. Seventy-five percent of people in state prisons have not completed high school. Seventy percent of inmates function at the lowest levels of literacy. Eighty percent of the felony criminal justice population cannot afford a lawyer. When the poor turn to the social safety net for help, moreover, they risk being surveilled and further criminalized. Sociologist Loïc Wacquant describes these collective phenomena as "the gradual replacement of a (semi-)welfare state by a police and penal state for which the criminalization of marginality and the punitive containment of dispossessed categories serve as social policy at the lower end of the class and ethnic order." In other words, we use crime policy to manage poor people.[8]

Nowhere is the crime-poverty nexus tighter than in the misdemeanor system. A host of petty offenses punish people for their inability to pay for things like car registration or insurance or for lacking key resources that the law says they should have, such as a place to sleep. By their nature, such offenses single out the poor—the wealthy can afford car insurance and housing. But formally they apply to everyone, and the Supreme Court has held that imposing financial burdens on the poor—including criminal fines—does not violate the Equal Protection Clause.[9] Or as novelist Anatole France facetiously remarked a hundred years ago, "The law, in its majestic equality, forbids the rich as well as the poor to sleep under bridges, to beg in the streets, and to steal bread."

Homelessness is perhaps the most obvious arena in which poverty is punished through misdemeanors. Sandy, for example, is a middle-aged homeless woman in Berkeley, California, where the shelters are full and it is illegal for her to sleep in her car. As she describes in a video interview, Sandy now has a pending criminal case and an outstanding warrant as a result of sleeping in a church:

> I sleep on the sidewalk, in a sleeping bag, [because I can't sleep in my car]. And I'm trying to . . . I don't use drugs. I don't use alcohol. I don't really do anything wrong. . . . I've got a warrant right

now for sleeping outside; basically it's a trespassing warrant. I was trying to get away from people who were, um, because of various reasons; drugs or whatever. . . . But I have to get away from them. And some nights you literally have to hide. It's not safe for women, especially older women. The police gave me a ticket one morning when I woke up. I had to hide from a crowd that was, whatever, I don't know what they were doing. But, you know, I just basically wanted to get in a little bit safer situation so I hid . . . in this church. And they gave me a ticket, and now I can't pay for this ticket; it's four-hundred bucks! You know, I can't pay eighty dollars. I have no income whatsoever.[10]

Misdemeanors that criminalize homelessness are on the rise. According to the National Law Center on Homelessness & Poverty, there has been a "rise in laws that impose city-wide bans on the basic human actions of homeless people," including camping, loitering, begging, and sleeping. Between 2012 and 2014, Minneapolis police arrested over 2,400 homeless people for violations related to not having a home, such as consuming alcohol in public, begging, and public urination. On Los Angeles's enormous Skid Row, sometimes referred to as the homelessness capital of the United States, locals are routinely arrested and jailed for the offense of sitting on the sidewalk. Juliette has lived on Skid Row for many years. She has been arrested over sixty times, most commonly for sitting, and has collectively spent over a year of her life in jail for that misdemeanor offense. As one researcher observed, "For most Americans, the sight of this proud grandmother sitting on the concrete handcuffed and sobbing is unfathomable. For those who live and work in Skid Row, it's just another Tuesday morning."[11]

Homelessness is also increasingly punished spatially and geographically, through the intersection of criminal misdemeanors such as loitering and trespassing with injunctions that ban people from specific spaces. Cities like Los Angeles, Portland, New York, and Cincinnati have created large swathes of public space where it is a crime for many homeless people to go. In Seattle, Washington, for example, police issued a seven-day exclusion order against a homeless man named Tom, making it a crime for the next week for him to return to the park where he and his friends ate and congregated. Eventually Tom was banned from all Seattle parks, the metro system, and the library, leading to numerous arrests and nights in jail.[12]

On any given night, over 600,000 people in the United States have nowhere to sleep; 1.6 million American children are homeless.[13] The misdemeanor system has become a frontline mechanism for managing this state of affairs as a criminal rather than a social welfare problem.

But the homeless are far from the only group punished for their poverty. The petty-offense process has injected the threat of criminalization into some of the most basic functions of modern life, especially driving. Damian Stinnie, for example, was twenty-four years old and had lymphoma. He lived with his twin brother in their car because they could not afford housing. Stinnie's troubles began when he was convicted of three traffic violations. He had recently lost his minimum-wage job at Walmart and had just begun working as a sales associate at Abercrombie & Fitch, where he earned approximately $300 per week. The fines and fees for those traffic violations totaled over $1,000. Because he could not pay, unbeknownst to him, the state of Virginia automatically suspended his license. He was diagnosed soon thereafter and underwent radiation and chemotherapy. After his release from the hospital, he was stopped again for speeding. Because his license was suspended, he was sentenced to jail as well as additional fees that he could not pay.[14]

In Virginia, license suspensions are a debt-collection tool: failure to pay any fine in any criminal or traffic proceeding automatically results in the indefinite suspension of a person's driver's license. Every year since 2010, Virginia has issued over 360,000 orders of suspension. Over 940,000 Virginians like Stinnie have a suspended license, which means they risk a criminal conviction if they need to drive.[15]

The city of Milwaukee likewise relies heavily on driver's license suspensions to collect unpaid traffic fines. In 2014 alone, the municipal court issued almost 48,000 suspensions. Many states, including Florida, Louisiana, North Carolina, Pennsylvania, Texas, and Washington, have similar laws that suspend driver's licenses for failure to pay fines and fees. Driving on a suspended license is, in turn, a crime in forty-six states. Such offenses represent a large percentage of local misdemeanor dockets—commonly as high as 30 percent and reaching 60 percent in some places. They impose billions of dollars of debt on the poor, and they send thousands of people to jail every year. The practice of suspending licenses for failure to pay is the subject of new civil rights litigation; in 2017, both California and Mississippi agreed to halt the practice.[16]

The misdemeanor system also issues millions of arrest warrants every year for people who have missed payments. In Ferguson, Missouri, the municipal court issued arrest warrants for 9,000 people in 2013, mostly for minor municipal violations, in a city with only 21,000 mostly low-income residents. These failure-to-pay warrants, sometimes called capias warrants, form an enormous cloud hanging over the heads of the poor. They can trigger the loss of welfare benefits, food stamps, and driver's licenses. Warrants may also cause people to avoid places and situations where they might be arrested such as hospitals, banks, or calling 911. In a scenario made tragically familiar by the shooting death of Walter Scott, a warrant issued for debt may even cause people to run from police. On April 4, 2015, during a routine traffic stop in Charleston, South Carolina, Scott ran from Office Michael Slager because he feared arrest on an outstanding failure-to-pay warrant. Slager shot Scott in the back and killed him, an act for which the officer was charged with murder.[17]

The misdemeanor system punishes poverty not only by turning various deprivations into crimes but by checking on the poor more often than it checks on the rich. This happens, for example, when police concentrate enforcement in low-income communities of color. Because residents of those neighborhoods are overexposed to police, they are more likely to be arrested, cited, and fined for common minor offenses. The neighborhood of Brownsville, New York, was so heavily policed that, before a court found the policy unconstitutional, police made approximately 13,000 stops a year in an area with 14,000 residents. In Newark, New Jersey, one of the country's poorest cities, police stopped over 50,000 pedestrians over a four-year period—approximately one-quarter of the adult population—and ran warrant checks on 40,000 of them.[18]

Of course not all misdemeanors are crimes of poverty. Domestic violence, drunk driving, and drug possession are committed by rich and poor alike. Indeed, several studies have found that wealthier and better-educated people are *more* likely to drive under the influence of alcohol.[19] Thousands of low-level offenses—from reckless driving to assault—target no particular economic class. But a large portion of the misdemeanor docket consists of offenses that the wealthy need never commit and over which the poor have little or no control.

GENERATING POVERTY

Not only do misdemeanors punish the poor, they tend to make them poorer. This is generally true of brushes with the criminal system. Any conviction—even for a minor offense—undermines a person's employability and credit. Some misdemeanors, particularly drug offenses, eliminate public benefits such as housing or financial aid. Even misdemeanor encounters that do not result in a conviction can exacerbate a person's disadvantage.

Alika was twenty-six years old and a single mother when two police officers stopped her in the courtyard of her Brooklyn housing development and asked for identification. When she produced it, they kept on her. "Then they asked me do I have anything else on me, like a gun or a knife. I told them I had a bag of marijuana in my purse. They said, 'Let's see it.' If I didn't show it to them, they were going to bring a lady cop to search me. If she found anything, they were going to send me direct to booking and spend the night." Alika's possession of marijuana was a decriminalized violation under New York law that could have earned her a ticket but no jail. But as soon as she took the marijuana out of her purse as she was ordered to do, her fine-only violation became the criminal misdemeanor of openly displaying the drugs. For this, she faced a potential sentence of ninety days in jail. She was handcuffed and taken to court, where her case was diverted for a year. The government agreed to drop the charges if she stayed out of trouble. For the duration of that year, however, the record of that charge would hamper her attempts to earn a living. She was, for example, promptly fired from her city job as a janitor, which had earned her $12 an hour.[20]

Misdemeanor dynamics like these strip people of their resources. Suspending a low-income person's driver's license does not just punish them for their inability to pay traffic tickets: it exacerbates their underlying poverty by preventing them from driving. Alyssa was a bus driver. When she moved to a new home, she missed the ten-day deadline to change her address with the California DMV. That triggered a $25 ticket that she did not know about, which got her license suspended. Lacking a license, she was fired, and without income she could not set up a payment plan to pay off the ticket and fees. Now she and her children are on public assistance, and her original $25 ticket has ballooned into a $2,900 fine.[21]

A New Jersey study found that following license suspension, 42 percent of people lost their jobs. Of those who lost their jobs, 45 percent could not find another one, and for those who did find another one, 88 percent earned less than they did when they had their license. As New Jersey resident Eddie Restrepo put it, "The more and more I kept trying to get out of it, it seemed like a bigger hole I was digging myself." Restrepo was a homeless Iraq War veteran who could not afford to renew his driver's license or pay his fines and fees. After he was caught driving twice without a valid license, a warrant was issued for his arrest. Before he turned himself in, he had accrued over $10,000 in criminal justice debt.[22]

The most obvious and direct way that the misdemeanor system makes people poorer is by taking their money. The use of fines, fees, surcharges, restitution, and interest, collectively known as legal financial obligations (LFOs), has exploded over the past few decades as more jurisdictions ratchet up misdemeanor punishments. Over 85 percent of misdemeanor defendants are reportedly charged monetary sanctions, although the actual percentage is likely higher due to underreporting.[23]

In Florida, for example, graffiti is a second-degree misdemeanor. By statute, punishment is up to sixty days in jail and up to a $500 fine. On top of that, a convicted person will face many or all of the following additional fees: a special $250 graffiti fine, a $50 application fee for the public defender, a $50 fee for using the public defender, a $50 prosecution fee, $60 in court costs, a $50 offender fee, a $20 crime-stopper fee, a $20 crime-prevention fee, a $10 county court fee, a $50 costs-on-conviction fee, a $124 community-control fee, and/or a $40-per-month probation fee. These additional fees can total over $750. Missing a payment deadline may generate a $30 late fee, a $7 license-suspension fee, a $60 license-reinstatement fee, and a $25 fee to initiate a payment program if a person cannot pay the full amount, bringing their total up to $850. If that sum remains unpaid after ninety days, the case will be referred to a private collections company, which can impose up to a 40 percent surcharge on the uncollected debt, or an additional $340. Similarly in Texas, a graffiti misdemeanor automatically triggers the application of at least nine and as many as twenty-three additional fees for a potential immediate surcharge of up to $444 in addition to the criminal fine. In Oklahoma, misdemeanor fees can total as much as $1,000.[24]

Some fees and assessments apply by their nature only to those too poor to pay their LFOs right away, a so-called poverty penalty. Most states charge late fees. Others impose collection fees, often paid to private collection companies. Other jurisdictions charge for creating a payment plan, with fees ranging from $10 in Virginia to $25 in Florida to $100 in New Orleans. Some jurisdictions issue failure-to-pay warrants and then charge defendants a fee for doing so. Washington charges 12 percent interest on outstanding LFOs. Michigan charges a 20 percent late fee after fifty-six days of nonpayment.[25] Because the wealthy can pay their obligations up front, such fees do not haunt them. But they magnify the burden on those who can least afford it.

If a person is placed on misdemeanor probation and then cannot pay their fines or fees, most states treat that failure to pay as a probation violation. This can lead to warrants, arrests, court hearings, and further incarceration. Under federal law, moreover, a probation violation disqualifies an individual from a wide range of welfare benefits, including Temporary Assistance to Needy Families, food stamps, low-income housing, and Supplemental Security Income (SSI) for the elderly and disabled. For example, Loretta was a forty-eight-year-old living in Waterbury, Connecticut, who subsisted on SSI and Old Age, Survivors, and Disability Insurance (OASDI), commonly known as Social Security. The average OASDI recipient receives approximately $12,500 annually, just above the federal poverty line. In 2009, Loretta learned that her benefits in Connecticut would be suspended because of an outstanding warrant issued by Florida in 1996. According to Florida officials, she owed $185 to the Salvation Army for supervising her misdemeanor probation, $50 to the state attorney's office, $54 to the St. Petersburg Police Department, and $354 to Pinellas County. Since Loretta had no income other than her benefits, she could not pay off the $643 demanded to clear the warrant and therefore faced the termination of those same benefits.[26]

The accumulation of LFOs can sink a person deeper into poverty in other ways. Like any unpaid debt, outstanding criminal fines can wreak havoc on people's credit scores, preventing them from getting jobs, renting homes, opening bank accounts, or taking out loans. Employer background checks increasingly include credit reports. Rental apartments and public housing authorities typically use credit scores to screen applicants. Outstanding criminal debt on a credit report also acts as a flag that the person has a conviction, which can further impede their access to jobs and housing.[27]

For people living on the economic margin, which includes nearly half the US population, the pressures of criminal justice debt can squeeze out other basic needs.[28] In order to pay misdemeanor fines and fees, many people divert scarce funds away from food, housing, child support, and health care or from education or buying a car or a home. John has criminal debt both from a past felony and from the accumulation of new misdemeanor fines and fees. He explains how he juggles his debt:

Interviewer: So how do you manage the payments?

John: I rob Peter to pay Paul.

Interviewer: What do you mean by that?

John: Gypping other obligations that I should have been responsible for.

Interviewer: What were the other responsibilities?

John: Rent, and car payments, insurance payments, and um, well you think it's only a couple days, but you get pulled over, and then you've got no insurance, so then you get another ticket, another court, another fine added on to that, and you know, it just snowballs.[29]

LFOs can even drive people to commit new crimes. In Childersburg, Alabama, one probationer expressed his frustration that others were committing crimes to pay their probation fees and getting away with it. "I know people selling drugs and paying [the probation company] every month. They like, 'Hey, I'm doing what they told me, ain't I?'" Or as one former offender aptly named Justice explains, "Frankly, I mean, I'm not trying or wanting to do any crime, and I still can't quite commit myself to do prostitution, but I think about it sometimes. . . . [A]t least that way I could pay some of these damn fines."[30]

In all these ways, the inability to pay a misdemeanor fine, ironically, can deprive a person of the life tools and public benefits they need to escape poverty. This is an important and underappreciated feature of the misdemeanor system: it covertly undermines other public policies aimed at alleviating economic disadvantage. It can even be seen as kind of an *anti*-welfare program since it strips the wealth of the very same people who most benefit from poverty assistance. The misdemeanor system has not been traditionally understood as a public welfare institution in this way, but it should be.[31] Because the system is so large and sweeps in so many people, its structural tendency to impoverish should be recognized as a form of national welfare policy in its own right, a way that federal, state, and local governments collectively, if perhaps unintentionally, decide how to manage the plight of the poor.

DEBTORS' PRISON

Fines and fees not only impoverish people but can land them in jail. Over the past few years, we have learned much more about how frequently people are incarcerated because they can't afford to pay criminal debt. As many as a quarter of misdemeanor jail inmates are incarcerated, not for their original offenses but because they failed to pay a fine or fee. In Rhode Island, 18 percent of all incarcerations are for debt. In Huron County, Ohio, 20 percent of jail bookings are for failure to pay fines and fees. In Benton County, Washington, approximately one-quarter of misdemeanor inmates are in jail for failure to pay.[32]

The phenomenon is referred to as the new debtors' prison, a caustic reference to the fact that civil debtors' prisons have long been deemed unjust, undemocratic, and unconstitutional. No one can be incarcerated for a civil debt like a car payment or a student loan. If you don't pay your credit card bill, the bank cannot put you in jail. That kind of debtors' prison was abolished in the United States in 1833 at the federal level, and all fifty states have constitutions or statutes that make it illegal to incarcerate a person solely because he or she owes a civil debt.[33] The use of fines and fees in the misdemeanor system has morphed into a way around that legal prohibition. By labeling the debt "criminal," the state has effectively made it possible to incarcerate people, not for their underlying crimes but for their poverty.

Stephen Papa, for example, was a homeless veteran of the Iraq War who lived in Grand Rapids, Michigan. One day he got drunk with friends, in what he sheepishly called "embarrassing behavior." He was convicted of destruction of property and resisting arrest. At his hearing, the judge imposed $2,600 in fines and court fees and asked Papa for an initial payment of $50. Papa, who was still homeless but on the verge of starting a new job, had only $25. Here is the conversation between him and the judge:

Papa: Your Honor, I tried really hard to get this job, and I'd really like to keep it. So I'm pretty much doing the best I can to take care of all the loose ends at once.

Judge: Mr. Papa, I want you to keep your job. The problem is, I have a certain kind of goal that I expect, and you were aware of it.

Papa: Roger that, sir. My finances are like absolutely zero.

Judge: [unintelligible] Cut grass. You know, make it work. How old are you.

Papa: I'll be twenty-seven, sir.

Judge: You didn't get to be twenty-seven and not having any initiative did you?

Papa: No, Your Honor.

Judge: You know how to hustle, legally, and earn some money. Make it work.

Papa: Roger that.

Judge: That's reality.

Papa was sentenced to twenty-two days in jail for failure to pay.[34]

As with so much of the petty-offense process, much of this incarceration for failure to pay occurs without defense counsel. While courts are not permitted to sentence people to jail in criminal cases without giving them a lawyer, we have seen that low-level courts routinely do so anyway. Holding people in civil contempt for failure to pay criminal fines—a proceeding that does not necessarily trigger the right to counsel—has become another common workaround.[35]

Debtors' prison practices vary from jurisdiction to jurisdiction. In some places, going to jail worsens defendants' debt: they are charged daily jail fees, meal fees, booking fees, and medical fees if they require health care during their incarceration. In other words, they must "pay to stay." Pete lives in Washington and describes the cycle: "And so I go back to jail, and by the time I left I owed $261 to the jail. OK? Do you know when I went in I owed $11. I stayed there one week, and by the time I checked out I owed $261, and I didn't see the doctor; I didn't dare see the doctor even though I needed medication and I had withdrawals from being on lithium . . . because that would cost me another $10 for the doctor visit. And I still racked up $261."[36]

The jail in Elko County, Nevada, charges inmates $6 a day for food, $10 for each doctor's visit, and a $5 booking fee. Sheriff Jim Pitts explains, "We're not the Hilton." At least forty-three states authorize room and board jail fees, and at least thirty-five authorize fees for medical care. Ninety percent of jails charge inmates some form of fee.[37]

Other jurisdictions, by contrast, maintain "pay-or-stay" systems in which defendants can work off their debt by going to jail, either by statute or as part of a plea. In California, a day in jail is worth a minimum of $30 of debt relief; in Ohio it is worth $50; in Missouri a day is worth $10. In New Orleans, this goes by the name "fines or time." Defendants are offered a sentence of either $100 in fines or thirty days in jail. Judge Calvin Johnson, former chief judge of the New Orleans criminal district court, mused, "Thirty days or $100—that was something I heard every day. Now, how can you describe a system where the City pays $23 a day to the Sheriff to house someone in the jail for 30 days to collect $100 as anything other than crazy?" According to a lawsuit against the Montgomery city jail in Alabama, an inmate named Tito Williams was offered credit toward his jail sentence if he would clean blood and feces from the jail floor.[38]

Some "pay-or-stay" jurisdictions simultaneously charge defendants for their jail stay so that they accrue new debt even as they work old debt off. In Michigan, for example, Kawana Young was the single mother of two young boys. Because she failed to pay three traffic tickets, three warrants were issued for her arrest. Brought to court, she was told either to pay $300 or spend three days in jail. When she went to jail, she was charged daily jail fees and a booking fee. Some defendants in Michigan are charged a $12 administrative fee to get out of jail; if they don't pay it, they remain incarcerated. In Ohio, defendant debtors are entitled by statute to receive $50 a day in credit for their incarceration, but dozens of Ohio jails simultaneously charge an average of $35 in daily jail fees.[39]

Once in jail, many low-level offenders who cannot pay their fines languish in dirty and dangerous conditions that rival those held unconstitutional in the prison context.[40] For example, a civil rights lawsuit challenging debtors' prison practices in Jennings, Missouri, described the local jail as "grotesque":

> [People] are kept in overcrowded cells; they are denied tooth-brushes, toothpaste, and soap; they are subjected to the stench of excrement and refuse in their congested cells; they are surrounded by walls smeared with mucus, blood, and feces; they are kept in the same clothes for days and weeks without access to laundry or clean undergarments; they step on top of other inmates, whose bodies cover nearly the entire uncleaned cell floor, in order to access a single shared toilet that the City does not clean; they huddle in cold temperatures with a single thin blanket even as they beg guards for warm blankets; they develop untreated illnesses and infections in open wounds that spread to other inmates; they sleep next to a shower space overgrown with mold and slimy debris; they endure days and weeks without being allowed to use the shower; women are not given adequate hygiene products for menstruation, and the lack of trash removal has on occasion forced women to leave bloody napkins in full view on the cell floor where inmates sleep; they are routinely denied vital medical care and prescription medication, even when their families beg to be allowed to bring medication to the jail.[41]

The new debtors' prison has come under sustained scrutiny. Civil rights challenges have been filed in states including Alabama, Arkansas, Louisiana, Mississippi, Missouri, Ohio, and Tennessee. In 2015, the Obama White House convened a conference titled "A Cycle of Incarceration: Prison, Debt, and Bail Practices." This was where Qiana Williams shared her story. At that same conference, then–US attorney general Loretta Lynch noted the irony that "in a country where we have ruled that debtors' prisons are unconstitutional, too many of our citizens are simply in jail because they don't have the money to get out."[42] Because the petty-offense process relies on those fines and fees for its own financial survival, however, reducing them and the debtors' prison practices they have engendered is no small task.

FUNDING THE BEAST: INSTITUTIONAL TAXATION AND PRIVATE PROFIT

The fines-and-fees phenomenon reaches deep into the heart of the petty-offense process. It is fueled by the incentives of the numerous official institutions that run the misdemeanor system: courts, jails, police, probation offices, prosecutor and public defender offices, and municipal governments themselves. Because misdemeanor fines and fees finance an ever-growing proportion of the budgets for these institutions—funding everything from salaries to retirement benefits to courthouse fitness centers—each has the incentive to widen the misdemeanor net and rush defendants through so as to meet their own financial needs. In times of recession, state fiscal crisis, or national economic upheaval, those pressures to find local revenue sources intensify.[43] The more that jurisdictions rely on the petty-offense process for funding, the more regressive the petty-offense process becomes.

Like everything about the sprawling misdemeanor system, funding arrangements vary widely from place to place. Sometimes individual offices depend on specific fines. In New Orleans, one-third of the public defender budget comes from defendant fees, and nearly two-thirds of the court's general operating budget comes from LFOs. In Mississippi, prosecutors got salary raises that were paid for by increasing penalties for littering and speeding. One prosecutor's office in Florida charges misdemeanor defendants a $50 fee to plead guilty. Half of

Texas's probation agencies' budgets come from offender fees. In Louisiana, judges who don't collect enough, so-called poor courts, get less funding for their courtrooms.[44]

Sometimes entire states depend on the revenue. In Alabama, state courts collected over $25 million a year in misdemeanor LFOs, more than the state collected in felony fines. Texas collects 30 percent of all fines and fees from low-level offenses and traffic tickets, a cut that amounted to $236 million in 2015. Statewide revenue arrangements can, in turn, change the way that certain fees are collected. In Michigan, rural courts are more aggressive about collecting court costs and defender fees, which go directly into the local court budget, than they are about collecting criminal fines, which go into a general statewide fund. By contrast, some cities and states do not rely on court revenues nearly so heavily. In Phoenix, Arizona, fines account for less than 2 percent of the city's general fund; Arizona cities typically raise less than 5 percent of their revenue through their municipal courts.[45]

The conflict over judicial revenue collection brewed quietly for years. Legal challenges in a handful of states ended some particularly egregious collections practices. In 2012, the Conference of State Court Administrators issued a critical report titled *Courts Are Not Revenue Centers*. Concerned about judicial integrity, the report complained that the proliferation of fines and fees "has recast the role of the court as a collection agency for executive branch services." The report warned in particular that "in traffic infractions, whether characterized as criminal or civil, court leaders face the greatest challenge in ensuring that fines, fees, and surcharges are not simply an alternative form of taxation."[46]

But the issue exploded onto the national scene in 2015 when the US Department of Justice published its *Investigation of the Ferguson Police Department*. Triggered by the police killing of eighteen-year-old Michael Brown in Ferguson and the wave of protests that swept the country afterward, the DOJ report zeroed in on the ways that the city's municipal court and policing apparatus openly extracted millions of dollars from its low-income African American population. As the report put it, "Ferguson's law enforcement practices are shaped by the City's focus on revenue rather than by public safety needs. This emphasis on revenue has compromised the institutional character of Ferguson's police department, contributing to a pattern of unconstitutional policing, and has also shaped its municipal court, leading to procedures that raise due process concerns and inflict unnecessary harm on members of the Ferguson community."[47]

Around the country, similar arrangements started to come to light, more lawsuits were filed, and the media zeroed in. As a result, we now know far more about how the institutions of the misdemeanor system fund themselves than we did just a few years ago.

In Ferguson, for example, the Department of Justice concluded that approximately one-fifth of the city's annual budget, over $2 million, came from criminal fines and fees generated by the municipal court. "The City budgets for sizeable increases in municipal fines and fees each year, exhorts police and court staff to deliver those revenue increases, and closely monitors whether those increases are achieved. City officials routinely urge [Police] Chief [Thomas] Jackson to generate more revenue through enforcement. In March 2010, for instance, the City Finance Director wrote to Chief Jackson that 'unless ticket writing ramps up significantly before the end of the year, it will be hard to significantly raise collections next year.'"[48] These policies pressured Ferguson police to make arrests and issue citations in order to raise revenue. As a result, "many officers appear[ed] to see some residents, especially those who live[d] in Ferguson's predominantly African-American neighborhoods, less as constituents to be protected than as potential offenders and sources of revenue."

Ferguson was far from alone. Numerous other towns similarly maintain speed traps, hot check courts, and other high-volume petty-offense mechanisms in order to generate revenue. Presiding judge John Bull of the San Antonio Municipal Court decried the top-down pressure on Texas judges to collect "the largest amount of money in the shortest amount of time." "Courts are not a Pay-Day Loan Company," he declared. The New York Times labeled the practice "for-profit policing" and "cash-register justice" and recently scolded, "Most states have done little or nothing to reform justice systems that clearly violate the Constitution."[49]

The private sector also increasingly drives the commodification of the petty-offense process as various industries feed off the revenue streams generated by misdemeanor fines and fees. Perhaps the most dramatic is the sort of private user-funded probation on display in Rutherford County, Tennessee, where Cindy Rodriguez sank into further destitution under the extractive thumb of PCC. In that arrangement, Rutherford County got its criminal fines collected for free, while PCC took its supervision fees directly from probationers. According to a civil rights lawsuit, the contract granted PCC an exclusive monopoly over probation cases in the county and in turn "require[d] Rutherford County and its court to ensure the full and total collection of PCC, Inc.'s profits." Courthouse officials, including judges and clerks, deferred to PCC and deprived defendants of their rights to counsel and due process so that PCC—and by extension the county—could collect its money. The lawsuit settled in 2017, requiring PCC to pay out $14 million to compensate the people it supervised.[50]

The PCC–Rutherford County scheme was an egregious example, but it was not an isolated one. Two small Georgia towns, Bainbridge and Pelham, had similar arrangements with the private company Red Hills Community Probation. Misdemeanor defendants there were sentenced to fines by the court, after which Red Hills immediately charged them hundreds of dollars in additional fees, detained them at the courthouse, and threatened them with jail if they did not pay.[51]

Over 1,000 court systems in over thirteen states use private probation companies like PCC and Red Hills. Some companies are particularly aggressive about converting the justice process into a moneymaker. Sentinel Offender Services had a special $1,000 "March Madness" bonus for probation officers who exceeded their collection goals. When two newly elected Arkansas judges tried to eliminate private probation in their jurisdiction, the probation company sued, arguing that the judges were interfering with their contractual right to profit off the probationers in the county. Alabama judge Hub Harrington called the private misdemeanor probation arrangement in Harpersville a "judicially sanctioned extortion racket." Often the whole arrangement is informal and unregulated: numerous counties in Kentucky use private probation companies, but no one keeps track of which counties, how many defendants they monitor, or how much they charge.[52]

Probation companies are just one of a number of private entities that feed off the misdemeanor revenue stream. Many courts outsource collections to private firms, which are permitted to tack on large fees of their own. Collection firms in Florida can levy a surcharge of up to 40 percent of the original debt; Alabama and Illinois permit a 30 percent surcharge. Only Texas expressly forbids imposing a collection surcharge if the defendant is too poor to pay.[53]

Similarly, the commercial bail bonds industry profits from the low-level misdemeanor process and the standardized bail schedules on which many low-level courts rely. While felony bonds are more profitable due to their larger amounts, commercial bail bonds for misdemeanors are widely available, and the industry has rallied against the threat posed by civil rights litigation and legislative reform to end money bail for misdemeanors. In 2016, the Professional Bail Agents of the United States (PBUS) held a conference in Biloxi, Mississippi, which had recently been sued for its debtors' prison practices. Titled "Ground Zero," the conference starred "Dog the Bounty Hunter," the bail bondsman star of the reality television show of the same name, and was part of the organization's campaign against proposed federal legislation that would have banned money bail. PBUS president Beth Chapman called the bail-reform movement "a disaster."[54]

More private entities are moving into the misdemeanor market. Private prison companies are expanding into punishment services commonly associated with low-level offenses such as day-reporting facilities, electronic monitoring, and halfway houses. Some places have even privatized the prosecutorial function. The California cities of Indio and Coachella hired a private law firm to act as municipal prosecutor for building-code crimes like overgrown weeds or improper signage. After people pled guilty, the law firm billed them thousands of dollars in prosecution fees and threatened to take their homes if they didn't pay. A few large retailers have taken matters into their own hands. Walmart and Bloomingdales, among others, have hired a company to run their own private criminal systems for suspected shoplifters, levying large fines and fees in exchange for not calling the police.[55]

The world of misdemeanor revenue is large and complex, involving numerous players, institutions, and incentives. Some jurisdictions rely more heavily on fines and fees than others. But the problem boils down to this. The petty-offense process extracts hundreds of millions of dollars from its low-income subjects not only as punishment for petty crimes, municipal violations, and traffic offenses but through a vast array of fees and surcharges designed to fund various aspects of the criminal system itself. Numerous private enterprises profit as well. This wealth transfer has become one of the primary motivating factors driving the nature and quality of misdemeanor justice. It explains much of the size and speed of misdemeanor dockets. It explains why so many poor and working people end up in jail. Indeed, it may entirely explain a city's decision to open a municipal court in the first place. This taxation function is thus a defining characteristic of today's misdemeanor system.

CAN THEY DO THAT? LEGAL CONSTRAINTS

As evidenced by the flurry of lawsuits and settlements in the past few years, many of the local practices described above are unconstitutional. At the same time, many are currently well within the legal authority of law enforcement officials, municipalities, and legislatures. On a basic level, it is legal to impose fines and fees for misdemeanors and minor violations, even on people who cannot afford to pay them. It is legal to channel those revenues to courts, jails, and other criminal justice institutions. And while there are limits on the extent to which poor people can be incarcerated for failing to pay, those limits are far from absolute.

Fines are a clearly permissible, long-standing form of punishment. The Eighth Amendment states, "Excessive bail shall not be required, nor excessive fines imposed, nor cruel and unusual punishments inflicted." A fine is only constitutionally "excessive" if it is too heavy given the gravity of the crime, not if the defendant can't afford to pay it. In other words, courts can legally impose fines that defendants cannot realistically pay. And those fines can amount to hundreds or even thousands of dollars for minor conduct.[56]

Fees and costs are also well established and legal. Fees may be authorized by state statute, municipal ordinance, or court rule; many states delegate authority to police, jails, prosecutors' offices, and other criminal justice institutions to set and charge their own fees. Because certain types of fees interfere with poor defendants' access to court—for example, filing and appellate transcript fees—a few have been struck down as unconstitutional. But fees that merely impose additional costs on the defendant as a way of defraying the court's expenses are allowed. States can even charge defendants for using a public defender, even though by definition public defense is available only to those who can't afford a lawyer in the first place.[57]

To the extent that there are legal limits on fees, they relate largely to judicial conflicts of interest. Straight up pay-per-conviction commissions are forbidden: judges cannot be paid per conviction or per warrant. Conflicts can also arise where the judge has an interest in raising money for the city. In *Ward v. Monroeville*, in 1972, the Supreme Court invalidated an arrangement in which a town mayor who also acted as the municipal court judge assessed fines and fees that comprised a substantial portion of the town's budget, finding that the judge was too "partisan" to be fair. But conflict is a matter of degree, and other similar arrangements have been upheld. Such limits, moreover, only apply to judicial decision-makers: no such restrictions apply to police or court clerks who receive commissions or fees.[58]

Some judicial decisions require fees to be reasonably related to the costs of the case at hand, although fees are rarely struck down on this basis. Other courts do not require any connection between the purpose of the fee and the case. The Florida Supreme Court approved a flat $1 fee for all cases to go into the state's general revenue fund, holding that "it is not unreasonable that one who stands convicted of such an offense should be made to share in the improvement of the agencies that society has had to employ in defense against the very acts for which he has been convicted."[59]

The central constitutional constraint on the misdemeanor system's ability to generate revenue occurs not at the point of sentencing but at the point of enforcement. Under the Equal Protection Clause, the state cannot incarcerate people merely because they are too poor to pay. In the 1983 case of *Bearden v. Georgia*, the Supreme Court held that a judge could not automatically revoke an offender's probation because he failed to pay his fines. Rather, the court had to determine whether the defendant had been willful or had failed to make good faith efforts to pay. If not, if the defendant authentically lacked the ability to pay, the court had to consider alternatives to incarceration. The restriction is even stronger when the underlying offense does not authorize incarceration. A defendant convicted of a fine-only offense cannot be jailed in order to pay off that fine.[60]

This prohibition against incarcerating the poor is the driving force behind recent lawsuits challenging misdemeanor money bail, debtors' prison, pay-or-stay schemes, and private probation. The main thesis of these cases is that using incarceration in each of these ways to punish the failure to pay, or the threat of it to extract payment, violates the Equal Protection Clause if poverty is the only reason people cannot pay. Because this is precisely the case for so many people, litigation rooted in *Bearden*'s prohibition is a powerful salvo against a key dynamic of the petty-offense process.

These limitations, however, are far from absolute. The Court in *Bearden* reaffirmed the state's power to impose fines, observing that "a defendant's poverty in no way immunizes him from punishment." While Danny Bearden's probation could not automatically be revoked for failure to pay, he could still be jailed if his failure was willful, if he did not make good faith efforts to come up with the money, or if the court determined that there was no reasonable alternative to incarceration. The concept of "too poor to pay," moreover, turns out to be spacious and slippery. Indigency determinations are left to judges who vary wildly in their evaluations of what defendants can afford. Judges have been known to infer the ability to pay because defendants had cable television, smoked cigarettes, or came to court in new sneakers.[61] Indeed, one judge (who was eventually sanctioned for repeated instances of this type of behavior) scolded a defendant for his food budget and for supporting his girlfriend:

> *Defendant:* I'm spending over a hundred dollars' worth of food a week.
>
> *Judge:* Why so much?
>
> *Defendant:* Because I have a girlfriend that lives with me.
>
> *Judge:* Ah, so you're supporting somebody else, why didn't you get rid of that? Is she employed?
>
> *Defendant:* She's trying to find work.
>
> *Judge:* So you're supporting somebody.
>
> *Defendant:* Yes.
>
> *Judge:* I'd suggest you get rid of her. So you're just throwing away money there. Why is she not working?
>
> *Defendant:* I don't know, sir, I really don't.
>
> *Judge:* Then why are you allowing her to live with you and freeloading off of you?[62]

The poor can also face incarceration, *Bearden* notwithstanding, through the mechanism of civil contempt. Civil contempt is a tool through which courts enforce their own orders; it is not considered punishment for the underlying crime. When that court order happens to be an order to pay a fine, defendants can be locked up for contempt of that order until they pay. Many states use this mechanism to incarcerate misdemeanor debtors; the law is still developing as to whether criminal defendants have a right to counsel during these contempt hearings.[63]

The availability of civil contempt creates a special paradox in the misdemeanor world, where many crimes are fine only, meaning that the defendant cannot be incarcerated for the underlying offense. Traffic offenses—for example, Gail Atwater's seatbelt violation—often do not carry jail time. Decriminalized offenses like marijuana possession do not carry jail time by definition: decriminalization means that such offenses are punished by fine alone and incarceration is taken off the table. Theoretically, incarceration should stay off the table even if the defendant is too poor to pay the fine. But using their contempt powers, courts can and do incarcerate defendants who fail to pay their fines and fees regardless of whether the underlying statute authorizes incarceration. Technically speaking, defendants are not being incarcerated for their traffic or marijuana offenses; by law they cannot be. Instead, they are being incarcerated for violating the court order to pay the traffic or marijuana fine. The contempt power thus represents a significant loophole.[64] To put it another way, people who plead guilty to fine-only traffic infractions or decriminalized marijuana-possession charges might be forgiven for thinking that they will never face jail. If they don't pay their fines, they will be wrong.

Finally, although the state is restrained in its power to enforce fines through incarceration, it has many other enforcement mechanisms at its disposal including wage garnishment, extended supervision, community service, and other alternative sanctions. The very existence of the debt, moreover, is punitive in its own right. The respite offered by *Bearden* and the equal protection principle is therefore inherently limited.

Even more fundamentally, the reality is that much of the misdemeanor system does not "care" whether its conduct is constitutional or not. Sometimes judges do not know the law. In Texas, for example, many judges incorrectly maintained that they did not have to assess defendants' ability to pay before incarcerating them, although Texas law expressly states that they do. When journalists pointed out the legal provision to one such judge, he responded, "That's a good point. That's a good point. That's a very good point." In Ohio, the state constitution prohibits debtors' prison, and the Ohio Supreme Court has expressly outlawed incarcerating people for failure to pay criminal court costs. Nevertheless, lower courts routinely sentence indigent defendants to jail for failure to pay in violation of state law. In Clinch County, Georgia, the sheriff decided to charge room and board to jail inmates although he lacked statutory authority to do so. Many of the law enforcement and judicial practices described in this chapter were clearly illegal, but only the threat of a lawsuit brought them to a halt, a lax attitude characteristic of misdemeanor culture at the bottom of the pyramid.[65]

At the end of the day, the most powerful source of the state's expansive misdemeanor funding authority is the ability to make commonplace behavior into a crime in the first place. Municipalities, counties, and states each possess the overlapping and redundant authority to criminalize minor, commonplace conduct and impose fines and fees as punishment. As long as they can make it a crime to spit or to litter, legal officials can make people pay for spitting and littering. Since they can require people to pay for car registration and insurance, they can haul people into court, and sometimes to jail, for failing to pay those costs. The power to criminalize behavior in which millions of people inevitably engage lets the state use the criminal system for all sorts of objectives, including the all-important one of collecting money.

THE PURPOSES OF PUNISHMENT

The revenue objective calls into question the true purposes of the criminal misdemeanor apparatus. Ask any first-year law student what the purposes of punishment are, and they will recite a well-established mantra: "retribution, deterrence, rehabilitation, and incapacitation."[66] This formula captures an important truth about what the criminal system is supposed to be doing. Punishing people who deserve it (retribution). Stopping people from committing new crimes (deterrence). Giving convicted people new tools to lead law-abiding lives (rehabilitation). And when all else fails, keeping dangerous people off the streets (incapacitation).

To state the obvious, the purpose of punishing murder is not revenue. Neither in theory nor in practice. Murder cases may well generate jobs or revenue, but that is not *why* there are murder cases. We punish murder for reasons that are central to why we have a criminal system in the first place: because it is wrong, because of the harm it inflicts on victims, in order to deter others from committing the crime, to punish the individual wrongdoer, and to maintain the social consensus that human life is valuable and sacred.[67] Even if punishing a murderer happens to generate police investigation funds, prosecutor salaries, or prison budgets, we don't prosecute murder for the money.

Of course, money is not irrelevant to our murder case. Investigations are expensive. Indeed, sometimes we *fail* to prosecute murder because its victims are poor or lack political clout. Law enforcement has historically devalued black homicides, and the lack of money and resources in poor communities can mean that homicides are never solved. Serious crimes are not immune from wealth effects—sometimes it takes money and power to get the criminal system's attention. But the primary guiding, motivating purpose of prosecuting serious crimes is not to generate revenue.[68]

Misdemeanors are different. The petty-offense apparatus has quietly expanded the purposes of punishment to include bureaucratic self-preservation and profit. The actual reasons and motivations for arresting and convicting millions of individuals now include police promotion policies and quotas, public and private revenue demands, and bureaucratic expansion—keeping the courthouse doors open. That does not mean that every arrest is about hitting a monthly target or that every conviction is about paying the courthouse bills. Nor does it mean that arrested individuals are necessarily innocent. It means, rather, that the culture of the misdemeanor process is suffused with pressures—implicit as well as explicit—to arrest, cite, convict, jail, and extract payments from criminal defendants in ways that dilute the traditional, legitimate goals of assessing guilt, promoting public safety, and doing justice.

This is a contentious point—it matters a lot to a lot of people *why* law enforcement and public officials make the decisions they do. In a Kansas City study of traffic stops, researchers found that blacks and whites felt very differently about being pulled over because they experienced the police as having different reasons for stopping them. Procedural justice theories tell us that people might even care more about law enforcement reasons than they care about outcomes. But identifying those reasons can be complicated. For example, I once received an offended email from a retired Massachusetts police offi-cer who objected to my observation in an interview that police stop people for all sorts of reasons that have nothing to do with whether that individual is committing a crime. He called my comments "in-flammatory and counterproductive" and said that academics needed to better "familiarize themselves with the police function."[69]

I took his comment to mean that he thought I was generally im-pugning the police and the job of policing. I did not intend to—I was describing what I thought to be an empirical fact about modern pro-fessional misdemeanor policing. Indeed, the US Supreme Court has said much the same thing, acknowledging that "encounters are initi-ated by the police for a wide variety of purposes, some of which are wholly unrelated to a desire to prosecute for crime."[70] But I under-stood why he took offense because stops and arrests are not *supposed* to be about anything other than crime. It was as if I had said that doctors perform operations for reasons unrelated to whether patients need surgery.

Because the misdemeanor world is enormous and diverse, no single description can capture all of its motivations, and jurisdictions grapple with financial questions very differently. In that retired officer's home state of Massachusetts, for example, the legislature faced a proposal to raise inmate fees. Instead of raising them, the state commissioned a comprehensive study, which concluded that imposing additional fees on a largely indigent population would be both ineffective and counterproductive. In Washington, DC, the city council slashed the fine for decriminalized marijuana possession from $100 to $25 on the theory that for much the District's low-income population, $100 was too punitive a burden.[71] Many public officials support decriminalization—imposing fines rather than incarceration—not for pecuniary reasons but because they consider fines fairer than jail for low-level offenses. In each of these examples, official actors are grappling with a wide array of legitimate policy goals while seeking to avoid further criminalizing poverty.

Even the decision to increase fines and fees is not always entirely about making money. Legislatures and courts often decide to impose financial burdens as part of defendants' punishment. The idea that criminals should be held responsible, pay their own way, and contribute to the system that adjudicates their cases has wide support. As the Oklahoma Supreme Court put it when it upheld fees assessed against drunk drivers, "We perceive no good reason why the legislature may not also require drunken drivers to share in the cost of maintaining agencies that society has had to create to make its highways safe from the risks those drivers impose upon the innocent, and to attempt to rehabilitate and treat those drivers."[72] While as a practical matter such justifications support increased revenue, they are also rooted in classic criminal justice concerns such as the desire to hold the guilty accountable or to send collective messages about right and wrong. Such arguments for increasing fines and fees should not be dismissed, as economists might say, as simple rent seeking. By contrast, in extreme jurisdictions like Rutherford County, Tennessee, it looks very much like the misdemeanor process has been co-opted into a tax system for both public and private gain and the patients, to mix metaphors, do not need surgery at all.

Private probation has come under increased fire because, like private prisons, it openly injects the profit motive into the criminal process in ways that incentivize criminalization, and it delegates the state's authority to punish—that quintessentially public function—to private actors. But privatization concerns do not fully capture the problem.

Even where all the players are government employees, pecuniary incentives do not disappear. Instead, they morph into other forms. Police are professionally evaluated and rewarded for arrests, prosecutors for convictions, clerks' offices for collections. Much of the modern misdemeanor commitment to productivity and taxation can be chalked up to this sort of institutional self-preservation. Bureaucracies naturally develop self-perpetuating practices that can stray far from their founding principles and mandates, and misdemeanor institutions are no different.[73] Cash-strapped courts and municipalities are tapping into a ready source of income over which they have near complete authority—a politically vulnerable population to which no one pays much attention. These tempting circumstances invite bureaucratic expansion, even where no individual official harbors any particular animus or exploitative tendency.

Monetary sanctions are not unique to misdemeanors, and misdemeanors are not the only crimes that criminalize poverty. Hefty fines and fees, often in the many of thousands of dollars, are imposed on felony defendants in ways that increase their poverty and impede their reentry into civic life. For many low-income felons, like many misdemeanor defendants, criminal debt is a lifelong punishment: they will never be able to pay it off. But philosophically the phenomenon is not quite the same. The primary punishment in most felony cases is incarceration; the average felony sentence in the United States is around four years. In such cases, prison does the bulk of the moral and instrumental work of punishment. It is therefore prison and all its harms that must be morally justified, that must constitute an adequate state response to those crimes, and that must bear the brunt of public criticism. To be sure, monetary sanctions sit on top of those sentences, complementing their effects. But burdensome as they are, fines and fees are adjuncts to the uniquely destructive experience of long-term incarceration.[74]

In misdemeanors, by contrast, the fine is often the primary punishment, and sometimes the only formal one. Monetary sanctions are commonly imposed instead of incarceration or probation, or may be the main reason that supervision is imposed at all. They are in no sense collateral. And the practice is indeed punishment in the fullest sense, with stigmatic and harmful effects involving personal suffering, civic exclusions, and often jail. Fines thus carry a lion's share of the moral weight of misdemeanor criminal punishment. When they are unfair or dysfunctional, it undermines the morality and legitimacy of the entire misdemeanor apparatus. Whether by design or by accident, the monetary sanction now sits at the heart of the work that the petty-offense process does, shaping its implications for our democracy as a whole.

It is now commonplace to point out that the United States incarcerates more people than any other country as a way of lamenting the generally punitive character of American society. The idea rests on the notion, to slightly misquote Dostoyevsky, that the degree of civilization in a society can be judged by how it punishes crime.[75] The fact that the misdemeanor system uses money in ways that punish, exacerbate, and tax poverty is also a defining characteristic of American "civilization." Although they have not received their fair share of attention, misdemeanor fines and fees determine the quality of American justice just as profoundly as mass incarceration or the war on drugs. Imagine what we would think about another country that rounded up its poorest citizens and prosecuted them in order to extract payment. To the extent that our misdemeanor system is motivated by money rather than the traditional purposes of punishment, it corrodes the character not only of that system but of our entire criminal justice apparatus.

RACE

THE MISDEMEANOR SYSTEM IS ONE OF THE GREAT THREATS to American racial equality. Arrest by arrest and case by case, it weaves an enormous net that sweeps millions of African Americans and other people of color into the criminal process. Based on common, often completely harmless conduct, the petty-offense machinery disproportionately marks people of color as criminals. It burdens them with arrests, fines, incarceration, and other punishments, making them poorer and more economically vulnerable. And it perpetuates old stereotypes that have historically undermined the social standing of African Americans and other racial minority groups by painting them with the brush of criminality. While mass incarceration is now widely recognized as one of the driving forces behind this country's racial inequities, the racialization of crime begins much earlier in the criminal process with low-level arrests and in misdemeanor courts, long before anyone goes to prison.[1]

The story of race and crime in this country is inextricably entwined with African American history and the black experience. It is also the racial group dynamic about which the system collects the most information, and this chapter spends the most time on it. But our criminal system also treats other racial and ethnic groups in disparate and harsh ways. Native American men are incarcerated at four times the rate of whites; they are killed by police at almost the same high rate as African Americans. Hispanics are more likely to be sent to prison than whites. In many cities, Latino drivers are racially profiled and stopped more often than white drivers. Arab and Muslim Americans are singled out in airports and at borders. Such phenomena have made the US criminal system internationally infamous. In 2014, the United Nations Committee on the Elimination of Racial Discrimination expressed its continuing concern with "the overrepresentation of racial and ethnic minorities in the [US] criminal justice system" and the fact "that members of racial and ethnic minorities, particularly African Americans, continue to be disproportionately arrested, incarcerated and subjected to harsher sentences."[2]

The human toll of these practices and histories is profound. The ubiquitous threat of being pulled over or stopped by police is a frightening and corrosive fact of life for many African Americans. The knowledge that a speeding ticket could lead to the deportation of a parent or child is a chilling reality for many Latino families, so much so that some people avoid driving to work or to school. For young people of color from Baltimore to Chicago to Seattle, a single encounter with police can mark them with a criminal record for life, threatening their educations and future livelihoods. And the fear that a child might be the next Tamir Rice—the twelve-year-old boy killed by Cleveland police while he played in the park with a toy gun—haunts parents of black children and casts a pall over the entire universe of police-community relations.

This chapter is devoted to race even though race does not operate independently or in a vacuum. As we have seen, the misdemeanor process tracks many different fault lines of social disadvantage. It traps hundreds of thousands of low-income and working-class whites who can't afford bail, fines, or fees. It targets homeless people of all races and ethnicities, the young, the addicted, and the unemployed. In effect, the misdemeanor process is the state-run machinery through which we begin to treat people as criminals, often without much evidence, based on their race, poverty, and other kinds of social vulnerability. Through it, we officially link race, class, and crime, infusing the experience of being poor with the threat of being criminalized and infusing the experiences of being black and Latino with distinctive fears and disadvantages. Throughout it all, race remains special, a uniquely influential and stratifying force without which the full implications of the misdemeanor machinery, and in turn the entire American criminal system, cannot be fully understood.

RACIAL DISPARITY

The racial disproportion in the misdemeanor process begins with low-level policing. Tyriel Simms, for example, lives in Baltimore. He is African American. He is tired of being arrested. "I have an extensive arrest history, but I do not have an extensive conviction rate," he explains to an interviewer. "That's normal for living in Baltimore City. It's normal to be arrested for something that you didn't do, to be looked at as a problem. It's normal to be in the wrong place at the wrong time, which is everywhere. And it's normal for guys to accept convictions for things that they didn't do."[3]

National arrest rates, generally high, are higher for minorities. By age twenty-three, 38 percent of white men, 44 percent of Latino men, and 50 percent of African American men can expect to be arrested at least once. Every year, police stop 12 percent of all drivers but 24 percent of minority drivers.[4]

In 2015, the US Department of Justice's investigation into the Ferguson Police Department revealed both openly racist official practices as well as the structural tendencies of that police department to focus on the black community. In a city where African Americans comprise 67 percent of the population, over 90 percent of arrests and citations were of black people. African Americans were also twice as likely as white drivers to be searched by police during vehicle stops, even though they were found in possession of contraband less often than white drivers.[5]

In Baltimore, where Simms lives, order-maintenance offenses like trespassing, disorderly conduct, and resisting arrest are heavily enforced against African Americans: between 80 and 90 percent of order-maintenance charges are brought against black defendants, although African Americans make up only 63 percent of Baltimore's population. Indeed, the assumption that trespassing is a black crime is so deeply ingrained in the Baltimore Police Department that it is written into the form that officers use when they make a trespassing arrest. The form contains blank spaces for the arrestee's name and the address of the arrest, but there are no spaces for race or gender. Instead, the form has already been filled in to read "BLACK MALE."[6]

Other places police in similar ways. African Americans comprise nearly 40 percent of the Durham, North Carolina, population but over 80 percent of resisting-arrest cases. In Nebraska, African Americans make up only 5 percent of the population but nearly 20 percent of all misdemeanor cases. Latinos make up 30 percent of the population in San Jose, California, but 70 percent of arrests for disturbing the peace, 57 percent of arrests for resisting, and 57 percent of arrests for public intoxication. In East Haven, Connecticut, a US Department of Justice investigation found pervasive discrimination against the Latino population, including racial profiling, intrusive traffic stops, and heavy-handed enforcement of minor offenses. Latino motorists throughout Oregon are twice as likely as white motorists to be charged with misdemeanors such as driving without a license, driving with a broken tail light, or making an improper lane change.[7]

Sometimes disparities occur in the policing of particular crimes. In Texas, misdemeanor shoplifting can be charged either as simple theft or as the more serious crime of "organized retail theft." Women of color are twice as likely as white women to be arrested and charged with the more serious version even when they have committed exactly the same offense. The disparities are even stronger when the arrests take place in wealthier neighborhoods.[8]

Jaywalking is a common culprit. In Urbana, Illinois, from 2007 to 2011, 91 percent of people ticketed for jaywalking were black, although only 16 percent of residents are. In Jacksonville, Florida, 55 percent of all pedestrian tickets are issued to African Americans, almost all of them in the city's poorest neighborhoods. Jacksonville is 29 percent black. The Department of Justice concluded that the Ferguson Police Department "appears to bring certain offenses almost exclusively against African Americans. For example, from 2011 to 2013, African Americans accounted for 95% of Manner of Walking in Roadway charges, and 94% of all Failure to Comply charges."[9]

Marijuana enforcement is also heavily skewed. Blacks and whites use marijuana just as often, but national black arrest rates for possession are four times higher than white arrest rates. In Iowa, Minnesota, and Illinois, African Americans are almost eight times more likely than whites to be arrested. In Van Zandt County, Texas, approximately fifty miles from Dallas, black people are *thirty-four times* more likely to be arrested for marijuana possession than white people.[10]

Even where marijuana possession has been decriminalized, disparities can persist or even, ironically, increase. After Illinois laws gave police discretion over whether to make arrests or issue citations for marijuana possession, arrest rates went down in white neighborhoods but actually went up in black neighborhoods. North Carolina similarly gives police a choice over whether to arrest or cite. Between 2014 and 2016, Charlotte police arrested African Americans for marijuana possession nearly three times as often as they did whites, 28 percent of the time compared to 10 percent.[11]

Although the FBI collects limited data on misdemeanor arrests, they show that key low-level offenses are overenforced nationally against African Americans, who make up approximately 12 percent

TABLE 6.1. FBI NATIONAL MISDEMEANOR ARREST DATA BY RACE AND ETHNICITY, 2015

	TOTAL	PERCENTAGE WHITE	PERCENTAGE BLACK OR AFRICAN AMERICAN	PERCENTAGE HISPANIC OR LATINO
US population	321,418,821	73.0	12.6	17.6
Total arrests counted	8,248,709	69.7	26.6	18.4
Arrests by misdemeanor				
Curfew and loitering	33,700	52.8	44.7	20.5
Disorderly conduct	295,835	64.0	31.0	12.6
DUI	825,218	82.6	13.2	22.7
Drug abuse	1,136,950	70.7	27.0	20.3
Drunkenness	313,390	76.4	14.3	22.7
Gambling	3,597	36.0	56.4	20.4
Suspicion	1,085	44.1	27.4*	5.7
Vagrancy	19,268	68.8	26.7	15.1
Vandalism	146,090	69.5	27.2	17.9

*In 2015, the black suspicion arrest percentage was uncharacteristically low, while suspicion arrests of American Indian and Alaska Natives (AIAN) leapt to an uncharacteristically high 27 percent. In contrast, for the previous decade AIAN suspicion arrests hovered around 1 percent, while African American suspicion arrests ranged between 35 and 55 percent of the total. See, for example, "Arrests by Race and Ethnicity—Table 43A," FBI Uniform Crime Reporting, 2014, https://ucr.fbi.gov/crime-in-the-u.s/2014/crime-in-the-u.s.-2014/tables/table-43 [https://perma.cc/TBX9-QZMX].

Sources: "Arrests by Race and Ethnicity—Table 43A," FBI Uniform Crime Reporting, 2015, https://ucr.fbi.gov/crime-in-the-u.s/2015/crime-in-the-u.s.-2015/tables/table-43 [https://perma.cc/86H7-7GLC]; "Annual Estimates of the Resident Population by Sex, Age, Race, and Hispanic Origin for the United States and States: 2015," US Census Bureau, 2015, https://factfinder.census.gov/faces/tableservices/jsf/pages/productview.xhtml?pid=ACS_16_1YR_B02001&prodType=table. Both total arrests and racial disparities in arrests have gone down over the past few years. "Arrests by Race and Ethnicity—Table 43A," FBI Uniform Crime Reporting, 2012, https://ucr.fbi.gov/crime-in-the-u.s/2012/crime-in-the-u.s.-2012/tables/43tabledatadecoverviewpdf [https://perma.cc/W5BF-JL4T].

of the US population but are typically arrested at double that rate, sometimes more.

Look carefully at gambling, vagrancy, and suspicion. There aren't many of these arrests, but they are revealing because the offenses are barely crimes. Gambling is a paradigmatically victimless offense. Vagrancy laws have been unconstitutional since 1972. Suspicion is not a crime at all.[12] None of these offenses constitute dangerous or blame-worthy conduct; the categories of vagrancy and suspicion are relics of a bygone constitutional era. All of them are enforced more often against African Americans.

High black arrest rates are an old and contentious story. Some interpret them as a form of racial discrimination; others interpret them to mean that African Americans commit more crimes. It can be a kind of chicken-and-egg problem because it is hard to establish underlying offense rates separate and apart from how often police make arrests. Do blacks and whites loiter at the same rates? How would we ever know, apart from looking at how often they get arrested?

Sometimes, however, we have more information. For certain violent felonies—murder and robbery in particular—surveys of victims indicate that higher black arrest rates do indeed reflect higher offense rates. For other crimes—most glaringly marijuana use—research shows that blacks and whites commit the underlying offense just as often, which means that high black arrest rates reflect skewed enforcement decisions. Studies of disorderly conduct, resisting arrest, and other "contempt-of-cop" offenses likewise conclude that the overenforcement of such offenses against black people is driven not by higher offending but by police discretion. This skew in misdemeanor arrests is not new—since the 1920s, scholars have pointed out that police overenforce minor offenses against black people and in black neighborhoods, resulting in artificially high arrest rates.[13] Misdemeanor arrest rates thus appear to be particularly attenuated from underlying offense rates and thus especially susceptible to racial distortion.

Put differently, order-maintenance arrests don't tell us much about group conduct, but they tell us a lot about police practices. In Baltimore, between 2010 and 2015, police arrested 657 people for "gaming" or "playing cards." Only five of those people were white.[14] That statistic obviously does not reveal how often white Baltimoreans gamble. Instead, such arrest rates provide information about the policing tools themselves, how those kinds of misdemeanors are deployed, and where they are used. When they are racially skewed, it indicates that enforcement biases, not crime, are driving the numbers.

Such enforcement disparities have become increasingly visible. In 2014, for example, a grand jury declined to indict the New York police officers who choked Eric Garner to death. In response, Twitter's highest-trending topic was the #CrimingWhileWhite feed. As a way of protesting racial disparities, white people confessed to minor crimes that police let them get away with. Reviewing the confessions, CNN concluded, "If you're white, you may be able to shoplift, drive drunk, even shove a police officer—and not suffer the same consequences a black person might." In 2018, two African American men were arrested in a Philadelphia Starbucks for "trespassing" because one of them asked to use the restroom without having placed an order, something that white people do all the time. The incident was captured on video; the public outcry caused Starbucks to shut down its operations for a day to conduct antibias training for its employees.[15]

Policing initiates the misdemeanor process, disproportionately filling the pipeline with people of color. This alone would generate more black and Latino convictions even if the rest of the process were entirely evenhanded. But it isn't. It is harder to find data on the racial dynamics of decision-making by prosecutors, defense attorneys, and judges, but there is evidence that disparities persist throughout. A study of Dane County, Wisconsin, showed that prosecutors charge African Americans more harshly than whites for the same low-level crimes. Whites charged with misdemeanors are 45 percent more likely than blacks to receive reduced charges or to have their cases dismissed entirely. The more minor the crime, the greater the racial disparity in prosecutorial decision-making. In Charlotte, North Carolina, prosecutors declined drug charges against whites more often than against blacks and *never* declined drug cases brought against African American women. New York prosecutors offer more lenient deals to whites than to blacks in marijuana cases.[16]

Defense attorneys are supposed to protect their clients against racial bias and governmental overreach, but even they may contribute to the problem. Scholars argue that overworked public defenders in high-pressure situations may represent their African American clients less aggressively due to unconscious racial bias. Everyone has implicit biases, and they can distort how public defenders evaluate the evidence and the strength of a case, their client's credibility, or the fairness of the punishment. And while there is not much research on misdemeanor judging—most attention is lavished on the stark racial disparities at the felony level—bias can affect those judges too. Ferguson municipal court judges were more likely to issue arrest warrants for and less likely to dismiss cases against African Americans. In Nebraska, Native American and Latino misdemeanor defendants were not only charged more often but also punished more heavily.[17]

The misdemeanor pipeline is built out of millions of decisions by police, prosecutors, defense attorneys, and judges. These decisions are typically highly discretionary; officials have a lot of room to make them as they see fit. At each stage, too many of those decisions tend to tilt against people of color. Not always, and not by everybody, but enough to distort the process as a whole. Because the misdemeanor process is so large, these judgments collectively shape the character of the vast majority of US criminal cases and convictions. Their cumulative effects account for much of the systemic racial skew that shapes the entire American criminal process.[18]

THE INEFFECTUAL CONSTITUTIONAL LAW OF RACE

Existing law on race and racial discrimination has been generally ineffectual in curbing the racial disproportion of the criminal system. On the one hand, the Supreme Court has reaffirmed the basic principle that race discrimination is wrong: "Discrimination on the basis of race, odious in all aspects, is especially pernicious in the administration of justice," the Court wrote in 2017.[19] But in practice, racial disparities are constitutionally tolerated in a wide variety of contexts. Indeed, in an earlier and still influential opinion, the Court called such disparities "inevitable": "There is, of course, some risk of racial prejudice influencing a jury's decision in a criminal case. There are similar risks that other kinds of prejudice will influence other criminal trials. The question is at what point that risk becomes constitutionally unacceptable. . . . Apparent disparities in sentencing are an inevitable part of our criminal justice system."[20]

There are two main provisions of the Constitution that might protect against racial disparities and discrimination in the criminal process. They have both turned out to be lame ducks. The Fourth Amendment governs the power of the police to stop and arrest people, but the Court has decided that it is not violated by race discrimination at all, even when that discrimination is outright and intentional. For example, police officers stopped Michael Whren and James Brown, young African American drivers in Washington, DC, for idling too long at a stop sign. The officers didn't care about the stop sign—that was a pretext. Rather, they had a hunch that young black men in that neighborhood might be drug dealers. In 1996, in *Whren v. United States*, the Supreme Court decided that pretextual stops are permissible as long as police have probable cause for *any* offense, no matter how minor. In this case the long idling was a civil traffic violation, so the officers could lawfully stop the car.[21] Since misdemeanor and traffic codes are so broad, there is almost always probable cause for some violation. Because of the *Whren* decision, officers have wide latitude to arrest people based on racial stereotypes, profiling, or even intentional racial hostility without violating the Fourth Amendment.

The other main constitutional provision that governs race is the Equal Protection Clause of the Fourteenth Amendment. That provision clearly prohibits race discrimination by any government actor, including criminal justice officials, but it only covers intentional or purposeful discrimination. Defendants must show that a police officer, prosecutor, or judge intentionally treated them differently based on race. The law makes such intentions difficult to prove. In Los Angeles in 1991, for example, every single federal crack cocaine defendant who came through the public defender office that year was black. This was due to prosecutorial decisions: prosecutors could choose whether to send crack cases to federal court, where penalties were higher, or whether to let defendants stay in state court where penalties were lower. The defendants sought records from the prosecutors regarding their intentions behind those racially skewed selection decisions, but the Supreme Court concluded that the all-black defendant pool was not enough evidence of discrimination to permit the defendants to get that additional information. As a result, such "selective prosecution" claims remain almost impossible to prove.[22]

Even racial disparities in the imposition of the most serious punishment of all, the death penalty, do not violate the Constitution. A 1987 study in Georgia showed that black defendants were more likely to get the death penalty, especially if the victims were white. But the Supreme Court decided that such racial disparities were constitutionally acceptable. Through decisions like these, the Court has curtailed constitutional litigation as a vehicle for challenging or reforming the criminal system's pervasive racial skew. It need not be this way. In other arenas such as voting, education, and affirmative action, the Court has been highly suspicious of race-based decision-making.[23] In the criminal context, however, the Equal Protection Clause mostly lacks bite.

The absence of constitutional remedies is particularly frustrating because improved data collection and behavioral science are providing new insights into how thoroughly racial decision-making affects the criminal process. For example, we now know much more about the powerful implicit racial biases that shape people's perceptions. As mentioned above, these unconscious associations, stereotypes, and assumptions can distort criminal justice decision-making in influential ways. Legal scholar L. Song Richardson explains that for police, "implicit stereotypes can cause an officer who harbors no conscious racial animosity . . . to unintentionally treat individuals differently based solely upon their physical appearance. As a result of implicit biases, an officer might evaluate behaviors engaged in by individuals who appear black as suspicious even as identical behavior by those who appear white would go unnoticed." Judges, prosecutors, and defense attorneys all harbor these same implicit biases that can tilt their decisions.[24]

Likewise, organizations and bureaucracies have their own internal demands and limitations that can exacerbate racial disparities, even if no person in the institution intends that result. Police are often under pressure to make large numbers of arrests, which turn out to be easier to make in low-income communities that lack strong social and economic organizations, which in turn are home to many people of color. Prosecutorial charging habits can have cumulative effects on minority groups. Judges making bail decisions typically have access to scant information about defendants, relying heavily on prior criminal records, income, and residence, all of which correlate with race.[25] Racial disparities are the product of all these forces, although they may not reflect the conscious intentions of any individual actor. As a result, a great deal of racially skewed decision-making is neither acknowledged by, nor amenable to challenge under, current constitutional law.

We are left then with a growing divide between cherished legal principles and the complex reality of racial inequality in the misdemeanor system. On the one hand, principles of equal protection and fair punishment demand that no one be criminalized or punished because of their race, gender, ethnicity, or religion. This is a precious commitment of constitutional democracy—you should be punished only for what you do, not for who you are or the group to which you belong. But because constitutional remedies are so constrained, these principles too often lack traction in the real-world operations of misdemeanor institutions.

THE HUMAN TOLL

The racial inequalities of the American criminal system take an enormous toll on individuals and their families, instilling a wide array of fears and insecurities. Nowhere is this fear more prominently displayed than in "The Talk," where parents explain to their black children that they need to protect themselves against potential violence during police encounters. Here is an excerpt from one of these painful rites of passage:

The reason we have to have this talk is because you are a black child in America. . . . I need you to always be prepared and always be on your guard and it takes away from you being a little kid, I know, but I'm trying to protect you right now.

If you are approached by police, just stay calm, don't fight back, don't give any rebuttals—you have to understand, if you want to stay alive, you have to do what they say. Because it could be the difference between me seeing you again and not seeing you again.

Sad to say sometimes that may not even work, I'm just going to be honest, it may not work at all. I know it's tough. And I know it sounds really scary. But it's not your fault.

Always stand with your head up and your shoulders back and be proud. We'll get through this and don't you ever ever blame yourself for what others do.[26]

The petty-offense process has long been a key ingredient in the criminalization of the black experience. African Americans learn from a young age that they may be singled out based on their race and that the misdemeanor enforcement apparatus not only has extensive power over their physical safety but can influence many aspects of their future. Law professor David Troutt describes how his own early encounters with law enforcement were setups for "a lifetime of suspicion, which, in the extreme, would be made easier by a rapidly growing record of minor arrests." Arrests are risky and frightening—police have the power to seize, search, handcuff, book, and jail a person. As "The Talk" warns, during an arrest police can even maim or kill. But arrests also informally determine a lot of other things, including the arrestee's future ability to get a job, a loan, or an apartment.[27] With an arrest, police can mark people in ways that society will never forget. In this manner, the misdemeanor process confers relatively unfettered authority on police to formally transform black men into petty criminals based on minor, often harmless conduct, and sometimes even when they are doing nothing at all.

It is hard to overstate how destructive this dynamic is or how early in life it kicks in. In a survey of 367 fifth graders in San Diego, children who identified as nonwhite scored police as less likeable, trustworthy, and fair than their white counterparts. Students from poorer schools also gave police lower marks.[28] High school students in Chicago say that police encounters are dehumanizing.

> *Christopher:* "It made me feel small. . . . I'm almost a man, but [being stopped] made me feel like less than a man. . . . It just makes you feel down, like you ain't nobody."
> *Jamari:* "They make you feel less of a person."
> *Ericka:* "You can't do what regular people do."[29]

Sociologist Victor Rios spent three years studying the experiences of black and Latino teenage boys in Oakland, California, some of whom received dozens of citations for "loitering, disturbing the peace, drinking in public, not wearing a properly fitted bicycle helmet, and violating curfew. . . . Minor citations for 'little shit' played a crucial role in pipelining many of the young men in this study deeper into the criminal justice system." Rios wrote, "The boys in this study felt outcast, shamed, and unaccepted, sometimes leading them to a sense of hopelessness."[30]

Adults voice fear and anger about being targeted based on their race. In the book *Pulled Over: How Police Stops Define Race and Citizenship*, African American residents of Kansas City describe their resentment of traffic stops and their knowledge that their race plays a role. "I felt violated," says Joe, who was pulled over even though he wasn't speeding. Deana was stopped twice within five minutes by two different officers who wanted to know where she was going. "I was pretty upset," she recalls. "And you know I was scared." The book's authors write, "Police stops convey powerful messages about citizenship and equality. Across millions of stops, these experiences are translated into common stories about who is an equal member of a rule-governed society and who is subjected to arbitrary surveillance and inquiry."[31]

Dr. Tiffany Chioma Anaebere is an emergency medical physician in Oakland and a graduate of Duke Medical School. In 2016, she recalled her own experience.

> I was stopped by a police officer a few weeks ago while driving in Chicago and the interaction was very pleasant. I was in a fancy dress driving back from a wedding. He was a white male cop who stopped me because I forgot to turn on the headlights to my rental car. What I can tell you is that before he came up to me, I was shaking. I was scared that this could be that cop, the one interaction that could change everything. There's a fear that if you aren't perfectly polite, if you move too quickly, if your cell phone is mistaken as a weapon, something could go horribly wrong.[32]

Today's public conversations about criminal reform increasingly include these kinds of stories and the recognition that misdemeanor and traffic enforcement are central to the racial contours of American criminal justice. Campaign Zero, a Black Lives Matter advocacy organization, argues that minor offenses like spitting and jaywalking should be eliminated altogether on the grounds that "[these] activities do not threaten public safety and are often used to police black bodies." When Cornell William Brooks was president of the National Association for the Advancement of Colored People, he zeroed in on the disproportion between the nature of misdemeanor conduct and the law enforcement response: "We have a number of incidents where we have young people who are at worst suspected of underwhelming, minor offenses who meet an overwhelming, major—sometimes lethal—use of force that leads to tragedy."[33]

The impact of misdemeanor enforcement spills out of the criminal system into the larger social milieu, with a variety of personal implications. As we have seen, one of the most common is that a misdemeanor record—of arrest as well as conviction—makes it harder to get a job. This is especially true for African Americans, who already face employment barriers due to racist stereotypes about criminality. In one well-known experiment, black and white college student "testers" with identical résumés and qualifications were sent out to see how employers responded to their job applications. The only difference between the testers was their race and whether they had a criminal record. The results were dramatic. Having a record made it more difficult for all testers, black and white, to get jobs. But the effect was stronger for the black testers. For white testers, having a record doubled the chance that they would not get the job, while for African American testers it tripled, as if the stigma took more strongly. Overall, the black men *without* criminal records had a harder time getting jobs than the white men *with* criminal records.[34] As the study's author put it, "Despite the fact that the white applicant revealed evidence of a felony drug conviction, and despite the fact that he reported having recently returned from a year and half in prison, employers seemed to view this applicant as no more risky than a young black man with no history of criminal involvement. . . . [B]eing black in America today is just about the same as having a felony conviction in terms of one's chances of finding a job."[35]

These dynamics are not just a distortion of the employment market, they are a devastating lesson in personal possibilities. As another researcher put it, "It was clear that to [Cameron], like many others with whom we spoke, his criminal record was a binding roadblock to a good and decent life—being able to support a family, having access to a green card, and being able to move freely without being 'watched.'" Ronnie is a young black woman in Virginia: "Getting a job is, oh God, getting a job is awful. When they ask you that one question—have you ever been convicted—some of them have gotten to the point where it's a misdemeanor. And they want you to pretty much give them a brief summary of what the charge was and what happened and the resolution. And if it had nothing to do with you working in a pie shop, you [still] can't work there."[36] People have a keen awareness that even a minor offense can stop them from getting a job, that they are permanently disabled in the employment arena, and that civil society will never really forgive their mistakes.

Being treated unequally based on race is a notoriously corrosive psychological experience. As the Supreme Court mused in the landmark desegregation case *Brown v. Board of Education*, to treat children differently "solely because of their race generates a feeling of inferiority as to their status in the community that may affect their hearts and minds in a way unlikely ever to be undone." One has to wonder whether those teenagers in Oakland and Chicago will ever feel equal in the eyes of the law. Adults from Kansas City to Baltimore disclose that being treated unequally in ways that threaten their safety and economic future, or those of their families and friends, makes them feel reduced and alienated. Fear, anger, shame, distrust, or even despair—these are all potential costs of the inequalities of the misdemeanor process.[37] While they do not show up in spreadsheets, courthouse budgets, or jailhouse population counts, they are nevertheless deeply expensive for each individual person and for our civic society as a whole.

THE DEMOCRATIC COST

The collective effect of these racial disparities and burdens is to make it harder for people of color to stand on equal political footing. When the misdemeanor system treats blacks more harshly than whites, it creates group-wide burdens and disadvantages. That same system also frequently deprives communities of color of the full benefits of robust and evenhanded law enforcement. And in a kind of vicious cycle, the petty-offense process erodes the political capital of society's most vulnerable members, making it harder for them to resist its incursions and injuries. In all these ways, misdemeanor inequities extend far beyond the criminal system to distort the entire public sphere.

Policing is a valuable benefit provided by the state to its citizens, a promise of safety and lawfulness. But throughout the United States, it is not provided equally or in the same fashion. The same communities that are heavily policed for low-level crimes commonly receive fewer law enforcement resources regarding serious ones: 911 response times are longer; homicide investigations are less effective. Carlos, for example, grew up in the New Jersey projects, and his brother is a police officer. Carlos describes what happens if you call the police in the wealthy suburbs nearby. "The police come right there, in five minutes. . . . In my area, it's different. You call the police, an hour later they come. Two hours later. . . . Depends on what town you call the police. . . . [L]ike here, they don't care about you."[38]

This underpolicing has long been understood as a form of official discrimination. "African Americans have always viewed the protection of black lives as a civil rights issue," writes law professor James Forman Jr., "whether the threat comes from police officers or street criminals." Professor Randall Kennedy goes further: "The principal injury suffered by African-Americans in relation to criminal matters is not overenforcement but underenforcement of the laws."[39] Too much policing may be discriminatory, but so is too little.

In other words, disadvantaged communities suffer simultaneously from overenforcement *and* underenforcement—too much intrusive misdemeanor policing as well as too little protection from serious crime. Indeed, sometimes overenforcement actually worsens underenforcement. Scholars conclude, for example, that overenforcing minor crimes can hamper the police's capacity to gather evidence and find witnesses willing to testify, making it harder to solve homicides. As a result, such communities may simultaneously resist misdemeanor policing even as they seek more policing for serious crimes and support a greater police presence in their neighborhoods aimed at preventing violence. As columnist Charles Blow writes, "Minority communities want policing the same as any other, but they want it to be appropriate and proportional."[40]

The takeaway is that overenforcement and underenforcement are not opposites. They are not cures for each other: overpolicing is not fixed by underpolicing. Rather, they are flip sides of the same coin of political and racial disadvantage, democratic deprivations that both occur because the state is insufficiently committed to getting the policing balance right.[41] The dynamic is a kind of racial tax exacted through the criminal process, through which residents of poor communities of color are punished twice: overpoliced for chump change, underprotected from serious threats.

Such deprivations are symptoms of political weakness—generally speaking, communities with more money and political clout get more responsive, balanced policing just like they get better schools and garbage collection.[42] But policing dysfunctions are special, self-reinforcing deprivations because they exacerbate the very political weaknesses from which they flow. Being overpoliced and overcriminalized destroys social capital. It makes it more difficult for individuals and communities to engage the political process and to make their voices heard. Overcriminalization thus deprives African Americans and other racial minorities of the very tools they would need to get the political branches of government to respond and change course.

The best-known mechanism of political exclusion is felony disenfranchisement, which currently deprives 2.2 million African Americans—over 7 percent of the black adult population—of the vote. But the criminal system excludes people of color from the democratic process in other, less overt ways. People who have encountered the criminal system are less likely to vote or serve on juries, even when they can. They are also less likely to work on political campaigns, attend a march or rally, band together to demand services from government, or otherwise participate in important forms of political engagement. Political scientists Amy Lerman and Vesla Weaver write that experiencing the criminal system makes people politically leery: "Instead of developing the tools and ethos of engaged citizens, they learn to stay quiet, make no demands, and be wary and distrustful of political authorities."[43]

At the same time, the criminal process exacerbates the stereotype of black criminality that has suppressed African American civic authority for over a century. Historian Khalil Gibran Muhammad explains that the very idea of a "black crime rate" has undermined the social and political status of African Americans since the Civil War. While politicians and the media rarely discuss "white crime rates," ubiquitous references to black incarceration rates, black arrest rates, and black crime rates consistently reinforce the notion that African Americans might be criminals. That stereotype, in turn, makes it harder for African Americans to collectively influence the political process and the public conversation around crime. Some politicians actively inject racial stereotypes into the political debate. When President George H. W. Bush used Willie Horton's mug shot in a campaign ad, and when President Donald Trump referred to Mexicans as "rapists" who bring crime and drugs across the border, they joined a long tradition of using crime rhetoric as a racial code, a way of signaling their views about which voters do and do not count.[44]

Misdemeanors drive this insidious cycle in a number of ways. It is, for example, the petty-offense process that overpolices African Americans for low-level crimes, arresting them and sending them to jail. These are the official practices that give initial substance to stereotypes about race and crime by dispensing arrest records and jail experiences to thousands of people of color each year. In a self-reinforcing cycle, neighborhoods characterized by high arrest rates then get treated as "high-crime" communities—an epithet that often triggers declining property values, middle-class flight, loss of public services, and yet more overpolicing.[45]

The petty-offense process then takes this same population and formally converts a large percentage into convicted criminals, adjudicating them in speedy, sloppy, disrespectful ways without careful attention to evidence or rules. In effect, the misdemeanor system *presumes* that poor black and brown people should be managed as criminals and then treats them so in a self-fulfilling manner by rushing them through the process, depriving them of robust counsel, pressuring them to plead guilty, and generally not bothering to test the evidence or the law that underlies their criminal convictions. This "presumption of guilt" generates millions of shaky convictions that fuel the "black crime rate" that has haunted American politics for decades.[46]

In this way, civic disrespect is built into the misdemeanor process itself. We don't usually think of the misdemeanor system as a political operation. But that speedy, sloppy process is politically tolerable only if we accept that all those millions of people deserve to be treated that way. The process embodies a contemptuous, dehumanizing stance toward the people who pass through it. Those individuals, in turn, learn that they do not matter to the official decision-makers who wield the power of the state. As Carlos said, "They don't care about you."[47]

Back in Baltimore, Tyriel Simms says the disrespect comes from all sides and from every player, from police to the public defender to the judge. He feels powerless. "The last time I was arrested, I was initially offered $150,000 bail, and then the judge changed it to no bail because he was in a *bad mood*. He said that. They say whatever they want to say to us. The toughest guy, the most confident person, is broken down in front of these judges, because they have the power to use that pen. It's not a sword; it's a nuclear bomb. They could ruin your life at any time, and you have to put in the work, time and money to get it back."[48]

Simms's experience exemplifies how legal rules offer a promise of equal treatment and how, when the state ignores the rules, it can be a kind of injury to democratic ideals. The judge was supposed to decide Simms's bail based on the rules that apply to everyone, not the judge's mood. This is a principle that sits at the heart of democracies, what scholars refer to as "rule of law," that we are all governed by the same public legal authority in the same ways. Ignoring the rules was disrespectful to Simms's standing as an equal citizen. Rules also promote equal treatment by requiring decision-makers to explain what they are doing, what evidence they are relying on, and why. Such rules guard against arbitrary official mistreatment, or in Simms's words, against that nuclear bomb that can ruin your life. And it is precisely these commitments to rules, evidence, and transparency that are habitually jettisoned by the petty offense process.[49]

To put it somewhat differently, being cavalier about evidence and procedure is a way of being cavalier about guilt and dignity. And being cavalier about a person's guilt and dignity *while we are convicting them of a crime* is a way of saying that we don't care much about them, what they did, or what happens to them. This sort of treatment is an undemocratic slap in the face. The government wouldn't do it to people with influence, who could push back, or who matter to decision-makers. And yet the misdemeanor system does do it, millions of times each year, especially to poor people of color but also to poor and vulnerable people of every race, ethnicity, and age in cities, counties, and states all across the country.

This disrespect reveals the tight connection between race and money. While poor people of color often fare the worst in the misdemeanor system, it is wealthy offenders—not white offenders—who typically fare the best. The rich are not punished for their poverty or their inability to pay fines and fees on time. Conduct deemed criminal when committed by the poor or the homeless—drinking in public for example—is often tolerated when committed by the wealthy, who are generally free to pop open a bottle of wine at an outdoor concert. When the wealthy do offend, courts may consider them lower risk and treat them more leniently; sometimes they can even buy their way out of the problem by paying for treatment, diversion, or private jails.[50] And of course, money provides access to well-resourced lawyers who can make the system work more smoothly and more fairly for their clients.

But most Americans don't have such options. Indeed, the persistent mistreatment of African Americans has arguably made it worse for almost everybody by weakening the system's general commitment to fairness and lawfulness. If a rising tide lifts all boats, a sinking one threatens them all too. When racial politics erode individual rights and legal procedures, vulnerable white people suffer alongside people of color. Local jails are filled with whites as well as blacks and Latinos who cannot afford to pay fines and fees. The pressure to plead guilty has convicted many an innocent white person. African American men may be the prime victims of overcriminalization, but it was Gail Atwater, a white mother of two, who the Supreme Court decided should go to jail for a seatbelt violation.[51] Because the petty-offense process sweeps so broadly, it renders all Americans vulnerable even as it has historically singled out and punished people of color.

HISTORY

THE MISDEMEANOR SYSTEM IS AN OLD BEAST. NONE OF its modern failings—its wrongful convictions, its regressive economics, its racial skew—are new. Rather, they are new iterations of old patterns. Legal historian Lawrence Friedman once wrote, "Every generation, in a sense, makes its own system of criminal justice. But on the whole, society cuts its products to old designs. The people are new, the events are new; but patterns, templates, and dies have a longer life. They wear out slowly, they change style slowly, they are never discarded all at once."[1] And so in order to understand the misdemeanor system we currently have, it helps to excavate what it used to be.

Modern misdemeanors have a deep backstory that stretches back centuries, long before the criminal system looked anything like it does today. In the Middle Ages, European feudal lords and governments used nonfelony offenses to exert control over and extract revenue from their subjects. English legal commentator William Blackstone described an elaborate eighteenth-century array of serious "misdemesnors," defined as all crimes for which the penalty did not include death. Those could include crimes as serious as kidnapping, extortion, and bribery.[2]

This chapter is not a history in that sense, a full accounting of that long pedigree. Rather, it tells the story of three select, distinctive historical phenomena in the United States—two old, one current—that together capture in high definition some of the perennial challenges of America's petty-offense process. The first began around 1865 after the Civil War and ended with World War II. During that period, southern states erected an enormous misdemeanor apparatus through which government and business interests effectively resurrected slavery by using petty-offense prosecutions and punishment. The second phenomenon, vagrancy law, is now unconstitutional. Vagrancy laws persisted through the 1960s; police used these laws indiscriminately to round up the unemployed, members of the LGBT community, people of color, political protesters, and a wide array of other socially disfavored individuals. Third and finally, the chapter explores the current controversy over broken windows policing and the use of order-maintenance offenses, a kind of narrower modern cognate of older, discredited practices. That ongoing debate reveals how long-standing misdemeanor conflicts over race, money, and social control have greatly changed and yet nevertheless continue to assert themselves in familiar ways.

The lessons of history have their limits: today's country is a far cry from 1950s America, certainly from the 1870s, and some very important things are completely different. US law has been substantially rewritten. Racial segregation and discrimination are illegal; laws and practices that once generated thousands of convictions have been declared unconstitutional. Meanwhile, police departments, prosecutors' offices, courts, and all the other institutions that make up the criminal system are much bigger, more powerful, professionalized, and technological. And yet at the same time, there is continuity. While much of our modern system would be unrecognizable to someone from fifty or one hundred years ago, an astonishing amount would look familiar.

These three examples are landmarks, not averages. The brutality of the postwar South, the now unconstitutional apparatus of vagrancy law, and the ongoing controversy over broken windows policing are illuminating precisely because they are extreme. They bring into relief the social and political significance of misdemeanors far beyond their role as conventional crime control. Landmark examples like these remind us what the misdemeanor system is capable of at its worst, its persistent economic and racial agendas, the unfettered quality of its legal authority, and its tendencies toward regressive social control. They also underscore just how influential misdemeanors have been in shaping our national character. Ultimately, they help us to better understand and judge the system that we currently have.

NEOSLAVERY AND ITS MISDEMEANOR INFRASTRUCTURE

In 1865, the Thirteenth Amendment abolished slavery and altered the course of American history. But it had one enormous loophole: "except as a punishment for crime." Southern states immediately exploited that loophole using misdemeanors to maintain the slavery economy for decades.

Green Cottenham, for example, was twenty-two years old in Alabama. Looking for work around the freight docks in Shelby County, Cottenham was arrested and charged with riding a freight train without a ticket. In fact he hadn't done any such thing, and so the charge was switched to vagrancy, the crime of lacking proof of employment. Cottenham spent three days in jail before a local judge found him guilty and sentenced him to thirty days of hard labor and $38.40 in fines and fees, almost $1,000 in current dollars. Since Cottenham couldn't pay, his hard labor sentence was extended to six months. The next day, a representative from Tennessee Coal, Iron & Railroad Co. agreed to pay $12 a month toward Cottenham's debt. In exchange, the court handed Cottenham over to the company, where he was put in chains and sent underground to mine for coal in Slope No. 12. Black prisoners like Cottenham worked all day underground in darkness, at gunpoint, subject to the whip, and chained to their beds at night. Four months later, Green Cottenham died in the mine of tuberculosis and lack of medical care. It was 1908, forty-three years after President Abraham Lincoln signed the Emancipation Proclamation.[3]

In his Pulitzer Prize–winning book *Slavery by Another Name: The Re-Enslavement of Black Americans from the Civil War to World War II*, Douglas Blackmon chronicles the forgotten history of misdemeanors as the legal infrastructure through which southern states re-enslaved African Americans after they had been freed. Local sheriffs and judges arrested and convicted African Americans for minor offenses like gaming, possessing alcohol, obscenity, and vagrancy. The courts imposed heavy fines. Defendants who could not pay were sold to farms, factories, mines, and other businesses as punishment. Officials tracked down black men and arrested them in order to fuel industry demands, and the state collected millions of dollars. White players also profited through an array of fees charged to defendants, including arrest, warrant, clerk, and jail fees. Deputy Sheriff Newton Eddings, who arrested Green Cottenham, for example, was paid by Tennessee Coal for every African American he arrested and transported for the company, plus expenses.[4]

According to Eric Foner, the preeminent historian of the Reconstruction period, converting criminal law into a form of labor control was part of the broader southern effort to subdue the newly freed African American population while finding new ways to extract work from them. "Virtually from the moment the Civil War ended," he writes, "the search began for legal means of subordinating a volatile black population that regarded economic independence as a corollary of freedom and the old labor discipline as a badge of slavery." Misdemeanors supplied those legal means. As a result, the southern judicial apparatus lost much of its connection to actual crime and criminal justice. Blackmon describes the details. "Instead of thousands of true thieves and thugs drawn into the system over decades, the records demonstrate the capture and imprisonment of thousands of random indigent citizens, almost always under the thinnest chimera of probable cause or judicial process. . . . Instead of evidence showing black crime waves, the original records of county jails indicated thousands of arrests for inconsequential charges or for violations of laws specifically written to intimidate blacks."[5]

Blackmon labels these postwar decades the "Age of Neoslavery" during which the petty-offense machinery brutally extorted labor from thousands of African Americans, many of whom died in the factories and mines to which they were sold. Northerners were complicit in various ways throughout. Immediately after the war, Freedmen's Bureau courts sent blacks to work on plantations in exchange for debt relief. In 1905, the Supreme Court held that peonage—forced labor in exchange for the payment of a debt—was a federal crime, but the federal government declined to enforce the law against southern interests. There was some respite when, at the height of Reconstruction, African Americans briefly achieved a measure of political power and some jurisdictions backed away from using criminal laws to extract forced labor. But by the late 1870s the federal government had adopted a laissez-faire approach to civil rights, and blacks lost many of the gains they had made. The practices of neoslavery did not fully die out until World War II when, under pressure to enlist African American soldiers, the federal government finally began enforcing the laws against slavery.[6]

This extortionate racial history may seem remote from modern concerns, but 1945 was not so long ago. If a twenty-two-year-old like Green Cottenham had been arrested that year, he would be ninety-five years old today. Perhaps even more disturbing are the resonances that persist as the misdemeanor system continues to convict African Americans for economic gain. In 1930s Shelby County, Alabama, poor blacks were incarcerated for minor offenses and charged coercive fines and fees so that local interests could profit off their criminalization. In 2012, a small town in Shelby County called Harpersville was sued for incarcerating poor blacks for misdemeanors, charging them coercively high probation fines and fees, and profiting off their criminalization. The judge presiding over the lawsuit called Harpersville's probation scheme "a judicially sanctioned extortion racket." Or recall the story of Cindy Rodriguez, the disabled woman stripped of her rights, liberty, and meagre income by Rutherford County, Tennessee, and its private probation company based on a single low-level misdemeanor. Such echoes from the past have not gone unnoticed. A group of sociologists recently mused that "although the criminally punished are no longer leased to corporations if they cannot pay their fees and fines, they are nonetheless saddled with a substantial financial debt, one that enhances their poverty and impairs their ability to extract themselves from the reach of the criminal justice system."[7]

Today, many recognize that mass incarceration and the racial skew in our criminal system flow in large part from that original loophole in the Thirteenth Amendment, permitting involuntary servitude to persist "as a punishment for crime."[8] Misdemeanors were and remain central to that exploitative legacy.

VAGRANCY: THE RISE AND FALL OF THE CATCHALL "CRIME"

The misdemeanor for which Green Cottenham was convicted in 1908 was vagrancy. At the time, vagrancy was the offense of being "without means" or lacking proof of employment. Although southern vagrancy law was racially neutral on its face—it technically applied to everyone—in reality it was overtly designed to control and conscript black labor: Foner notes, "The vagrant contemplated was the plantation negro." But the South was not alone. In the West, nineteenth-century settlers used vagrancy and other public-order laws, such as disorderly conduct and drunkenness, to strip indigenous residents of their land and force them to work. Up north, vagrancy enforcement swept up poor whites.[9]

The United States did not invent vagrancy—it repurposed European laws with old roots. In eighteenth-century England it was a crime to be an "idle person." As described in *Blackstone's Commentaries*, "Idleness in any person whatsoever is . . . a high offense against the public economy. . . . All idle persons or vagabonds are . . . divided in three classes, *idle* and *disorderly* persons, *rogues* and *vagabonds*, and *incorrigible rogues*; all these are offenders against the good order, and blemishes in the government, of any kingdom."[10]

Vagrancy laws continued to be reused and recycled in the United States long into the twentieth century. In 1972, sixty-four years after Green Cottenham's arrest, Florida's vagrancy statute criminalized sprawling classes of people, including

> rogues and vagabonds, or dissolute persons who go about begging, common gamblers, persons who use juggling or unlawful games or plays, common drunkards, common night walkers, thieves, pilferers or pickpockets, traders in stolen property, lewd, wanton and lascivious persons, keepers of gambling places, common railers and brawlers, persons wandering or strolling around from place to place without any lawful purpose or object, habitual loafers, disorderly persons, persons neglecting all lawful business and habitually spending their time by frequenting houses of ill fame, gaming houses, or places where alcoholic beverages are sold or served, persons able to work but habitually living upon the earnings of their wives or minor children.

Such people could be arrested, jailed, and fined. In some cities, vagrants were banished.[11]

Until the Supreme Court declared such statutes unconstitutional in 1972, the vagrancy offense was an enormously popular and powerful law enforcement tool. Vagrancy laws, which existed in every state, effectively granted the police unfettered power to arrest anyone who appeared poor, out of place, undesirable, or otherwise deviant. In Vagrant Nation: Police Power, Constitutional Change, and the Making of the 1960s, historian Risa Goluboff emphasizes just how broadly the police used the tool not only to control the poor but to regulate social convention and to stifle political dissent.[12] Vagrancy enforcement was such a pervasive fact of life that disadvantaged and minority groups trained themselves and their children to respond, generating a plethora of eerily familiar "talks":

> Working-class immigrant families warned their maturing children not to leave home without money that could inoculate them from

vagrancy arrests. Early "homophile" organizations educated their gay and lesbian members about "lewd vagrancy" arrests and how to avoid them—"wear at least three items of the clothing of your own sex" was a common refrain. Black newspapers warned their readers that vagrancy arrests were a likely consequence of any racially presumptuous behavior. Civil rights organizations tried to head off seemingly inevitable vagrancy arrests of workers heading south by providing "vagrancy forms" that attested to the workers' standing as "reputable members of the community."[13]

As Goluboff describes it, the demise of vagrancy law was a key legacy of the 1960s. Over decades, a diverse and decentralized array of activists, lawyers, and individuals resisted the legal conformity and authoritarian premises of the vagrancy policing model. Mobilized around issues ranging from sexual freedom to civil rights, poverty, and the Vietnam War, a wide assortment of groups produced a sustained, bottom-up campaign against vagrancy that generated hundreds of judicial decisions and ultimately resulted in its legal elimination.[14]

These groups had a key supporter in Supreme Court justice William O. Douglas, who made it part of his life's work to go after vagrancy and other vague public-order laws. In 1960 he wrote an article excoriating the undemocratic nature of such crimes. "The persons arrested . . . are not the sons of bankers, industrialists, lawyers, or other professional people," he fumed. "They . . . come from other strata of society, or from minority groups who are not sufficiently vocal to protect themselves, and who do not have the prestige to prevent an easy laying-on of hands by the police."[15] In 1972, Justice Douglas authored the Court's unanimous opinion in *Papachristou v. City of Jacksonville*, which held that the offense of vagrancy conferred too much vague, unfettered discretion on police, permitting them to impose their will arbitrarily on too many people. The opinion concluded,

The implicit presumption in these generalized vagrancy standards—that crime is being nipped in the bud—is too extravagant to deserve extended treatment. Of course, vagrancy statutes are useful to the police. Of course, they are nets making easy the roundup of so-called undesirables. But the rule of law implies equality and justice in its application. Vagrancy laws . . . teach that the scales of justice are so tipped that even-handed administration of the law is not possible. The rule of law, evenly applied to minorities as well as majorities, to the poor as well as the rich, is the great mucilage that holds society together.[16]

Papachristou was one of a series of cases in which the Supreme Court struck down similarly broad and vague criminal misdemeanor laws. In 1971, the Court invalidated a Cincinnati municipal ordinance that made it a crime for "three or more persons to assemble on any of the sidewalks and there conduct themselves in a manner annoying to persons passing by." In 1983, the Court found unconstitutional a California loitering statute that required anyone "who loiters or wanders upon the streets or from place to place without apparent reason or business" to provide the police with "'credible and reliable' identification and to account for their presence." In 1999, the Court invalidated a gang loitering statute that made it a crime for gang members to "loiter," which the ordinance defined as "remain[ing] in any one place with no apparent purpose." The Court noted that "the freedom to loiter for innocent purposes is part of the 'liberty' protected by the Due Process Clause of the Fourteenth Amendment."[17]

Collectively, these vagrancy and loitering decisions constrained the kinds of laws that had long given police broad power to make misdemeanor arrests. But striking down those laws did not, in practice, always curtail police discretion on the street. Instead, policing shifted toward other laws—updated versions of order-maintenance crimes—that technically met constitutional requirements while still preserving enormous police discretion.[18] Recall, for example, New York's heavy-handed trespass policies, and how Baltimore order-maintenance laws are used to "clear corners." The statutes are constitutional—the trouble lies in the realities of enforcement.

Moreover, even as the Supreme Court restricted the scope of some policing statutes, it was expanding police authority under the Fourth Amendment. The Court's 1968 decision in *Terry v. Ohio* authorized police to seize people based only on reasonable suspicion rather than the higher standard of probable cause. Because so little evidence is needed, the precise contours of statutes now matter less, giving low-level offenses like disorderly conduct and loitering enormous reach. In this sense, *Terry* effectively guaranteed to police much of what *Papachristou* tried to take away. Not surprisingly, Justice Douglas didn't like *Terry*. He penned a scathing dissent in the case, arguing that conferring this new power on police represented "a long step down the totalitarian path."[19]

Meanwhile, as we have seen throughout this book, the legal mechanisms for enforcing the constitutional standards demanded by *Papachristou* and similar cases are often simply lacking. High-volume, speedy misdemeanor courts are poorly suited to contest the niceties of statutory language. People under pressure to plead guilty in order to get out of jail are less likely to invest the time to mount legal challenges. New York's loitering ordinance, for example, was declared unconstitutional in 1992. Nevertheless, for years the city continued making hundreds of loitering arrests; one man alone, Eddie Wise, was convicted of loitering seven times between 1992 and 2005.[20] The subtleties of formal law demanded by the Constitution lack traction in a system that doesn't pay much attention to rules in the first place.

In some places, the spirit of vagrancy policing has been resurrected even more directly through the creation of "banishment" laws and practices. Through this panoply of criminal and civil tools, police and courts can exclude individuals from public spaces like parks and libraries and even entire downtown neighborhoods. Aimed largely at the homeless and the addicted, these tools include civil injunctions, exclusion orders, drug loitering ordinances, trespassing contracts, and other spatial bans. While many of these legal orders are technically civil, violations of them are often criminal offenses and land violators in jail. In cities from Seattle to Cincinnati to Los Angeles, thousands of individuals are banned from public areas, gentrified neighborhoods, and even entire cities in the ways that vagrancy laws used to permit.[21]

As such examples show, vagrancy statutes may be gone, but the pressure to arrest and control disfavored populations is not. The high-volume street arrests permitted by vagrancy laws were not entirely abandoned but rather displaced to other narrower enforcement vehicles with new justifications. One study concludes that after vagrancy laws were declared unconstitutional, major declines in vagrancy arrest rates were more than compensated for by increases in arrests for disorderly conduct, loitering, and other low-level crimes. Even when legal rules are transformed, actual practices don't always change that much. And even the law on the books hasn't changed as much as it might have: 33 percent of US cities still ban loitering in public.[22] It is this conflicted legacy over the proper scope and purposes of low-level policing that is currently on prominent display in the ongoing debate over order-maintenance policing and its most controversial iteration, the "broken windows" theory.

BROKEN WINDOWS, ZERO-TOLERANCE, AND ORDER-MAINTENANCE POLICING

In 1982, James Wilson and George Kelling wrote a now famous article titled "Broken Windows: The Police and Neighborhood Safety" in which they argued that the appearance of disorder breeds crime. An unrepaired broken window on a house suggests that the neighborhood is not cared for, which in turn promotes other forms of disorder and, eventually, lawbreaking. The strict policing of low-level disorders such as loitering, graffiti, littering, and public drinking should therefore not only lead to more orderly appearing communities but reduce serious crime. Broken windows theory is, in effect, a rationale for heavy misdemeanor enforcement. Sometimes referred as "quality-of-life" or "zero-tolerance" policing, in its most aggressive form the strategy intentionally overenforces low-level offenses above and beyond their intrinsic threat or value in order to reduce crime up the food chain. Such policing is also closely associated with the widespread use of stop-and-frisk. Police departments often use both tactics in the same neighborhoods or against the same groups, and they proceed on the similar principle that intrusive low-level policing decreases serious crime.[23]

Broken windows policing is heavily contested both as an idea and as public policy. It was widely endorsed by numerous public officials and scholars in the 1990s and eventually adopted by various police departments, including New York, Chicago, and Los Angeles. Since then, it has been just as widely criticized as inaccurate, racist, counterproductive, and the source of police-community tensions. Numerous organizations, including Black Lives Matter and Harvard Law School's Fair Punishment Project, have called for its abolition. By contrast, when President Donald Trump was running for office he called for more stop-and-frisk.[24]

The largest-scale implementation of broken windows policing took place in New York City in 1994 when Mayor Rudolph Giuliani and Police Commissioner William Bratton embraced the approach. Misdemeanor arrests in New York leapt from approximately 125,000 in 1993 to 225,000 in 2001, peaking at nearly 250,000 in 2010. New York's crime rate fell significantly around the same time, which Giuliani, Bratton, and many others attributed to the new order-maintenance arrest policy.[25]

By contrast, numerous scholars and officials have challenged broken windows policing both as an empirical and philosophical matter. Recall the Supreme Court's comment in *Papachristou* that "the implicit presumption in these generalized vagrancy standards—that crime is being nipped in the bud—is too extravagant to deserve extended treatment." Broken windows theory explicitly resurrects this presumption, and an enormous literature has arisen arguing over its accuracy. In the book *Illusion of Order: The False Promise of Broken Windows Policing*, legal scholar Bernard Harcourt concludes that broken windows is a powerful rhetorical strategy lacking proof that it actually works. Crime dropped in New York, to be sure, but it dropped all around the country at the same time, including in cities that did not adopt the policy. Various studies have failed to demonstrate a causal connection between broken windows policing and crime reduction. Sociologists Robert Sampson and Stephen Raudenbush likewise agree that "the current fascination in policy circles on cleaning up disorder through law enforcement techniques appears simplistic and largely misplaced, at least in terms of directly fighting crime."[26] In sum, the claim that overenforcing misdemeanors reduces serious crime remains, at best, a matter of dispute.

At the same time, broken windows, zero-tolerance, and quality-of-life policing have proven to be very expensive. In New York, they led to an extreme racial skew in the city's stop-and-frisks and arrests, numerous civil rights lawsuits, and ultimately a federal court's conclusion that the New York Police Department had engaged in unconstitutional practices. Broken windows policy has eroded the relationship between police and residents in cities from Seattle to Chicago to Baltimore. Many argue that it reinforces racist stereotypes of black criminality because it is deployed predominantly in black neighborhoods and results in large-scale stops and arrests of black people for minor or harmless conduct.[27]

Part of the problem is that a number of questionable assumptions are packed into the broken windows strategy. For one thing, *disorder* is not the same thing as *crime*. Sometimes disorder can threaten public safety or make crime more likely, but it can also be innovative, vibrant, or welcoming. A group of young people standing on the street corner might be perceived as disorderly and threatening, but they could also be seen as vivacious friends, children of the community, or just plain neighborly, depending on who is doing the perceiving and where. "The exuberant diversity" of cities is full of seeming disorder, wrote Jane Jacobs in *The Death and Life of Great American Cities*, a disorder that is really an intricate and complex order composed of people, movement, and change. There are, moreover, lots of kinds of disorder. Broken windows focuses on street activity, but crime and disorder occur in shopping malls, on the Internet, and on Wall Street where there are no "zero-tolerance" policing efforts. Indeed, the very term "quality-of-life policing" assumes a kind of us-them group conflict: arrests might improve some group's quality of life, but they destroy the quality of life of the people being arrested. Or as *New York Times* columnist Clyde Haberman remarked, "If we are to have quality-of-life campaigns . . . may we get straight whose life we're talking about, anyway?"[28]

Perhaps most importantly, our shared understandings and fear of disorder are generated in part by the policies of the misdemeanor system itself. Neighborhoods where police decide to overenforce disorder offenses become labeled as "disorderly communities." The people who sustain arrests and convictions for order-maintenance crimes carry those criminal labels into society with them. That labeling tells employers, schools, and landlords to worry about that conduct and to treat it as harmful or frightening. The petty-offense process, in other words, is not merely responding to disorder—it is defining and enforcing a particular version of it.[29]

The broken windows era is not over, so we don't know how the story ends. Perhaps broken windows will be legally and intellectually discredited the way vagrancy laws were. Or perhaps the policy will— as some already predict—morph into more diffuse forms of surveillance and marking that deploy different policing tactics but target the same populations.[30] Whatever happens, the controversy is the latest iteration of the perennial challenge of petty-offense enforcement: balancing the need for safety and crime control against the requirements of democratic, egalitarian governance.

LESSONS FROM THE VAULT

These three examples illuminate the long-standing and critical significance of the misdemeanor institution. First, developments within the misdemeanor system are important to the arc of American history and politics. Sometimes those developments look like progress. For all its flaws, broken windows policing today is a far cry from the lawless sweeps of the vagrancy era. Vagrancy, in turn, was an improvement over the brutal forced-labor machinery of the postbellum South. While each iteration preserves many of its predecessors' flaws, the petty-offense process has evolved as America has deepened its commitments to civil rights, egalitarianism, and constitutional governance. Indeed, it is one of the vehicles for that advancement.[31]

Sometimes modern developments don't look as much like progress. Today's petty-offense system still rounds up, incarcerates, and punishes many of the same classes of people in ways that shockingly resemble old discredited practices. Some things change, some things don't. But for better or for worse, the enormous misdemeanor system remains an influential player in the historical drama over class and race in America. Getting misdemeanors right or wrong is a way of getting these thorny issues right or wrong.

These examples also reveal a powerful recurring theme: how the petty-offense process repeatedly uses its criminal authority to accomplish noncriminal policy ends. Southern states deployed misdemeanors to reinstate slave labor practices that were otherwise illegal—strategically treating common conduct as "criminal" in pursuit of racial and commercial goals. That era stands as a dramatic reminder that the petty-offense process is available as a cover for disreputable social and economic agendas that might not pass muster on their own terms. The vagrancy apparatus deployed criminal law to impose economic, political, and social controls on disfavored and disadvantaged populations based not on their criminal conduct but on their unpopularity. Today, the economic motivations behind a great deal of misdemeanor enforcement remain alive and well. Much of the distrust of order-maintenance policing similarly flows from its tenuous connection to crime reduction. In other words, the misdemeanor system still does a lot of work that is only loosely tied to crime control.

The misdemeanor process lends itself to this sort of pretext and co-optation precisely because many of its crimes are so petty. Spitting and jaywalking are not particularly dangerous or morally bad. We do not need to fully enforce laws against disorderly conduct; in fact, most of the time we don't enforce them rigorously at all, and we probably wouldn't want to live in a restrictive society that did. Because actual enforcement isn't all that pressing, law enforcement has a lot of leeway. The enormous reach of the process, moreover, makes it ripe for distortion. Most people never commit serious crimes, but misdemeanor prohibitions against common conduct expose nearly everyone to the authority of the petty-offense process. That gives every police department, every low-level court, every municipality a ready-made pool of easy-to-reach subjects. It did in 1870, and it still does today. It is perhaps unsurprising that such a decentralized, unregulated, yet powerful infrastructure has historically been coopted for all sorts of purposes.

On the other hand, the modern misdemeanor system is not *just* a pretext, not just a way of sneaking in other agendas. The enforcement of low-level crime remains a valuable public service in its own right.[32] Just because the misdemeanor process continues to do all sorts of covert and inegalitarian work does not mean it should be thrown out with the bathwater. Instead, it needs a framework of strong principles to sort out which of its aspects are legitimate and necessary to a safe and democratic society and which lend themselves too easily to distortion. The next chapter takes a step back to consider what that framework might look like and what it reveals about the capacity of the misdemeanor process to achieve meaningful justice.

| 8 |

JUSTICE

HAVING CONFRONTED THE MISDEMEANOR PROCESS IN all its complexity, we now face foundational theoretical questions. What is the right way to run a low-level criminal system in a democracy? Our misdemeanor system is deeply flawed. What would make it fair, principled, and good, or at least good enough? Misdemeanors have largely escaped such scrutiny, slipping beneath the radar of big philosophical conversations about criminal justice and democratic principles. But the petty-offense process is too important and influential to be left out of such debates. It deserves to be brought into the theoretical fold, to take its place alongside other major public institutions and practices that are routinely subjected to sustained, principled analysis. This chapter is an effort to begin that process.

The good news is that there is no need to reinvent the wheel. We have been having rigorous conversations about justice for a long time, especially within criminal legal theory, in sociology, and in democratic theory. Together these three different perspectives offer a combination of basic principles, ways of asking about the fairness and legitimacy of major social institutions, through which we can evaluate the misdemeanor system as a legal and democratic phenomenon. They give us a vocabulary to explain more precisely why so many aspects of the petty-offense process seem unjust, in recognizable terms that have long been used to make such arguments. They also can help clarify more precisely where the petty-offense process offends basic precepts of law and democracy and where it is merely flawed in the all-too-common way of human institutions and around which it is the business of government to tinker.

Of course, these three approaches are not the only perspectives from which we could ask such questions. Economics and psychology, for example, offer important insights into the nature of criminal justice as well.[1] But these three are the legs of the misdemeanor justice stool, as it were. Each one goes to a fundamental feature of the misdemeanor system. It is, first, a *criminal system* and therefore needs to comport with basic criminal legal principles. Second, it exerts an enormous amount of stratifying social control over the disadvantaged. This fact requires sustained attention of the kind that sociology provides. And third, because of these first two features, it is an integral, influential part of our larger democracy, which means that it should obey basic democratic principles. Whatever else it might include, any framework for misdemeanor justice will need to engage these sorts of legal, sociological, and democratic issues.

We start with the classic legal justifications for state punishment.[2] We begin there in order to remind ourselves that the criminal system wields special authority, that it has a unique moral, normative heft, that through its coercive and stigmatic powers, it enables the government to turn millions of people into *criminals*. In addition to its many other costs, the sheer enormity of the American penal institution has normalized this singular function of the state. With millions of people in prison and jail, we have become numbed to the violent quality of criminalization and to just how awful it is when the state treats you as a criminal. We have lost sight, in other words, of the extraordinary power that motivates the unique rules and philosophies of the criminal law. Beginning with those rules and philosophies is a way, I hope, of regaining our sensitivities.

CRIMINAL JUSTICE AT THE BOTTOM OF THE PYRAMID

Short of the military, the criminal system is the most coercive, violent arm of the state. It is therefore subject to some special constraints. It can't just behave any old way. As legal philosopher Sharon Dolovich points out, criminal punishment can include "extended deprivations of liberty, ongoing hardship and humiliation, and even death. Ordinarily, such treatment would be judged morally wrong and roundly condemned, yet in the name of criminal justice, it is routinely imposed."[3] In order to retain and justify this unique authority, the criminal process must meet certain bedrock demands to ensure its fairness and legitimacy. These are classically understood in terms of three core commitments: to the *rule of law*, to *factual evidence*, and to *criminal blameworthiness*. Each of these has long been seen as a basic requisite for a legitimate criminal system. Each is routinely flouted by the petty-offense process.

A legitimate criminal system needs to have and follow universal, neutral rules and procedures. It should, as the Supreme Court wrote in the landmark case *Marbury v. Madison*, be a "government of laws and not men," governed by legality and not human or political caprice. Legal scholar William Stuntz explained this commitment, sometimes referred to as the "legality principle," to mean that "when the state deprives one of its citizens of life, liberty, or property, the deprivation is primarily the consequence of a legal rule, not a discretionary choice." If the monarch waves her hand and declares a person criminal on a whim, that wouldn't really be criminal *justice* in the modern, legal sense of the word. This legality principle is expressed in the Latin maxim *nulla poena sine lege*, "no punishment without law," sometimes rendered as "no punishment with crime." The late Justice Antonin Scalia called this principle "one of the most widely held value judgments in the entire history of human thought."[4]

The second bedrock commitment of criminal justice is to evidence. "It is beyond question, of course," says the Supreme Court, "that a conviction based on a record lacking any relevant evidence as to a crucial element of the offense charged would violate due process." It seems too obvious for words that criminal convictions require factual evidence of guilt, but it is worth remembering why this is so. A conviction is a public announcement that a person engaged in bad behavior for which they should be punished. This is what gives convictions social and moral meaning: they purport to reflect what the individual person *actually did*. Evidence is that all-important factual link between a legal conviction and an individual's bad behavior. Without evidence to back them up, convictions are just empty labels. Accordingly, a legitimate criminal system will only convict people based on evidence, facts, proof that the person engaged in the behavior condemned by law.[5]

Finally, the conduct that we punish as criminal must be, in fact, worthy of punishment. People should be at fault before we blame and punish them. While we punish for many reasons, the classic ones are retribution, deterrence, rehabilitation, and incapacitation. Or in less legalistic terms, we punish people because they did bad things and deserve it, or to deter future crimes, or to give people second chances, or when all else fails, to get dangerous people off the streets. Underlying all these reasons sits the notion that the person has *done* something culpable that is worth punishing. In paradigmatic examples like homicide, that culpability is very great and clearly morally wrong, which gives the criminal label its classic stigmatic character. In practice, we criminalize a lot of conduct that is not so obviously wrong or immoral, but the idea of personal criminal fault is nevertheless special, distinguished from other kinds of wrongs by its moral weight and the stigma it concomitantly confers.

Of course there is wide disagreement over exactly what sort of behavior does or does not belong in the special criminal category. A crime, as one scholar put it long ago, "is not simply anything which a legislature chooses to call a 'crime.'" It must invite "community condemnation," either because it is morally bad or especially harmful. A system that only punished people for entirely blameless, harmless conduct—catching a cold, for example, or breaking eggs at the small end—would not qualify as a proper criminal system in the philosophical sense because those people haven't done anything to deserve condemnation.[6]

Perhaps most importantly, the public, commonsense understanding of criminality retains that special moral and stigmatic weight. "Criminal justice," writes legal scholar and federal judge Stephanos Bibas, "more than almost any other area of law, is morally freighted in the popular imagination, and its moral significance is linked closely to its legitimacy." Criminal convictions are not technocratic, bureaucratic incidents: they morally matter. Indeed, this is precisely why they generate so many social, economic, and personal consequences. Or as philosopher Michael Walzer once put it, when we punish "it is critically important that we find the right people, that we put the mark of Cain *on Cain*."[7]

To recap, then, these are the ABCs of criminal legitimacy: rule of law, evidence, and blameworthiness. Of course this is an excessively, perhaps unconscionably condensed version of a vast world of criminal legal theory. Many volumes have been devoted to rule of law and its nuances, the complexities of evidentiary requirements, and the highly contested nature of criminal culpability. Many other important requirements could be added to the list, such as the presumption of innocence, proportionate punishment, and democratic accountability.[8] But these three basic commitments remain necessary, if not sufficient, to establish the legitimacy of criminal decision-making. A system that ignores them, one might say, has no business calling itself "criminal justice."

The crazy thing is how often the misdemeanor system violates these basic requirements. As we have seen, rule of law is weak in those many lower courts where speed and informality are the norm. From substantive law to constitutional procedures, legal rules are openly ignored, even by judges. Recall Chief Justice Jean Hoefer Toal of the South Carolina Supreme Court, who explained that she disagreed with the constitutional right to counsel in low-level cases and, as she put it, had "simply told my magistrates that we just don't have the resources to do that. So I will tell you straight up we [are] not adhering to" the constitutional rule. This is a shocking admission from a state's highest judicial official that the government is "straight up" ignoring the Constitution. Eddie Wise was convicted of loitering in New York seven times *after* the state's loitering statute was declared unconstitutional.[9] Such lawlessness, a key characteristic of the petty-offense process, means that many misdemeanor convictions are being produced in violation of the system's own core legitimating rules. The title of this book is, among other things, a reference to this failure of the legality principle *nulla poena sine lege*: the misdemeanor system commonly inflicts punishment without crime and in the absence of law.

The misdemeanor process also flouts the basic commitment to evidence, to the factual question of whether people are actually guilty. Again, we have seen how the process regularly pressures innocent people into pleading guilty without evidence or even despite the evidence. Thousands of guilty pleas are taken without anyone checking the evidence, so we will never know whether the defendants were guilty or not. We can understand this as a wrongful conviction problem, but it is deeper than that. The way that the system has abandoned evidentiary integrity represents the weakening of the fault model itself, the core notion that we punish people *because* they have done something blameworthy. If we never check to see what defendants actually did but just go ahead and punish them regardless, it suggests that the system is not really committed to punishing the guilty. That, to say the least, is a very weird sort of criminal justice.

Inattention to evidence and guilt also creates room for other, inappropriate things to matter. When the decision to convict is only weakly constrained by guilt, other factors can creep in and influence that decision, factors such as law enforcement selection policies, bad lawyering, money, and race. In the worst-case scenario, we can no longer say that a person was convicted *because* there was evidence that they committed a crime. Instead, it becomes more accurate to say that they were convicted *because* they were arrested, that they might well have been arrested for any number of reasons unrelated to the evidence, and that they pled guilty not necessarily because they were guilty but because the process exerted such strong pressures on them to do so.

Finally, the misdemeanor system often flouts the blameworthiness requirement. Even when we do check the evidence, many misdemeanor offenses do not define bad, dangerous, or blameworthy conduct in the first place. Offenses like loitering, disorderly conduct, spitting, and walking in the middle of the street are hard to square with classic notions of criminal culpability, blame, and danger. Indeed, dozens of states increasingly consider marijuana possession—for decades one of the largest misdemeanor categories—not to be a crime at all. Instead, such offenses are better understood as law enforcement tools, empowering police to interfere with, stop, and arrest broad classes of people in much the same way that vagrancy laws once did.[10]

To be clear, empowering police in this way could in theory be positive policy. We might decide that there are good reasons for police to have or keep these types of street-clearing, interventionist powers. But we shouldn't confuse this with individual *criminality*. Many people subject to such police powers will not be guilty of anything at all. Others may have technically violated a criminal statute but will still not have done anything harmful or wrong.

For all these reasons, much of the misdemeanor system is not really "criminal" at heart. It is called a criminal system, it confers criminal convictions, but it doesn't do the basic things that a true criminal system is supposed to do. It doesn't adhere to rule of law. It doesn't pay attention to evidence. And often it doesn't really care about blameworthiness, danger, or actual guilt—the criteria that make people worthy of social condemnation and therefore justify the state in exercising its criminal powers over them. Consequently, many of the people who emerge from the petty-offense process with convictions cannot really be said to be "criminals," not in the blameworthy, weighty sense that the term has come to and should mean.

If nothing else, this sleight of hand should generate a healthy skepticism about the significance of misdemeanor convictions, an appreciation of just how little information many of them convey about the people to whom they are attached. While some minor convictions are produced in relatively robust ways—drunk driving and domestic violence, for example, typically command more serious attention and resources—many are not. Convictions for disorderly conduct, loitering, trespassing, resisting arrest, spitting, and jaywalking are routinely generated in a low-quality fashion and thus tell us little about the person's actual conduct. Instead, they are reminders of the system's habits: that order-maintenance policing tends to sweep up the poor and people of color; that public defenders often lack the time and resources to contest cases; that the process pressures people into pleading guilty. Although these convicted people are now technically "criminals," that label should be understood not as a reflection of their personal blameworthiness, as criminal law promises, but as an artifact of the misdemeanor institution itself.

More philosophically, the weakened legitimacy of the misdemeanor process—all that flouting—is a reason to object to petty convictions on principle, to see them as distractions from what our criminal system ought to be doing and an abuse of the system's enormous authority. There is a lot of slippage between what the misdemeanor system says it does—managing crime—and the wide ranging social and economic work it actually performs. This slippage is worse at the bottom of the penal pyramid than it is at the top. Serious crimes and the law enforcement apparatus devoted to them are generally not pretextual: we *really* want to catch the murderer; we *really* want to punish the Wall Street inside trader. Indeed, much of the criminal system's importance and authority flows from this sincerity of function. Of course even that sincerity is far from absolute. The death penalty is in many ways a historical descendent of lynching. The modern war on drugs and mass incarceration, with their devastating impact on the African American community, have been decried as "the new Jim Crow." But much of the felony apparatus remains authentically motivated by crime and justice, which is to say constrained by rules, driven by evidence, and concerned with actual blameworthiness.[11]

Conversely, the disregard of basic criminal justice principles enables the slippage at the bottom. If the system paid more attention to rules, evidence, and blameworthiness, it would have a more limited reach. It would be more authentically *criminal*. These insights should inform our willingness to delegate authority to that system. If the petty-offense process is not going to act like a proper criminal system, then it shouldn't get the powers and benefits that we confer on authentically criminal institutions: extensive discretion over people's lives, liberty, and property; authority to punish and impose moral and social stigma; and the many special exemptions from the constraints that limit other state functions. Most other governmental institutions—administrative, civil, bureaucratic—are subject to far greater restrictions while they make important decisions about people's lives.[12] Whatever else it can do to you, the Department of Motor Vehicles can't pluck you off the street, put you in jail, and label you a criminal for the rest of your life. When the misdemeanor system declines to subject itself to the constraints and commitments of criminal justice, it should lose its special criminal status. It shouldn't get to have it both ways.

SOCIAL AND ECONOMIC CONTROL

Legal principles are not the only theoretical lens through which the misdemeanor system can be understood. Sociology has a long tradition of conceptualizing the criminal process as a means of social control, which is to say, as a far-reaching economic, cultural, and political institution whose raison d'être is not strictly limited to managing and reducing crime. The stories that sociology tells about the criminal system take us far beyond the constraints of the legal paradigm, revealing just how influential the criminal system really is.

Sometimes that system changes the way our entire society works. Sociologist David Garland, for example, argues that the economic and social upheavals of modern life have given rise to a "culture of control," filled with "our obsessive attempts to monitor risky individuals, to isolate dangerous populations, and to impose situational controls." This concern with control means that all of us now live "in a mode that is more than ever defined by institutions of policing, penality and prevention." In a similar vein, legal scholar Jonathan Simon describes how the United States now "governs through crime," not only through policing and prisons but in "office buildings, universities, day-care centers, medical complexes, apartment buildings, factories and airports. . . . [C]rime has become . . . central to the exercise of authority in America, by everyone from the president of the United States to the classroom teacher."[13] In these views, criminal justice is not so much a method of crime control as it is a collective and rather fearful way of life.

The criminal system exerts such broad cultural influence in part because it performs so many social and economic regulatory functions. The criminal process disciplines the labor supply; it maintains class and racial stratifications; it produces cultural norms and civic values. We use it to manage poverty, addiction, unemployment, racial tension, urban gentrification, family life, and all sorts of communal risks. While this infrastructure affects everyone, it primarily impacts the disadvantaged. In *Punishing the Poor: The Neoliberal Government of Social Insecurity*, sociologist Loïc Wacquant charts how criminal systems in the United States and to a lesser extent Europe have displaced the welfare state as the central mechanisms for regulating the lives and behavior of the poor and dispossessed. Even more pointedly, he characterizes this policy shift as a form of racial control, a new way of managing underemployed and disadvantaged African American communities after the demise of Jim Crow legal segregation.[14]

Such conceptual frameworks—governing through crime, the culture of control, punishing the poor, the new Jim Crow—describe a criminal system very different from the one contemplated by legal theory. Sociology offers a kind of exposé, revealing how criminal justice is not just about individual criminality and harm but the management and control of society in general and of disfavored groups, poverty, and race in particular.

Note how this flips the legal story on its head. Rather than chasing crime and criminals, the system is preemptive, predictive, and actuarial, devoted to managing people it deems risky.[15] Some of those individual people may indeed commit low-level crimes, but that is not *why* they are watched, stopped, marked, and disciplined—they are already in the crosshairs of the criminal system whether they commit crimes or not. As a matter of legal principle, of course, this is backward. The criminal system is supposed to go *after* criminals, not decide who they are beforehand and mark them for future reference.

Although much of the social control literature focuses on mass incarceration and violent crime, the petty-offense process has long provided one of the clearest examples of how the criminal system functions as a mode of social control in general and as a means of controlling the disadvantaged in particular.[16] Indeed, sociology is one of the few intellectual disciplines that has taken misdemeanors seriously. This is how Caleb Foote described vagrancy courts in 1956: "Philadelphia magistrates . . . viewed their function as a deterrent one to banish 'bums' from Philadelphia and keep them out ('After this you stay where you belong'), or as a form of civic sanitation ('I'll clean up this district if I have to stay here until 5 o'clock every afternoon'), or as control of suspicious persons ('There have been a lot of robberies around here. I'm going to have you investigated—three months'), or as humanitarian ('I'm saving his life by sending him where he can't booze')."[17]

By 1979, when Malcolm Feeley examined New Haven's lower court, vagrancy laws were unconstitutional and defendants had many more legal rights. Nevertheless, the lower-court process had not become significantly more formal—courts were still meting out summary low-level punishments to the poor, the working-class, and the disorderly, a process largely designed to "put an end to bothersome behavior" and to "[subject] the accused . . . to some minimal degree of public accountability." As Feeley writes, "One sad fact of social life is that criminal courts everywhere are populated by the poor and the disadvantaged and the problems that bring them into contact with the criminal court do not vary radically. Indeed, the courts are one of society's primary institutions for managing such people and their continuing problems." A few years later, in 1985, John Irwin characterized the jail—the institution that houses petty offenders—as a means not of controlling dangerous criminals but of "managing the underclass in American society." "Jail was invented," he concluded, "and continues to be operated, in order to manage society's rabble."[18]

More recently, scholars have documented social control impulses at every stage of the low-level justice process. Professor Issa Kohler-Hausmann describes lower courts in New York as "managerial," aimed not so much at determining guilt or imposing convictions as at giving the state a way to keep track of disadvantaged people: "an opportunity to sort and assess people hauled in from policing of disorderly places, seeing over time what sort of people they are, and keeping records of them in the process. [The managerial model] operates on the basis of a presumption of need for social control over the population brought into misdemeanor court." Other scholars have shown how numerous cities use banishment techniques to "move people around," keeping the homeless and the addicted out of gentrified and downtown areas: "[These] new social control techniques allow legal actors to create a new status that does not depend on criminal conviction or even arrest." Many describe stop-and-frisk policing as a form of racial discipline, a way of training African Americans to walk, drive, and behave defensively and to accept various kinds of disrespectful treatment.[19]

In effect, sociology documents the various stratifying functions of the petty-offense process. This book could likewise be read as a kind of global mapping of the many ways that the petty-offense process exerts control over the working poor, people of color, immigrants, the homeless, and other vulnerable groups. Part of that control flows from the extensive personal burdens imposed by the system, including the accumulation of criminal records, the loss of income, jobs, and housing, and all the other consequences of a misdemeanor encounter that shape a person's behavior, options, and place in society. Part of that control flows from the sheer scale of an institution that touches 13 million people every year. Every step of the official process, moreover, imposes its own kind of discipline, from stop-and-frisk to arrest and jail, the economics of bail, and the pressures to plead guilty. The technologies of the modern petty-offense process add new layers of on-going oversight, making it possible to identify, mark, follow, burden, and keep track of people in intrusive and long-lasting ways. The fact that the system routinely convicts the innocent is, among other things, a kind of pernicious social-marking policy—an official decision that notwithstanding the lack of evidence, such people should nevertheless be labeled as criminal, tracked, and punished. The control is also economic. The imposition of fines and fees is not merely a revenue-raising ploy but a way of claiming the resources of the poor and vulnerable to fuel the very system that, ironically, ensures that they remain poor and vulnerable. The same could be said for the overpolicing of black people and black neighborhoods, a long-standing systemic habit of governing people of color through the criminal system in ways that distort their personal, economic, and political trajectories. And in case we thought any of this was new, history offers dramatic examples of how the petty-offense process has been used to label, move, control, displace, and even enslave entire groups and populations for centuries.

Because of its intimate relationship to social disadvantage, the misdemeanor system turns out to be one of the main public institutions through which the United States covertly manages poverty. Typically this is thought to be the job of the welfare state—that network of schools, hospitals, housing, welfare programs, and other vehicles through which the government handles poverty, social disadvantage, and marginal groups. On paper, the criminal system and the welfare state are two separate worlds: one goes after criminals; the other takes care of people who need it. But because crime and poverty in the

United States are inextricable, the two institutions are intimately intertwined. Indeed, as we have seen, the misdemeanor system has become a kind of reverse-welfare program.[20] It disproportionately goes after poor people and makes people poorer. It affirmatively strips people of their resources, imposing fines and fees and curtailing employment and housing options, all the while criminalizing conduct associated with being low-income.

At the same time, sociology tells us that the welfare state itself has become harsher and more like the criminal system. The criminalization of poverty exemplifies the punitive creep identified by Garland and Simon, part of the "culture of control" and one of the ways that we "govern through crime." Police, prosecutors, and probation officers have taken up residence within public schools. Welfare recipients are heavily punished for minor violations of the welfare rules. In public hospitals, poor pregnant women of color have been drug tested and referred for prosecution when they test positive. Urban police sometimes monitor hospitals and emergency rooms for people with outstanding warrants, while ER nurses have been seen allocating and withholding emergency medical treatment depending on whether they think a patient is connected to the criminal system. In all these ways, the social safety net itself has become criminalized, extending the reach of criminal processes and surveillance deep into the economic and personal lives of the most vulnerable.[21]

This creep has deep implications for misdemeanor justice. The tight connection between crime and poverty, between the criminal system and the welfare state, enmeshes the petty-offense process in the long historical battle over the public obligation to and concern for the poor.[22] The wide net of petty-offense enforcement and the heavy-handedness of misdemeanor punishments are as integral to this harsh trajectory as any welfare reform.

The bottom of the pyramid, however, is a sociologically complicated place. Even as the criminal and welfare systems have grown harsher in tandem, criminal institutions quietly perform a lot of classic welfare functions. Services like drug treatment, health care, job training, and housing for the homeless are now often provided as a condition not of poverty or need but of arrest and incarceration, especially for minor offenses. Specialized courts and diversion programs offer health care and job training, police route the homeless into shelters, while probation officers send offenders to drug treatment. Some prosecutors run community programs, while public defenders have long served as de facto social workers for their clients. All of this can get ideologically confusing. In the land of misdemeanors, it is common for lawyers and law enforcement to use punishment as an opportunity to get poor people government benefits, even as welfare providers leverage benefits to get poor people punished.[23]

In all these many ways, the petty-offense process exceeds its boundaries as a criminal justice institution, serving as a vehicle both for giving and taking away wealth, public benefits, and other social resources. Many have asked whether the criminal system in general is the proper public institution to be handling such things. The question is even more pressing with respect to the misdemeanor system in particular, since misdemeanors do so much of this redistributive work for so many.

DEMOCRATIC GOVERNANCE

Criminal justice has always been an important measure of democratic health. "It is generally agreed," writes philosopher Nicola Lacey, "that the humanity, fairness and effectiveness with which governments manage their criminal justice systems is a key index of the state of a democracy."[24] Or as protesters have chanted for decades, "No justice, no peace."

The operations of today's misdemeanor system give rise to some troubling antidemocratic dynamics. By now they will sound familiar. The system is highly stratifying, reducing people's life opportunities and social status based on wealth and race. It covertly taxes the poor. And it empowers local officials to act without accountability or transparency and even in violation of law. Taken together, such dynamics suggest that on top of everything else, the petty-offense process has a democracy problem.

While democracy has no single definition, it does have some basic, well-recognized principles. Broadly speaking, they locate governance authority in the citizenry and thus in responsive public institutions rather than, for example, an elite aristocracy or authoritarian government. If democracy had a bumper sticker, it would read, "Of the people, by the people, for the people." Philosopher Amartya Sen writes that democracy represents a rejection of authoritarianism and an embrace of participatory governance and human equality. Legal philosopher John Rawls similarly conceptualizes democracy as "a fair system of cooperation" in which "citizens [are] free and equal persons" with the ability to "take part in society as equal citizens." Lacey adds, "Adherence to the rule of law and respect for human rights."[25]

These commitments both describe how people in a democracy must be treated—equally and without discrimination or caste—and how government must behave—responsively and without authoritarianism. Such democratic principles have urgent implications for the criminal process because it is inherently coercive, highly discretionary, and historically stratifying. In other words, the very nature of criminal justice poses built-in democratic risks. In *Democracy and the Police*, law professor David Sklansky points out that policing is special because it can both improve and undermine democracy: "The police are both a uniquely powerful weapon against private systems of domination and a uniquely frightening tool of official domination."[26] The founding fathers were so worried about the government's ability to abuse its crime-control authority that they devoted nearly half the Bill of Rights to constraining it.

Democracy also has its downsides. Popular politics are notoriously prone to racism and hot-button policy extremes; they can eclipse the voices of experts, legal professionals, and even the power of legal rules themselves. Many blame American tough-on-crime politics for mass incarceration, the result of politicians ratcheting up anticrime rhetoric in order to win votes. Historian James Whitman warns that "there is . . . an intimate nexus between the politics of mass mobilization . . . and the making of harshness in criminal punishment; . . . a fact that should raise some uncomfortable questions for any of us who like to think of ourselves as committed to the values of democracy." To be sure, this is not true for all social mobilizations—today's Black Lives Matter movement adamantly opposes harsh punishment. But the fear that politicians will sacrifice minority voters and pluralist values as a way of courting majority sentiments is an old one. In the United States, criminal justice has been a prime example of precisely this problem.[27]

The petty-offense process turns out to be the quintessential risky democratic exercise. The misdemeanor system is a core expression of the state's authority that deprives millions of their liberty and property. It addresses many highly contested political issues—money, race, privacy, public order—involving vulnerable populations. It is an influential citizenship regulator, determining who is labeled a criminal and thus restricted from full participation in social, economic, and political life. It does its work in highly local and often unaccountable ways, heavily influenced by each jurisdiction's particular history, politics, budget, and demographics. And it exercises all that coercive, intrusive authority in response to low-level, often harmless, and highly common individual behaviors—not the murders, rapes, and robberies that clearly demand and justify government intervention. All these features should make us worry about whether the petty-offense process is operating in sufficiently accountable and democratic ways.

This worry, of course, has long overshadowed the state's exercise of its general criminal authority. People have argued for decades that the US criminal system is undemocratic, especially with regard to mass incarceration and its racial skew, that it is flawed as a governance mechanism, that its harshness is democratically unjustified.[28] But because the misdemeanor system has been largely left out of that discourse, its specific transgressions have not received the scrutiny they deserve.

Three antidemocratic features of the misdemeanor system merit special attention. First, the petty-offense process officially produces and maintains social inequality on a large scale. Second, it represents an undemocratic form of taxation and the regressive redistribution of wealth. And third, it creates and tolerates informal local authoritarianism. Each argument could fairly command an entire book in its own right—the following are merely opening salvos.

The first and perhaps most obviously antidemocratic feature of misdemeanors is how they create and maintain social inequality. As we have seen, the petty-offense process reinforces economic disadvantage, perpetuates racial stereotypes about black criminality, and generally operates as a massive labeling system for the poor, the working-class, and others without the resources to escape its touch. This is an old democracy problem: all men may be created equal, but they don't stay that way, and persistent social and racial inequality is a challenge for every diverse polity. As constitutional scholar Jack Balkin puts it, "If social hierarchy is a sin to democratic ideals, then democracy always exists in a fallen condition, a penitent perpetually in hope of redemption. Democracies are always unfinished projects; they are always, in some sense, antidemocratic."[29]

Of course, not every social inequality triggers the same democratic concerns. Individual differences flow from a wide array of sources, including natural endowments, the vagaries of the market, personal choices, and luck. But when state action cements inequality, especially along predictable lines of wealth and race, we have a governance problem.[30]

The petty-offense process has not gotten its fair share of attention or blame for American inequality. First and foremost, it deprives millions of vulnerable people of their liberty, the quintessential democratic entitlement. But it does more. It strips people of their money, time, ability to drive, and capacity to work. By marking people of color with permanent records and stigma, it perpetuates old stereotypes and creates new racial burdens. In the age of "crimmigration," the petty-offense process has become a net of exclusion through which noncitizens are intimidated, disciplined, and expelled. The misdemeanor system intimately shapes what it means to be poor, unemployed, homeless, undocumented, or otherwise socially disadvantaged in this country. It should thus take its place alongside other major structural phenomena such as inadequate public schools and the lack of affordable housing as one of the great engines of American social and racial inequality.

The second antidemocratic feature is related to the first. A robust democracy should not let its criminal system moonlight as a regressive tax system and an anti-welfare machine.[31] The covert redistribution of wealth away from the poor under cover of criminalization is inegalitarian in precisely the ways forbidden by democratic principles: it creates and reinforces material inequality, and it does it without taking public responsibility for doing so, while simultaneously undermining other, more publicly accountable governmental functions such as the welfare state and the official tax system.

As a way of raising public revenue, misdemeanor fines and fees are a form of taxation largely untethered from political accountability, a suspicious move to which the founding fathers were particularly sensitive. Indeed, in Federalist No. 10, James Madison worried explicitly about the antidemocratic tendencies of majority factions to impose unfair taxes. "There is, perhaps, no legislative act," he wrote, "in which greater opportunity and temptation are given to a predominant party, to trample on the rules of justice. Every shilling with which they overburden the inferior number, is a shilling saved to their own pockets."[32]

When laundered through the judiciary, taxation raises even greater concerns. It is the job of the courts to interpret and enforce the law, not to decide fiscal policy. As the Conference of State Court Administrators points out, "Courts are not revenue centers." In a political system committed to the separation of powers, the judicial branch is not the appropriate vehicle for such a large-scale redistribution of wealth. Neither are police, sheriffs, court clerks, probation officers, bail bondsmen, or any of the other myriad players who have morphed into revenue collectors throughout the misdemeanor process. Yet each of these players now collects their covert taxes backed up by the state's coercive criminal power to incarcerate and punish, an enforcement power sparingly and parsimoniously allocated to the civil tax-collection system.[33]

As the misdemeanor system strips people of their wealth through criminalization and taxation, it also distorts the workings of the welfare state. First and foremost, it undermines the public commitment to help the needy and to lift the poor out of poverty. The United States spends billions of dollars on education, housing, food stamps, and financial aid in order to make our society more equal. Misdemeanors undermine that work by criminalizing and impoverishing the already poor and depriving them of those very same benefits. On top of that, the misdemeanor process has taken over some of those welfare functions, for example by providing job training, drug and mental health treatment, and other benefits. This takeover is a double-edged sword. On the one hand, it is a much-needed recognition that so many people in the petty-offense process have pressing needs. On the other hand, it obscures the allocation of those benefits—how will we even know if welfare programs are working if they are buried in the criminal process? It also distorts the benefits themselves by making access to food, housing, health care, and employment contingent upon criminalization. The poor should not have to get arrested in order for the state to take their needs seriously. Bottom line, none of this is responsive, transparent governance.

Put another way, the misdemeanor system is making enormously important political decisions for the country outside the established political process. Whether to tax the poor is a bellwether political choice for any democracy. So is establishing the reach and generosity of the social safety net. However we resolve such fundamental issues, the misdemeanor process should not decide them for us covertly or by accident.

Third, the misdemeanor process contradicts democratic principles by quietly tolerating abuses of power by unaccountable local officials. As we have now seen, police, prosecutors, sheriffs, clerks, and judges routinely make decisions in violation of basic legal rules and norms—

including rules contained in the Constitution—without oversight or restraint, decisions that result in people going to jail, getting convicted, and losing their money. While there are plenty of "bad apple" stories in which individual local officials abuse their authority, the problem is structural because the misdemeanor system both incentivizes such abuses and lacks strong mechanisms to prevent and discipline them. This is low-grade, informal authoritarianism: public officials with unchecked authority over the most profound matters of individual liberty and property.[34]

This lack of accountability is a direct result of the misdemeanor system's cultural disregard of rule of law. We have already explored how rule of law is vital to the legitimacy of criminal systems. This is because rule of law is, more generally, a bulwark against official tyranny: Rawls identifies it as one of the "basic liberties" required by a just democracy. Rules are a form of public accountability imposed on the coercive sovereign, a way to restrain the proverbial Leviathan from violating individual liberties.[35] Where the petty-offense process flouts rule of law, it vests unchecked power in local officials. Because the system lacks transparency and other mechanisms of accountability, the phenomenon persists under the radar.

Such lawlessness is not exactly a new problem for criminal justice—it is a risk that comes with giving broad, relatively unregulated discretion to police and prosecutors as our criminal system historically has. Scholars often worry that police and prosecutorial discretion is so broad as to be immune from rule of law constraints; others have made similar points about lower courts.[36] But even law enforcement discretion is not supposed to be absolute. Rather, it is coupled with other kinds of checks and balances and fairness guarantees that are routinely evaded by the misdemeanor process—the adversarial system itself, judicial review, neutral public officials, transparency, and political accountability. These mechanisms, which make official discretion defensible in theory, are often missing from the petty-offense process in practice. Moreover, that unchecked authority is not limited to police and prosecutors but pervades the entire misdemeanor apparatus, from jails and court administrators to clerks and probation officers. That so much of the criminal system operates informally, off the record, subject to the whims of official actors, unbound by the rules of law and procedure established over decades of judicial and public debate is paradigmatically undemocratic.[37]

THE BIG INJUSTICE

The misdemeanor system's violation of legal principles, its spread of inegalitarian social control, and its threat to democratic ideals are each deeply problematic in their own right. But they converge in a particularly tragic sort of injustice: the pervasive risk of wrongful conviction disproportionately aimed at the most vulnerable people. Wrongful minor convictions flow from the structural erosion of basic protections against error and unjust punishment: a lack of due process and defense counsel, inattention to evidence, and a generally cavalier attitude toward guilt and innocence. These protections, however, have always been about far more than accuracy. The Bill of Rights and due process are benefits of citizenship, a floor of dignity and constitutional protection beneath which no member of the community should have to fall. The presumption of innocence is, as one Supreme Court justice put it, a constitutional lesson "about the limits a free society places on its procedures to safeguard the liberty of its citizens."[38] The fact that the bottom of the pyramid is permitted to operate with such open disregard for these legal and democratic entitlements reflects a deep civic disrespect for the millions of Americans who pass through the petty-offense process every year. This is a failure of our democracy.

To put it more concretely, a single police officer's assertion of probable cause is simply not enough to generate a criminal conviction against the wealthy, the favored, or the powerful. Such individuals have at their disposal a wide array of protective devices to check the evidence, enforce the rules, and take advantage of the public adversarial process. This is how robust criminal systems should work: it is *supposed* to take more than a police officer's word to produce a permanent criminal conviction. But for poor, undereducated, black, brown, and other vulnerable people, that's often all it takes. This is undemocratic. It violates basic legal principles. It has vast sociological ramifications. And it is a reminder of the sordid history of the petty-offense process that we glimpsed in the previous chapter, with its legacy of economic and racial oppressions. Green Cottenham, after all, did not commit the crime for which he was arrested.

Through this framework of legal principle, sociological insight, and democratic theory, it becomes clear how many misdemeanor injustices are not anomalies. Rather, they flow intrinsically from the structures of the petty-offense process, the result of weighty institutional decisions and troubling compromises made along the way. They will not be alleviated by tweaking the rules or by superficial reforms that leave the underlying weaknesses in place. The next and last chapter is devoted to fundamentally rethinking the policies and practices of the misdemeanor system in this light.

| 9 |

CHANGE

CHANGE HAPPENS IN THE MISDEMEANOR WORLD ALL the time. It usually begins when someone—often a group of some-ones—decides to think differently. To reframe the status quo as unfair, illegal, expensive, anachronistic, or otherwise unacceptable. And then to do something about it.

In 1980, a coalition of parents decided that the misdemeanor system needed to change. Specifically, they disagreed with the tolerant attitude toward drunk driving, which they believed should count as a more serious offense. In what is now a well-recognized political and legal success story, Mothers Against Drunk Driving (MADD) launched a multidecade campaign that completely transformed how we understand, manage, and punish millions of misdemeanor cases. When MADD began, driving under the influence was often a fine-only civil infraction no weightier than a speeding ticket.[1] Today it is a serious misdemeanor that can trigger heavy punishment and social stigma.

In 1995, at the height of the war on drugs, marijuana possession was illegal in most states for nearly every purpose. Twenty years later, twenty-eight states had legalized marijuana for medical purposes; eight of those states legalized it completely for adults. Yet another thirteen states decriminalized the possession of small amounts for personal use. This radical turnaround was the result of numerous forces, including widespread grassroots advocacy, medical and scientific research, and public education.[2] As a result, this enormous aspect of the misdemeanor process now works very differently than it once did in the majority of states, and the social meaning of conduct once uniformly considered criminal has been thoroughly altered.

More change is in the works. The third-largest jail in America is in the city of Houston in Harris County, Texas. Until 2017, Harris County routinely incarcerated nearly half of the 50,000 people arrested for misdemeanors every year, largely those too poor to make bail. On April 28, 2017, Lee Rosenthal, chief judge of the US District Court for the Southern District of Texas, declared the Harris County misdemeanor bail system unconstitutional. Thousands of people have since been released. Across the country, dozens of other jurisdictions have agreed to eliminate bail schedules, capias warrants, failure-to-pay sentences, and other debtors' prison practices.[3]

Law enforcement, prosecutors, judges, and other officials are starting to speak out against other excesses of the misdemeanor system. In New York, a group of minority police officers sued their own police department, arguing that quotas pressure them to make low-level arrests and issue citations for the wrong reasons. As Officer Edwin Raymond put it, "You don't get recognized and rewarded for helping a homeless person get permanent housing, but you get recognized for arresting them again and again and again."[4]

The CEO of the Association of Prosecuting Attorneys has called the misdemeanor plea system dysfunctional. It is "a significant systemic malfunction," he writes, "which causes an inordinate amount of guilty pleas and threatens individuals, communities, [and] public trust in the judicial system." New York judge Joseph Bellacosa has taken aim at the system's speed: "A system of 'meet 'em, greet 'em, and plead 'em' . . . where overworked defense attorneys actually don't even meet clients before disposition hearings—is a recipe for wrongful convictions."[5]

In Murfreesboro, Tennessee, Sheriff Robert Arnold publicly complained that his jail was overcrowded because Providence Community Corrections, Inc., the private probation company, was overusing incarceration. In the Harris County bail lawsuit, Sheriff Ed Gonzalez switched sides and testified against the county because, as he put it, "when most of the people in my jail are there because they can't afford to bond out, and when those people are disproportionately black and Hispanic, that's not a rational system."[6]

Two leading judicial leadership organizations, the Conference of Chief Justices and the Conference of State Court Administrators, have announced their opposition to the current reliance on fines and fees, stating that "court functions should be funded from the general operating fund of state and local governments to ensure that the judiciary can fulfill its obligation of upholding the Constitution and protecting the individual rights of all citizens." California state senator Bob Hertzberg is blunt about the fact that levying fines and fees is often ineffectual since most people can't pay them: "We're not even getting the dough. How intelligent is that?" he asks. "We're just ruining people's lives."[7]

In sum, people are starting to change their minds about the petty-offense process, how it should work, and what it represents. If you've read this far, then you've been following a long argument about all the ways and reasons we should think differently about misdemeanors. This last chapter distills those insights and broadly considers what might be done in their wake.[8]

CHANGING HOW WE THINK

Misdemeanors invite different thinking about a number of large issues. These include reconsidering what we mean by the "criminal system," what we mean when we talk about criminals and punishment, and whose interests we believe to be at stake throughout the whole endeavor.

PETTY IS IMPORTANT. The first and most important change in thinking about misdemeanors is to appreciate their importance. Petty convictions shape individual lives, families, communities, and the criminal system as a whole. It is time to put to bed the discredited notion that getting a minor conviction is no big deal.

Misdemeanors should also take their rightful conceptual place as central to the broader criminal justice endeavor. Serious crimes will always carry special meaning—they represent both the worst of human behavior and the state's strongest response to it. But felony-centric thinking mistakenly treats serious offenses as the model for how to evaluate the whole criminal justice process, whether it is working, and whether it is fair. Misdemeanors actually do the bulk of the system's work, touch the most people, generate the most convictions, and do so in their own highly specific ways. While law books and popular culture instinctively treat murder and rape as the paradigmatic crimes, with their high-visibility investigations and courtroom drama, the much larger bottom of the pyramid is very different, a nearly invisible world of stop-and-frisk, bail schedules, speedy court proceedings, and debtors' prisons. From this vantage point, the paradigmatic American crimes are jaywalking and disorderly conduct, marijuana possession, driving on a suspended license, and even speeding. While they may never be the subject of an episode of *Law & Order* or *CSI*, these sorts of crimes must be handled right for the system to be truly just.

Giving the lowly misdemeanor its due reorients many of the big structural problems of crime and punishment. Misdemeanor thinking is first and foremost a front-end exercise, a reconsideration of why we run so many people through the criminal system in the first place and why we treat low-level behaviors as criminal instead of managing them in some other, less costly way. Felony thinking, by contrast, is largely concerned with back-end matters of process and punishment because there is little question that bank robbers, kidnappers, and multimillion-dollar embezzlers belong in the criminal system one way or another. They should definitely be handled *as criminals*—the only question is what to do with them. But it is not at all clear that people who commit misdemeanors should be in the criminal system at all, that conviction and punishment are correct responses to loitering or littering, or that jail should follow the failure to pay a fine. Misdemeanor thinking requires us to question not just how we punish but why we have a criminal system in the first place and who belongs in it—matters largely settled in the serious felony context.

MAYBE THEY AREN'T REALLY CRIMINALS. The second step in misdemeanor thinking is to recognize that guilt means something very different at the top and bottom of the pyramid. At the top, when a person is properly convicted of a serious felony, it signifies bad behavior and blameworthiness, a reason to treat them with caution. At the bottom by contrast, the fact that a person is guilty does not necessarily mean any such thing. They may have engaged in entirely blameless, harmless conduct. They may well be innocent and have pled guilty because the process costs were too high. In other words, they may technically be a "criminal"—a person legally convicted of a crime—but without any of the harmful, blameworthy, scary content that the term conveys.

In effect, the concepts of "guilt" and "criminal" and "offender" have been forged in the context of serious offenses. They draw their intuitive meaning and social weight from crimes like murder and rape, and from robust court processes that give us faith in the accuracy of outcomes. They are top-of-the-pyramid terms. The petty-offense system borrows those terms as if it were the same sort of institution—but it isn't. Convictions at the bottom are not produced with the same care and attention to evidence or process; most minor crimes do not carry the same blameworthiness; people obey and disobey minor prohibitions for different reasons than they obey and disobey serious ones.[9] It is sloppy thinking—and increasingly unjustifiable—to label people "criminals," with all the moral and threatening weight of that term, when they have been convicted through the petty-offense process.

THE CURE IS WORSE THAN THE DISEASE. The third step in misdemeanor thinking flows from the second. If people who commit misdemeanors are not all that blameworthy or dangerous, then we are punishing them too much. For too long, the harsh excesses of mass incarceration have made misdemeanor punishments look lenient by comparison. But they are not lenient. The array of consequences—from incarceration to wealth-stripping fines to criminal records that mark and burden people for life—are too crushing to be justified as a response to most of the underlying crimes. The Eighth Amendment prohibits "cruel and unusual punishment," and the Supreme Court has held that "grossly disproportionate" sentences are indeed cruel and unusual.[10] Part of the misdemeanor reorientation is to appreciate just how "grossly disproportionate" misdemeanor punishments have become by measuring the true extent of that punishment in its actual operations, including all the formal and informal burdens that accrue to people convicted of minor offenses. This means accounting not only for legal sentences but also for pretrial detention, fees as well as fines, the costs of bail, immigration implications, the impact of arrest and conviction records, and the wide array of formal and informal civil consequences. In other words, the full extent of the actual grueling punishment entailed by going through the process from beginning to end. That full accounting reveals just how heavy-handed and unjustifiable the systemic response to petty crimes has become and the pressing need to roll it back.

WE ARE ALL PETTY OFFENDERS. The misdemeanor system touches everyone. Wealthy college kids who smoke weed, undocumented laborers who drive over the speed limit, single mothers who live in heavily policed public housing, and prosperous lawyers who drive home after a scotch. To be sure, the system affects these groups differently—some people are less likely to be touched at all, and the impact of a misdemeanor encounter depends heavily on wealth and race—but everybody is potentially exposed to the low-level criminal system. This is just not true of felonies. Very few people in the general population commit serious crimes. But almost everybody commits minor offenses.

Between traffic codes and urban ordinances, it is almost impossible not to. Part of misdemeanor thinking, therefore, is to be inclusive, much more inclusive than the felony-centric "us-them" approach that dominates debates over mass incarceration and serious crime. In the misdemeanor world there is nothing special about offenders. We don't need criminologists to figure out the mystery of why people commit minor crimes—once in a while we all jaywalk, litter, loiter, spit, trespass, act disorderly, and, of course, speed. At the bottom of the pyramid, our neighbors, coworkers, schoolmates, and family members are the offenders.

WITH LIBERTY AND JUSTICE FOR ALL. In his groundbreaking treatise *A Theory of Justice*, philosopher John Rawls proposed a way of figuring out what a fair and just society would look like. Put everyone behind a "veil of ignorance," he said. No one knows who they will be in life—rich, poor, black, white, male, female, good, or bad. From this "original position," ask everyone how the world should work. If nobody knows who they will be beforehand, Rawls reasoned, then they will construct a world that is fair to every sort of person, just to be on the safe side.[11]

Rawls didn't consider misdemeanors, but his thought experiment makes for a nice exercise. Since the misdemeanor system makes potential offenders of us all, it is in everyone's interest that the process work properly. Not just a theoretical, wouldn't-it-be-nice interest but a visceral, there-but-for-the-grace-of-God interest. That shared destiny can help alter what we will tolerate and what we imagine to be just. Mass incarceration, after all, requires an enormous amount of dehumanization—how else could we treat so many people so terribly? Bryan Stevenson is a MacArthur Genius Fellow and a renowned public interest lawyer. "Mass incarceration and extreme punishment in America," he muses, "[are] about how easily we condemn people in this country and the injustice we create when we allow fear, anger, and distance to shape the way we treat the most vulnerable among us."[12] Or as the artist Common rapped in his Emmy-Award-winning song about the criminal system,

We ain't seen as human beings with feelings
Will the U.S. ever be us? Lord willing!
For now we know, the new Jim Crow
They stop, search and arrest our souls.[13]

Misdemeanors' inclusiveness is a potential antidote to the dehumanizing psychology of mass incarceration. In effect, it reduces the distance between us. Chances are high that the process will eventually touch us or our kids or someone else we care about or know. The bigger the system is, the greater our collective interest in its integrity. Accordingly, it had better be fair, just to be on the safe side.

Admittedly it has not always worked this way. History shows a high tolerance for the petty-offense system at its worst, as a vehicle for forced labor, as a way of rounding up the poor, as a way of marking young black men and locking up the vulnerable. In its more mundane operations, the process is allowed to be sloppy, inaccurate, unpredictable, and disrespectful. These are not acceptable modes for a democratic institution, especially one that affects so many. Human beings do not belong behind bars for no good reason. Individuals are not reducible to revenue sources when a cash-strapped government decides it needs some money. Minor transgressions do not authorize the state to run roughshod over the humanity of its subjects. Innocent people should not be punished for things they didn't do. The criminal system is one of our most important collective vehicles for protecting human dignity; it's time that the misdemeanor machine started behaving that way.[14] Every year, 13 million people—along with their families, friends, and all the people who depend on them—need it to be so. Ultimately, we all pay the price when it isn't.

ACCIDENTAL CHANGE: BE CAREFUL WHAT YOU WISH FOR

Before exploring how new ways of thinking might translate into concrete change, it is important to note that none of these criticisms and arguments are completely new and that people have tried to improve the criminal system before with mixed results. It turns out that changing criminal justice is tricky, like a game of whack-a-mole. Ban one practice, another one springs up to take its place. Tweak a rule, institutions adapt to get the same result anyway.[15] The system is enormous and flexible; decision-makers have a lot of discretion and therefore many choices. New rules do not necessarily produce better outcomes. To avoid fixatives and band-aids, the hydraulic forces of the entire process must be taken into account.

Sometimes, for example, making the process more lenient or easier to navigate can have the unintended effect of making the system bigger. This phenomenon is called "net widening," and it happens when reforms designed to soften the impact of criminal encounters also make it easier to instigate them. Common examples include decriminalization, diversion, and community corrections such as probation and drug treatment: they punish people less harshly than incarceration, but they also make it easier to sweep people up in the first place. Each of these reforms makes room for more people in the system. Cases are cheaper and easier to process; they don't fill up expensive jail beds, while people are more likely to accept diversionary or community dispositions instead of going to court to fight it out. Reforms aimed at making the system more lenient can thus paradoxically lead to the punishment of more people. The current scale of mass incarceration and the last thirty years of criminal justice expansion more generally are due in part to this perverse dynamic.

Like so many misdemeanor challenges, this is an old one. In 1985, Stanley Cohen described the criminal system as a "gigantic fishing net . . . cast by an army of different fishermen and fisherwomen working all day and even into the night." Cohen had noticed that the criminal net had co-opted the progressive reforms of the 1970s to make itself bigger and more powerful. Those reforms included decriminalization, diversion, community treatment, and decarceration—basically the same reforms being considered today. By the mid-1980s, things hadn't turned out the way reformers intended. The net swept up more people, many of whom would previously have been left alone. The levels of intervention and control got ratcheted up. In the end, Cohen worried, "The system enlarges itself and becomes more intrusive, subjecting more and newer groups of deviants to the power of the state and increasing the intensity of control directed at former deviants." Other sociologists agreed. An article titled "Wider, Stronger, and Different Nets" showed that diversion programs captured people whose cases might otherwise have been dismissed or never brought in the first place. Probation, halfway houses, and treatment programs accommodated new classes of defendants and created new institutions to manage them. "Widening the net," the article concluded, "describes the nightmare of the benevolent state gone haywire."[16]

These tensions have not gone away. Many commentators have pointed out that drug court—a highly popular diversionary program often credited with resounding, humane successes—is a net widener. Judge Morris Hoffman is a longtime critic. "The very presence of the drug court," he writes, "with its significantly increased capacity for processing cases, has caused police to make arrests in, and prosecutors to file, the kinds of $10 and $20 hand-to-hand drug cases that the system simply would not have bothered with before." Or as Professor Eric Miller puts it, drug courts "'widen the net' by providing the police and prosecutor with a costless alternative to dismissal for those cases that would not go to court." As drug courts proliferate around the country, they show how reforms that do positive work along one dimension can have unintended, even contradictory consequences along another.[17]

A paradigmatic example of this tension is decriminalization—one of the most important misdemeanor reforms. Decriminalization has enormous potential to stem the flow of people into the system, improve public defense, reduce incarceration, ease racial disparities, and save the state money. At the very same time it also has the potential to *increase* the flow of people into the system, undermine due process, harshen punishments, exacerbate racial disparities, and distort economic incentives. It is both promising and threatening, a win-win and a double-edged sword. It thus requires special, detailed consideration.[18]

The most important thing to remember about misdemeanor decriminalization is that it is not legalization. The underlying conduct is still forbidden—we just punish it differently, centrally by eliminating incarceration. The term can be confusing because other areas of law use the terms "decriminalization" and "legalization" interchangeably. When people talk about "decriminalizing" abortion or same-sex intimacy or political speech, they mean that such conduct should be legal and the state should get out of the business of forbidding it.[19] By contrast, there is a long tradition of decriminalizing misdemeanors short of full legalization. In jurisdictions that have decriminalized but not legalized marijuana, for instance, possession is still against the law, even if the consequence is a civil infraction or a fine. Similarly, traffic decriminalization does not authorize people to speed or drive without a license. It just reduces the penalties for engaging in that still-impermissible behavior.

The difference between legalization and decriminalization is enormous. In its historic decision *Griswold v. Connecticut*, for example, the Supreme Court struck down a Connecticut law that made it a crime (a misdemeanor as it happens) for married couples to use contraception. The Court *legalized* the use of contraception, holding that states cannot criminalize such conduct at all because couples have a constitutional right to privacy.[20] Imagine if the Court had merely *decriminalized*. Then married couples could still be given tickets and fines for using birth control. We would not be appeased by the benefit—"at least they won't go to jail"—because decriminalization would have left the offending state intrusion and enforcement apparatus in place.

Misdemeanor decriminalization takes two main forms. The fullest, most robust form occurs when an offense is taken out of the criminal code and reclassified as a civil offense. The conduct remains prohibited, but the consequences are civil in nature, typically the imposition of a fine without the creation of a criminal record. These "infractions," "citations," and "violations" are often compared to getting a traffic ticket. Massachusetts, for example, has decriminalized the first-time offenses of disturbing the peace and operating a vehicle while uninsured or with a suspended license.[21] More commonly, however, legislatures engage in partial decriminalization by simply eliminating jail time as possible punishment for an offense. Such offenses, often referred to as "nonjailable misdemeanors," remain fully criminal. They generate criminal records and all the attendant consequences; you just don't go to jail for them.

The benefits of decriminalization are large. It is an obvious counterweight to three decades of criminal law expansion and mass incarceration. It reduces incarceration and arrest rates. When offenses are converted into civil infractions, this "full" decriminalization eases many of the additional burdens that come with formal criminal convictions. It is an especially promising way of slowing the criminal branding of so many young men of color who tend to get swept up and incarcerated for petty crimes such as marijuana possession, disorderly conduct, and other order-maintenance offenses.

Decriminalization also offers the government financial benefits because of the special legal feature of misdemeanors explained earlier: minor offenses that carry no possibility of jail time do not trigger the Sixth Amendment right to counsel. Accordingly, even "partial" decriminalization (eliminating incarceration as punishment) looks like a kind of win-win. Defendants don't go to jail, while the state saves millions of dollars in defense, prosecution, and jail costs. Because it can negate the constitutional requirement for counsel in hundreds of thousands of cases, decriminalization also promises a much-needed reprieve for the struggling public defense bar. It is for all these kinds of reasons that decriminalization is fairly viewed as a progressive silver bullet.

But decriminalization has a dark side in both its partial and full forms. Nonjailable misdemeanors are still crimes that trigger the usual array of burdens, including arrest, probation and fines, criminal records, and employment consequences. Even civil infractions can still derail a defendant's job, education, and immigration status, while the failure to pay fines can lead to contempt citations and incarceration.

These burdens, moreover, can be imposed on offenders quickly, informally, and without counsel, so that the standard procedural safeguards against wrongful conviction and overpunishment are lessened if not eliminated altogether.

Decriminalization is a well-known "net widener." Because issuing a ticket is a cheap and simple way of charging someone with an offense, it makes it easier to reach more people. Since those people are not entitled to lawyers, they are more likely to plead guilty. The widening net, moreover, is not colorblind: as we've seen in states like Illinois and North Carolina, decriminalization empowers police to stop and cite black men more often, all without the constraints of criminal adjudication or the threat of defense counsel.[22]

Finally, decriminalization makes it easier for the criminal process to engage in regressive taxation. For jurisdictions that rely on fines and fees, decriminalization offers a tempting revenue stream. Without the protections of defense counsel and the other resource constraints of the criminal process, courts and law enforcement are free to mete out fines for decriminalized infractions to an ever-widening population. That, paradoxically, can make decriminalization a kind of regressive economic policy masquerading as progressive penal reform.

The benefits of decriminalization are thus unequally distributed. Decriminalization permits minor offenders to avoid heavier punishments, typically through payment of a fine. Wealthy and otherwise socially secure defendants can exit the system relatively easily because they can pay. But for defendants who can't, decriminalization is not really an authentic exit strategy. Instead, they may well end up being punished in traditionally harsh ways, through onerous debt, long-term supervision, and even incarceration. Indeed, this is true more generally of low-level punishments since small burdens are always more expensive for the socially disadvantaged than they are for the well-off. Fines exert little or no influence over those who can easily pay them, but even small fines can be life-altering events for the poor and underemployed. A monthly meeting with a probation officer is straightforward for someone with a car and a stable job but challenging for an impoverished single parent with no transportation. An infraction or citation record may have little impact on the job prospects of a well-educated white college graduate but can make all the difference to a black candidate already stigmatized by the association between race and crime.

Because decriminalization is conflicted in all these ways, many people do not understand its true significance. Individuals may think that racking up minor decriminalized offenses will have no impact on their records or futures, even though it very likely will. Policymakers may promote decriminalization as an egalitarian and racially healing reform, even though it doesn't always shake out that way. Voters and legislators may embrace decriminalization proposals in lieu of legalization in the mistaken belief that they are equivalent. Ironically, the very promise of decriminalization—to reduce the punishment and stigma associated with criminal convictions—makes sweeping people into the petty-offense system logistically, politically, and psychologically more acceptable.

The conflicted lessons of decriminalization and net widening should be recalled every time a misdemeanor reform is proposed. For example, in response to new pressures to eliminate money bail, some have proposed across-the-board electronic monitoring—for instance, with ankle bracelets—that would permit arrestees to remain free until trial. While such a reform would obviously reduce incarceration, it would also make it easier to impose pretrial restrictions rather than simply releasing individuals on their own recognizance. It would create an enormous class of people under intrusive governmental surveillance that would track them into every place they visit, from churches, synagogues, and mosques to strip clubs, Alcoholics Anonymous meetings, and the homes of their friends and families.[23] And it would expand an already vibrant and powerful industry with a vested economic interest in promoting the intrusion. The point is not necessarily to reject electronic monitoring but to be clear-eyed about its downsides. Progress rarely comes in neat packages.

Indeed, many such misdemeanor reforms can be seen not so much as a commitment to rolling back the enormous petty-offense machinery but as an upgrade: a move to more diffuse and less formal modes of punishment as a way of adapting America's massive criminal apparatus to a new age of resource scarcity and unease about mass incarceration.[24] Think of decriminalization, diversion, and community corrections as "Punishment 2.0," a vast, growing net of formal and informal burdens, intrusions, and stigmatic labels imposed on millions of offenders, even those who never spend a day in jail. These impositions include criminal records and employment stigma, long-term legal debt, surveillance, and a variety of social exclusions, all of which extend the consequences of a minor brush with the criminal system deep into a person's future. Such reforms are not antithetical to the "culture of control" or "governing through crime"; they are just newer, different ways of doing it. As mass incarceration becomes increasingly expensive, discredited, and politically unsustainable, these new kinds of marking, surveillance, and social control are primed to take its place.

Such upgrades are made both possible and attractive by modern advances in surveillance, data collection, and finance. New technologies permit the criminal system to use monitoring, treatment, and economic constraints in lieu of physical restraints and jail. In other words, mass incarceration looks less attractive in part because it is becoming less necessary. In this age of GPS, electronic monitoring, big data, and individual debt, the penal state can potentially track and influence people, monitor their behavior, and take their money, all without the need to lock them up at all. That new digitized Leviathan could be worse in some ways than the old analog one.

LESS IS MORE: CHANGING HOW THE PETTY-OFFENSE SYSTEM WORKS

With these cautionary tales in mind, we can broadly rethink how basic features of the petty-offense system might work. Or more specifically, how to change its most destructive habits: its scale, its harshness, its regressive economics and racial skew, its sloppiness, and its opacity. No single policy reform or court case can change such things. Rather, at each crucial juncture the misdemeanor system must adopt different priorities and mechanisms.[25] The proposals below will sound familiar: they encapsulate the analyses of the previous chapters and reflect many efforts already occurring around the country. The notes include details for those interested in the specifics, but these are not meant to be blueprints or formulas. Rather, these are basic frameworks for structural change and descriptions of how such change might occur.

One way is through litigation. Courts and constitutional litigation are traditional vehicles for social change in this country, and they are already playing an influential role throughout the misdemeanor arena. Dozens of recent lawsuits have successfully challenged the constitutionality of cash bail, debtors' prison, and license-suspension practices, and many jurisdictions have instituted reforms as a result. When a federal judge declared New York's stop-and-frisk practices unconstitutional, it was a bellwether moment for low-level policing. Decades of civil rights advocacy and litigation around the right to counsel have produced not only court victories but a growing bipartisan consensus that the core constitutional right to a lawyer has been woefully underenforced.[26] Other areas are similarly ripe for judicial intervention, from wrongful convictions to racially skewed policing.

But litigation has its limits. The misdemeanor apparatus is highly decentralized, really hundreds of small local systems each operating more or less on their own terms, making them resistant to top-down legal change. Even when a law like loitering or a practice like cash bail is declared unconstitutional in one jurisdiction, there is no guarantee that others will alter course. Moreover, sometimes misdemeanor laws and constitutional rules themselves are the problem since they often permit or even encourage egregious practices. As a result, many misdemeanor changes will of necessity be bottom-up, driven by local residents, advocates, and public officials insisting on new laws and new approaches to criminal justice. The beauty of localism, however, is that it offers enormous room for creativity and experimentation;

each jurisdiction can implement change in its own ways, given its own population, history, needs, and resources. It is an approach consistent with deep features of American federalism. As Justice Louis Brandeis wrote in 1932, "It is one of the happy incidents of the federal system that a single courageous State may, if its citizens choose, serve as a laboratory; and try novel social and economic experiments without risk to the rest of the country."[27] In the misdemeanor world, every police department, prosecutor's office, courthouse, and municipality can launch its own experiment.

A big part of changing the petty-offense system will entail paying closer attention to its true costs. Cost has long been an impediment to certain kinds of criminal reform in general and to misdemeanor reform in particular. It is often thought that stronger procedures, more defense counsel, data collection, and individuated justice are too expensive, especially given the petty nature of the underlying offenses. But many misdemeanor reforms save the state money, especially those that reduce incarceration. Pretrial release is cheaper than holding people on bail. "It makes no sense," observes the Harris County district attorney, "to spend public funds to house misdemeanor offenders in a high-security penal facility when the crimes themselves may not merit jail time." Community service is less expensive than incarcerating people who cannot afford to pay fines and fees. Albuquerque, New Mexico, saved over $600,000 when it stopped jailing homeless people and found them shelter instead. Legalization and decriminalization mean that the state no longer has to pay for defense counsel, prosecutorial resources, or jail. Professor Robert Boruchowitz estimates that increasing misdemeanor diversion and decriminalization alone could save over $1 billion nationwide.[28]

Although the misdemeanor system relies on fines and fees as a source of revenue, doing so is rarely cost-effective because so many people cannot afford to pay. It often costs the government more in the aggregate to arrest, process, and incarcerate the poor than the system will ever be able to collect from them. The city of Milwaukee, Wisconsin, for example, spent $10.2 million over five years to incarcerate 22,000 people for failing to pay $5.7 million in fines. The White House Council of Economic Advisors concluded that "in many cases, the costs of collection may exceed revenues from fines and fees due to the high direct costs of collecting debt and the low rate of collection."[29] Notice that losing money like this does not pose the same kind of problem in murder cases—we do not expect serious felonies to be moneymakers. But the misdemeanor process has expanded the purposes of punishment to include revenue generation, and it often doesn't work.

At the same time, the individual and social costs of misdemeanor overcriminalization are staggering. Society—especially local budgets—bears the cost when millions are incarcerated, impoverished, and rendered jobless by the misdemeanor experience. But individual police, prosecutors, and judges rarely know or weigh the full social costs when they are deciding whether to arrest, prosecute, and punish. Because decision-makers don't have to pay the full costs of their punishment decisions, they punish too much—scholars call this getting a "correctional free lunch." In the misdemeanor context, that free lunch encourages too many arrests, too much incarceration, and imposition of too many fines and fees. Were the officials and institutions of the petty offense process held accountable for the full costs of their decisions, there would be stronger incentives to avoid overpunishment. If prosecutors had to balance jail budgets, for example, or if courts had to identify social services for people with convictions, they might punish fewer people in the first place.[30]

For all these kinds of reasons, the key to strengthening the fairness, accuracy, and efficacy of the misdemeanor system is to make it smaller. The following proposals show how we can shrink the enormous pipeline that routes millions of people into the system; shrink the punitive impact on individuals of going through the process; reduce the incentives to use the misdemeanor system as a covert tax mechanism; and strengthen the constitutional and informational constraints on the process.

1. Fewer People

The misdemeanor system sweeps in too many people for the wrong reasons. The US Supreme Court, among others, has missed this important fact. In Gail Atwater's case, the Court permitted her arrest for a seatbelt violation in part because it didn't think misdemeanors posed much of a national problem. "Surely," reasoned the Court, "the country is not confronting anything like an epidemic of unnecessary minor-offense arrests."[31] Actually, it is.

There are at least three key moments of decision, spigots if you will, that generate the enormous flow of people into the petty-offense process. These spigots are controlled respectively by legislatures, police, and prosecutors. Legislatures decide the number of crimes, police decide the number of arrests, and prosecutors decide the number of cases. Each has plenty of room for change.

First, legislatures can reduce the number of crimes that subject people to criminal charges in the first place through legalization or, where legalization is not feasible, full decriminalization. This process is already in full swing with respect to marijuana; order-maintenance offenses are obvious candidates as well. The Supreme Court has already declared certain forms of order statutes, such as vagrancy, to be unconstitutionally vague, but many remain alive and well on the books, including loitering-type crimes, disorderly conduct, and resisting arrest. Like vagrancy, such crimes come uncomfortably close to criminalizing free speech and other liberties while exacerbating some of the system's worst inequities. Some jurisdictions have already taken up the challenge. Philadelphia has decriminalized disorderly conduct and public drunkenness; disorderly conduct in New York is a noncriminal violation; Massachusetts has decriminalized disorderly conduct and disturbing the peace for first-time offenders. Order-maintenance offenses are especially good candidates for legalization because they are just one set of policing tools in an enormous arsenal; even without them, police retain broad authority to stop and detain anyone posing a threat or suspected of a crime.[32]

Traffic is also an obvious opportunity. Twenty-five states treat some or all forms of speeding as a crime carrying a potential jail sentence. In Georgia, where the entire traffic code is criminal, most traffic violations are classified as misdemeanors carrying up to one year in jail. In 2011, over 1.3 million such cases were filed in Georgia's municipal courts. In such states, decriminalizing the traffic code offers enormous potential for improved efficiency, savings, and fairness. Since 1970, twenty-two states have done so. Some have gone farther. Hawaii undertook a comprehensive review of its noncriminal codes—including traffic—in order to eliminate incarceration for regulatory offenses. As a result, the state decriminalized many agricultural, animal, and conservation as well as transportation offenses.[33]

Legalization and decriminalization retract the punitive arm of the state, but that does not mean they are "soft on crime." Nobody wants a free-for-all, and minor misconduct should not be ignored. But the criminal misdemeanor process has shown itself to be a poor regulator, imposing crushing punishments for behavior that does not deserve it and distorting the social fabric far beyond the seriousness of the antisocial conduct at issue. Legalization and decriminalization are ways of checking the scope of that government intrusiveness, calibrating the means by which we maintain a safe, civilized, and inclusive public sphere. The late Chief Justice William Rehnquist thought that legalization and decriminalization were sensible responses to an overreaching state, particularly in connection with minor offenses like marijuana possession and prostitution. "This approach," he wrote, "falls generally under what might be called the head of individual freedom or 'libertarianism.' . . . It has the great virtue of dealing straightforwardly with the basic issue at stake—whether the conduct in question should or should not be subject to regulation by the government." Even former president Richard Nixon, whom many credit with inventing tough-on-crime politics, supported decriminalization. "We have to find ways to clear the courts of the endless streams of what are termed 'victimless crimes' that get in the way of serious consideration of serious crimes," he told the National Conference on the Judiciary in 1971. "There are more important matters for highly skilled judges and prosecutors than minor traffic offenses, loitering and drunkenness."[34] Legislatures thus have strong reasons as well as numerous tools at their disposal to recalibrate the size of the misdemeanor criminal net.

Second, police can shrink the pipeline by arresting fewer people. Or rather, police can adopt policies that better select who gets arrested and why. As we have seen throughout this book, of the 11 million people arrested in 2015, many were arrested not because they posed a threat but in order to clear a street corner, because they were too poor to pay a fine, or because of internal police promotion policies. Former prosecutor, now law professor Rachel Harmon argues that arrests have been around for so long that their effectiveness has gone largely unquestioned: "Arrest is often unnecessary to achieve our law enforcement goals," she writes, "and we have not yet seriously explored the range of possible alternatives."[35]

This is especially true for misdemeanors. Policing experts conclude that large-scale, indiscriminate misdemeanor arrests are not very good at stopping crime. Criminologists Cynthia Lum and Daniel Nagin argue that police overrely on arrest, using it as a "key metric of success" at the expense of more targeted, proactive, and effective tools such as problem solving and hot spot policing. As do many scholars, Lum and Nagin zero in on broken windows and zero-tolerance policing as particularly ineffective—expensive, high-volume, indiscriminate arrest practices that do not demonstrably reduce crime.[36]

Police can also reduce the flow of people into jails by substituting citations for arrests. The President's Task Force on 21st Century Policing, the American Bar Association, and the Pretrial Justice Institute all recommend greater reliance on citation in lieu of arrest. According to the International Association of Chiefs of Police, "Citation . . . is a good tool to be used to divert nonviolent misdemeanor offenders whom an officer determines are not a public safety risk and who would only increase jail overcrowding." States can also encourage citations. Maryland law, for example, requires police to use citations instead of arrests for all fine-only offenses and for most misdemeanors that carry up to ninety days in jail.[37]

As we've seen, many police departments use arrests and citations to measure officer productivity, imposing formal or informal quotas that determine officers' ability to get raises and promotions. Such personnel policies can force police into making unfair arrests or issuing unnecessary tickets.[38] Eliminating such quotas and pressures would stem the flow of unnecessary and unfounded arrests into the petty-offense system in the first place. The President's Task Force specifically recommended such changes: "Law enforcement agencies and municipalities should refrain from practices requiring officers to issue a predetermined number of tickets, citations, arrests, or summonses, or to initiate investigative contacts with citizens for reasons not directly related to improving public safety, such as generating revenue."[39]

Such proposals are realistic. National arrest levels have gone down over the past decade. Arrests for order-maintenance offenses may also be falling. Although the system remains enormous, it has demonstrated its ability to shrink.[40]

The third major spigot filling up the misdemeanor pipeline is the prosecutorial charging decision. Once a person is arrested, prosecutors decide whether that arrest should be declined or converted into a formal criminal case. Because misdemeanor arrests are easy to make and can occur for all sorts of reasons, this initial screening is an especially vital regulator. Prosecutors should have the time and incentives to screen carefully before those arrests ever enter the formal legal system. Declination rates should be correspondingly high, particularly for offenses related to order maintenance and drug possession whose value often lies primarily in their role as policing tools. While many jurisdictions rely on dismissals later in the process rather than declinations up front, dismissals exact a higher price all around. Prosecutors and defense attorneys still have to manage and negotiate those cases, while defendants remain under pressure to plead guilty and will already have begun to pay a price in time, resources, and fear. Declinations thus provide the strongest upfront protection against bloated dockets, overcriminalization, and wrongful conviction.[41]

Strong declination practices not only keep bad cases out of the system but can improve the integrity of the entire process. For example, the Vera Institute study of Milwaukee, Wisconsin, found that low declination rates in drug-paraphernalia cases were also racially skewed. When the office assigned more experienced attorneys to better train the new prosecutors, declination rates rose, and racial disparities declined. Similarly, a study in Charlotte, North Carolina, revealed that the prosecutors' office was pursuing every single drug arrest against black women. Many of those cases were ultimately dismissed, but not before the women paid the price of going through the criminal process. The office instituted a more vigorous screening process, and declination rates rose overall, including in cases against black women.[42]

A stronger commitment to screening and declinations would bring misdemeanor culture closer to the more rigorous approach accorded felonies at the top of the pyramid. While every jurisdiction is different, serious crimes typically get strong screening; going forward with a homicide case takes evidence and resources. By contrast, drug, public-order, and other low-level offenses often get less screening, not because the cases are stronger but because screeners have less time or less experience.[43] Devoting more resources to declinations would thus acknowledge the importance and impact of misdemeanors in a particularly fruitful way.

Reducing the flow from these three spigots—crimes, arrests, and declinations—could elevate the entire petty-offense process. Having fewer cases in the pipeline would ease the pressures experienced by every player to clear dockets and move cases along and would make more resources available to handle the cases that are left. Those remaining cases would be more substantial and benefit from a greater consensus that they should be in the criminal system in the first place. More broadly, reducing the influx of minor cases could ease the dismissive attitude toward misdemeanors, elevate the stature of the people who incur and handle them, and infuse the entire process with more resources and dignity.

2. Less Jail

The misdemeanor system operates its own version of mass incarceration: it locks people up before conviction, it locks them up during their formal sentences, and it locks them up again when they can't afford to pay their fines and fees. This overuse of jail drives much of the system's harshness and inhumanity; in the words of one leading civil rights lawyer, "Putting a human being in a cage is brutal business."[44] It should be a last resort, not the default, and the default can be changed at each step along the way.

Many jurisdictions are already restricting or eliminating money bail for low-level offenses. A California court called the bail process a "deformity" and a "blight on the system." In 2016 Maryland's attorney general wrote that his state's use of money bail to incarcerate the poor was probably unconstitutional; in 2017 the Maryland Court of Appeals changed the rules to curtail the use of money bail. New Jersey recently eliminated its heavy reliance on cash bail and replaced it with a risk-assessment system. In 2017, bipartisan federal legislation was introduced that would have provided grant money for states to engage in bail reform along these lines. In jurisdictions that have embraced more pretrial release, such as Washington DC and Colorado, people continue to show up to court, and the state has experienced significant savings.[45]

Converting misdemeanors to fine-only offenses—the heart of decriminalization—also reduces incarceration. But the move to financial penalties mostly helps the rich unless jurisdictions also reject the debtors' prison model and stop locking people up to enforce payment. If people cannot pay fines and fees, incarceration is not so much eliminated as postponed. States should thus restrict their courts from using incarceration, including for civil contempt, to enforce the payment of legal financial obligations. Constitutional law already puts limits on locking defendants up when they cannot pay, but state law can go farther. Every state, for example, already bans debtors' prison for civil debt either by constitutional provision or by statute. Such bans could be applied to the civil fees and costs routinely imposed on defendants and to the civil fines associated with decriminalized offenses and many municipal ordinances.[46] In each of these ways—through bail reform, decriminalization, and ending debtors' prison—the misdemeanor system can wean itself off the incarceration cage.

3. Less Punishment

The misdemeanor system punishes people too heavily and in too many ways for minor, common, and often harmless conduct. There are numerous opportunities to roll back this harshness. Decriminalization does it directly by eliminating jail time, while diversion does it indirectly by postponing conviction and giving defendants the chance to avoid a criminal record. Fines can also be lowered, replaced with community-service options, or keyed to individual income.

Diversion is a popular form of leniency that permits defendants to avoid formal convictions by submitting to a period of supervision. When the supervision ends, charges are dismissed. Through diversion, prosecutors can funnel people out of the criminal system even if outright declination or dismissal is inappropriate, so people can keep their records clean. Some drug courts work on a diversion model, providing treatment as well as the opportunity to avoid conviction. The suspended-license diversion program in King County, Washington, has permitted thousands of defendants to keep their licenses, avoid criminal conviction, and pay off their fines, while saving the county over $300,000.[47]

Many jurisdictions are already turning to diversion as an obvious way to shrink the punitive impact of the petty-offense process. The Law Enforcement Assisted Diversion Bureau provides support and training to dozens of offices around the country. But like all reforms, diversion has its challenges. In New York, for example, a diversion marks the defendant's record during the diversion period, so people still sometimes lose their jobs. While most diversion programs promise that defendants will not sustain a permanent record, the realities of commercial data collection and inaccurate databases make such promises hard to keep. As a result, even diversions and dismissals can leave a permanent criminal mark, sometimes unbeknownst to defendants.[48]

Diversion programs, moreover, are not always equally available to rich and poor. A *New York Times* investigation concluded that some prosecutors' offices have turned diversion programs into revenue sources, charging defendants for the opportunity to keep their records clean. Fees for participating in a diversion program can reach $5,000 for a single offense.[49]

While not perfect, diversion remains a central and powerful means for reducing the punitive impact of a misdemeanor charge. Because how and when to charge a crime is a discretionary decision, diversion is largely controlled by the prosecutorial branch. The Association of Prosecuting Attorneys recommends more prosecution-led diversion efforts.[50]

A wider array of institutions has the power and opportunity to ease the impact of fines and fees. Legislatures can lower statutory fines. Courts can evaluate the individual's ability to pay before imposing financial sanctions. Criminal fines can be made interchangeable with community service.[51]

An even deeper commitment to proportionality would be to assess fines based on a defendant's income through the use of so-called day fines. While courts already have the authority to tailor fines to a defendant's ability to pay, they typically impose the flat and therefore regressive fines set by statute. In Europe, by contrast, some countries levy fines that are fixed fractions of a person's daily earnings, punishing rich and poor proportionately to their ability to pay. In a high-profile Finnish case, a wealthy businessman was fined $58,000 for speeding—based on his $7 million annual income. In a few US jurisdictions that experimented with day fines in the 1980s, payment rates often improved, and collection costs decreased. Day fines thus ensure that defendants are punished on the same financial scale rather than over-punishing the poor and letting the rich off the hook.[52]

Fees are different. Unlike fines, which are legal punishment, fees are revenue-generating mechanisms that force a largely impoverished defendant population to subsidize its own punishment. Such fees should be eliminated for the indigent, who by definition cannot pay them. Specifically, indigent defendants should not be charged fees for counsel, diversion, community service, jail, probation, drug testing, electronic monitoring, or any other aspect of their own adjudication and punishment. If a court wants to sentence a person to financial punishment, it should do so openly and honestly by imposing criminal fines, not surreptitiously through hidden costs and fees.[53]

Judges and prosecutors get to decide whether a person will be sentenced to jail, probation, or fines. But the true impact of misdemeanor punishment extends far beyond these legal sentences. The full consequences of a misdemeanor conviction are wide-ranging, from the stigma of a criminal record to license suspensions to the loss of benefits, housing, jobs, and immigration status. Because the criminal system does not control all of those consequences, change must come from many additional sources.

The first sort of damage—the stigma of a criminal record—is arguably both the most nebulous and the most pervasive and therefore the hardest to change. It is widely recognized that criminal records can have a devastating and unfair effect on employment, and jurisdictions are experimenting with various remedies. Laws that "ban the box" prohibit employers from asking applicants about criminal records. Many jurisdictions offer sealing and expungement of records so as to minimize the impact of a conviction on future employment, housing, and credit. Scholars have proposed additional reforms. For example, misdemeanor criminal records for all but the most serious offenses could be routinely expunged after an appropriate waiting period. The juvenile system seals and expunges many of its records so that young people are not burdened by their mistakes for life; similar principles could be applied to petty offenses.[54]

Unfortunately, these kinds of genie-back-in-the-bottle reforms don't work very well. In the modern era of commercial data collection and internet searches, a damaging record, once created, is very difficult to cabin or erase. Employers have easy access to background checks. Sealing and expungement are often ineffective in the face of a massive data-collection industry that scoops up arrest and conviction records as soon as they are generated. In *The Eternal Criminal Record*, James Jacobs concludes that "expunging or sealing criminal records is largely futile." Law professor Jenny Roberts calls expungement and sealing "the giant band-aid."[55] While records should still be expunged, sealed, and regulated, the only certain way to stem their harm is to avoid creating them in the first place. Which takes us back to step one: reducing the number of people swept up into the process and subject to those records to begin with.

Other types of consequences are rooted in law and therefore more amenable to control. Legislatures and courts should stop using license suspensions to enforce debt collection or as supplemental punishment for crimes that are unrelated to dangerous driving. At least one federal court has already declared failure-to-pay license suspensions unconstitutional when people cannot afford to reinstate their licenses, calling the practice destructive and irrational.[56]

The Council of State Governments maintains a database listing nearly 9,000 additional statutory consequences that can kick in following a misdemeanor conviction. For all but the most serious offenses, those should be repealed. Immigration law and policy are largely federal matters, but many state and local governments have agreed not to use traffic and low-level law enforcement as a vehicle for immigration enforcement or deportations.[57] The particularly vicious feedback loop in which a misdemeanor probation violation triggers the loss of welfare benefits should be eliminated. Housing, financial aid, food stamps, and other crucial life resources should not be jeopardized by low-level convictions that typically do not even merit incarceration.

At the end of the day, the most important thing to change is our attitude: stop piling on. For decades, courts and legislators piled new consequences on top of minor convictions without considering—or even knowing—the aggregate effect on individuals or the systemic significance of the practice. Now that we know, it's time to reverse the process.

4. Less Taxation

The misdemeanor process has become a covert mechanism for regressive taxation. Courts, jails, police, public defender and prosecutor offices, and many local governments rely on criminal fines and fees for substantial portions of their revenue. The dynamic is not a stand-alone phenomenon: it is connected to broader state and local fiscal challenges and is also part of the historic underfunding of the public defense bar.[58] But incentivizing government entities to raise funds through criminalization is not just about finding new money—it is a distortion of the criminal process itself.

Severing the linkages between fines, fees, and local budgets would reduce those incentives. The Conference of Chief Justices and the Conference of State Court Administrators recommend that the judiciary be funded from general state funds to ensure its stability and neutrality. The National Center for State Courts, in its recommendations for best court practices, states that "municipal courts should not be deemed revenue generators for cities." Instead, local courts should be funded by general government revenues, fees should be waived for indigent litigants, and judges should never be evaluated based on their ability to generate revenue for a city.[59]

Instead of flowing to individual agencies and cities, fines and fees can go into a general state fund used to support criminal justice institutions and improve the criminal process. The state, in turn, can distribute the revenues more equitably to the institutions that need them, rather than forcing agencies themselves to act as collection entrepreneurs. In Maryland, for example, fines from decriminalized marijuana offenses go into a drug-treatment fund controlled by the Department of Health and Mental Hygiene. In California, Proposition 47 reduced many drug crimes from felonies to misdemeanors; the savings are earmarked for drug treatment. Fines and fees can also be capped. After Ferguson, the state of Missouri passed a law capping the percentage of municipal revenues that can be derived from traffic fines. "Under this bill," said then-governor Jay Nixon, "cops will stop being revenue agents and go back to being cops." Such measures would not entirely eliminate the challenge: as long as the criminal system collects fines and fees, state governments will have incentives to rely on them. But state officials lack the direct control over arrest, prosecution, and punishment that local officials exercise and that causes the most severe conflicts of interest.[60]

5. More Justice

One of the greatest failings of the low-level criminal court environment is its undignified, disrespectful culture of lawlessness. The speedy herding of defendants, the lack of attorney engagement or the straight-up lack of attorneys, routine violations of rules and constitutional principle: these breakdowns convey disrespect for individual defendants and for the rule of law itself. Even something as seemingly trivial as noise can make a difference: observers report that some courts are so loud and crowded that no one can hear what the judge is saying. That is not the public, accountable system of justice contemplated by the founders when they ensconced the right to a public trial in the Constitution.[61]

The National Center for State Courts emphasizes that fairness is not a luxury. "High performing courts are procedurally fair. They treat those who appear before the court with respect, dignity, and understanding. Procedural fairness is not a feel-good, vague ideal; it is a tangible operational philosophy that promotes the highest ideals of justice."[62]

The primary, traditional way of enforcing lawfulness in criminal proceedings is through the Sixth Amendment right to counsel, the right that ensures that "all other rights of the accused are protected." As numerous national reports and investigations have demonstrated, that constitutional right is routinely flouted in lower courts around the country. Judiciaries and state governments must therefore find the resources to provide meaningful counsel to the thousands of defendants who come before lower courts and who are entitled to counsel by law. This includes reducing defender caseloads to American Bar Association–recommended levels of three hundred cases per year; the right to counsel is not satisfied by an overworked lawyer without time or resources.[63]

Under current Supreme Court precedent, defendants facing jail time have the right to a lawyer; defendants who are not incarcerated do not. But this distinction verges on the incoherent in a world where the consequences of a criminal misdemeanor conviction can ruin people's lives even if they never spend a day in jail. Many jurisdictions, including the federal system, recognize that the right to a lawful and fair proceeding should not depend on the ultimate punishment. These jurisdictions provide counsel up front to everyone facing criminal charges, regardless of the sentence.[64] States and localities should move beyond the Supreme Court's outdated assumptions and make counsel available to everyone in misdemeanor court.

But lawyers are not enough. Indeed, if we gave every single misdemeanor defendant an attorney, it would not solve many of the problems we've seen throughout this book. Defense counsel can do nothing about docket size and speed, bail amounts, the pressure on their clients to plead guilty, or courts' reluctance to take time to hear legal issues.[65] Prosecutors wield enormous power over the legality and fairness of misdemeanor proceedings. Doing justice is their job too. Judges are ultimately responsible for ensuring that the rules are honored, that attorneys on both sides have the time and opportunity to raise legal issues, that unrepresented defendants understand their rights and the nature of the proceedings, and that the courtroom is a place where defendants can be confident of respectful treatment.

Calling for more justice is, at the end of the day, a call to every legal player in the drama to treat misdemeanors like they matter. There are, to be sure, many high-performing misdemeanor courtrooms around the country, but in too many others the legal profession has fallen down on the job. Prosecutors always need to screen and exercise their discretion thoughtfully; public defenders always need to be zealous advocates; judges always need to run their courtrooms in lawful, rigorous, and respectful ways. This is the full expression of individuated justice where every legal player contributes to the just adjudication of every single defendant. It might take ten minutes or ten months, but everybody should behave like it matters all along the way.

6. More Information

The criminal system is one of our most important and powerful public institutions. But because the petty-offense process has escaped oversight and scrutiny, the people who pass through it often do not know how it works.[66] Defendants typically do not know their rights, what to expect when they get to court, or the potentially severe consequences of pleading guilty. Onlookers do not know how decisions are being made. Even legal professionals are often working blind. Prosecutors and judges don't know much if anything about defendants or their families. Lawyers and law enforcement may not appreciate how the law affects people's lives or how the system looks from afar. Indeed, many legislators and judges do not realize the enormous and influential scope of the misdemeanor institution and thus the significance of their various decisions to preserve or change it.

This collective ignorance afflicts the entire criminal process but is especially prevalent in the case of misdemeanors. As we saw in Chapter 2, there is no national mechanism for collecting data on low-level courts; data on misdemeanors are scarce, disorganized, and difficult to find. The closest thing to a national accounting is the effort of the National Center for State Courts, to which thirty-three states now voluntarily report their aggregate misdemeanor filings.[67] In states that do not have unified court systems, hundreds of minor courts do not make their caseload data public or may not even collect them at all. Such courts—municipal courts, summary courts, justice courts, mayor's courts—may issue thousands of convictions without public transparency or oversight.

The first step toward lifting the veil from the misdemeanor system is making more information available. States should pass legislation mandating that every court at every level collect, report, and make public their data through a centralized repository. Data should be collected and reported on the most salient and influential aspects of misdemeanor dockets, including the number of cases filed, declinations, dismissals, guilty-plea rates, trial rates, diversionary dispositions, the punishment imposed, whether defendants had counsel, and defendant characteristics such as gender, race, ethnicity, and age.[68] When I asked for this data in December 2016, many states responded that they did not collect this range of information, and several courts told me that they lacked the infrastructure to assemble it. This is the type of data needed to fully understand the workings of the enormous misdemeanor system and its impact on millions of Americans every year.

Just as importantly, those millions of Americans need to know how the system works, what it means, and what can happen to them and their families when they encounter it. Like knowing how to vote, file your taxes, or register your car, understanding misdemeanors is part of the civic knowledge base necessary to survive and thrive in American democracy. I hope that this book will help make that knowledge more accessible.

7. More Engagement

Alec Karakatsanis is the founder of Civil Rights Corps, the organization behind dozens of lawsuits challenging money bail and debtors' prison practices across the country. I asked him why those lawsuits have been so successful. "Virtually everywhere the misdemeanor system is operating in flagrant violation of the Constitution," he explained. "So when you come into court and show that, courts basically have no choice." Then how come it took so long? I asked. Since it's all so clearly unconstitutional, why didn't this change happen years ago? He thought for a minute. "Good question. I think people became desensitized, it was so common, the everyday brutality became normalized. It took a lot of hard work and a lot of bad things to wake people up. [But] once you shook some of the blind faith in what the system was doing, it opened things up. People looked around and said, well wait a second. How can we be doing this to human beings?"[69]

Change is always an uphill battle. But changing the criminal system is particularly challenging because the people who suffer most from its excesses often have the fewest resources to push back. People touched by the criminal process tend to be less wealthy, less educated, and thus less equipped to make the gears of the political process work on their behalf. Criminal defendants are not a popular constituency; many a politician has built their career by being tough on crime. Indeed, the criminal system affirmatively deprives its subjects of their social capital, stripping people of their jobs, money, and other resources, undermining community networks, and otherwise ensuring that the constituencies with the greatest interest in change will have the toughest time getting heard.[70]

But the misdemeanor arena also offers important and inspiring counterexamples. Don't forget that the petty-offense process is very old and that most of its positive change has occurred relatively recently. The forced labor apparatus in the South was dismantled less than one hundred years ago. After centuries of unquestioned authority, vagrancy laws were held unconstitutional as recently as 1972. The right to counsel was firmly extended to misdemeanors in that same year. Today, broken windows and stop-and-frisk policies are being rethought. The future of misdemeanor cash bail is looking shaky. In each of these scenarios, some combination of lawyers, grassroots organizations, poor people, politicians, activists and journalists, police, prosecutors, judges, and sheriffs cooperated to challenge some of the criminal system's most entrenched and persistent injustices.

In other words, change is happening right under our noses, even though much of it remains unsung, veiled by misdemeanors' general obscurity. This inattention is ironic considering the global infamy of the US criminal system. The whole world noticed when the American polity turned against mass incarceration: that bipartisan consensus made international headlines. But there is a quieter, lower-profile consensus gaining steam that the petty-offense process governing the lives of millions of regular Americans should work better, more fairly, in less inegalitarian and racist ways, and closer to how we expect a proper criminal system to behave. It's an exciting moment with enormous possibilities.

Because misdemeanors are so local, moreover, they are good candidates for the impatient. Legal change never occurs at the push of a button, but some kinds take longer than others. It took over twenty years, for example, to reduce the crack-cocaine disparity in the US Sentencing Guidelines.[71] By contrast, even though as of this writing the Harris County bail litigation is far from over, obtaining the court order that resulted in the release of thousands of people from a single jail took only about a year. Municipalities can unilaterally improve their practices whenever they choose, with immediate effect on the lives of local residents. In this sense, misdemeanor change is uniquely accessible. The president of the United States does not control local misdemeanor practices, so it matters less who he or she is. No one needs to wait for Congress, the Department of Justice, or the Supreme Court—regular people can engage their local police, prosecutors, judges, and city councils to do things differently. Seen through this lens, the misdemeanor system is a place of hope.

EPILOGUE

IT WOULDN'T BE PERRY'S FIRST GUN CONVICTION, BUT IT
was about to be mine.[1] Stuck on a long, dark, winding road, Perry
had accidentally driven up to the entrance of a heavily guarded military base. Having no way to turn around, Perry was stopped and
searched by police, who found an illegal weapon in the car. Now
Perry was in federal misdemeanor court with me as his newly minted
public defender. A quiet, lanky man, Perry was clearly resigned to
adding yet another conviction to his lengthy record. But I was push-
ing a Hail Mary argument that the unavoidable encounter had violated his constitutional rights. After all, I argued, the winding road
had prevented Perry from exercising his right to turn around and
avoid the police, effectively depriving him of his Fourth Amendment
protections against search and seizure. The judge had a reputation as
a careful jurist, and he listened thoughtfully, nodding. He called my
arguments "interesting" and "novel." Then he denied my motion to
suppress the gun.

I had failed Perry. Crushed, I began apologizing to him for the loss. But Perry's eyes were shining. "No," he said. "Thank you. That was great. I never had anyone make me a constitutional argument before."

From 2000 until 2003, I worked as an assistant federal public defender in Baltimore, Maryland. As do most public defenders, I trained in misdemeanors—drunk driving, petty theft, driving on a suspended license, trespassing. Like most low-level defendants, my clients were often guilty, trials were occasional, and people mostly pled. Once in a while people went to jail, but probation and fines were more common punishments. In these ways, federal misdemeanor court looked a lot like thousands of low-level courts around the country.

But in vital ways it was completely different. Federal court is the top of the pyramid, there were lots of resources, and everything mattered, even misdemeanors. My misdemeanor caseload consisted of dozens, not hundreds, of cases. I had plenty of time to talk to my clients, investigate, and prepare. Every official player in the courtroom—me, the prosecutor, the judge—had the wherewithal to take each case seriously. My office expected me to litigate zealously when issues arose, and the prosecutors and judges expected that to happen. There were motions and hearings and trials and appeals.

My colleagues in the public defender's office were some of the best lawyers I ever met, and I've met a lot of good lawyers. They were knowledgeable, hardworking, dedicated, occasionally ornery independent thinkers who relished standing up on behalf of the underdog. I learned from them the beauty of the well-litigated case, even the cases we lost (we lost a lot). The misdemeanor prosecutors were top-notch lawyers too and generally thoughtful: they followed the rules, they weren't obsessed with winning (they won a lot), and they cared about fair outcomes. Like me, they were learning their craft.

My first assignment was to cover misdemeanor court on a military base, presided over by a federal magistrate judge (the one who heard Perry's case). The judge was courteous, highly skilled, and rigorous. He listened to everyone and addressed every defendant with respect. I loved practicing law in that courtroom because I knew I could do good work as an attorney and that my clients had a fair shot: legal issues would be aired, facts would be valuable, the equities would be considered. Innocent people stood a strong chance of acquittal (it's never guaranteed). Many of my clients walked out of that courtroom feeling that they had been heard, even when they had just been convicted and sentenced. "That was fair," they often conceded.

I learned the most from my clients. I could not have written this book without them. It turns out that many of them had trained in misdemeanors too, but not in a good way. Their previous experiences in lower state courts had frequently taught them that they were unimportant, that law didn't matter, that outcomes were forgone conclusions. They expected to be thrown in jail, to be punished too harshly, to remain unheard. They taught me the messy calculus of punishment: sometimes going to jail for a few weeks is better than probation for a year if you don't have a car and can't get to appointments with a probation officer. Sometimes, no matter how many jobs you are working, you will never have the money to fix that suspended license. Sometimes it takes the somber gaze of a judge and the quiet seriousness of a courtroom to make you realize that you need help with your drinking. Sometimes, as for Perry, the immediate need to carry a gun to protect yourself from your neighbors is more pressing than the need to avoid a federal gun charge. My clients were smart, scared, thoughtful, reckless, young, old, black, white, Asian, Latino, male, and female. I worked with veterans and students, mechanics and nurses. For the most part, they were entirely regular people who had gotten unlucky or made a bad decision along the way, or both.

These experiences first impressed upon me the wide-ranging significance of misdemeanors. Eventually I moved on to more serious cases like bank robbery and drug dealing, but in some ways the misdemeanors turned out to be just as weighty, sometimes more so. I never won a felony trial, but I won a few misdemeanor ones. I could help my trespassing clients get their lives back on track or make sure they weren't derailed in the first place, but for my bank robbery clients there typically wasn't much I could do. In my brief career as a practicing criminal attorney I only litigated one case that set a significant legal precedent: it was a misdemeanor.

Ironically, in some ways the misdemeanor process was fairer than the felony process. The federal felony system is famed for its astronomical sentences, its coercive plea bargaining dynamics, and especially in drug cases, its racial disparities. Going to trial can mean risking decades of additional punishment. There is, after all, plenty of unfairness at the top of the pyramid, even when the law is working exactly the way it is supposed to. But my misdemeanor clients weren't facing thirty-year sentences. They didn't have to take a deal and plead guilty to avoid years in prison. They could exercise their rights, defend themselves, and have their day in court without sacrificing their entire lives.

It would be naive to think that the whole criminal system could work like that courtroom. After all, the top of the pyramid is expensive; federal courts do not face the crush of cases and resource deprivations that state and local courts do. But much of that positive culture flowed not just from material resources but from the habits and commitments of the legal players involved. Everyone agreed that the people and their cases mattered, and everyone acted that way to the best of their abilities. Of course it wasn't the same as felony practice—on average we spent less time and money on misdemeanors. It wasn't perfect—people were jerks, made mistakes, overreached, and occasionally slacked off. And it wasn't always fair. But in that particular misdemeanor court, I got a glimpse of what justice could look like. The culture was respectful and law-abiding. The commitment to fairness felt alive even when it didn't necessarily prevail.

If there is a moral to this story, to this book, it is that the bottom of the pyramid should work more like the top. It doesn't at the moment because that takes time and money and, above all, an appreciation of the importance of misdemeanors and the dignity of the people who are swept up into the petty-offense process. But there is no principled reason why the bottom couldn't be a better place or why we shouldn't try to make it so. Every year, 13 million Americans deserve at least that much.

APPENDIX

THIS APPENDIX SUMMARIZES THE DATA I COLLECTED ON the size of state misdemeanor dockets in the United States for 2015. To my knowledge, it is the most comprehensive effort of its kind. It offers the fullest, up-to-date estimate of the total size of the 2015 US misdemeanor docket: 13,240,034 criminal filings.

DATA COLLECTION

On December 6, 2016, I sent a records request letter to the Administrative Office of the Court (AOC) for all fifty states and the District of Columbia. The AOC is the state oversight entity responsible for, among other things, collecting data regarding state and local court operations. From each AOC I requested the following data for 2015: total state filings for all misdemeanors, infractions, and violations for all courts; case dispositions (trials, convictions, acquittals, guilty pleas, dismissals, nolle prosequi, declinations, and diversionary dispositions); total filings by type of offense; punishments imposed, including incarcerations, probations, diversionary dispositions, and fines; and total fines assessed and collected. In addition, I specifically requested these data for the following subsets of cases: driving on a suspended license, possession of marijuana, disorderly conduct, loitering, trespassing, and resisting arrest.

Fourteen states sent me some of the data requested.[*] South Carolina and Tennessee denied my request. Eight states did not respond at all, even after follow-up emails.[†] Several states indicated that such data could only be assembled at significant cost. When the bill was a few hundred dollars, I paid for the data. When it was much more, I didn't. The majority of state AOCs responded by directing me to their public websites, which typically housed an annual judicial report. Many (but not all) of those reports provided that state's annual misdemeanor caseload, but those reports and websites rarely contained the other data I requested. Moreover, the information in judicial reports was often partial. Some states do not have unified court systems, which means that there are municipal and other local courts—typically dozens—that do not provide data to the AOC and whose misdemeanor caseloads are therefore not included in state totals. In some of those states, AOC representatives indicated that municipal caseloads could only be obtained, if at all, by calling dozens or sometimes hundreds of municipal courts individually.

I also relied on data from the Court Statistics Project, a joint project of the National Center for State Courts (NCSC) and the Conference of State Court Administrators. The Court Statistics Project is a public, centralized repository of data on state caseloads including misdemeanor caseloads.[‡] Thirty-five states reported 2015 data to the NCSC.[§] Those totals are included in the table below. The NCSC also

---

[*] Arkansas, Connecticut, Florida, Hawaii, Idaho, Kentucky, Michigan, Nebraska, North Carolina, North Dakota, Ohio, Oregon, Texas, and Utah.

[†] Iowa, Louisiana, Mississippi, New Hampshire, Oklahoma, Rhode Island, South Dakota, and Wisconsin.

[‡] "About the Court Statistics Project," Court Statistics Project, http://www.courtstatistics .org [https://perma.cc/V363-VNWV].

[§] Including the District of Columbia. West Virginia and Arkansas previously reported their caseloads to the NCSC; although that data is no longer on the NCSC website, I include it in the table.

estimates misdemeanor filing rates per 100,000 population for each state: those estimates are included in the table.

In addition to NCSC data and the AOC responses, I supplemented the results for each state with data from other sources. These included state judicial annual reports, reports by nonprofit and other independent organizations, local governmental sources, public defender offices, and Google searches—pretty much anything I could think of. For states that did not provide data either to the NCSC or in response to my formal request, I made special efforts to locate statewide data elsewhere. Each of those sources is documented in the footnotes. The table provides both NCSC totals and the totals that I arrived at based on AOC and all other sources. They often differ significantly. Sometimes I found evidence of higher misdemeanor filings. Sometimes I was unable to locate as many filings on the public record as the NCSC totals reflect. Either way, when my totals differed from those reported to the NCSC, I relied on NCSC data to calculate the national total.[*]

For thirteen states for which the NCSC did not have data, I estimate filing rates based on the data that I collected independently and on 2015 census data. For three additional states—Louisiana, Oklahoma, and Tennessee—no statewide filing data were available at all. For those, I used the average filing rate of the other forty-eight states and the District of Columbia (4,124 per 100,000 population) and extrapolated a misdemeanor caseload based on those three states' populations.[†]

---

[*] For five of the states that did not report to the NCSC (Alabama, Colorado, Mississippi, South Dakota, Wyoming), caseload data was available only by fiscal year and not by calendar year. For those states I include caseload data from FY 2015.

[†] The median filing rate for those forty-eight states is 3,228 per 100,000. The 2009 report *Minor Crimes, Massive Waste* used a national median misdemeanor rate of 3,544 to extrapolate a national misdemeanor caseload based on data from twelve states. Robert C. Boruchowitz et al., *Minor Crimes, Massive Waste: The Terrible Toll of America's Broken Misdemeanor Courts* (Washington, DC: National Association of Criminal Defense Lawyers, April 2009), 11. My thanks to Dr. Julianne Ohlander for her assistance with various calculations.

THE EVALUATIVE CHALLENGE

In assembling these data I have tried to be both thorough and conservative. The goal is to provide an accurate sense of the scale of the criminal misdemeanor apparatus, how often states and localities wield their coercive criminal powers through low-level offenses, and how many individuals go through the experience. The task is challenging in part because states categorize and count low-level offenses differently. This lack of uniformity is due to two structural features of the petty-offense process, both of which I discuss in detail in Chapter 2. First, there are assorted offenses with various labels, including "misdemeanors," "infractions," "violations," and "traffic," each of which may have different definitions and features in different states or even jurisdictions within states. Some are jailable; some are fine only; some are labeled "non-criminal" but can still result in punishment and even jail; some, such as speeding, can technically be "criminal misdemeanors" but are nevertheless handled in largely administrative ways by clerks. Traffic codes in particular—both state and local—can be either criminal or civil or a mixture of both and contain both relatively serious offenses, such as DUI or driving on a suspended license, as well as minor violations.

Second, low-level court systems are not unified or consistent. Many states have multiple levels of trial courts—some state, some local—each of which handles, categorizes, and counts low-level offenses in different ways. Of particular note are those states that authorize individual cities to create independent municipal courts to adjudicate local ordinance violations. Those ordinances define offenses, some or all of which may technically be criminal misdemeanors but which can range from traffic offenses to littering to assault. Moreover, at least ten state systems are not unified in the sense that not all local courts report their data to the central state repository; therefore their misdemeanor caseload counts are necessarily partial. Those states are identified in the table.

In light of this definitional chaos, counting state misdemeanors can be a somewhat artful exercise. I handle it as follows. Where states clearly and substantively distinguish between criminal misdemeanors and all other offenses, I adopt their categorizations. Otherwise I make various judgments depending on the data available to me. For example, twenty-five states classify speeding as a crime, and many states categorize all traffic violations as misdemeanors, often carrying potential jail time. Nevertheless, when I have a choice, I exclude speeding and other low-level traffic offenses, such as running a stop sign, from state totals even when they are technically criminal. I do so because they are a class unto themselves, they would swamp the results, and including them would obscure the insights into scale that the narrower count provides. This approach is also consistent with that taken by the states themselves, which typically do not include speeding and other "ordinary traffic" offenses in their misdemeanor totals. Conversely, I include what some states refer to as "serious traffic," namely, driving on a suspended license or without insurance, drunk driving, and other offenses that states often punish harshly and that more closely resemble what most Americans understand to be minor crimes. Again, this is consistent with the approach of most states. I exclude civil ordinance violations that do not carry jail time. As a default, I tend to exclude cases rather than include them, and I document those decisions in the footnotes. As a result, these results understate the scale on which state and local governments wield their criminal powers through the petty-offense process.

I had hoped to obtain a more granular picture of the misdemeanor apparatus but the information I received was too scattered and partial. For example, I asked each state for the racial composition of its misdemeanor population and for various offenses, but most did not provide that information. I asked for the total number of order-maintenance offenses such as disorderly conduct and trespassing, but I rarely got that either. Where states did give me answers to specific questions, I include them in the text.

Above all, I hope that these data—and documenting my efforts and sources in some detail—will support further research. This appendix is a distillation: I am happy to share more information with those who are interested.

TABLE A.1. 2015 STATE MISDEMEANOR CASELOAD DATA

STATE	2015 CASELOAD— NCSC DATA[*][1]	2015 CASELOAD— NON-NCSC SOURCES	FILINGS PER 100,000 POPULATION[†][2]	AOC RESPONSE TO DATA REQUEST	UNIFIED COURT SYSTEM[†]
Alabama	—	**239,150**[3]	4,926	Email with link to website	Yes
Alaska	24,555	25,887[4]	3,325	Email with link to website	Yes
Arizona	486,853	307,435[5]	7,130	Email with link to website	Yes
Arkansas	387,077	403,530[6]	12,997	Spreadsheet	No
California	1,147,794	922,730[7]	2,932	Email with link to website	Yes
Colorado	—	**73,030**[8]	1,340	Email with link to website	No
Connecticut	91,795	96,225[9]	2,556	Spreadsheet	Yes
Delaware	147,160	142,125[10]	15,557	Email with link to website	Yes
District of Columbia	21,231	13,342[11]	3,158	Email with link to website	Yes
Florida	569,661	612,070[12]	2,810	Spreadsheet	Yes
Georgia	299,649	333,383[13]	2,933	Email with link to website	Yes
Hawaii	68,287	64,345[14]	4,770	Spreadsheet	Yes
Idaho	73,756	105,200[15]	4,457	Spreadsheet	Yes
Illinois	246,716	243,707[16]	1,918	Email	Yes
Indiana	146,390	140,161[17]	2,211	Email with link to website	Yes
Iowa	103,067	n/a[18]	3,299	No response	Yes
Kansas	25,945	157,517[19]	891	Email with link to website	Yes
Kentucky	254,505	n/a[20]	5,751	Spreadsheet	Yes
Louisiana	—	**[192,641**[21]**]**	[4,124[22]]	No response	No

[*] A dash in this column indicates that the state did not report to the NCSC, and the corresponding total in the next column is set in bold to indicate that it is included in the final national total.

[†] Where the state reported to the NCSC, this column contains the NCSC estimate. Where there was no NCSC data, I estimate based on the US Census's 2015 state population estimates.

[‡] For the purposes of this table, a unified system is one in which all courts report caseload data to the AOC or other state central judicial authority. In a non-unified system, the AOC does not collect data from all courts.

TABLE A.1. 2015 STATE MISDEMEANOR CASELOAD DATA (CONTINUED)

STATE	2015 CASELOAD— NCSC DATA[*1]	2015 CASELOAD— NON-NCSC SOURCES	FILINGS PER 100,000 POPULATION[†2]	AOC RESPONSE TO DATA REQUEST	UNIFIED COURT SYSTEM[†]
Maine	41,051	n/a[23]	3,088	Email with link to website	Yes
Maryland	252,114	165,281[24]	4,197	Email with link to website	Yes
Massachusetts	157,978	n/a[25]	2,325	Email with no data	Yes
Michigan	—	**491,961[26]**	4,960	Spreadsheet	Yes
Minnesota	151,882	121,007[27]	2,767	Email with link to website	Yes
Mississippi	—	**324,097[28]**	10,841	No response	Yes
Missouri	111,309	116,686[29]	1,830	Email with link to website	Yes
Montana	—	**69,551[30]**	6,738	Email with link to website	Yes
Nebraska	99,388	211,093[31]	5,241	Spreadsheet	Yes
Nevada	131,122	88,346[32]	4,536	Email with link to website	Yes
New Hampshire	30,810	n/a	2,315	No response	Yes
New Jersey	475,830	675,258[33]	5,312	Email with link to website	Yes
New Mexico	46,930	59,111[34]	2,251	Email with link to website	No
New York	—	**332,703[35]**	1,684	Email with link to website	Yes
North Carolina	—	**387,040[36]**	3,856	Spreadsheet	Yes
North Dakota	—	**42,000[37]**	5,549	Spreadsheet	No
Ohio	603,987	**1,054,221[38]**	5,201	Spreadsheet	Yes
Oklahoma	—	**[161,016[39]]**	[4,124[40]]	No response	No
Oregon	—	**50,335[41]**	1,250	Report	No

* A dash in this column indicates that the state did not report to the NCSC, and the corresponding total in the next column is set in bold to indicate that it is included in the final national total.

† Where the state reported to the NCSC, this column contains the NCSC estimate. Where there was no NCSC data, I estimate based on the US Census's 2015 state population estimates.

‡ For the purposes of this table, a unified system is one in which all courts report caseload data to the AOC or other state central judicial authority. In a non-unified system, the AOC does not collect data from all courts.

TABLE A.1. 2015 STATE MISDEMEANOR CASELOAD DATA (CONTINUED)

STATE	2015 CASELOAD— NCSC DATA[*1]	2015 CASELOAD— NON-NCSC SOURCES	FILINGS PER 100,000 POPULATION[†2]	AOC RESPONSE TO DATA REQUEST	UNIFIED COURT SYSTEM[†]
Pennsylvania	285,801	n/a[42]	2,232	Email with link to website	Yes
Rhode Island	24,173	24,173[43]	2,288	No response	Yes
South Carolina	—	**226,979[44]**	4,637	Denied	Yes
South Dakota	—	**20,979[45]**	2,445	No response	Yes
Tennessee	—	**[271,802[46]]**	[4,124[47]]	Denied	No
Texas	2,647,081	2,034,609[48]	9,637	Spreadsheet	Yes
Utah	91,498	110,512[49]	3,054	Spreadsheet	Yes
Vermont	12,831	12,761[50]	2,050	Denied; link to website	Yes
Virginia	—	**579,891[51]**	6,930	Email with link to website	Yes
Washington	193,471	205,264[52]	2,698	Email with link to website	Yes
West Virginia	230,321[53]	230,321[54]	12,489	Report	No
Wisconsin	73,689	81,832[55]	1,277	No response	Yes
Wyoming	—	**21,152[56]**	3,609	Email with link to website	No
SUBTOTALS	9,755,707	**3,484,327[57]**	[4,124] (average)		
NATIONAL TOTAL	13,240,034				

[*] A dash in this column indicates that the state did not report to the NCSC, and the corresponding total in the next column is set in bold to indicate that it is included in the final national total.

[†] Where the state reported to the NCSC, this column contains the NCSC estimate. Where there was no NCSC data, I estimate based on the US Census's 2015 state population estimates.

[‡] For the purposes of this table, a unified system is one in which all courts report caseload data to the AOC or other state central judicial authority. In a non-unified system, the AOC does not collect data from all courts.

NOTES TO TABLE A.1

1. R. Schauffler et al., eds., "Court Statistics Project DataViewer," Court Statistics Project, last modified January 11, 2017, http://www.ncsc.org/Sitecore/Content/Microsites/PopUp/Home /CSP/CSP_Intro [https://perma.cc/EML6-25U3] (accessed December 1, 2016, August 24, 2017, and March 2, 2018).

2. "Annual Estimates of the Resident Population: April 1, 2010 to July 1, 2017," US Census Bureau, December 2017, https://factfinder.census.gov/faces/tableservices/jsf/pages/productview.xhtml?pid=PEP_2017_PEPANNRES&src=pt [https://perma.cc/F3B6-2FKU].

3. *Alabama Unified Judicial System, Fiscal Year 2015, Annual Report and Statistics* (Montgomery: Alabama Administrative Office of Courts 2015), 156, 163, http://www.alacourt.gov/Annual%20Reports/2015AOCAnnualReport.pdf [https://perma.cc/DPA9-T6E5]. Includes district court criminal filings (143,643) and municipal court DUI and nontraffic filings (95,507).

4. *Alaska Court System Annual Report FY 2015* (Anchorage: Alaska Court System, 2015), 125 and Table 5.04, https://public.courts.alaska.gov/web/admin/docs/fy15.pdf [https://perma.cc/6RH2-WCYP]. Includes DUI, driving with a suspended license, and some other serious motor vehicle offenses but not speeding. Alaska designates the vast majority of its traffic offenses as "minor offenses," not misdemeanors.

5. *Limited Jurisdiction Courts: Narrative Summary* (Arizona: Arizona Court Services Division, 2015), 3, http://www.azcourts.gov/Portals/39/2015DR/LJCaseActivity.pdf#page=3 [https://perma.cc/B6LD-V6NN]. The total caseload that Arizona reported to the NCSC appears to include "other traffic," "misdemeanor FTA [failure to appear]," and "traffic FTA." When I included only criminal misdemeanors, serious traffic violations, and DUIs, I arrived at this lower number.

6. Spreadsheet provided by Arkansas Administrative Office of the Court, on file with author. Includes 38,576 local ordinance misdemeanors. Annual statistical reports for 2015 are not yet available on the public website. "Calendar Year 2015 Annual Report," Arkansas Judiciary, https://courts.arkansas.gov/forms-and-publications/annual-reports/calendar-year-2015-annual-report [https://perma.cc/96SF-JQ6L] (accessed March 26, 2018). Some local district courts report only partial data to the state central repository. Diane Robinson, Arkansas Administrative Office of the Courts, email, December 20, 2016, on file with author.

7. *2016 Court Statistics Report: Statewide Caseload Trends 2005–2006 Through 2014–2015* (San Francisco: Judicial Council of California, 2016), 5, 110, and Table 7a, http://www.courts.ca.gov/documents/2016-Court-Statistics-Report.pdf [https://perma.cc/7BUL-S86K]. Includes nontraffic and traffic misdemeanors but not infractions.

8. *Judicial Branch Annual Statistical Report Fiscal Year 2015* (Denver: Colorado Judicial Department, 2015), Table 26, https://www.courts.state.co.us/userfiles/file/Administration/Planning_and_Analysis/Annual_Statistical_Reports/2015/FY2015%20Annual%20Statistical%20Report.pdf [https://perma.cc/38X7-SPSF] (county court filings). This number is incomplete. Colorado has 225 municipal courts, which do not report data to the state judicial data system. *Justice Derailed: A Case Study of Abusive and Unconstitutional Practices in Colorado City Courts* (Denver, CO: American Civil Liberties Union, October 5, 2017), 4, https://aclu-co.org/wp-content/uploads/2017/10/JUSTICE-DERAILED-web.pdf [https://perma.cc/2L87-J3D5]. These courts process thousands of criminal misdemeanors. See, e.g., *Pueblo Municipal Court 2014 Annual Report* (Pueblo, CO: Pueblo Municipal Court, February 27, 2015), 4, https://www.pueblo.us/ArchiveCenter/ViewFile/Item/1334 [https://perma.cc/U5HW-Q5G2] (reporting 4,700 adult criminal cases filed in 2014).

9. Spreadsheet provided by AOC, on file with author.

10. *Annual Report 2015* (Wilmington: Delaware Administrative Office of the Courts, 2015), 34, 40, http://courts.delaware.gov/aoc/annualreports/FY15/doc/AnnualReport2015.pdf [https://perma.cc/PB28-R7VD]. Includes courts of common pleas and justice of the peace courts. In addition, Delaware has six alderman's courts, which are not part of the state judiciary but do report their caseloads to the Administrative Office of the Court. They filed a total of 26,951 civil and criminal cases in 2015. *2015 Annual Report Statistics Information* (Wilmington: Delaware Administrative Office of the Courts, 2015), 71, http://courts.delaware.gov/aoc/annualreports/FY15/doc/2015-Statistical-Report.pdf [https://perma.cc/5Z7T-H5BK].

11. *District of Columbia Courts: Statistical Summary 2015* (Washington, DC: District of Columbia Courts, 2015), 12, https://www.dccourts.gov/sites/default/files/matters-docs/2015-Statistical-Summary.pdf [https://perma.cc/4RPL-XXG3]. New filings and cases only, not pending cases.

12. Spreadsheet provided by AOC, on file with author. Includes 327,793 county court total criminal filings, including municipal ordinances, and 284,277 criminal traffic filings.

13. "Caseload Reports," Judicial Council of Georgia, http://www.georgiacourts.org/content/caseload-reports [https://perma.cc/J56K-AJL7]. Includes cases filed in superior court, state court, magistrate court, and municipal court. Includes serious traffic offenses.

14. Spreadsheet provided by AOC, on file with author. Includes misdemeanors and petty misdemeanors filed in circuit and district court.

15. Spreadsheet provided by AOC, on file with author. Compare *2015 Annual Statistical Report: Idaho Judiciary* (Boise: Idaho Judiciary, 2015), 15, https://isc.idaho.gov/annuals/2015/ISC_Annual_Report_Appendix_2015.pdf [https://perma.cc/AEM3-ZYFJ] (reporting 72,632 Magistrate Division case filings).

16. *Annual Report of the Illinois Courts, Statistics Summary—2015* (Springfield: Administrative Office of the Illinois Courts, 2015), 47, http://www.illinoiscourts.gov/SupremeCourt/AnnualReport/2015/2015_Statistical_Summary.pdf [https://perma.cc/8BCV-Y9DH]. Does not include another 64,987 quasi-criminal ordinance cases. Municipal ordinance violations can carry up to six months' incarceration. 65 Ill. Comp. Stat. § 5/1-2-1.

17. *2015 Indiana Judicial Service Report*, vol. 1: *Judicial Year in Review* (Indianapolis: Office of Judicial Administration, 2015), 71, http://www.in.gov/judiciary/rpts-ijs-2015-judicial-v1-review.pdf [https://perma.cc/TEP6-93DW].

18. The NCSC issued a report on Iowa court workloads in which it reported 172,459 simple misdemeanors and 46,179 aggravated misdemeanors filed in 2015, but that first category appears to include an indeterminate number of traffic offenses. *Iowa Judicial Officer Workload Assessment Study, 2016* (Williamsburg, VA: National Center for State Courts, June 2017), 4, https://www.iowacourts.gov/collections/242/files/428/embedDocument [https://perma.cc/N33R-BRYX].

19. *Annual Report for the Courts of Kansas Fiscal Year 2015* (Topeka: Office of Judicial Administration, 2015), http://web.kscourts.org/stats/15/15%20T%20OF%20C%20for%20web.pdf [https://perma.cc/6RBC-DLSC]. The report documents an annual district court misdemeanor caseload of 14,372 and an additional 69,989 criminal traffic misdemeanors, including DUIs. This does not include traffic infractions such as speeding. Approximately 385 municipal courts separately reported an additional 73,156 criminal filings in 2016 and 72,529 in 2017. *Annual Report of the Kansas Municipal Courts FY 2016* (Topeka: Office of Judicial Administration, 2016), 12, http://www.kscourts.org/Kansas-Courts/Municipal-Courts/FY_2016_MuniCtCaseloadSummaryReport.pdf [https://perma.cc/YPC6-RRA2]; *Annual Report of the Kansas Municipal Courts FY 2017* (Topeka: Office of Judicial Administration, 2017), 12, http://www.kscourts.org/kansas-courts/municipal-courts/MunicipalCaseloadAnnualReport.pdf [https://perma.cc/BWR3-M6UC] (accessed February 28, 2018). I was unable to locate a municipal court caseload report for 2015.

20. Due to a miscommunication, the Kentucky AOC provided me with selected offense breakdowns but not a statewide total caseload.

21. Extrapolated. I was unable to find aggregate caseload statistics for Louisiana. *2015 Annual Report of the Judicial Council of the Supreme Court* (New Orleans: Louisiana Office of Judicial Administration, 2015), https://www.lasc.org/press_room/annual_reports/reports/2015_Annual_Report.pdf [https://perma.cc/6QF5-96B3] (providing misdemeanor caseloads for city and parrish courts but not mayor's and justice of the peace courts).

22. Average state filing rate used to extrapolate state caseload.

23. *Maine Judicial Branch 2015 Annual Report* (Portland: Maine Administrative Office of the Courts, 2015) http://www.courts.maine.gov/reports_pubs/reports/annual_reports/ar2015.pdf [https://perma.cc/SC2H-PEFX]. Does not contain misdemeanor caseloads. In a telephone conversation, a representative of the Maine AOC informed me that the office's computer system was outdated and unable to aggregate misdemeanor data. Notes to author, December 16, 2016.

24. *Maryland Judiciary Annual Statistical Abstract FY 2015* (Annapolis: Maryland Administrative Office of the Courts, 2015), Tables DC-2, DC-4, and DC-5, http://mdcourts.gov/publications/annualreport/reports/2015/fy2015statisticalabstract.pdf [https://perma.cc/RY72-WVH6]. Includes 147,155 criminal filings and 18,126 DWI filings. Criminal filings in Maryland District Courts include some felonies.

25. Massachusetts provides reports on total criminal court caseloads that do not distinguish between misdemeanors and felonies. "Trial Court Case Statistics: A Listing of Case Statistics for Trial Court Departments by Fiscal Year," Mass.gov, http://www.mass.gov/courts/court-info/court -management/case-stats/case-stats-2015-gen.html [https://perma.cc/R2TF-KUGZ] (accessed March 26, 2018).

26. Spreadsheet provided by AOC, on file with author. See also *2015 Annual Statistical Report, Statewide District Court Summary* (Lansing: Michigan Administrative Office of the Courts, 2015), http://courts.mi.gov/education/stats/Caseload/Documents/Caseload/2015/Statewide.pdf [https://perma.cc/BLA2-PWQC] (reporting a total of 498,142 misdemeanor filings).

27. "Annual District Court Statistics," Minnesota Judicial Branch, http://mncourts.gov/help -topics/data-requests/dashboards.aspx [https://perma.cc/5JP9-V9C9]. Includes all nontraffic "minor criminal" filings.

28. Data collected and disseminated by AOC pursuant to Miss. Code Courts § 9-1-46.

29. *Missouri Judicial Report: Supplement Fiscal Year 2015* (Jefferson City: Missouri Administrative Office of the Courts, 2015), Table 16, http://www.courts.mo.gov/file.jsp?id=83240 [https://perma.cc/29WL-5RZ6]. Includes misdemeanor filings in circuit court and alcohol/drug -related traffic filings in the Municipal Division. It does not include an additional 283,905 nontraffic ordinance cases filed in the Municipal Division because that total does not distinguish between civil and criminal filings.

30. *2015 Case Filing Statistical Summary* (Helena: Montana Administrative Office of the Courts, 2015), http://courts.mt.gov/Portals/189/lcourt/stats/2015/CrimViolations.pdf [https:// perma.cc/N35Z-MNFH]. Includes criminal filings (53,181) and local ordinance filings (16,370), but not traffic filings, in all Montana courts of limited jurisdiction. Montana cities appear to define local ordinance violations as criminal misdemeanors. See, e.g., Missoula Municipal Code § 1.20 (all violations of municipal code are misdemeanors punishable by up to $500 fine and six months' imprisonment); City of Whitefish Municipal Code § 1-4-1 (same).

31. Spreadsheet provided by AOC, on file with author. The Nebraska AOC provided several different spreadsheets, some of which stated a total 2015 misdemeanor caseload on the order of 80,000, and others of which described a larger criminal category of misdemeanor, which included over 200,000 misdemeanor filings.

32. *Annual Report of the Nevada Judiciary FY 2015* (Carson City: Nevada Administrative Office of the Courts, 2015), Table 1 (justice and municipal court filings); *Annual Report of the Nevada Judiciary: Fiscal Year 2015 Appendix Tables* (Carson City: Nevada Administrative Office of the Courts, 2015), Tables A2-1, A6-1, A6-2, A8-1, and A8-2, http://nvcourts.gov/Supreme /Reports/Annual_Reports/2015_Annual_Report [https://perma.cc/9Y5Q-PVBB]. While Nevada is technically a non-unified judicial system, local courts do report their caseload data to the Administrative Office of the Court. Rebecca Love Kourlis and Pamela Gagel, "Reinstalling the Courthouse Windows: Using Statistical Data to Promote Judicial Transparency and Accountability in Federal and State Courts," *Villanova Law Review* 53 (2008): 969–970.

33. *Municipal Court Statistics July 2014–June 2015* (Trenton: New Jersey Administrative Office of the Courts, 2015), https://www.judiciary.state.nj.us/assets/stats/munc1506.pdf [https:// perma.cc/9LT9-YNDQ]. Includes municipal court filings of 429,407 disorderly persons and petty disorderly persons, 213,357 other criminal, and 32,494 DWI offenses. See also *Annual Report of the New Jersey Courts 2014–2015* (Trenton: New Jersey Administrative Office of the Courts, 2015), 79, https://www.judiciary.state.nj.us/public/assets/annualreports/AnnualReportCY15_web .pdf [https://perma.cc/YTY2-GFG6].

34. *New Mexico Judiciary Statistical Addendum to the 2015 Annual Report* (Santa Fe: New Mexico Administrative Office of the Courts, 2015), https://www2.nmcourts.gov/newface/annualrp /ar2015/FY2015_Statistical_Addendum.pdf [https://perma.cc/9NG6-QRU7]. Does not include eighty-one municipal courts, which do not report filings to the central state data repository.

35. *New York State Adult Arrests Disposed: Misdemeanors* (New York: New York State Division of Criminal Justice Services, 2015), 5 (332,703 adult misdemeanor dispositions), http:// www.criminaljustice.ny.gov/crimnet/ojsa/dispos/nys.pdf [https://perma.cc/CKF7-T6LJ]. Does not

include 327,306 criminal summons filings in New York City's Criminal Court. *Criminal Court of the City of New York: Annual Report 2015* (New York: New York City Criminal Court, 2015), 7, https://www.nycourts.gov/COURTS/nyc/criminal/2015_crim_crt_ann_rpt_%20062316_fnl2.pdf [https://perma.cc/LPS4-EKFN].

36. *Statistical and Operational Report of the North Carolina Trial Courts* (Raleigh: North Carolina Administrative Office of the Courts, 2015), 3, 6, http://www.nccourts.org /Citizens/SRPlanning/Documents/2014-15_trial_courts_statistical_and_operational_report.pdf [https://perma.cc/4QS7-RT92]. Does not include DWI, which North Carolina categorizes as a "traffic misdemeanor," together with speeding and other low-level traffic violations.

37. Spreadsheet provided by AOC, on file with author. Includes filings from all district courts and sixteen municipal courts. Does not include fifty-seven additional municipal courts that do not use the state case-management system. Letter from Sally Holewa, state court administrator, March 10, 2017, on file with author. See also *North Dakota Court System 2015 Annual Report* (Bismarck: Office of the State Court Administrator, 2015), 17, https://www.ndcourts.gov/court /News/AnnualReport2015.pdf [https://perma.cc/Q7EJ-4TC9] (reporting 21,113 district court misdemeanor filings).

38. Letter from Michael Buenger, administrative director, Supreme Court of Ohio, December 16, 2016, on file with author. Includes 888,178 misdemeanors and 166,043 operating -vehicle-under-the-influence cases. Excludes other traffic offenses. The misdemeanor category includes nonjailable misdemeanors. Totals include reporting from municipal, county, and mayor's courts.

39. Extrapolated. I was unable to locate public caseload data for Oklahoma state courts. Oklahoma also has hundreds of municipal courts, both of record and not of record, which also do not make their caseloads public. "The Oklahoma Court System," Oklahoma State Courts Network, http://www.oscn.net/courts [https://perma.cc/3VBH-6Y6X] (accessed March 27, 2018).

40. Average filing rate.

41. *Oregon Judicial Branch 2015 Annual Report* (Salem: Oregon Judicial Department, 2015), 57, http://www.courts.oregon.gov/about/Documents/2015_AnnualReport%20(6).pdf [https:// perma.cc/VB7Q-394C] (reporting 50,335 misdemeanors filed in circuit courts). See also *Analysis of Charges Filed in State Trial Courts, Calendar Years 2014, 2015 and 1st Half of 2016* (Salem: Oregon Judicial Department, Office of the State Court Administrator, 2016), 1 (reporting 45,880 misdemeanors filed) (report provided by Office of the State Court Administrator, on file with author). Oregon has thirty-two justice courts and many municipal courts, neither of which are included in these reports.

42. *2015 Caseload Statistics of the Unified Judicial System of Pennsylvania* (Harrisburg: Administrative Office of Pennsylvania, 2015), http://www.pacourts.us/assets/files/setting-768/file -6170.pdf?cb=24a86d [https://perma.cc/C45V-VY7B]. Does not provide misdemeanor breakdowns for magisterial courts.

43. *Rhode Island Judiciary 2015 Annual Report* (Providence: State Court Administrator, 2015), 26, https://www.courts.ri.gov/PublicResources/annualreports/PDF/2015.pdf [https://perma.cc/5BL5 -REK9]. Rhode Island has twenty-six municipal courts, which appear to handle mostly traffic.

44. Alisa Smith et al., *Rush to Judgment: How South Carolina's Summary Courts Fail to Protect Constitutional Rights* (Washington, DC: National Association of Criminal Defense Lawyers, 2017), 10, https://www.nacdl.org/RushToJudgement [https://perma.cc/S5P5-HU5C]. Includes criminal and DUI cases; does not include traffic or ordinance cases. Also does not include more serious misdemeanor cases that are heard in the General Sessions Court.

45. *South Dakota Courts: State FY 2015 Annual Statistical Report of the South Dakota Unified Judicial System* (Pierre: Office of the State Court Administrator, November 2015), 3, 11, 13, https://cld.bz/mfuEl6y/22 [https://perma.cc/27MZ-NGK7]. Includes 20,979 Class 1 misdemeanors (punishable by up to one year), which includes DUI cases. There were also 112,323 Class 2 misdemeanors, punishable by up to thirty days and a $500 fine (S.D. Code § 22-6-2). Of those Class 2 misdemeanors, 88,747 were uncontested and processed by the clerks of court. Class 2 misdemeanors, however, appear to be almost entirely speeding or other low-level traffic offenses. See *Class 2 Misdemeanor and Petty Offense Violations and Municipal Ordinance Violations Traffic Violations Summary from 07/01/2014 to 06/20/2015* (Pierre: South Dakota Unified Judicial System,

July 1, 2015), http://www.ujs.sd.gov/uploads/annual/fy2015/FY2015%20Traffic%20Violations .pdf [https://perma.cc/RD35-5K4J] (listing 110,177 traffic violations filed in FY 2015).

46. Extrapolated. See *Annual Report of the Tennessee Judiciary Fiscal Year 2014–2015* (Nashville: Administrative Office of the Courts, 2015), 20, http://www.tncourts.gov/sites/default/files /docs/annual_report_fy2015-1.pdf [https://perma.cc/TPT5-A48T] (reporting statewide criminal court filings without distinguishing between case types); see also *The Need for Standardized Caseload Data in Tennessee Courts* (Nashville: Comptroller of the Treasury, May 2001), i, http://www .comptroller.tn.gov/Repository/RE/judcase2001.pdf [https://perma.cc/X65B-PL7D] (noting that Tennessee does not collect caseload data from its low-level general sessions misdemeanor courts).

47. Average filing rate.

48. Spreadsheet provided by AOC, on file with author. Includes fine-only nontraffic criminal misdemeanors filed in municipal and justice courts. Does not include traffic misdemeanors. See also *Annual Statistical Report for the Texas Judiciary Fiscal Year 2015* (Austin: Office of Court Administration, 2015), http://www.txcourts.gov/media/1308021/2015-ar-statistical-print.pdf [https:// perma.cc/Q2K7-XN4F].

49. Spreadsheet provided by AOC, on file with author. Includes misdemeanors and DUIs. See also *2016 Annual Report to the Community: Courts Taking a Leadership Role in Reform Efforts* (Salt Lake City: Utah Administrative Office of the Courts, 2015), 25, https://www.utcourts.gov /annualreport/2016-CourtsAnnual.pdf [https://perma.cc/NG95-G2LX].

50. *Vermont Judiciary Annual Statistical Report for FY 2015* (Montpelier: Vermont Judiciary, 2015), 24, https://www.vermontjudiciary.org/sites/default/files/documents/FY15_Statistical_Report .pdf [https://perma.cc/6KPV-883B].

51. *2015 Caseload Statistics of the General District Courts* (Richmond: Office of the Executive Secretary, 2015), http://www.courts.state.va.us/courtadmin/aoc/judpln/csi/stats/district/dbr1 _2015.pdf [https://perma.cc/5SFU-Q6YL]. Includes district court general misdemeanors (221,052) and traffic misdemeanors (319,140) but not traffic infractions (1.3 million). Also includes 39,699 circuit court misdemeanor filings. *Virginia State of the Judiciary Report 2015* (Richmond: Office of the Executive Secretary, 2015), 64 and Table 8, www.courts.state.va.us/courtadmin/aoc/judpln /csi/sjr/2015/state_of_the_judiciary_report.pdf [https://perma.cc/RU98-DAZX]. In 2012, Virginia also reported 202,008 misdemeanor "processes" in magistrate courts (not included), where some misdemeanors are resolved. *Virginia 2012 State of the Judiciary Report Magistrates* (Richmond: Office of the Executive Secretary, 2012), http://www.courts.state.va.us/courtadmin/aoc/judpln/csi /stats/mag/mag_caseload_rpt_2012.pdf [https://perma.cc/W8D6-5GXZ].

52. *Courts of Limited Jurisdiction 2015 Annual Caseload Report* (Olympia: Washington Administrative Office of the Courts, 2015), 17, http://www.courts.wa.gov/caseload/content/archive /clj/Annual/2015.pdf [https://perma.cc/JPW3-BN88]. Includes misdemeanor traffic but not traffic infractions.

53. No longer available on the NCSC website. I obtained and printed this data when I visited the NCSC website in December 2016, when it was still available.

54. Spreadsheet provided by the AOC, on file with author. Includes motor vehicle misdemeanors filed in magistrate court. Does not include municipal courts, which do not report to the AOC.

55. *Circuit Court Statistics 2015: Misdemeanor Disposition Summary* (Madison: Wisconsin Administrative Office of the Courts, 2015), https://www.wicourts.gov/publications/statistics/circuit /docs/misdemeanorstate15.pdf [https://perma.cc/ZE6Q-H72W]. Includes 72,623 misdemeanor cases opened in circuit court. Also includes 9,209 DWI cases disposed of in municipal court. *2015 Municipal Statistics Summary* (Madison: Wisconsin Administrative Office of the Courts, 2015), https://www.wicourts.gov/publications/statistics/municipal/docs/caseload15.pdf [https://perma.cc /HBW6-VSHL]. An additional 87,822 nontraffic cases were disposed of in municipal court.

56. *Wyoming Circuit Court Statistics FY 2015* (Cheyenne: Wyoming Administrative Office of the Court, 2015), 4, http://www.courts.state.wy.us/wp-content/uploads/2017/04/CCFY2015 .pdf [https://perma.cc/T9EK-LUYQ]. Total includes DUIs. The Wyoming AOC does not maintain reports for its eighty-two municipal courts.

57. Includes only caseloads for those **bolded** sixteen states that did not report caseloads to the NCSC.

ACKNOWLEDGMENTS

THIS BOOK WAS MADE POSSIBLE BY THE GENEROSITY OF a number of institutions and more people than I can possibly thank here. In 2016, I was honored to receive a fellowship from the John Simon Guggenheim Memorial Foundation. I was fortunate to begin this project at Loyola Law School, Los Angeles, where for years I received extraordinary intellectual, financial, and personal support. I finished the book at the University of California, Irvine School of Law, which has done everything imaginable to help me complete the project. In particular, the UC Irvine staff has been spectacularly helpful: special thanks to Julianne Ohlander, Adelina Tomova, and the library staff. Deshani Senewiratne and Chris Smallwood were excellent research assistants. As I researched this book, administrators and statisticians at various state Administrative Offices of the Court magnanimously shared their time, data, and expertise with me. Prosecutors and public defenders from offices across the country provided unique insights. So did numerous other criminal justice advocates and experts. My agent Sam Stoloff gave great advice. My editor Brian Distelberg believed in the idea of this book from the beginning and devoted countless hours to strengthening the manuscript.

This project has been a long time in the making and many friends and colleagues contributed along the way by reading chapters, opening doors, offering wisdom, and generally helping out at crucial moments. My deepest thanks to Rachel Barkow, Sylvia Brownrigg, Laura Cadra, Seth Davis, Kathy Frey-Balter, Kaaryn Gustafson, Rick Hasen, Alec Karakatsanis, Gerry Leonard, Ingrid Lobet, Mona Lynch, Song Richardson, Dan Richman, Dan Simon, and Bob Weisberg.

In particular, to Brie Clark, Sharon Dolovich, Don Herzog, and Doug NeJaime I owe an unpayable debt. Each took an extraordinary amount of time and energy out of their own endeavors to read and comment on the entire manuscript. The book is much better for their thorough, pointed, and incredibly generous interventions. I am better for their friendships.

I am especially grateful to and for my partner Charles Holland. Not only was he unflaggingly empathetic and enthusiastic about the project, he was always willing to put down his manuscript and help me come up with better words for mine.

As always, this book is dedicated to my son Raphael, who makes everything worthwhile.

NOTES

INTRODUCTION

1. Atwater v. City of Lago Vista, 532 U.S. 318, 346–347, 353, 369–370 (2001); Marcia Coyle, "The Perfect Case," *National Law Journal* (2001): 16.

2. Benjamin Weiser, "Class-Action Lawsuit, Blaming Police Quotas, Takes on Criminal Summonses," *New York Times*, May 17, 2015; Memorandum Opinion, Stinson v. City of New York, No. 10-CV-4228 (RWS), 2017 WL 2985751 (S.D.N.Y. 2017) (approving $75 million settlement); Complaint at 39–40, Stinson v. City of New York, No. 10-CV-4228 (S.D.N.Y. August 31, 2010).

3. The appendix contains state-by-state misdemeanor filing data. More than 13 million total misdemeanor cases were filed in 2015, but some could have involved the same people passing through the system more than once.

4. Argersinger v. Hamlin, 407 U.S. 25, 34–35 (1972) (internal quotations and citations omitted).

5. Diane DePietropaolo Price, *Summary Injustice: A Look at Constitutional Deficiencies in South Carolina's Summary Courts* (Washington, DC: National Association of Criminal Defense Lawyers and American Civil Liberties Union, 2016), 8. The report refers to Grandma G as "SG."

6. Alisa Smith and Sean Maddan, *Three-Minute Justice: Haste and Waste in Florida's Misdemeanor Courts* (Washington, DC: National Association of Criminal Defense Lawyers, July 2011), 15; David Koon, "'Million-Dollar Thursday': A Visit to Sherwood's Hot Check Court," *Arkansas Times*, August 25, 2016; Complaint at 14, Dade v. City of Sherwood, Arkansas, No. 4:16-CV-602 (E.D. Ark., August 23, 2016); *Public Safety—Municipal Courts: A Report on St. Louis County Municipal Courts* (St.

Louis, MO: Better Together, October 2014), 3, 33–34, http://www.bettertogetherstl.com/studies/public-safety/municipal-courts-report [https://perma.cc/6R5T-FDBC].

7. William Glaberson, "How a Reviled Court System Has Outlasted Critics," *New York Times*, September 27, 2006; Alisa Smith et al., *Rush to Judgment: How South Carolina's Summary Courts Fail to Protect Constitutional Rights* (Washington, DC: National Association of Criminal Defense Lawyers, 2017), 16–19. The Supreme Court upheld the constitutionality of nonlawyer judges in North v. Russell, 427 U.S. 328 (1976).

8. Robert C. Boruchowitz et al., *Minor Crimes, Massive Waste: The Terrible Toll of America's Broken Misdemeanor Courts* (Washington, DC: National Association of Criminal Defense Lawyers, April 2009), 21–22.

9. "2015 Statewide Misdemeanor Bench Trials and Rates" and "2015 Statewide Misdemeanor Jury Trials and Rates," *2015 Criminal Caseloads—Trial Courts* (Williamsburg, VA: National Center for State Courts, Court Statistics Project, 2015) (documenting state misdemeanor bench and jury trial rates of 2 percent or less), http://www.ncsc.org/Sitecore/Content/Microsites/PopUp/Home/CSP/CSP_Criminal [https://perma.cc/YR4U-PWDH].

10. Eve Brensike Primus, "Our Broken Misdemeanor System: Its Problems and Some Potential Solutions," *Southern California Law Review Postscript* 85 (2012): 81.

11. Robert L. Spangenberg et al., *Contracting for Indigent Defense Services: A Special Report* (Washington, DC: Spangenberg Group, April 2000), 1.

12. Smith et al., *Rush to Judgment*, 17–19.

13. *In for a Penny: The Rise of America's New Debtors' Prisons* (Washington, DC: American Civil Liberties Union, October 2010), 29–30.

14. *Investigation of the Baltimore City Police Department* (US Department of Justice, Civil Rights Division, 2016), 37–38.

15. Alexandra Natapoff, "The Penal Pyramid," in *The New Criminal Justice Thinking*, ed. Sharon Dolovich and Alexandra Natapoff (New York: New York University Press, 2017), 71–98. On federal misdemeanor representation, see 18 U.S.C. § 3006A (providing counsel for misdemeanors); Erica J. Hashimoto, "The Price of Misdemeanor Representation," *William & Mary Law Review* 49 (2007): 461 (on federal misdemeanor practice).

16. The serious felony machinery, for example, is notorious for its coercively long sentences, racial disparities, and dehumanizing harshness, much of which is consistent with existing criminal law. That unfairness is countered but not cured by good lawyering. Bryan Stevenson, *Just Mercy: A Story of Justice and Redemption* (New York: Spiegel & Grau, 2014), 15; David Cole, *No Equal Justice: Race and Class in the American Criminal Justice System* (New York: New Press, 1999).

17. Explored in Chapter 5 ("Money"). "The New Debtors' Prison: If You Are Poor, Don't Get Caught Speeding," *The Economist*, November 16, 2013.

18. According to a 2016 civil rights lawsuit filed by the American Civil Liberties Union and the Lawyers Committee for Civil Rights. Complaint, at 16, 25, Dade v. City of Sherwood, No. 4:16-CV-602 (E.D. Ark., August 23, 2016). See also Alex Campbell and Kendall Taggart, "The Ticket Machine," *BuzzFeed*, January 26, 2016 (describing Port Arthur ticketing practices), https://www.buzzfeed.com/alexcampbell/the-ticket-machine?utm_term=.ylxKPlzw9#.oqxPYxwJK [https://perma.cc/GAJ6-3962].

19. See Chapter 7 ("History"); Douglas A. Blackmon, *Slavery by Another Name: The Re-enslavement of Black Americans from the Civil War to World War II* (New York: Doubleday Publishing Group, 2009).

20. The system's racial disparities and implications are explored at length in Chapter 6 ("Race"). The juvenile system similarly sweeps in young people of color. Tamar R. Birckhead, "The Racialization of Juvenile Justice and the Role of the Defense Attorney," *Boston College Law Review* 58 (2017): 379. See also *The War on Marijuana in Black and White* (New York: American Civil Liberties Union, June 2013), 4 (describing Chicago enforcement disparities); Anita Chabria et al., "'Racial Profiling'? Jaywalking Tickets Disproportionately Given to Black People in Sacramento," *Sacramento Bee*, April 16, 2017, http://www.sacbee.com/news/local/crime/article144743834.html [https://perma.cc/5D3P-9D3Q].

21. Chapter 8 ("Justice") discusses at length how the criminal process has historically performed numerous social and political functions.

22. Boruchowitz et al., *Minor Crimes*, 11 (2009 report). A forthcoming law review article also estimates a national docket of approximately 13 million based on some but not all of the same data. Megan Stevenson and Sandra Mayson, "The Scale of Misdemeanor Justice," *Boston University Law Review* 98 (forthcoming 2018), draft available at https://papers.ssrn.com/sol3/papers.cfm?abstract_id=3146057. The National Center for State Courts (NCSC) reported approximately 2.7 million felony criminal filings for thirty-nine states in 2015 with an average filing rate of 1,083 per 100,000 population, which would translate into approximately 3.5 million cases filed nationwide. "Statewide Felony Caseloads and Rates," in *2015 Criminal Caseloads—Trial Courts* (Williamsburg, VA: NCSC, Court Statistics Project, 2015), http://www.ncsc.org/Sitecore/Content/Microsites/PopUp/Home/CSP/CSP_Intro [https://perma.cc/5B4Z-V7B9].

23. Malcolm M. Feeley, *The Process Is the Punishment: Handling Cases in a Lower Criminal Court* (1979; rpt. New York: Russell Sage Foundation, 1992), 5–9 (discussing the history of study of low-level courts).

24. Alexandra Natapoff, "Misdemeanors," *Southern California Law Review* 85 (2012); Alexandra Natapoff, "Aggregation and Urban Misdemeanors," *Fordham Urban Law Journal* 40 (2013); Alexandra Natapoff, "Gideon Skepticism," *Washington and Lee Law Review* 70 (2013); Alexandra Natapoff, "Misdemeanors," *Annual Review of Law and Social Science* 11 (2015); Alexandra Natapoff, "Gideon's Servants and the Criminalization of Poverty," *Ohio State Journal of Criminal Law* 12 (2015); Alexandra Natapoff, "Misdemeanor Decriminalization," *Vanderbilt Law Review* 68 (2015); Alexandra Natapoff, "Criminal Misdemeanor Theory and Practice," in *Oxford Handbook of Criminal Law*, ed. Markus Dubber and Tatjana Hörnle (Oxford: Oxford University Press, 2016); Alexandra Natapoff, "Negotiating Accuracy: DNA in the Age of Plea Bargaining," in *Wrongful Convictions and the DNA Revolution: Twenty-Five Years of Freeing the Innocent*, ed. Daniel Medwed (Cambridge: Cambridge University Press, 2017); Alexandra Natapoff, "Misdemeanors," in *Reforming Criminal Justice*, ed. Erik Luna (Phoenix: Arizona State University, 2017), 1:71–98; Alexandra Natapoff, "A Stop Is Just a Stop: Terry's Formalism," *Ohio State Journal of Criminal Law* 15 (2017); Natapoff, "The Penal Pyramid."

25. Tracey L. Meares and Dan M. Kahan, *Urgent Times: Policing and Rights in Inner-City Communities* (Boston: Beacon Press, 1999) (on balancing crime control

and democracy in low-income communities of color); Alexandra Natapoff, "Underenforcement," *Fordham Law Review* 75 (2006): 1715–1775 (on policing as a valuable public entitlement and the symbiotic relationship between over- and underenforcement). The relationship between over- and underenforcement is discussed in Chapter 6 ("Race").

26. Griswold v. Connecticut, 381 U.S. 479 (1965); Lawrence v. Texas, 539 U.S. 558 (2003); Ruth Bader Ginsburg, "Remarks on Women's Progress in the Legal Profession in the United States," *Tulsa Law Journal* 33 (1997): 18.

27. Some accounts, for example, are taken from legal documents filed in recent lawsuits and may still be in dispute.

CHAPTER 1: IMPACT

1. Duncan v. Louisiana, 391 U.S. 145 (1968); Scott v. Illinois, 440 U.S. 367 (1979).

2. Nick Pinto, "The Bail Trap," *New York Times*, August 13, 2015.

3. Danielle Kaeble and Lauren Glaze, *Correctional Populations in the United States, 2015* (Washington, DC: Bureau of Justice Statistics, December 2016), 2; Todd D. Minton and Zhen Zeng, *Jail Inmates in 2015* (Washington, DC: Bureau of Justice Statistics, December 2016), 1, 4 (27 percent of jail inmates held for misdemeanors regardless of conviction status); Todd D. Minton and Zhen Zeng, *Jail Inmates at Midyear 2014* (Washington, DC: Bureau of Justice Statistics, June 2015), 1–4; Christian Henrichson et al., *The Price of Jails: Measuring the Taxpayer Cost of Local Incarceration* (New York: Vera Institute of Justice, May 2015), 7; Ram Subramanian et al., *Incarceration's Front Door: The Misuse of Jails in America* (New York: Vera Institute of Justice, February 2015), 5 (in New York 50 percent of cases involving jail were for misdemeanors).

4. Doris James, *Special Report: Profile of Jail Inmates, 2002* (Washington, DC: Bureau of Justice Statistics, 2004).

5. John Gibbons and Nicholas de B. Katzenbach, *Confronting Confinement: A Report of the Commission on Safety and Abuse in America's Prisons* (New York: Vera Institute of Justice, 2006), 6; Sharon Dolovich, "Two Models of the Prison: Accidental Humanity and Hypermasculinity in the L.A. County Jail," *Journal of Criminal Law and Criminology* 102, no. 4 (2012) (describing special jail unit designed to protect gay and transgender inmates that created a less violent, more humane subculture within the larger jail); Jonathan Abel, "Staph Infection Sends Pinellas Jail Inmate into Coma," *Tampa Bay Times*, February 27, 2008; "Presumed Innocent, Found Dead: Counting Jail Deaths in the Year Since Sandra Bland's Death," *Huffington Post*, 2016, http://data.huffingtonpost.com/2016/jail-deaths/landing [https://perma.cc/8FG8-SH2S].

6. Christopher T. Lowenkamp et al., *The Hidden Costs of Pretrial Detention* (Houston, TX: Laura and John Arnold Foundation, 2013); Megan Comfort, "A Twenty-Hour-a-Day Job: The Impact of Frequent Low-Level Criminal Justice Involvement on Family Life," *Annals of the American Academy of Political and Social Science* 665, no. 1 (2016): 67–68; David Murphey and P. Mae Cooper, *Parents Behind*

Bars: What Happens to Their Children? (Bethesda, MD: Child Trends, October 2015); Hon. Marguerite D. Downing, "Barriers to Reunification for Incarcerated Parents—a Judicial Perspective," *Family Court Review* 50, no. 1 (2012): 71; Michael Pinard and Anthony C. Thompson, "Offender Reentry and the Collateral Consequences of Criminal Convictions: An Introduction," *N.Y.U. Review of Law and Social Change* 30 (2006): 599–600; Ann Cammett, "Expanding Collateral Sanctions: The Hidden Costs of Aggressive Child Support Enforcement Against Incarcerated Parents," *Georgetown Journal on Poverty Law and Policy* 13, no. 2 (2006): 328–331.

7. Shaila Dewan, "Probation May Sound Light, but Punishments Can Land Hard," *New York Times*, August 2, 2015.

8. Danielle Kaeble and Thomas P. Bonczar, *Probation and Parole in the United States, 2015* (Washington, DC: Bureau of Justice Statistics, December 2016), 5; Michelle S. Phelps, "Mass Probation: Toward a More Robust Theory of State Variation in Punishment," *Punishment & Society* 19, no. 1 (2017): 59; Fiona Doherty, "Obey All Laws and Be Good: Probation and the Meaning of Recidivism," *Georgetown Law Journal* 104, no. 2 (2016): 340 (as much as 80 percent of misdemeanor convictions result in probation).

9. Michelle S. Phelps, "The Paradox of Probation: Community Supervision in the Age of Mass Incarceration," *Law & Policy* 35, no. 1–2 (2013): 51; Dewan, "Probation May Sound Light."

10. Ken Armstrong, "The Woman Who Spent Six Years Fighting a Traffic Stop," Marshall Project, August 10, 2015, https://www.themarshallproject.org/2015/08/10/the woman-who-spent-six-years-fighting-a-traffic-stop [https://perma.cc/C7PY-Z6UF].

11. *Not Just a Ferguson Problem: How Traffic Courts Drive Inequality in California* (San Francisco: Lawyers Committee for Civil Rights et al., 2015), 4, http://www.lccr.com/wp-content/uploads/Not-Just-a-Ferguson-Problem-How-Traffic-Courts-Drive-Inequality-in-California-4.20.15.pdf [https://perma.cc/D4BV-FH5Z]; Beth A. Colgan, "Reviving the Excessive Fines Clause," *California Law Review* 102 (2014): 277–350.

12. *Not Just a Ferguson Problem*, 10. The Supreme Court recently decided that the state cannot keep court costs and fees if the defendant is ultimately found innocent. Nelson v. Colorado, 137 S. Ct. 1249, 1251–1252 (2017).

13. Utah v. Strieff, 136 S. Ct. 2056, 2068 (2016) (Sotomayor, J., dissenting).

14. *Investigation of the Ferguson Police Department* (Washington, DC: US Department of Justice, Civil Rights Division, 2015), 55; Kendall Taggart and Alex Campbell, "In Texas It's a Crime to Be Poor," *BuzzFeed*, October 5, 2017, https://www.buzzfeed.com/kendalltaggart/in-texas-its-a-crime-to-be-poor?utm_term=.qxRWR5zQ4#.ghY50Ldlk [https://perma.cc/529Q-PBEN]; Joseph Shapiro, "As Court Fees Rise, the Poor Are Paying the Price," National Public Radio, May 19, 2014, https://www.npr.org/2014/05/19/312158516/increasing-court-fees-punish-the-poor [https://perma.cc/9MSP-8R2W] (accessed January 26, 2018); Respondent's Brief, Utah v. Strieff, No. 14-1373 (January 22, 2016), 5; Radley Balko, "How Municipalities in St. Louis County, Mo., Profit from Poverty," *Washington Post*, September 3, 2014.

15. *Investigation of the Ferguson Police Department*, 47, 55; Herring v. United States, 555 U.S. 135, 155 (2009) (Ginsburg, J., dissenting).

16. Michelle Natividad Rodriguez and Maurice Emsellem, *65 Million "Need Not Apply": The Case for Reforming Criminal Background Checks for Employment* (New York: National Employment Law Project, March 2011).

17. Rodriguez and Emsellem, *65 Million*, 4.

18. James B. Jacobs, *The Eternal Criminal Record* (Cambridge, MA: Harvard University Press, 2015), 1 (estimating that 20 million Americans have felony records); Joe Palazzolo, "Criminal Records Haunt Hiring Initiative: Insurance Background Checks Thwart Laws Aimed at Giving Second Chance to Ex-Offenders," *Wall Street Journal*, July 12, 2015.

19. Jenny Roberts, "Why Misdemeanors Matter: Defining Effective Advocacy in the Lower Criminal Courts," *U.C. Davis Law Review* 45 (2001): 300.

20. SEARCH et al., *Report of the National Task Force on the Commercial Sale of Criminal Justice Record Information* (Sacramento, CA: National Consortium for Justice Information and Statistics, 2005); Jacobs, *Eternal Criminal Record*, 4.

21. SEARCH et al., *Report of the National Task force*, 76 (internal quotation marks omitted).

22. Jacobs, *Eternal Criminal Record*, 36–37; Elizabeth E. Joh, "Should Arrestee DNA Databases Extend to Misdemeanors?," *Journal of Recent Advances in DNA & Gene Sequences* 8, no. 2 (2015): 2; 34 U.S.C. § 40702 (federal DNA collection statute); Andrea Roth, "Maryland v. King and the Wonderful, Horrible DNA Revolution in Law Enforcement," *Ohio State Journal of Criminal Law* 11 (2013): 301–303 (describing potential consequences of being in a DNA database); Kimberly Edds, "Rackauckas Gets $1.38 Million for 'Spit and Acquit,'" *Orange County Register*, December 16, 2010; Stephen Mercer and Jessica Gabel, "Shadow Dwellers: The Underregulated World of State and Local DNA Databases," *NYU Annual Survey of American Law* 69 (2014); Sarah Gannett, "Brief for the National Association of Federal Defenders as Amicus Curiae Supporting Respondent," Maryland v. King, No. 12-207 (February 1, 2013), 20.

23. 42 U.S.C. § 608(a)(9)(A) (forbidding assistance to "any individual who is violating a condition of probation"); Rebekah Diller et al., *Criminal Justice Debt: A Barrier to Reentry* (New York: Brennan Center for Justice, 2010), 28, notes 202–204; 21 U.S.C. § 862.

24. *The War on Marijuana in Black and White* (New York: American Civil Liberties Union, 2013), 82–84.

25. "National Inventory of Collateral Consequences of Conviction," Council of State Governments, https://niccc.csgjusticecenter.org/search [https://perma.cc/52VT -3DPB] (accessed January 27, 2018).

26. Michael Pinard, "Collateral Consequences of Criminal Convictions: Confronting Issues of Race and Dignity," *N.Y.U. Law Review* 85 (2010): 491 (on collateral housing consequences in New York and Baltimore).

27. Ginger Thompson and Sarah Cohen, "More Deportations Follow Minor Crimes, Records Show," *New York Times*, April 6, 2014.

28. Jason A. Cade, "The Plea-Bargain Crisis for Noncitizens in Misdemeanor Court," *Cardozo Law Review* 34, no. 5 (2013): 1758–1759; Thompson and Cohen, "More Deportations."

29. Thompson and Cohen, "More Deportations."

30. *Consequences and Costs: Lessons Learned from Davidson County, Tennessee's Jail Model 287(g) Program* (Nashville: American Civil Liberties Union of Tennessee, December 2012).

31. Cade, "The Plea-Bargain Crisis," 1773–1776.

32. Padilla v. Kentucky, 559 U.S. 356 (2010); Cade, "The Plea-Bargain Crisis," 1776–1781.

33. Jacobs, *Eternal Criminal Record*, 2–3 (on police and prosecutorial decision-making).

34. Nichols v. United States, Petitioner's Brief, 1993 WL 657283, at 5 and n.2; Nichols v. United States, 511 U.S. 738 (1994).

35. Alexandra Natapoff, "Misdemeanor Decriminalization," *Vanderbilt Law Review* 68, no. 177 (2015): 1091 and n.177.

36. Devon W. Carbado, "Blue-on-Black Violence: A Provisional Model of Some of the Causes," *Georgetown Law Journal* 104 (2016): 1485–1498 (documenting African American overexposure to repeated police contact); Andrew E. Taslitz, "Wrongly Accused Redux: How Race Contributes to Convicting the Innocent: The Informants Example," *Southwestern University Law Review* 37 (2008): 122–124 (describing the ratchet effect); Joseph Fox, "NYPD Transit Recidivist Policy Memorandum," NYPD Police Department Memorandum, January 27, 2012; Rocco Parascandola and Graham Rayman, "NYPD Arrests Mostly People of Color for Fare Beating: Stats," *New York Daily News*, February 12, 2016; *Profile of General Population and Housing Characteristics: 2010, New York City, NY* (Washington, DC: US Census Bureau, May 12, 2011), http://www1.nyc.gov/assets/planning/download/pdf/data-maps/nyc-population/census2010/t_sf1_dp_nyc.pdf [https://perma.cc/XH42-EU99].

37. Paul Butler, *Let's Get Free: A Hip-Hop Theory of Justice* (New York: New Press, 2009), 4–5, 8–26.

38. Jonathan Simon, "Misdemeanor Injustice and the Crisis of Mass Incarceration," *Southern California Law Review Postscript* 85, no. 5 (2012): 116.

39. According to the federal civil rights lawsuit filed against the county, which subsequently settled. Complaint at 30–31, Rodriguez v. Providence Cmty. Corr., No. 3:15-CV-01048 (M.D.Tenn., October 1, 2015).

40. Sarah Brayne, "Surveillance and System Avoidance: Criminal Justice Contact and Institutional Attachment," *American Sociological Review* 79, no. 3 (2014): 367–391; Amy E. Lerman and Vesla M. Weaver, *Arresting Citizenship: The Democratic Consequences of American Crime Control* (Chicago: University of Chicago Press, 2014), 4, 15–17 (interviews).

41. Malcolm M. Feeley, *The Process Is the Punishment: Handling Cases in a Lower Criminal Court* (1979; rpt. New York: Russell Sage Foundation, 1992), 30–31.

42. Gabriel J. Chin, "The New Civil Death: Rethinking Punishment in the Era of Mass Conviction," *University of Pennsylvania Law Review* 160 (2012): 1789–1791.

43. See Megan Comfort, "Punishment Beyond the Legal Offender," *Annual Review of Law and Social Science* 3 (2007): 271–289 (charting the spillover effects of criminal justice contact on children and families).

44. Barack Obama, *Dreams from My Father: A Story of Race and Inheritance* (New York: Crown Publishers, 2004), 93–94; Katie Zezima and Juliet Eilperin,

"Obama Says That Without Family Support He Could Have Been in Prison," *Washington Post*, July 16, 2015.

CHAPTER 2: SIZE

1. *Missouri Municipal Courts: Best Practice Recommendations* (Williamsburg, VA: National Center for State Courts, November 2015), 10.

2. Robert C. Boruchowitz et al., *Minor Crimes, Massive Waste: The Terrible Toll of America's Broken Misdemeanor Courts* (New York: National Association of Criminal Defense Lawyers, 2009), 11 (based on data collected by NCSC in 2006 from twelve states, estimating a median misdemeanor filing rate of 3,544 per 100,000 and extrapolating that rate to the national population); *2015 Statewide Felony Caseloads and Rates* (Williamsburg, VA: NCSC, Court Statistics Project, 2015) (reporting a total caseload of 2,690,000 felonies for thirty-eight states); Sean Rosenmerkel et al., *Felony Sentences in State Courts, 2006—Statistical Tables* (Washington, DC: Bureau of Justice Statistics, 2010), 2 (estimating 1.1 million felony sentences entered in 2006); *Federal Judicial Caseload Statistics 2015* (Washington, DC: Administrative Office of the US Courts, 2015), http://www.uscourts.gov/statistics-reports/federal-judicial-caseload-statistics-2015 [https://perma.cc/VTE9-D2J3] (accessed January 29, 2018) (reporting 80,081 criminal filings in US District Courts, including nearly 10,000 misdemeanors); *2015 Sourcebook of Federal Sentencing Statistics*, Table 10, US Sentencing Commission, https://www.ussc.gov/sites/default/files/pdf/research-and-publications/annual-reports-and-sourcebooks/2015/Table10.pdf [https://perma.cc/WQ9Z-VAP2] (reporting 71,003 federal convictions). The NCSC reported approximately 2.7 million felony criminal filings for thirty-seven states in 2015, with an average filing rate of 1,083 per 100,000 population, which would translate into approximately 3.5 million cases filed nationwide. "2015 Statewide Felony Caseloads and Rates," in *2015 Criminal Caseloads—Trial Courts* (Williamsburg, VA: National Center for State Courts, Court Statistics Project, 2015), http://www.ncsc.org/Sitecore/Content/Microsites/PopUp/Home/CSP/CSP_Intro [https://perma.cc/5B4Z-V7B9]; "2015 Crime in the United States, Table 1 by Volume and Rate per 100,000 Inhabitants, 1996–2015," FBI Uniform Crime Reporting, 2015, https://ucr.fbi.gov/crime-in-the-u.s/2015/crime-in-the-u.s.-2015/tables/table-1 [https://perma.cc/6JVU-VB4B] (accessed January 30, 2018) (reporting 15,696 murder/manslaughter cases and 124,047 rape cases); Danielle Kaeble and Lauren Glaze, *Correctional Populations in the United States, 2015*, NCJ 250374 (Washington, DC: Bureau of Justice Statistics, December 2016), 2 (incarcerated population in 2015 comprised 1,526,800 people in state and federal prisons and 728,200 people in local jails).

3. A forthcoming law review article also estimates a national docket of approximately 13 million based on some, but not all, of the same data. Megan Stevenson and Sandra Mayson, "The Scale of Misdemeanor Justice," *Boston University Law Review* 98 (forthcoming 2018), draft available at https://papers.ssrn.com/sol3/papers.cfm?abstract_id=3146057. See "Estimated Influenza Illnesses, Medical Visits, Hospitalizations, and Deaths Averted by Vaccination in the United States," Centers for Disease Control and Prevention, National Center for Immunization and Respiratory

Diseases, https://www.cdc.gov/flu/about/disease/2015-16.htm#table3 [https://perma
.cc/M2G9-TBYV] (accessed January 30, 2018); Nick Bunkley and Lindsay Chappell,
"Americans Will Buy 10 Million Trucks (and SUVs) This Year," *Autoweek*, http://
autoweek.com/article/car-news/people-will-buy-10-million-trucks-year[https://perma
.cc/LF3K-ENFV] (accessed January 30, 2018); "Enrollment in Elementary, Secondary,
and Degree-Granting Postsecondary Institutions," National Center for Education Statistics, https://nces.ed.gov/programs/digest/d16/tables/dt16_105.20.asp https://perma
.cc/T4Z5-3RRN] (accessed January 30, 2018).

4. See note 2 of this chapter for felony filing rates. See also Stevenson and
Mayson, "Scale of Misdemeanor Justice," 10 (estimating an average filing rate of
4,261 misdemeanors per 100,000 population). The appendix documents individual
state filing rates. See also "2015 Statewide Misdemeanor Caseloads and Rates," in
2015 Criminal Caseloads—Trial Courts (Williamsburg, VA: National Center for
State Courts, Court Statistics Project, 2015), http://www.ncsc.org/Sitecore/Content
/Microsites/PopUp/Home/CSP/CSP_Criminal [https://perma.cc/5B4Z-V7B9]. Kansas
reports the lowest number of misdemeanor filings to the NCSC of any state, but its
reported caseload diverges so greatly from the data in its annual report and other
sources that it may be unreliable.

5. State Disposition Tables, § 1.11(c–1), text accompanying note 40.1380, in
Wayne R. LaFave et al., *Criminal Procedure, 2017–2018*, 4th ed. (Eagan, MN: West
Group, 2017) (concluding that approximately one-third of state misdemeanors are
diverted or dismissed based on data from thirteen states); "New York County
Adult Arrests Disposed," New York Division of Criminal Justice Services, 2016,
http://www.criminaljustice.ny.gov/crimnet/ojsa/dispos/newyork.pdf [https://perma
.cc/2JZH-54TD]. In Connecticut, approximately 60 percent of misdemeanors are
"nolle prossed," which in other jurisdictions typically means they are dismissed outright but in Connecticut means that "the prosecutor agrees to drop the case against
the defendant but keeps the right to reopen the case and prosecute at any time during
the next thirteen months." Joseph Greelish, deputy director, Connecticut Judicial
Branch, email, September 5, 2017; see also spreadsheet from Connecticut Administrative Office of the Courts on file with author (containing Connecticut disposition data). Professor Issa Kohler-Hausmann argues that dismissals and diversions
are powerful forms of marking and social control even though they do not result
in formal conviction. Issa Kohler-Hausmann, "Managerial Justice and Mass Misdemeanors," *Stanford Law Review* 66 (2014): 646–650.

6. See appendix for state-by-state details. See also State Disposition Tables,
§ 1.11(c–1) in LaFave et al., *Criminal Procedure* (describing misdemeanor dockets
for thirteen states); Diane DePietropaolo Price et al., *Summary Injustice: A Look at
Constitutional Deficiencies in South Carolina's Summary Courts* (Washington, DC:
National Association of Criminal Defense Lawyers and American Civil Liberties
Union, 2016), 9–10; Alisa Smith et al., *Rush to Judgment: How South Carolina's
Summary Courts Fail to Protect Constitutional Rights* (Washington, DC: National
Association of Criminal Defense Lawyers, 2017), 10; Miss. Code Courts § 9–1–46.
The default punishment for a traffic offense in Mississippi, if no other punishment
is specified, is up to $250 plus costs and between one and six months incarceration.
Miss. Code Traffic § 63–1–69.

7. Compare "2015 Crime in the United States, Table 29," FBI Uniform Crime Reporting, 2015, https://ucr.fbi.gov/crime-in-the-u.s/2015/crime-in-the-u.s.-2015/tables/table-29 [https://perma.cc/7LWS-T5HG] (accessed January 28, 2018) (10,797,088 US arrests), with "2006 Crime in the United States, Table 29," FBI Uniform Crime Reporting, 2006, https://ucr.fbi.gov/crime-in-the-u.s/2006 [https://perma.cc/UXY2-SP7C] (accessed January 28, 2018) (14,380,370 US arrests), and "2015 Crime in the United States, Table 32, Ten-Year Arrest Trends, Totals, 2006–2015," FBI Uniform Crime Reporting, 2015, https://ucr.fbi.gov/crime-in-the-u.s/2015/crime-in-the-u.s.-2015/tables/table-32 [https://perma.cc/CCF4-V43M]. See also Stevenson and Mayson, "Scale of Misdemeanor Justice," 11–12 (concluding that overall criminal filing rates have decreased since 2006); John F. Pfaff, *Locked In: The True Causes of Mass Incarceration and How to Achieve Real Reform* (New York: Basic Books, 2017), 70–72 (documenting a rise in felony filing rates between 1998 and 2008).

8. State Disposition Tables, § 1.11(c–1), in LaFave et al., *Criminal Procedure*, 40.1200 (noting that state misdemeanor disposition tables are both under- and overinclusive).

9. *Summary of State Speed Laws* (Washington, DC: US Department of Transportation, National Highway Traffic Safety Administration, April 2011), v–ix; Miss. Code Traffic §§ 63-3-201, 63-9-11; Ga. Code Ann. § 40-6-1 (traffic code penalty section); "2015 Statewide Traffic Caseloads and Rates," in *Traffic/Violations Caseloads—Trial Courts* (Williamsburg, VA: National Center for State Courts, Court Statistics Project, 2015), http://www.ncsc.org/Sitecore/Content/Microsites/PopUp/Home/CSP/CSP_Intro [https://perma.cc/N9UJ-WCDU] (accessed June 5, 2018) (showing total traffic caseload of approximately 20 million for twenty-one states that potentially impose jail for speeding).

10. See appendix for state details (e.g., Kansas and Montana appear to exclude serious traffic misdemeanors from their total counts). See also State Disposition Tables, § 1.11(c-1), in LaFave et al., *Criminal Procedure* (describing "gaps in coverage" in state misdemeanor reporting). See also Milwaukee Code of Ordinances § 106-1; John Pawasarat and Marilyn Walzak, *Cited in Milwaukee: The Cost of Unpaid Municipal Citations* (Milwaukee, WI: Justice Initiatives Institute, June 2015).

11. William Blackstone, *Commentaries on the Laws of England*, Book IV, Chap. 1 § I (1769; rpt. Chicago: University of Chicago Press, 1979), 5; William Oldnall Russell, *Russell on Crime*, 3rd ed. (London: Stevens, 1845), 44–45; William Oldnall Russell, *Russell on Crime*, 12th ed. (London: Stevens, 1964), 4; Humphry W. Woolrych, *A Practical Treatise on Misdemeanors* (London: Shaw and Sons, 1842); see also United States v. Watson, 423 U.S. 411, 438–440 (1976) (Marshall, J., dissenting) (noting that at common law "many crimes now classified as felonies . . . were treated as misdemeanors").

12. Samuel J. Barrows, *New Legislation Concerning Crimes, Misdemeanors, and Penalties* (Washington, DC: Government Printing Office, 1900), viii–ix.

13. 18 U.S.C. §§ 3559, 3571.

14. John Chisholm, "Judicial Responsibility for Justice in Criminal Courts" (Public remarks, Hofstra University, Maurice Deane School of Law, April 6, 2017).

15. Brian A. Reaves, *Felony Defendants in Large Urban Counties, 2009—Statistics Tables* (Washington, DC: Bureau of Justice Statistics, December 2013), 26

(mean felony prison sentence in 2009 was fifty-two months); Pfaff, *Locked In*, 56 (same-year felony releases); John F. Pfaff, "The Myths and Realities of Correctional Severity: Evidence from the National Corrections Reporting Program on Sentencing Practices," *American Law and Economics Review* 13, no. 2 (2011): 499–502 (on sentence length); Ronald F. Wright and Rodney L. Engen, "The Effects of Depth and Distance in a Criminal Code on Charging, Sentencing, and Prosecutor Power," *North Carolina Law Review* 84, no. 6 (2006): 1982 (out of 41,661 felony arrests, 15,144, or 36.4 percent, ended in a misdemeanor conviction); Thomas H. Cohen and Tracey Kyckelhahn, Table 11 in *Felony Defendants in Large Urban Counties, 2006—Statistical Tables* (Washington, DC: Bureau of Justice Statistics, 2010), 11 (in seventy-five large urban counties, approximately one-sixth of convicted felony defendants were convicted of misdemeanors).

16. Jeannie Suk, "Criminal Law Comes Home," *Yale Law Journal* 116, no. 2 (2006): 2–70.

17. For definitions of these minor order offenses, see N.Y. Penal Law § 240.20; Ferguson, Mo., Code of Ordinances § 1-15 and § 44-344 (2015) (repealed April 26, 2016, by consent decree); see also Molly Hennessy-Fiske, "Walking in Ferguson: If You're Black, It's Often Against the Law," *Los Angeles Times*, March 5, 2015. For an analysis of the group orientation of low-level policing, see Bernard E. Harcourt, *Illusion of Order: The False Promise of Broken Windows Policing* (Cambridge, MA: Harvard University Press, 2001), 16; John Irwin, *The Jail: Managing the Underclass in American Society* (Berkeley: University of California Press, 1985), 10 ("The 'criminalization' of drug and alcohol use was intended to control classes of people as much as to punish deviant social behavior of individuals."). Because risk is a loaded social construct, preventative penal policies that aim at risk can serve as vehicles for bias and discrimination. See Sonja B. Starr, "Evidence-Based Sentencing and the Scientific Rationalization of Discrimination," *Stanford Law Review* 66, no. 4 (2014): 822–842; Bernard E. Harcourt, *Against Prediction: Profiling, Policing, and Punishing in an Actuarial Age* (Chicago: University of Chicago Press, 2007). See also Robert J. Sampson and Stephen W. Raudenbush, *Research in Brief: Disorder in Urban Neighborhoods— Does It Lead to Crime?* (Washington, DC: National Institute of Justice, 2001), 5 ("Public disorder may not be so 'criminogenic' after all."). Chapter 7 ("History") discusses broken windows policing at greater length, and Chapter 8 ("Justice") discusses the sociological view.

18. The FBI reported 1.16 million larceny-thefts, 1.08 million nonaggravated assaults, and 1.09 million DUI arrests in 2015. "2015 Crime in the United States, Table 29," FBI Uniform Crime Reports, https://ucr.fbi.gov/crime-in-the-u.s/2015/crime-in -the-u.s.-2015/tables/table-29 [https://perma.cc/7LWS-T5HG]. See also Stevenson and Mayson, "Scale of Misdemeanor Justice," 18–19 (comparing various misdemeanor arrest rates).

19. Robert Boruchowitz, "Diverting and Reclassifying Misdemeanors Could Save $1 Billion per Year: Reducing the Need for and Cost of Appointed Counsel," *American Constitution Society for Law & Policy* (December 2010) (Washington State data); Alisa Smith and Sean Maddan, *Three-Minute Justice: Haste and Waste in Florida's Misdemeanor Courts* (Washington, DC: National Association of Criminal Defense Lawyers, July 2011), 21; spreadsheet from Connecticut Administrative

Office of the Courts on file with author; James J. Fazzalar, "Violations Resulting in a Suspended Driver's License and Penalties for Driving While Under Suspension," Connecticut General Assembly, last modified November 30, 2007, https://www.cga .ct.gov/2007/rpt/2007-R-0636.htm [https://perma.cc/H3HN-VN69] (28,000 cases filed every year); *Consequences and Costs: Lessons Learned from Davidson County, Tennessee's Jail Model 287(g) Program* (Nashville: American Civil Liberties Union of Tennessee, December 2012), 8. Chapter 5 ("Money") discusses the economic consequences of getting a suspended license in more detail.

20. "2015 Crime in the United States," FBI Uniform Crime Reporting, 2015, https://ucr.fbi.gov/crime-in-the-u.s/2015/crime-in-the-u.s.-2015 [https://perma.cc /6JVU-VB4B] (accessed January 30, 2018) (marijuana possession comprised 38.6 percent of all drug arrests); Brendan Cheney, "For Non-White New Yorkers, Marijuana Arrests More Often Lead to Conviction," *Politico*, September 21, 2017, https://www.politico.com/states/new-york/city-hall/story/2017/05/04/racial -disparities-in-marijuana-convictions-in-all-five-boroughs-111807[https://perma.cc /7R4P-BNB6]; spreadsheet from Texas Administrative Office of the Courts on file with author; spreadsheet from Kentucky Administrative Office of the Courts on file with author.

21. Kathleen Kane-Willis et al., *Patchwork Policy: An Evaluation of Arrests and Tickets for Marijuana Misdemeanors in Illinois* (Chicago: Illinois Consortium on Drug Policy, May 2014), 8, 11; Lauren Del Valle, "Marijuana-Related Summonses on the Rise in NYC, East New York; Minority Nabes Feeling the Heat," *News21*, http:// www.amny.com/news/decriminalization-of-marijuana-nypd-summonses-for-pot -violations-up-in-early-2015-1.10741116 [https://perma.cc/ECY3-3UAM] (accessed August 16, 2015).

22. For FBI crime statistics and definitions, see "2015 Crime in the United States, Table 29"; *FBI Uniform Crime Reporting Handbook, 2004* (Clarksburg, WV: US Department of Justice, Federal Bureau of Investigation, 2004), 139–147. See also William O. Douglas, "Vagrancy and Arrest on Suspicion," *Yale Law Journal* 70, no. 1 (1960) (explaining why suspicion arrests are unconstitutional). For Seattle, Baltimore, Kentucky, Connecticut, and Wisconsin data, see "Seattle Municipal Court, Civility Criminal Charges, 2011–2017, 2018 Q3," tableau public, 2018, https://public .tableau.com/profile/nickz#!/vizhome/SeattleCivilityCharges/Criminal[https://perma .cc/A2PM-YK4W] (accessed January 30, 2018); *Investigation of the Baltimore City Police Department* (Washington, DC: US Department of Justice, Civil Rights Division, August 10, 2016), 26; spreadsheets from Kentucky and Connecticut Administrative Offices of the Courts on file with author (Kentucky and Connecticut data); "2015 Misdemeanor Disposition Summary, Statewide Report," Wisconsin Court System Statistics, 2015, https://www.wicourts.gov/publications/statistics /circuitcircuitstats.htm#2015 [https://perma.cc/4K43–6Y2N].

23. See Chapters 6 ("Race") and 7 ("History").

24. Table 42 (arrests by sex) and Table 43 (arrests by race and ethnicity), "2015 Crime in the United States, Persons Arrested," FBI Uniform Crime Reporting, 2015, https://ucr.fbi.gov/crime-in-the-u.s/2015/crime-in-the-u.s.-2015/persons-arrested /persons-arrested [https://perma.cc/Z8U7-6D5M and https://perma.cc/3NTE-H7UF]. Chapter 6 provides further breakdowns by race and ethnicity.

25. Daniel Kreps, "Justin Bieber Pleads Guilty to Careless Driving in Miami," *Rolling Stone*, August 13, 2014, https://www.rollingstone.com/music/news/justin-bieber-pleads-guilty-to-reckless-driving-in-miami-20140813 [https://perma.cc/6RLH-7GXL?type=image]; Stuart Silverstein, "Kiefer Sutherland Pleads No Contest to DUI Charge; New Judge Could Void Plea Deal," *Los Angeles Times*, October 10, 2007; Jason Rodrigues, "Hugh Grant Arrested with Sex Worker 20 Years Ago," *The Guardian*, June 26, 2015; Hilary Moss, "Jessica White Gets Anger Management, Community Service & Fine After Assault Charges," *Huffington Post*, June 16, 2011, https://www.huffingtonpost.com/2011/06/16/jessica-white-anger-management-assault_n_877960.html [https://perma.cc/X9CF-3XAS].

26. Tabatha Abu El-Haj, "All Assemble: Order and Disorder in Law, Politics, and Culture," *University of Pennsylvania Journal of Constitutional Law* 16, no. 4 (2014): 961–962 (on the Occupy movement); Coretta S. King, "The Meaning of the King Holiday," King Center, http://www.thekingcenter.org/meaning-king-holiday [https://perma.cc/735T-8TLW] (accessed February 6, 2018) (regarding twenty-nine arrests); "Rev. King Given Four Months for Driving Without License," *Stanford Daily* 138, no. 25 (1960), https://stanforddailyarchive.com/cgibin/stanford?a=d&d=stanford19601027-01.2.30 [https://perma.cc/2UMK-YNKN]; "Today We Honor Martin Luther King," *Ascheman Law*, http://www.aschemanlaw.com/today-we-honor-martin-luther-king-jr [https://perma.cc/B9EX-R689] (accessed January 31, 2018) (regarding Alabama license).

27. Dana Hunt et al., *ADAM II: 2010 Annual Report, Arrestee Drug Abuse Monitoring Program II* (Washington, DC: Office of National Drug Control Policy, 2011), viii–xii; Eric Dunleavy et al., *Literacy Behind Bars: Results from the 2003 National Assessment of Adult Literacy Prison Survey* (Washington, DC: US Department of Education, 2007), 7, 12, 13; Doris J. James and Lauren E. Glaze, *Special Report: Mental Health Problems of Prison and Jail Inmates* (Washington, DC, Bureau of Justice Statistics, 2006), 1; Caroline Wolf Harlow, *Special Report: Defense Counsel in Criminal Cases* (Washington, DC, Bureau of Justice Statistics, 2000), 1.

28. Andra Sparks, "Judicial Responsibility for Justice in Criminal Courts" (public remarks, Hofstra University, Maurice Deane School of Law, April 6, 2017).

29. Katherine M. Keyes and Deborah S. Hasin, "Socio-Economic Status and Problem Alcohol Use: The Positive Relationship Between Income and the DSM-IV Alcohol Abuse Diagnosis," *Addiction* (2008): 7; see Chapter 6.

CHAPTER 3: PROCESS

1. Amy Bach, *Ordinary Injustice: How America Holds Court* (New York: Henry Holt, 2009); Steve Bogira, *Courtroom 302: A Year Behind the Scenes in an American Criminal Courthouse* (New York: Knopf, 2005). Sometimes the felony world is sloppy about even its most serious cases. Stephen Bright, "Counsel for the Poor: The Death Sentence Not for the Worst Crime but for the Worst Lawyer," *Yale Law Journal* 103 (1994): 1835–1836.

2. United States v. Sharpe, 470 U.S. 675, 684, 686 (1985); Terry v. Ohio, 392 U.S. 1, 13 (1968); Alexandra Natapoff, "A Stop Is Just a Stop: Terry's Formalism," *Ohio State Journal of Criminal Law* 15 (2017): 113.

3. *Terry*, 392 U.S. at 27, 21; Floyd v. City of New York, 959 F. Supp. 2d 540 (S.D.N.Y. 2013) (finding that "time of day" and other factors cited by police were insufficient to support stops); Illinois v. Wardlow, 527 U.S. 1062 (1999) (upholding stop of fleeing person); Whren v. United States, 517 U.S. 806 (1996) (holding that any traffic violation suffices to authorize car stop). For a discussion of racial profiling and pretextual traffic stops, see Charles R. Epp, et al., *Pulled Over: How Police Stops Define Race and Citizenship* (Chicago: University of Chicago, 2014); Ian Ayres and Jonathan Borowsky, *A Study of Racially Disparate Outcomes in the Los Angeles Police Department* (Los Angeles: American Civil Liberties Union, October 2008).

4. Joseph Goldstein, "Trial to Start in Class Suit on Stop-and-Frisk Tactic," *New York Times*, March 17, 2013 (12 percent of stops resulted in arrest or summons). For legal standards governing arrest, see Illinois v. Gates, 462 U.S. 213, 238, 243 n.13 (1983); Maryland v. Pringle, 540 U.S. 366 (2003); Ybarra v. Illinois, 444 U.S. 85 (1979).

5. Eisha Jain, "Arrests as Regulation," *Stanford Law Review* 67 (2015): 809; Arizona v. Gant, 556 U.S. 332 (2009); Atwater v. Lago Vista, 532 U.S. 318, 364–365 (2001) (O'Connor, J., dissenting) (internal citations omitted).

6. As Jeff Fagan points out, "The Terry Court never said *which* crimes had to be 'afoot' to justify a stop." Jeffrey Fagan, "Terry's Original Sin," *University of Chicago Legal Forum* 43 (2016): 93.

7. *Atwater*, 532 U.S. at 346–347, 353, 369–370.

8. *Terry*, 392 U.S. at 26 ("An arrest is the initial stage of a criminal prosecution"). Many scholars and policymakers argue that given the high costs of arrest to both individuals and the state, summonses and citations should be used more often. See Chapter 9 ("Change").

9. Katherine Beckett and Steve Herbert, *Banished: The New Social Control in Urban America* (Oxford: Oxford University Press, 2009), 85.

10. Graham Rayman, "The NYPD Tapes, Part 2," *Village Voice*, May 11, 2010; *Investigation of the Baltimore City Police Department* (Washington, DC: US Department of Justice, Civil Rights Division, August 10, 2016), 41; *Investigation of the Ferguson Police Department* (Washington, DC: US Department of Justice, Civil Rights Division, March 4, 2015), 2.

11. Rayman, "The NYPD Tapes" (quoting sections of tape recordings made by an officer in Brooklyn's 81st Precinct).

12. *Terry*, 392 U.S. at 14, n.11; Peter Moskos, *Cop in the Hood: My Year Policing Baltimore's Eastern District* (Princeton, NJ: Princeton University Press, 2008), 55, 120.

13. Christy Lopez, "Disorderly (mis)Conduct: The Problem with 'Contempt of Cop' Arrests," *American Constitution Society Issue Brief* (2010); Eric Nadler, "Obstruction of Justice: Blacks Are Arrested on 'Contempt of Cop' Charges at Higher Rate," *Seattle Post-Intelligencer*, February 28, 2008.

14. Julie Dressner and Edwin Martinez, "The Scars of Stop-and-Frisk," Opinion Video, *New York Times*, June 12, 2012, https://nyti.ms/2jXgd7V.

15. City of Houston v. Hill, 482 U.S. 451, 462–463 (1987).

16. Lewis v. City of New Orleans, 415 U.S. 130, 135 (1974); see also Natapoff, "A Stop Is Just a Stop," 120–122 (describing police ability to generate evidence through allegations of disorder).

17. "2015 FBI Crime in the United States, Table 29, Persons Arrested," FBI Uniform Crime Reporting, 2015, https://ucr.fbi.gov/crime-in-the-u.s/2015/crime-in-the -u.s.-2015/tables/table-29 [https://perma.cc/UXY2-SP7C] (10,797,088 arrests); "2014 FBI Crime in the United States, Table 29, Persons Arrested," FBI Uniform Crime Reporting, 2014, https://ucr.fbi.gov/crime-in-the-u.s/2014/crime-in-the-u.s.-2014/tables /table-29 [https://perma.cc/5ZFT-PA5C] (11,205,833 arrests); Robert Brame et al., "Demographic Patterns of Cumulative Arrest Prevalence by Ages 18 and 23," *Crime & Delinquency* 60, no. 3 (January 2014): 471–486; Robert Brame et al., "Cumulative Prevalence of Arrest from Ages 8 to 23 in a National Sample," *Pediatrics* 129, no.1 (December 2011): 21–27. FBI arrest data does not expressly distinguish between felony and misdemeanor arrests, but many arrest categories such as "Disorderly Conduct" are misdemeanors, and some categories such as "Other Assaults" (non-aggravated) are largely misdemeanors. *FBI Uniform Crime Reporting Handbook, 2004* (Clarksburg, WV: US Department of Justice, Federal Bureau of Investigation, 2004), 139–147. By way of example, Maryland has a relatively average misdemeanor filing caseload of 4,197 per 100,000. Its FBI-reported arrest data for 2015 showed the majority of its arrests to be for misdemeanor-type offenses, largely drug abuse, other assaults, driving under the influence, and disorderly conduct. *Crime in Maryland 2015 Uniform Crime Report* (Pikesville: Maryland State Police, 2016), 108–109. Cherise Burdeen, CEO of the Pretrial Justice Institute, estimates that over 90 percent of national arrests are for misdemeanors. *Bailing on Baltimore: Voices from the Front Lines of the Justice System* (Washington, DC: Justice Policy Institute, September 2012), 23 (quoting Burdeen). See also Stevenson and Mayson, "Scale of Misdemeanor Justice," 11–13 (estimating misdemeanor arrest rates based on FBI Uniform Crime Reporting data and comparing them to lower violent-crime arrest rates).

18. Thomas H. Cohen and Brian A. Reaves, *Special Report: Pretrial Release of Felony Defendants in State Courts* (Washington, DC: Bureau of Justice Statistics, November 2007), US DOJ, NCJ 214994; Paul Heaton, Sandra G. Mayson, and Megan Stevenson, "The Downstream Consequences of Misdemeanor Pretrial Detention," *Stanford Law Review* 69 (2017): 711; Jocelyn Simonson, "Bail Nullification," *Michigan Law Review* 115 (2017): 585; Douglas L. Colbert, "Thirty-Five Years After Gideon: The Illusory Right to Counsel at Bail Proceedings," *University of Illinois Law Review* 1 (1998): 1.

19. United States v. McConnell, 842 F.2d 105, 107 (5th Cir. 1988) (bail not excessive merely because defendant could not afford to pay it). In United States v. Salerno, the Supreme Court held that bail must be set at an amount "reasonably calculated to ensure the defendant's presence at trial," United States v. Salerno, 481 U.S. 739, 752–754 (1987), and that pretrial detention is "regulatory in nature, and does not constitute punishment before trial." Ibid. at 747–748. See also Bell v. Wolfish, 441 U.S. 520, 535 (1979) ("Under the Due Process Clause, a detainee may not be punished prior to an adjudication of guilt").

20. Ram Subramanian et al., *Incarceration's Front Door: The Misuse of Jails in America* (New York: Vera Institute of Justice, February 2015), 34.

21. Bail Reform Act, 18 U.S.C. § 3141 et seq. (governing federal jurisdictions); "2016 Bail Schedule for Infractions and Misdemeanors," Superior Court of Califor-

nia, County of Los Angeles, 2018, https://www.lacourt.org/division/criminal/pdf/misd
.pdf [https://perma.cc/SC4A-HW8F]; *Chicago Police Department Bail Bond Manual—General Bonding Procedures*, CPD-11.909 (Chicago Police Department, October 13, 2010), 3, http://directives.chicagopolice.org/forms/CPD-11.909.pdf [https://perma.cc/LT69-3WHS]; Rothgery v. Gillespie County, 554 U.S. 191 (2008) (declining to decide whether defendants are entitled to counsel's presence at bail hearings); Diane DePietropaolo Price, *Summary Injustice: A Look at Constitutional Deficiencies in South Carolina's Summary Courts* (Washington, DC: National Association of Criminal Defense Lawyers and American Civil Liberties Union, 2016), 15; Heaton, Mayson, and Stevenson, "Downstream Consequences," 730 (on Harris County bail hearings); Subramanian et al., *Incarceration's Front Door*, 29 (documenting various actors with the authority to set bail).

22. Odonnell v. Harris Cty., 2017 WL 1735456, *2 (S.D.Tex., April 28, 2017); Heaton, Mayson, and Stevenson, "Downstream Consequences," 716, 732–733 (Harris County); Jamie Fellner, *The Price of Freedom: Bail and Pretrial Detention of Low Income Nonfelony Defendants in New York City* (New York: Human Rights Watch, December 2010).

23. Adam Liptak, "Illegal Globally, Bail for Profit Remains in U.S.," *New York Times*, January 29, 2008.

24. Heaton, Mayson, and Stevenson, "Downstream Consequences," 717–718.

25. Debbie Nathan, "What Happened to Sandra Bland?," *The Nation*, April 21, 2016; Opinion, Jones v. City of Clanton, Case No. 2:15cv34-MHT (M.D.Ala. September 14, 2015); Leon Neyfakh, "Is Bail Unconstitutional?," *Slate*, June 30, 2015; Advice Letter from Sandra Benson Brantley, Counsel to the General Assembly, Office of the Maryland Attorney General, October 11, 2016 http://www.marylandattorneygeneral.gov/News%20Documents/Rules_Committee_Letter_on_Pretrial_Release.pdf [https://perma.cc/4RL4-6NS5]; Kevin Rector, "Maryland Judges, Commissioners Shifting Away from Cash Bail as Reform Debate Continues," *Baltimore Sun*, February 25, 2017. See www.civilrightscorps.org for additional litigation.

26. Simonson, "Bail Nullification," 589 ("For most indigent defendants, bail is the ballgame.").

27. Ron Paschal, phone interview with the author, January 24, 2017, transcript on file with author.

28. Angela J. Davis, *Arbitrary Justice: The Power of the American Prosecutor* (Oxford: Oxford University Press, 2007); William Stuntz, "The Pathological Politics of Criminal Law," *Michigan Law Review* 100 (2001): 505, 509; Imbler v. Pachtman, 424 U.S. 409, 427 (1976); Bordenkircher v. Hayes, 434 U.S. 357, 364 (1978).

29. Berger v. United States, 295 U.S. 78, 88 (1935).

30. I have explored the significance of misdemeanor overcriminalization in depth in Alexandra Natapoff, "Misdemeanors," *Southern California Law Review* 85 (2012): 1357–1361.

31. See "2015 Statewide Misdemeanor Bench Trials and Rates" and "2015 Statewide Misdemeanor Jury Trials and Rates," in *2015 Criminal Caseloads—Trial Courts* (Williamsburg, VA: National Center for State Courts, Court Statistics Project, 2015), http://www.ncsc.org/Sitecore/Content/Microsites/PopUp/Home/CSP/CSP_Criminal [https://perma.cc/YR4U-PWDH] (accessed February 2, 2018) (documenting typical

state misdemeanor bench and jury trial rates of 2 percent or less). For an analysis of the various psychological pressures that can distort plea bargaining, see Stephanos Bibas, "Plea Bargaining Outside the Shadow of Trial," *Harvard Law Review* 117 (2004): 2496–2519.

32. *Rothgery*, 554 U.S. 191 (2008).

33. See US Attorneys' Manual § 9-27.220 (describing the factors that go into deciding whether to charge a federal case); *How Many Cases Should a Prosecutor Handle? Results of the National Workload Assessment Project* (Alexandria, VA: American Prosecutors Research Institute, 2002), 22. On federal declination rates, see Mark Motivans, *Federal Justice Statistics, 2009* (Washington, DC: Bureau of Justice Statistics, December 2011), NCJ 234184, at 7, Table 5. See also Daniel Richman, "Prosecutors and Their Agents, Agents and Their Prosecutors," *Columbia Law Review* 103 (2003): 762–765 (describing the federal prosecutorial declination process).

34. Bruce Frederick and Don Stemen, *The Anatomy of Discretion: An Analysis of Prosecutorial Decision Making—Technical Report, Final Report to the National Institute of Justice Grant No: 2009-IJ-CX-0040* (New York: Vera Institute of Justice, December 2012), 134–135.

35. Frederick and Stemen, *Anatomy of Discretion*, 134; Joan Jacoby et al., *Prosecutor's Guide to Misdemeanor Case Management* (Washington, DC: Jefferson Institute for Justice Studies, September 2001), 33–34 (nine-jurisdiction study of prosecutors' offices).

36. Interviews with prosecutors in Riverside, California, and Wichita, Kansas, transcripts on file with author; *How Many Cases*, 6.

37. Ronald F. Wright and Kay L. Levine, "The Cure for Young Prosecutors' Syndrome," *Arizona Law Review* 56 (2014): 1065, 1107.

38. Wright and Levine, "Cure," 1103–1104 and n.12, 1101 and n.190.

39. *Racial Disparities in the Criminal Justice System: Hearing Before the Subcomm. on Crime, Terrorism, and Homeland Security of the Comm. on the Judiciary H.R.*, 111th Congress, First Session, 111-78 (2009), 6 (statement of Wayne S. McKenzie, Director, Program on Prosecution and Racial Justice), https://judiciary.house .gov/_files/hearings/printers/111th/111-78_53093.PDF [https://perma.cc/H55M-6JB4] (on Mecklenburg study); Josh Bowers, "Legal Guilt, Normative Innocence, and the Equitable Decision Not to Prosecute," *Columbia Law Review* 110 (2010): 1717 (Iowa declination rates); *Alaska Court System Annual Report FY 2015* (Anchorage: Alaska Court System 2016), 135, Table 5.12, http://www.courtrecords.alaska.gov/webdocs /admin/docs/fy15.pdf [https://perma.cc/FW5K-Z6Y5] (misdemeanors dismissed at or before arraignment). Alaska eventually dismisses another 30.6 percent of misdemeanor cases.

40. On declinations, see *Investigation of the Baltimore City Police Department*, 26; spreadsheet from Florida Administrative Office of the Courts on file with author (cases designated as "before trial no file"). On dismissals and diversions, see *Maryland Judiciary Annual Statistical Abstract Fiscal Year 2015* (Annapolis, MD: Court Operations Department, 2015), Table DC-4; Wayne R. Lafave et al., *Criminal Procedure, 2017–2018*, 4th ed. (Eagan, MN: West Group, 2017), 114, § 1.11(c–1).

41. Jonathan Abel, "Cops and Pleas: Police Officers' Influence on Plea Bargaining," *Yale Law Journal* 126 (2017): 1743. By contrast, Justice Lewis Powell once

noted that the state sometimes permits police rather than prosecutors to present minor cases, suggesting that such cases are insufficiently unimportant to warrant full prosecutorial attention. Argersinger v. Hamlin, 407 U.S. 25, 49 (1972) (Powell, J., concurring the result).

42. Andrew Horwitz, "Taking the Cop Out of Copping a Plea: Eradicating Police Prosecution of Criminal Cases," *Arizona Law Review* 40 (1998): 1306 ("Twelve percent of the judges sitting in misdemeanor criminal courts [nationally] indicated that a prosecuting attorney 'infrequently' or 'never' conducted the trial of misdemeanor defendants"; 75 percent of the time the case was prosecuted by police). On South Carolina see Price, *Summary Injustice*, 19; see also Alisa Smith et al., *Rush to Judgment: How South Carolina's Summary Courts Fail to Protect Constitutional Rights* (Washington, DC: National Association of Criminal Defense Lawyers, 2017), 16.

43. *A Citizen's Guide to Municipal Court* (Santa Fe: New Mexico Municipal Courts, 2008), 3, https://municipal.nmcourts.gov/publication-.aspx [https://perma.cc/97U6-MGEL]; Nikolas Frye, "Allowing New Hampshire Police Officers to Prosecute: Concerns with the Practice and a Solution," *New England Journal on Criminal & Civil Confinement* 38 (2012): 339; Price, *Summary Injustice*, 19–20.

44. *Imbler*, 424 U.S. at 424–425; Buckley v. Fitzsimmons, 509 U.S. 259, 273–274 (1993).

45. Gideon v. Wainwright, 372 U.S. 335, 344 (1963); Jonathan Rapping, "Public Defenders: The Vanguard of Redemption," *Ohio State Journal of Criminal Law* 15 (2017): 201 ("The public defender was birthed as a civil rights hero."); Barbara Babcock, "'Defending the Guilty' After 30 Years," in *How Can You Represent Those People?*, ed. Abbe Smith and Monroe H. Freedman (New York: Palgrave MacMillan, 2013), 3. See also Penson v. Ohio, 488 U.S. 75, 84 (1988) ("It is through counsel that all other rights of the accused are protected.").

46. Powell v. Alabama, 287 U.S. 45, 68–69 (1932).

47. Argersinger v. Hamlin, 407 U.S. 25, 34 (1972).

48. *Gideon*, 372 U.S. at 344; *Argersinger*, 407 U.S. at 31–33 (establishing right to counsel for misdemeanors); Scott v. Illinois, 440 U.S. 367 (1979) (no right to counsel where defendant is not actually incarcerated); Alabama v. Shelton, 535 U.S. 654, 661–662 (2002) (right to counsel for jailable probation).

49. Alexandra Natapoff, "Gideon's Servants and the Criminalization of Poverty," *Ohio State Journal of Criminal Law* 12 (2015): 445; Smith and Freedman, *How Can You Represent Those People?*.

50. Charles J. Ogletree, "Beyond Justifications: Seeking Motivations to Sustain Public Defenders," *Harvard Law Review* 106 (1993): 1271–1272.

51. Robin Steinberg, "Beyond Lawyering: How Holistic Representation Makes for Good Policy, Better Lawyers, and More Satisfied Clients," *New York University Review of Law & Social Change* 30 (2006): 625.

52. United States v. Ross, Case No. 13-MJ-3055-SAG (D. Md. July 15, 2015), https://casetext.com/case/united-states-v-ross-153 [https://perma.cc/3MPM-R7VN] (finding insufficient evidence of disorderly conduct and a fatal variance between the charges and the charging document).

53. See, e.g., *No Day in Court: Marijuana Possession Cases and the Failure of the Bronx Criminal Courts* (New York: Bronx Defenders Office, 2013) (outlining sophisticated impact litigation strategy designed to challenge misdemeanor case processing).

54. Wilbur v. City of Mt. Vernon, 989 F. Supp. 2d 1122, 1124 (W.D.Wash. 2013).

55. *A Race to the Bottom: Speed and Savings over Due Process: A Constitutional Crisis* (Washington, DC: National Legal Aid & Defender Association, 2008), ii–iii, http://www.mynlada.org/michigan/michigan_report.pdf [https://perma.cc/B8FF-XSHG] (on per capita spending); Tracey Kyckelhahn, *Justice Expenditure and Employment Extracts, 2012—Preliminary* (Washington, DC: Bureau of Justice Statistics, 2015), NCJ 248628 (spending on criminal justice), https://www.bjs.gov/index.cfm?ty=pbdetail&iid=5239 [https://perma.cc/7ZDR-BRC7]; *ABA Standards for Criminal Justice Providing Defense Services* (Washington, DC: American Bar Association Criminal Justice Standard Committee, 1992), § 5–5.3 comment., at 72 and n.13 (recommended caseloads); Robert C. Boruchowitz et al., *Minor Crimes, Massive Waste: The Terrible Toll of America's Broken Misdemeanor Courts* (Washington, DC: National Association of Criminal Defense Lawyers, April 2009), 21 (on caseloads), 26–27 (on triage), 38 (on investigative resources).

56. *Contracting for Indigent Defense Services: A Special Report* (Washington, DC: Bureau of Justice Assistance, 2000), 1 (prepared by the Spangenberg Group) (California); *Wilbur*, 989 F. Supp. 2d at 1124 (Washington State litigation).

57. Boruchowitz, *Minor Crimes*, 39.

58. Boruchowitz, *Minor Crimes*, 39.

59. Abbe Smith, "Too Much Heart and Not Enough Heat: The Short Life and Fractured Ego of the Empathetic, Heroic Public Defender," *University of California Davis Law Review* 37 (2004): 1259; Eve Brensike Primus, "Culture as a Structural Problem in Indigent Defense," *Minnesota Law Review* 100 (2016): 1771.

60. "Affidavit of Rodney J. Uphoff," at 9, ¶ 25, Lewis v. Hollenbach, Civil Action No. 08-CI-1094 (Franklin Circuit Ct., Div. II, Ky., January 15, 2009).

61. "Uphoff Affidavit," 13 ¶ 30.

62. *Bailing on Baltimore*, 22 (quoting Tyriel Simms).

63. Eve Brensike Primus, "Our Broken Misdemeanor System: Its Problems and Some Potential Solutions," *Southern California Law Review Postscript* 85 (2012): 81.

64. Boruchowitz, *Minor Crimes*, 23 (describing facts of Ohio v. Jones, Case No. 2008-P-0018 [Ohio Ct. App. December 31, 2008], http://www.sconet.state.oh.us/rod/docs/pdf/11/2008/2008-ohio-6994.pdf [https://perma.cc/4K9B-TAWU]).

65. *No Day in Court*, 3.

66. Boruchowitz, *Minor Crimes*, 19 (Mississippi defendant detained eleven months); *Gideon's Broken Promise: America's Continuing Quest for Equal Justice* (Chicago: American Bar Association, 2004), 24, http://www.americanbar.org/content/dam/aba/administrative/legal_aid_indigent_defendants/ls_sclaid_def_bp_right_to_counsel_in_criminal_proceedings.authcheckdam.pdf [https://perma.cc/CWD5-NF6T] (jailed Georgia defendant waited thirteen months to receive counsel); Boruchowitz, *Minor Crimes*, 15 (quoting Monahan).

67. Boruchowitz, *Minor Crimes*, 17 (Pennsylvania prosecutor negotiating deals in basement); *Gideon's Broken Promise*, 24–25 (Georgia mass arraignment).

68. Boruchowitz, *Minor Crimes*, 15.

69. Youngstown Sheet & Tube Co. v. Sawyer, 343 U.S. 579, 635 (1952) (Jackson, J., concurring). Separation-of-powers principles may not apply in quite the same way to local municipal courts. Moreau v. Flanders, 15 A.3d 565, 580 (R.I. 2011).

70. Republican Party of Minnesota v. White, 536 U.S. 765, 798 (2002) (Stevens, J., dissenting).

71. *Republican Party of Minnesota*, 536 U.S. at 803–804 (Ginsburg, J., dissenting) (internal quotations and citations omitted).

72. Boruchowitz, *Minor Crimes*, 30 (cattle auction); Hon. Shelley C. Chapman, "I'm a Judge and I Think Criminal Court Is Horrifying," Marshall Project, August 11, 2016, https://www.themarshallproject.org/2016/08/11/i-m-a-judge-and-i-think-criminal-court-is-horrifying [https://perma.cc/PDL9-AKNC]; Emily DePrang, "Poor Judgment," *Texas Observer*, October 12, 2015 (Harris County judge who never showed up); Alisa Smith and Sean Maddan, *Three Minute Justice: Haste and Waste in Florida's Misdemeanor Courts* (Washington, DC: National Association of Criminal Defense Lawyers, July 2011), 8 (quoting Justice Kogan).

73. Bogira, *Courtroom 302*, 12, 17, 39 (describing Chicago felony court); Bach, *Ordinary Injustice*, 26–28, 35–36, 259; Lawrence M. Friedman and Robert V. Percival, *The Roots of Justice: Crime and Punishment in Alameda County, California, 1870–1910* (Chapel Hill: University of North Carolina Press, 1981), 120–125; Caleb Foote, "Vagrancy-Type Law and Its Administration," *University of Pennsylvania Law Review* 104 (1956): 603, 605.

74. Malcolm M. Feeley, *The Process Is the Punishment: Handling Cases in a Lower Criminal Court* (1979; rpt. New York: Russell Sage Foundation, 1992), 9–11. Feeley likened the process to a speedy and informal "supermarket"—he thought the "assembly line" metaphor misleadingly suggested uniformity and thus "ignores the complexity of the criminal process, and the casualness and confusion characteristic of decision making in the lower criminal courts." Feeley, *The Process Is the Punishment*, 13, 187.

75. Smith and Maddan, *Three Minute Justice*, 15, 22.

76. Primus, "Our Broken Misdemeanor Justice System," 81; Brendan Smith, "Legislative Efforts Requiring Judges to Hold JD Meet with Mixed Results," *ABA Journal*, July 1, 2011, http://www.abajournal.com/magazine/article/is_there_a_lawyer_in_the_court [https://perma.cc/6ESP-B97A] (twenty-four states do not require judges to have a law degree). See also Price, *Summary Injustice*, 10.

77. Lawrence R. Jones, "Reassessing and Reforming the Structure of New Jersey's Municipal Courts," *New Jersey Lawyer Magazine* 232 (February 2005): 41. See also *Missouri Municipal Courts: Best Practice Recommendations* (Williamsburg, VA: National Center for State Courts, 2015), 14, 18; Ethan Leib, "Local Judges and Local Government," *New York University Journal of Legislation and Public Policy* 18 (2015): 707 (interviewing local New York judges and describing local political arrangements); Mark Flatten, *City Court: Money, Pressure and Politics Make It Tough to Beat the Rap* (Phoenix: Goldwater Institute, 2017).

78. Boruchowitz, *Minor Crimes*, 19; *No Day in Court*, 6.

79. "Types of Drugs Courts," National Association of Drug Court Professionals, http://m.nadcp.org/learn/what-are-drug-courts/types-drug-courts [https://perma.cc/SC8D-9P79] (stating that 2,734 drug courts will serve over 136,000 people in 2017).

See also *Census of Problem-Solving Courts, 2012* (Washington, DC: Bureau of Justice Statistics, 2016): 1, 7, NCJ 249803, https://www.bjs.gov/content/pub/pdf/cpsc12.pdf [https://perma.cc/NH2W-MT2A] (counting 1,722 nondrug problem-solving courts, most of which serve fifty people or fewer). The Pratt and Calabrese courtrooms are described in Tina Rosenberg, "The Simple Idea That Could Transform US Criminal Justice," *The Guardian*, June 23, 2015.

80. Judge John B. Van de North Jr., "Problem-Solving Judges: Meddlers or Innovators?," *William Mitchell Law Review* 32 (2006): 957–960; Leon Neyfakh, "The Custom Justice of 'Problem-Solving Courts,'" *Boston Globe*, March 23, 2014; Eric J. Miller, "Embracing Addiction: Drug Courts and the False Promise of Judicial Interventionism," *Ohio State Law Journal* 65 (2004): 1479.

81. "Red Hook Community Justice Center: Documented Results," Center for Court Innovation, http://www.courtinnovation.org/sites/default/files/RH_Fact_sheet .pdf [https://perma.cc/T3XF-NFSH]; *Census of Problem-Solving Courts*, 7.

82. Gayle Williams-Byers, "Judicial Responsibility for Justice in Criminal Courts" (public remarks, Hofstra University, Maurice Deane School of Law, April 6, 2017).

83. Nancy J. King and Ronald F. Wright, "The Invisible Revolution in Plea Bargaining: Managerial Judging and Judicial Participation in Negotiations," *Texas Law Review* 95 (2016): 325–326, 374 (studying judicial role in managing felony dockets in ten states); Judith Resnik, "Managerial Judges," *Harvard Law Review* 96 (1982): 380, 395–399 ("Judicial management may be teaching judges to value their statistics, such as the number of case dispositions, more than they value the quality of their dispositions."); Bogira, *Courtroom 302*, 39, 16 (quoting Chicago judge).

CHAPTER 4: INNOCENCE

1. Not the defendant's actual name. This vignette is drawn from a telephone interview with Sarah Elkins, December 9, 2016, notes on file with author. For a definition of burglary, see Md. Code Crim. § 6-205; Herd v. State, 125 Md. App. 77, 92 (1999).

2. Justin Fenton and Luke Broadwater, "Gov. Hogan Announces 'Immediate' Closure of Baltimore Jail," *Baltimore Sun*, July 30, 2015.

3. Albert W. Alschuler, "A Nearly Perfect System for Convicting the Innocent," *Albany Law Review* 79 (2017): 919.

4. David Polin, *Challenges to Use of Breath Tests for Drunk Drivers Based on Claim That Partition or Conversion Ratio Between Measured Breath Alcohol and Actual Blood Alcohol Is Inaccurate*, 90 A.L.R.4th 155 (1991).

5. Daniel S. Medwed, ed., *Wrongful Convictions and the DNA Revolution: Twenty-Five Years of Freeing the Innocent* (Cambridge: Cambridge University Press, 2017); Dan Simon, *In Doubt: The Psychology of the Criminal Justice Process* (Cambridge, MA: Harvard University Press, 2012); Brandon Garrett, *Convicting the Innocent: Where Criminal Prosecutions Go Wrong* (Cambridge, MA: Harvard University Press, 2011); Barry Scheck et al., *Actual Innocence: Five Days to Execution, and Other Dispatches from the Wrongly Convicted* (New York: Doubleday, 2000).

6. Samuel Gross is founder of the National Registry of Exonerations. Samuel R. Gross and Barbara O'Brien, "Frequency and Predictors of False Conviction: Why We

Know So Little, and New Data on Capital Cases," *Journal of Empirical Legal Studies* 5, no. 4 (December 2008): 941 (noting lack of attention to misdemeanors); "About," National Registry of Exonerations, https://www.law.umich.edu/special/exoneration /Pages/about.aspx [https://perma.cc/JDM3-DZ4P]. The past few years have seen some changes. The National Registry has begun to include misdemeanor exonerations. Barry Scheck, founder of the Innocence Project, has called attention to the high rate of wrongful misdemeanor guilty pleas. Barry Scheck, "Four Reforms for the Twenty-First Century," *Judicature* 96 (May–June 2013): 325.

7. Ryan Gabrielson and Topher Sanders, "How a $2 Roadside Drug Test Sends Innocent People to Jail," *New York Times*, July 7, 2016.

8. *Exonerations in 2015* (Irvine, CA: National Registry of Exonerations, Newkirk Center for Science and Society, 2016), 9–11. See also Samuel R. Gross, "Opinion: The Staggering Number of Wrongful Convictions in America," *Washington Post*, July 24, 2015 (discussing the Harris County exonerations); Ryan Gabrielson, "Houston Police End Use of Drug Tests That Helped Produce Wrongful Convictions," *ProPublica*, July 14, 2017.

9. Gabrielson and Sanders, "How a $2 Roadside Drug Test."

10. Ryan Gabrielson, "Unreliable and Unchallenged," *ProPublica and Las Vegas Review-Journal*, October 28, 2016.

11. Gabrielson, "Unreliable and Unchallenged."

12. Cal. Health & Safety Code § 11350; Or. Rev. Stat. § 475.752; 18 U.S.C. § 844; Matthew R. Durose, "State Court Sentencing of Convicted Felons 2004—Statistical Tables, Felony Case Processing in State Courts, Table 4.3," Bureau of Justice Statistics, July 1, 2007, NCJ 217995, https://www.bjs.gov/content/pub/html/scscf04/tables /scs04403tab.cfm [https://perma.cc/JZF4-RVBP]; *Exonerations in 2015* (documenting Harris County sentences of a few days or weeks).

13. Gabrielson, "Unreliable and Unchallenged," 8.

14. United States v. Horn, 185 F. Supp.2d 530, 533 (D. Md. 2001) (field sobriety tests did not constitute scientific evidence proving blood alcohol content to which police could testify as experts); "Tests for Driving Under Influence of Marijuana Questioned," *Fortune Magazine*, May 10, 2016; Lara Bazelon, "Testing, Testing: The Sweat Patch Was Supposed to Solve the Problems of Urinalysis, but It Created a Host of Its Own," *Legal Affairs*, July–August 2003.

15. Complaint, Rothgery v. Gillespie County, No. A04CA456LY (W.D.Tx. July 15, 2004); Rothgery v. Gillespie County, 554 U.S. 191 (2008); Michael Graczyk, "High Court Hears Case of Texan Denied a Lawyer," *Laredo Morning Times*, March 16, 2008.

16. Herring v. United States, 555 U.S. 135, 155 (2009) (Ginsburg, J., dissenting).

17. *License Plate Seizure Program's Error Rate Still High; Program Should Be Abolished, Office of Program Policy Analysis and Government Accountability* (Tallahassee: Florida Legislature, December 2000); Melanie Payne, "Driver's License Suspensions Could Be Mistake," *News-Press*, November 2, 2015; State v. Pitcher, 379 N.J. Super. 308 (2005); State v. Petterson, 256 Or. App. 385 (Or. 2013); Commonwealth v. Wilkerson, 436 Mass. 137 (2002).

18. Madeline Neighly and Maurice Emsellem, *Wanted: Accurate FBI Background Checks for Employment* (New York: National Employment Law Project,

2013), 1; James B. Jacobs, *The Eternal Criminal Record* (Cambridge, MA: Harvard University Press, 2015), 133–140.

19. Or. Rev. Stat. § 166.270; Minn. Stat. § 624.713; N.Y. Penal Law § 265.01; W. Va. Code § 61-7-7.

20. *Herring*, 555 U.S. at 155 (Ginsburg, J., dissenting); Kevin Lapp, "Databasing Delinquency," *Hastings Law Journal* 67 (2015): 210–211 (on gang databases); *Investigation of the Ferguson Police Department* (Washington, DC: US Department of Justice, Civil Rights Division, 2015) 47, 55 (on the lack of accurate warrant data).

21. Albert Samaha, "Blue Lies Matter," *BuzzFeed*, January 17, 2017, https://www.buzzfeed.com/albertsamaha/blue-lies-matter?utm_term=.psGY8o54M#.hr7l0KrG2 [https://perma.cc/UL9G-6L6D] (documenting sixty-two incidents where video footage contradicted police accounts); James C. McKinley, "New York Officer Is Charged in Arrest of Man Who Tried to Film Him," *New York Times*, December 22, 2015.

22. Ligon v. City of New York, 925 F. Supp. 2d 478 (S.D.N.Y. 2013): Davis v. City of New York, 902 F. Supp. 2d 405 (S.D.N.Y. 2012); M. Chris Fabricant, "Rousting the Cops: One Man Stands Up to the NYPD's Apartheid-Like Trespassing Crackdown," *Village Voice*, October 30, 2007.

23. *Ligon*, 925 F. Supp. 2d at 490 (internal citations and quotations omitted); N.Y. Penal Law § 140.15[1].

24. *Ligon*, 925 F. Supp. 2d at 497–498; "A Plaintiff Reflects on Judge Scheindlin's Clean Halls Decision," Bronx Defenders, February 13, 2013, https://www.bronxdefenders.org/a-plaintiff-reflects-on-judge-scheindlins-clean-halls-decision[https://perma.cc/ZDB4-XTRH].

25. Complaint, Ligon v. City of New York, No. 12 Civ. 2274, *35 (March 28, 2012); "New York County Adult Arrests Disposed," New York State Division of Criminal Justice Services, 2016, http://www.criminaljustice.ny.gov/crimnet/ojsa/dispos/newyork.pdf [https://perma.cc/2JZH-54TD].

26. *Ligon*, 925 F. Supp. 2d at 540.

27. Joseph Goldstein, "Prosecutor Deals Blow to Stop-and-Frisk Tactic," *New York Times*, September 25, 2012.

28. Peter Moskos, *Cop in the Hood: My Year Policing Baltimore's Eastern District* (Princeton, NJ: Princeton University Press, 2008), 114–115, 119–120, 55.

29. Complaint at 33, NAACP v. Baltimore Police Dep't, Case No. 06-1863 (D. Md., December 18, 2007).

30. NAACP Complaint, 44–45.

31. *Investigation of the Baltimore City Police Department* (Washington, DC: US Department of Justice, Civil Rights Division, 2016), 17, https://www.justice.gov/crt/file/883296/download [https://perma.cc/XSK4-S5C5].

32. *Investigation of the Baltimore City Police Department*, 29.

33. *Investigation of the Baltimore City Police Department*, 17, 24, 26. Overall, BPD made over 200,000 total arrests during this period.

34. Balt. City Code, Police Codes, Art. 19 § 25-1.

35. City of Chicago v. Morales, 527 U.S. 41 (1999).

36. Williams v. State, 140 Md. App. 463, 477 (2001); *Investigation of the Baltimore City Police Department*, 36–37.

37. *Investigation of the Baltimore City Police Department*, 35–36; *City of Chicago*, 527 U.S. 41 (1999) (striking down loitering statute); Papachristou v. City of Jacksonville, 405 U.S. 156 (1972) (striking down vagrancy statute).

38. Natalie Finegar, phone interview with author, December 1, 2016, notes on file with author.

39. *Investigation of the Baltimore City Police Department*, 35, 26, 35.

40. *Maryland Judiciary Annual Statistical Abstract Fiscal Year 2015* (Annapolis: Court Operations Department, 2015), Table DC-4. The Maryland judiciary provides aggregate data on criminal case filings and dispositions but not on the specific offenses of trespassing, loitering, or other order-maintenance crimes. If cases are initially well screened, prosecutors later in the process may be less likely to dismiss them once they get to court. See, e.g., Bruce Frederick and Don Stemen, *The Anatomy of Discretion: An Analysis of Prosecutorial Decision Making—Technical Report* (New York: Vera Institute of Justice, December 2012), 256.

41. *Maryland Judiciary Annual Statistical Abstract*, Table DC-4 (documenting 5,297 guilty pleas in 2015).

42. Interview with Natalie Finegar; *Bailing on Baltimore: Voices from the Front Lines of the Justice System* (Washington, DC: Justice Policy Institute, September 2012), 22 (quoting Baltimore resident).

43. *Investigation of the Newark Police Department* (Washington, DC: US Department of Justice, Civil Rights Division, 2014); *Investigation of the Seattle Police Department* (Washington, DC: US Department of Justice, Civil Rights Division, 2011), 9–11, 25–26 (finding that Seattle police use excessive force in response to minor offenses and overuse pedestrian stops against minorities); Eric Nalder et al., "The Strong Arm of the Law: 'Obstructing' Justice: Blacks Are Arrested on 'Contempt of Cop' Charge at Higher Rate," *Seattle Post-Intelligencer*, February 28, 2008.

44. *Investigation of the Baltimore City Police Department*, 55–56.

45. Christy E. Lopez, "Disorderly (mis)Conduct: The Problem with 'Contempt of Cop' Arrests," *American Constitution Society Issue Brief* (2010): 5–6 (Seattle), 7 (San Jose); Floyd v. City of New York, 959 F. Supp. 2d 540, 558 (S.D.N.Y. 2013).

46. Gabrielson and Sanders, "How a $2 Roadside Drug Test," 12–13 (Houston exonerations); "2014 Crime in the United States, Table 49," FBI Uniform Crime Reporting, 2014, https://ucr.fbi.gov/crime-in-the-u.s/2014/crime-in-the-u.s.-2014/tables/table-49 [https://perma.cc/B695-RD83] (arrests by race); Cassia Spohn, "Race, Crime, and Punishment in the Twentieth and Twenty-First Centuries," *Crime and Justice* 44 (2015): 49, 64–66 (on drug use and prosecution by race); Michelle Alexander, *The New Jim Crow: Mass Incarceration in the Age of Colorblindness* (New York: New Press, 2012), 7 and n.10 (on drug use and prosecution by race).

47. Disparate misdemeanor arrest rates for African Americans are discussed further in Chapter 6 ("Race"). Although they are a numeric minority in the criminal system, black women are increasingly criminalized and labor under a unique set of criminalized stereotypes. See Stephanie Clifford and Jessica Silver-Greenberg, "Foster Care as Punishment: The New Reality of 'Jane Crow,'" *New York Times*, July 21, 2017 (on the criminalization of the parenting choices of women of color); Priscilla A. Ocen, "The New Racially Restrictive Covenant: Race, Welfare, and the Policing of Black Women in Subsidized Housing," *UCLA Law Review* 59 (2012):

1540, 1548 ("contest[ing] the distinction that is often implicit in social welfare and criminal justice scholarship that suggests that Black men and women are regulated on the separate and gendered tracks of the criminal justice and the social welfare systems").

48. "2015 Statewide Misdemeanor Bench Trials and Rates," National Center for State Courts, Court Statistics Project, 2015, http://www.ncsc.org/Sitecore/Content /Microsites/PopUp/Home/CSP/CSP_Criminal [https://perma.cc/YR4U-PWDH] (documenting typical state misdemeanor trial rates of 2 percent or less).

49. *No Day in Court: Marijuana Possession Cases and the Failure of the Bronx Criminal Courts* (New York: Bronx Defenders Office, 2013), 1–2. The report states that "Angel Cardona" is not the client's actual name.

50. *No Day in Court*, 2–3.

51. Lafler v. Cooper, 132 S. Ct. 1376, 1388 (2015) (on national plea rates); "List of Exonerations in the United States," National Registry of Exonerations, http://www.law.umich.edu/special/exoneration/Pages/browse.aspx [https://perma.cc /KG3W-7BJH] (accessed February 20, 2018).

52. The public defender in Jack Ford's case, for example, informed the judge that he had a valid defense. See also Robert C. Boruchowitz et al., *Minor Crimes, Massive Waste: The Terrible Toll of America's Broken Misdemeanor Courts* (Washington, DC: National Association Criminal Defense Lawyers, April 2009), 33 (quoting Judge Joseph Bellacosa); Josh Bowers, "Punishing the Innocent," *University of Pennsylvania Law Review* 156 (2008): 1119–1120 (arguing that it is often in the interests of innocent misdemeanor defendants to plead guilty). The National Registry of Exonerations lists eighty-five misdemeanor exonerations out of 2,144. "List of Exonerations in the United States."

CHAPTER 5: MONEY

1. Qiana Williams, "A Cycle of Incarceration: Prison, Debt and Bail, White House Conference," video posted to YouTube by "The White House," December 3, 2015, https://www.youtube.com/watch?v=ErcSHP12deE.

2. Neal Gabler, "The Secret Shame of Middle-Class Americans," *The Atlantic* (May 2016), http://www.theatlantic.com/magazine/archive/2016/05/my-secret-shame /476415 [https://perma.cc/NKS3-YCLW].

3. Thomas B. Edsall, "The Expanding World of Poverty Capitalism," *New York Times*, August 26, 2014.

4. Richard A. Webster, "Judicial Funding 'Scheme' Dismantled in Ascension Parish," *Times-Picayune*, July 5, 2016; Amended Complaint, Williams v. Lambert, No. 16-CV-251 (M.D.La., April 19, 2016). In 2016, subsequent to the filing of the Williams lawsuit, the Louisiana legislature changed the rules so that Judge Lambert no longer controlled the fund.

5. David Koon, "'Million-Dollar Thursday': A Visit to Sherwood's Hot Check Court," *Arkansas Times*, August 25, 2016, https://www.arktimes.com/ArkansasBlog /archives/2016/08/25/million-dollar-thursday-a-visit-to-sherwoods-hot-check -court [https://perma.cc/T8SB-ZSFF]; Complaint at 7, 33–36, Dade v. City of Sherwood, No. 4:16-CV-602 (E.D.Ark., August 23, 2016); "Hot Check Division," City of

Sherwood, http://www.cityofsherwood.net/162/Hot-Check-Division [https://perma.cc /46FA-F6P3].

6. Browning-Ferris Industries v. Kelco Disposal, 492 U.S. 257, 287 (1989) (O'Connor, J., dissenting).

7. These facts are taken from the complaint in Rodriguez v. Providence Cmty. Corr., Inc., No. 3:15-cv-01048 (M.D.Tenn., October 1, 2015). The case settled in 2017. Adam Tambourin, "Probation Company, Rutherford County Paying $14.3 Million to Settle Extortion Lawsuit," *The Tennessean*, September 19, 2017, https:// www.tennessean.com/story/news/local/rutherford/2017/09/19/probation-company -rutherford-county-paying-14-3-million-settle-extortion-lawsuit/682379001 [https:// perma.cc/QHG2-869V].

8. Loïc Wacquant, *Punishing the Poor: The Neoliberal Government of Social Insecurity* (Durham, NC: Duke University Press, 2009), 11, 41; Kaaryn S. Gustafson, *Cheating Welfare: Public Assistance and the Criminalization of Poverty* (New York: New York University Press, 2011); Peter Edelman, *Not a Crime to Be Poor: The Criminalization of Poverty in America* (New York: New Press, 2017). For income and educational data on prisoners, see Darren Wheelock and Christopher Uggen, "Race, Poverty and Punishment: The Impact of Criminal Sanctions on Racial, Ethnic, and Socioeconomic Inequality" (Working Paper 6-15, National Poverty Center, 2006), 13, fig. 3; Bruce Western and Christopher Wildeman, "Punishment, Inequality, and the Future of Mass Incarceration," *Kansas Law Review* 57 (2009): 860 (30 percent unemployment rate); Bernadette Rabuy and Daniel Kopf, *Prisons of Poverty: Uncovering the Pre-Incarceration Incomes of the Imprisoned* (Northampton, MA: Prison Policy Initiative, July 9, 2015) (average preincarceration income of an incarcerated man is $19,650, less than half the average for a nonincarcerated man). On prisoner literacy, see Caroline Wolf Harlow, *Special Report: Education and Correctional Populations* (Washington, DC: Bureau of Justice Statistics, 2003) (75 percent of state prison inmates did not complete high school); Second Chance Act of 2007, § 231, 42 U.S.C.A. § 1750 (citing National Institute of Literacy on low inmate literacy). See also Caroline Wolf Harlow, *Special Report: Defense Counsel in Criminal Cases* (Washington, DC: Bureau of Justice Statistics, November 2000) (80 percent of felony defendants qualified for appointed counsel).

9. Bearden v. Georgia, 461 U.S. 660 (1983) (equal protection prohibits the incarceration of indigent defendant too poor to pay fine but not the imposition of the fine itself); Tate v. Short, 401 U.S. 395 (1971) (same). See also San Antonio Indep. School District v. Rodriguez, 411 U.S. 1, 24 (1973) ("Where wealth is involved, the Equal Protection Clause does not require absolute equality or precisely equal advantages.").

10. Sandy, interview by invisiblepeople.tv, *Invisible People*, March 2010, https:// invisiblepeople.tv/2010/03/sandy-homeless-berkley [https://perma.cc/3RUQ-VP7M].

11. *No Safe Place: The Criminalization of Homelessness in U.S. Cities* (Washington, DC: National Law Center on Homelessness and Poverty, 2014), 17; *Picking Up the Pieces, Policing in America: A Minneapolis Case Study* (American Civil Liberties Union, 2016); Forrest Stuart, *Down, Out, and Under Arrest: Policing and Everyday Life in Skid Row* (Chicago: University of Chicago Press, 2016), ix; Los Angeles Muni. Code, Chap. IV § 41.18(D) ("No person shall sit, lie or sleep in or upon any street, sidewalk or other public way").

12. Katherine Beckett and Steve Herbert, *Banished: The New Social Control in Urban America* (Oxford: Oxford University Press, 2010), 5–6, 8. Seattle Municipal Code § 18.12.278 authorizes park police to issue exclusion orders.

13. *No Safe Place*, 12–13.

14. Memorandum Opinion, Stinnie v. Holcomb, No. 3:16-CV-00044, 2017 WL 963234 (W.D.Va., March 13, 2017); see also Complaint at *7–13, Stinnie v. Holcomb, No. 3:16-cv-00044 (W.D.Va. July 6, 2016). The case was dismissed on procedural grounds in 2017; as of this writing litigation is ongoing. Stinnie v. Holcomb, App. No. 17-1740 (4th Cir. May 23, 2018) (unpublished opinion).

15. Va. Code Ann. § 46.2-395(B); Dahlia Lithwick, "Punished for Being Poor: The Virginia Scheme That Suspends the Driver's License of Anyone Who Can't Pay Trivial Fines," *Slate*, July 16, 2016, http://www.slate.com/articles/news_and_politics /jurisprudence/2016/07/the_virginia_driver_s_license_scheme_that_punishes_poor _people.html [https://perma.cc/RNQ9-8RCP].

16. Vivian Wang, "Ticket to Nowhere: The Hidden Cost of Driver's License Suspensions," *Milwaukee Journal Sentinel*, August 15, 2015 (Milwaukee license suspensions); Alicia Bannon et al., *Criminal Justice Debt: A Barrier to Reentry* (New York: Brennan Center for Justice at New York University School of Law, 2010), 24–25 and n.161 (identifying states that suspend licenses for nonpayment); "Driving While Revoked, Suspended or Otherwise Unlicensed: Penalties by State," National Conference of State Legislatures, http://www.ncsl.org/research/transportation /driving-while-revoked-suspended-or-otherwise-unli.aspx [https://perma.cc/QBF7 -KAYE]; Robert C. Boruchowitz et al., *Minor Crimes, Massive Waste: The Terrible Toll of America's Broken Misdemeanor Courts* (Washington, DC: National Association Criminal Defense Lawyers, April 2009), 26 (describing size of driving-on-suspended dockets in various jurisdictions); Robert C. Boruchowitz, *Diverting and Reclassifying Misdemeanors Could Save $1 Billion per Year: Reducing the Need for and Cost of Appointed Counsel* (Washington, DC: American Constitution Society for Law and Policy Issue Brief, December 2010), 1, n.1 (driving on suspended constituted 30 percent of Washington State's 2007 misdemeanor docket). On states that have retracted the practice, see the Southern Poverty Law Center, "SPLC Reaches Agreement with Mississippi to Reinstate over 100,000 Driver's Licenses Suspended for Non-Payment of Fines," December 19, 2017, https://www.splcenter.org/news /2017/12/19/splc-reaches-agreement-mississippi-reinstate-over-100000-driver%E2 %80%99s-licenses-suspended-non [https://perma.cc/4CBQ-8HS9]; Sophia Bollag, "California to Stop Suspending Licenses for Traffic Fines," *Associated Press*, June 28, 2017, https://www.usnews.com/news/best-states/california/articles/2017-06-28 /california-to-stop-suspending-licenses-for-traffic-fines [https://perma.cc/8A6J-UGZE]; Fowler v. Johnson, No. CV 17-11441, 2017 WL 6379676 (E.D.Mich. December 14, 2017) (preliminary injunction barring Michigan from suspending driver's licenses of people unable to pay traffic debt).

17. *Investigation of the Ferguson Police Department* (Washington, DC: US Department of Justice, Civil Rights Division, March 4, 2016), 3, 66, 55. On the effects of having an outstanding warrant, see Alexes Harris, Heather Evans, and Katherine Beckett, "Drawing Blood from Stones: Legal Debt and Social Inequality in the Contemporary United States," *American Journal of Sociology* 115, no. 6 (2010):

1761–1762; Bannon et al., *Criminal Justice Debt*, 23, n.145. See also Sarah Brayne, "Surveillance and System Avoidance: Criminal Justice Contact and Institutional Attachment," *American Sociological Review* 79 (2014): 367; Armando Lara-Millan, "Public Emergency Room Overcrowding in the Era of Mass Imprisonment," *American Sociological Review* 79, no. 5 (2014): 866, 873 (study of police surveillance and enforcement activities in public hospitals); Alice Goffman, *On the Run: Fugitive Life in an American City* (Chicago: University of Chicago Press, 2014), viii, 34–35 (describing police hospital surveillance in Philadelphia). In South Carolina, Officer Slager ultimately pled guilty to using deadly force in violation of Mr. Scott's civil rights. Alan Blinder, "Ex-Officer Who Shot Walter Scott Pleads Guilty in Charleston," *New York Times*, May 2, 2017.

18. Ray Rivera et al., "A Few Blocks, 4 Years, 52,000 Police Stops," *New York Times*, July 11, 2010 (describing Brownsville); *Investigation of the Newark Police Department* (Washington, DC: US Department of Justice, Civil Rights Division, and US Attorney's Office District of New Jersey, 2014), 9, 19; Utah v. Strieff, 136 S. Ct. 2056, 2068 (2016) (Sotomayor, J., dissenting). For additional examples of heavy misdemeanor policing of low-income neighborhoods, see Abdallah Fayyad, "The Criminalization of Gentrifying Neighborhoods," *The Atlantic*, December 20, 2017; *Cited in Milwaukee: The Cost of Unpaid Municipal Citations* (Milwaukee, WI: Justice Initiatives Institute, June 2015); *Picking Up the Pieces*; Saki Knafo, "A Black Police Officer's Fight Against the N.Y.P.D.," *New York Times Magazine*, February 18, 2016.

19. Katherine M. Keyes and Deborah S. Hasin, "Socio-Economic Status and Problem Alcohol Use: The Positive Relationship Between Income and the DSM-IV Alcohol Abuse Diagnosis," *Addiction* 103, no. 7 (2008).

20. Jim Dwyer, "Side Effects of Arrests for Marijuana," *New York Times*, June 16, 2011. The *New York Times* did not publish Alika's last name.

21. *Not Just a Ferguson Problem: How Traffic Courts Drive Inequality in California* (San Francisco: Lawyers Committee for Civil Rights et al., 2015), 17. The report did not publish Alyssa's last name.

22. Alan M. Voorhees et al., *Motor Vehicle Affordability and Fairness Task Force Final Report* (New Brunswick, NJ: Edward J. Bloustein School of Planning and Public Policy, Rutgers University, 2006), 38; "Profiles of Those Forced to 'Pay or Stay,'" National Public Radio, May 19, 2014, http://www.npr.org/2014/05/19/310710716/profiles-of-those-forced-to-pay-or-stay [https://perma.cc/ENJ2-KGRH] (profiling Restrepo).

23. Harris, Evans, and Beckett, "Drawing Blood from Stones," 1770–1771; Joseph Shapiro, "As Court Fees Rise, the Poor Are Paying the Price," National Public Radio, May 19, 2014, https://www.npr.org/2014/05/19/312158516/increasing-court-fees-punish-the-poor.

24. Fla. Stat. Ann. §§ 806.13, 775.082 (2016); Rebekah Diller, *The Hidden Costs of Florida's Criminal Justice Fees* (New York: Brennan Center for Justice, 2010); "Texas County Clerks' Misdemeanor Conviction Court Costs Chart," *Texas Courts*, January 1, 2016, http://www.txcourts.gov/media/1437645/cc-misd-ct-cst-orig-010116.pdf [https://perma.cc/TC7R-MDJJ]; Laura I. Appleman, "Nickel and Dimed into Incarceration: Cash-Register Justice in the Criminal System," *Boston College Law Review* 57, no. 5 (2016): 15 (on Oklahoma fines and fees).

25. Bannon et al., *Criminal Justice Debt*, 15, n.65; Diller, *Hidden Costs*, 15; Harris, Evans, and Beckett, "Drawing Blood from Stones," 1759, n.7.

26. Bannon et al., *Criminal Justice Debt*, 28 (noting that all fifteen states in study made payment a condition of probation and describing consequences of probation violation); Harris, Evans, and Beckett, "Drawing Blood from Stones," 1787 (nonpayment constituted 12 percent of technical probation violations in Washington); Brief for Empire Justice et al. as Amici Curiae Supporting Plaintiff-Appellant, 2009 WL 8144027 at 17–18, Clark v. Astrue, No. 08-5801-cv (2nd Cir. 2010) (describing Loretta's situation). The brief refers to Loretta as "Loretta R."

27. Bannon et al., *Criminal Justice Debt*, 27–28.

28. Gabler, "The Secret Shame of Middle-Class Americans," 5 ("[T]he evidence strongly indicates that either a sizable minority or a slim majority of Americans are on thin ice financially.").

29. Harris, Evans, and Beckett, "Drawing Blood from Stones," 1789.

30. *Profiting from Probation: America's "Offender-Funded" Probation Industry* (New York: Human Rights Watch, February 2014), 46 (quoting Alabama probationer); Harris, Evans, and Beckett, "Drawing Blood from Stones," 1785 (quoting Justice).

31. Wacquant, *Punishing the Poor*, 6 (arguing that in the United States the welfarist left hand of the state has been supplanted by the punitive right hand); Alexandra Natapoff, "Gideon's Servants and the Criminalization of Poverty," *Ohio State Journal of Criminal Law* 12 (2015): 445 (articulating the intimate connections between the criminal system and the welfare state); Elizabeth Hinton, *From the War on Poverty to the War on Crime: The Making of Mass Incarceration in America* (Cambridge, MA: Harvard University Press, 2016) (describing how the welfare programs of Lyndon Johnson's Great Society morphed into the criminal justice apparatus of mass incarceration). The welfarist role of the misdemeanor system is explored in more depth in Chapter 8.

32. Bannon et al., *Criminal Justice Debt*; *In for a Penny: The Rise of America's New Debtors' Prisons* (Washington, DC: American Civil Liberties Union, October 2010); Shaila Dewan, "Court by Court, Lawyers Fight Policies That Fall Heavily on the Poor," *New York Times*, October 23, 2015; "The New Debtors' Prison: If You Are Poor, Don't Get Caught Speeding," *The Economist*, November 16, 2013; *Fines, Fees, and Bail: Payments in the Criminal Justice System That Disproportionately Impact the Poor* (Washington, DC: White House Council of Economic Advisers, December 2015), 4 (on Rhode Island and Huron, Ohio); *The Outskirts of Hope: How Ohio's Debtors' Prisons Are Ruining Lives and Costing Communities* (Cleveland, OH: American Civil Liberties Union, 2013) (studying Huron County); Shapiro, "As Court Fees Rise," 8–9 (documenting Benton County, Washington).

33. Bannon et al., *Criminal Justice Debt*, 19. But see Jennifer Turner, *A Pound of Flesh: The Criminalization of Private Debt* (Washington, DC: American Civil Liberties Union, 2018), 5 (documenting the use of arrest warrants by private debt collectors).

34. "Profiles of Those Forced to 'Pay or Stay,'" National Public Radio, May 19, 2014, http://www.npr.org/2014/05/19/310710716/profiles-of-those-forced-to-pay-or-stay [https://perma.cc/ENJ2-KGRH].

35. Alabama v. Shelton, 535 U.S. 654 (2002). See Chapter 3 for the law and practices governing the appointment of counsel. See also *In for a Penny*; text accompanying notes 123–127 infra (on the use of civil contempt).

36. Harris, Evans, and Beckett, "Drawing Blood from Stones," 1784. The interviewers do not provide Pete's last name.

37. Lauren-Brooke Eisen, *Charging Inmates Perpetuates Mass Incarceration* (New York: Brennan Center for Justice at New York University School of Law, 2015), 3–5 (quoting Sheriff Pitts in Elko, Nevada, and describing legal landscape); Barbara Krauth and Karin Stayton, *Fees Paid by Jail Inmates: Fee Categories, Revenues, and Management Perspectives in a Sample of U.S. Jails* (Washington, DC: US Department of Justice, National Institute of Corrections, December 18, 2005).

38. Cal. Penal Code § 1205(a); Ohio Rev. Code Ann. § 2947.14(D); Mo. Rev. Stat. Ann. § 543.270(1). That particular New Orleans practice was purportedly halted after a civil rights lawsuit in 2007, although observers say it persists. *In for a Penny*, 23–24. On the Montgomery jail, see Complaint at 7–8, Mitchell v. City of Montgomery, No. 2:14-cv-186 (M.D.Ala. March 18, 2014).

39. *In for a Penny*, 29–30 (describing Kawana Young); *In Jail and in Debt: Ohio's Pay-to-Stay Jail Fees* (Cleveland, OH: American Civil Liberties Union, Fall 2015), 5.

40. See, e.g., Brown v. Plata, 563 U.S. 493 (2011) (prison overcrowding and lack of medical care violated Eighth Amendment).

41. Complaint at 1–2, Jenkins v. Jennings, No. 4:15-cv-00252 (E.D.Mo. February 8, 2015). The case settled in 2016. Chris King, "Nov. 24 Deadline to Collect in Jennings Settlement, $4.7M to Compensate Those It Wrongly Jailed," *St. Louis American*, September 16, 2016.

42. For additional civil rights litigation, see Civil Rights Corp. (http://www.civilrightscorps.org) and Equal Justice Under Law (http://www.equaljusticeunderlaw.org). To hear former US attorney Lynch's comments, see Loretta Lynch, "A Cycle of Incarceration: Prison, Debt and Bail, White House Conference," video posted to YouTube "The White House," December 3, 2015, https://www.youtube.com/watch?v=ErcSHP12deE.

43. See Michelle Wilde Anderson, "Losing the War of Attrition: Mobility, Chronic Decline, and Infrastructure," *Yale Law Journal Forum* 127 (2017): 528 (describing urban fiscal declines); Michelle Wilde Anderson, "The New Minimal Cities," *Yale Law Journal* 123 (2014): 1120–1125 (describing the challenges of insolvent cities); see also Darrick Hamilton and Michael Linden, "Issue Brief: Hidden Rules of Race Are Embedded in the New Tax Law" (New York: Roosevelt Institute, May 2018), 6–7 (citing studies that show that reduced state and local tax revenues lead to higher fees and fines).

44. On New Orleans, see *In for a Penny*, 8, 27–28; Derwyn Bunton, "When the Public Defender Says, 'I Can't Help,'" *New York Times*, February 19, 2016 (fines and fees pay for two-thirds of the Louisiana public defender system). On Mississippi, see Vershal Hogan, "State Gives Judges, District Attorneys First Raise in Ten Years," *Natchez Democrat*, February 17, 2013. On Florida, see Diller, *Hidden Costs*, 10. On Texas, see Shapiro, "As Court Fees Rise." On Louisiana, see *In for a Penny*, 25. See also Alexes Harris, *A Pound of Flesh: Monetary Sanctions as Punishment for the Poor*

(New York: Russell Sage Foundation, 2016), 112 (interview with Washington judge who described pressure from the county council to raise money through LFOs).

45. Claire Greenberg et al., "The Growing and Broad Nature of Legal Financial Obligations: Evidence from Alabama Court Records," *Connecticut Law Review* 48 (2016): 1108; Kendall Taggart and Alex Campbell, "Judge Blasts Texas for Using Courts to Make Money off Poor," *BuzzFeed News*, April 19, 2016, https://www .buzzfeed.com/kendalltaggart/texas-judge-blasts-state-for-profiting-from-poorest -defendan?utm_term=.vwXQ3ozqK#.wlvkKmPlJ [https://perma.cc/2858-2CYG]; *In for a Penny*, 38 (on Michigan); Mark Flatten, *City Court: Money, Pressure and Politics Make It Tough to Beat the Rap* (Phoenix: Goldwater Institute, 2017), 9 (on Phoenix, Arizona).

46. *Profiting from Probation*, 47, 60–61 (describing litigation in Georgia and Alabama); see also *In for a Penny*, 53 (describing pay-to-stay litigation against Hamilton County, Ohio). Carl Reynolds and Jeff Hall, *2011–2012 Policy Paper: Courts Are Not Revenue Centers* (Williamsburg, VA: Conference of State Court Administrators, 2012), 1, 9.

47. *Investigation of the Ferguson Police Department*, 2.

48. *Investigation of the Ferguson Police Department*, 2.

49. *Investigation of the Ferguson Police Department*, 2; Hon. John Bull to Daphne Webber, February 23, 2016, Regional Collections Specialist, Office of Court Administration, https://www.documentcloud.org/documents/2805102-Judge-John -Bull-Letter-to-OCA.html [https://perma.cc/79QW-WWL2]; "Ending Cash-Register Justice," *New York Times*, October 17, 2017; "The Problem Is Bigger Than Ferguson," *New York Times*, March 12, 2015.

50. Complaint at 6, Rodriguez v. Providence Cmty. Corr., Inc.; Adam Tamburin, "Probation Company, Rutherford County Paying $14.3 Million to Settle Extortion Lawsuit," *The Tennessean*, September 19, 2017, https://www.tennessean.com/story /news/local/rutherford/2017/09/19/probation-company-rutherford-county-paying -14-3-million-settle-extortion-lawsuit/682379001 [https://perma.cc/QHG2-869V].

51. Carrie Teegardin, "Ticket Torment: Georgia Probation Systems Ensnares Those Too Poor to Pay Traffic Fines," *Atlanta Journal-Constitution*, November 22, 2014; see also Edwards v. Red Hills Community Probation, No. 1:15-CV-67 (M.D.Ga., April 10, 2015).

52. *Profiting from Probation*, 16, n.20 (listing states that use private probation); Carrie Teegardin, "March Madness Bounty Put Squeeze on Sentinel Probationers," *Atlanta Journal-Constitution*, March 4, 2016; *Profiting from Probation*, 19; Andrew Cohen, "Is There a Constitutional Right to Cash In on the Poor?," Marshall Project, September 11, 2017, https://www.themarshallproject.org/2017/09/11/is-there -a-constitutional-right-to-cash-in-on-the-poor [https://perma.cc/KBZ4-6ZRC] (describing lawsuit against Arkansas judges); *Profiting from Probation*, 60 (quoting Judge Harrington); James McNair, "Inside Kentucky's Unregulated Private Probation Industry," Kentucky Center for Investigative Reporting, January, 20, 2016, http:// kycir.org/2016/01/20/inside-kentuckys-unregulated-private-probation-industry [https://perma.cc/E9B4-85YP].

53. Bannon et al., *Criminal Justice Debt*, 17, n.94.

54. Beth Chapman, press release, Duane "Dog" Chapman Facebook page, July 10, 2016, https://www.facebook.com/OfficialDogTheBountyHunter/posts /1072234586202898 [https://perma.cc/LM67-R9GF]; "Newly-Elected Chairperson and President Beth Chapman to Preside over PBUS Mid-Year Conference July 10–13 in Biloxi, MS," *NBC-2*, January 3, 2018, http://www.24-7pressrelease.com/press -release/newlyelected-chairperson-and-president-beth-chapman-to-preside-over-pbus -midyear-conference-july-1013-in-biloxi-ms-425444.php [https://perma.cc/8LAF-5QRX].

55. Joshua Holland, "Private Prison Companies Are Embracing Alternatives to Incarceration," *The Nation*, August 23, 2016; see also Paul Barrett, "Private Prisons Have a Problem: Not Enough Inmates," *Bloomberg Businessweek*, September 9, 2016, https://www.bloomberg.com/news/articles/2016-09-08/private-prisons-have-a -problem-not-enough-inmates [https://perma.cc/R8HS-46XG]; Brett Kelman, "They Confessed to Minor Crimes. Then City Hall Billed Them $122K in 'Prosecution Fees,'" *Desert Sun*, November 15, 2017, http://www.desertsun.com/story/news/crime _courts/2017/11/15/he-confessed-minor-crime-then-city-hall-billed-him-31-k-his-own -prosecution/846850001 [https://perma.cc/58XV-EWU7]; Jessica Pishko, "'Restorative Justice' for Shoplifting? A Court Calls It Extortion," Marshall Project, October 30, 2017, https://www.themarshallproject.org/2017/10/30/restorative-justice-for-shoplifting -a-court-calls-it-extortion [https://perma.cc/VE9R-C6GU]; Jessica Silver-Greenberg, "In Prosecutors, Debt Collectors Find a Partner," *New York Times*, September 15, 2012 (California proscutors let private debt companies use letterhead with district attorney seal to collect debt and share the proceeds); Sarah Stillman, "Get Out of Jail, Inc.," *New Yorker* (June 2014); John Rappaport, "Criminal Justice, Inc.," *Columbia Law Review* 118 (forthcoming) (on privatized criminal adjudication).

56. United States v. Bajakajian, 524 U.S. 321, 334, 336 (1998). See Beth A. Colgan, "The Excessive Fines Clause: Challenging the Modern Debtors' Prison," *UCLA Law Review* 65 (2018): 47–76 (arguing that ability to pay should be part of the excessiveness inquiry); Beth A. Colgan, "Reviving the Excessive Fines Clause," *California Law Review* 102 (2014): 295; Wayne A. Logan and Ronald F. Wright, "Mercenary Criminal Justice," *Illinois Law Review* 2014 (2014): 1204. The First Circuit has held otherwise, stating that "a court should also consider whether forfeiture would deprive the defendant of his or her livelihood." United States v. Levesque, 546 F.3d 78, 83–85 (1st Cir. 2008) (invalidating a $3 million judgment against an unemployed low-level drug mule). See also Nicholas M. McLean, "Livelihood, Ability to Pay, and the Original Meaning of the Excessive Fines Clause," *Hastings Constitutional Law Quarterly* 40 (2013): 835. For examples of fines upheld and struck down, compare Commonwealth v. Eisenberg, 98 A.3d 1268 (Pa. 2014) (invalidating mandatory minimum fine of $75,000 for misdemeanor theft of $200), with State v. Adams, 2004 WL 1380494 (Ohio Ct. Ap. 7th Dist., June 14, 2004) (upholding fines of up to $600 for operating car stereo at excessive noise level), and State v. Cotton, 198 So.3d 737, 739 (Fla. Dist. Ct. App. 2016) (Fla. June 15, 2016) (upholding $5,000 statutory fine for second-degree misdemeanor of soliciting prostitution). See also Colgan, "Reviving the Excessive Fines Clause," 18–46 (arguing that a broad range of economic sanctions should be considered "fines" for constitutional purposes).

57. Logan and Wright, "Mercenary Criminal Justice," 1185–1196 (describing who is authorized to impose fees); Schilb v. Kuebel, 404 U.S. 357, 370–372 (1971)

(approving a 1 percent administrative fee charged against those who posted bail bonds); Fuller v. Oregon, 417 U.S. 40 (1974) (approving public defender recoupment fee).

58. Connally v. Georgia, 429 U.S. 245 (1977) (invalidating arrangement where judge's salary depended entirely on how many warrants he issued); Tumey v. Ohio, 273 U.S. 510 (1927) (invalidating arrangement where judge received conviction fee in addition to salary); Ward v. Monroeville, 409 U.S. 57, 60–61 (1972) (invalidating mayor/judge conflict but reaffirming mayoral judgeship in Dugan v. Ohio, 277 U.S. 61 [1928]). On nonjudicial actors, see Brown v. Edwards, 721 F.2d 1442, 1451 (5th Cir. 1984) (upholding $10 fee paid to police for every arrest resulting in conviction); Logan and Wright, "Mercenary Criminal Justice," 1202–1203.

59. On fee arrangements, see Reynolds et al., *Courts Are Not Revenue Centers*, 5–6; Logan and Wright, "Mercenary Criminal Justice," 1206–1208; State v. Young, 238 So. 2d 589, 590 (Fla. 1970) (approving $1 flat fee).

60. *Bearden*, 461 U.S. at 672; *Tate*, 401 U.S. at 398–399 (defendant could not be sentenced to incarceration for failing to pay fine on fine-only offense).

61. Bannon et al., *Criminal Justice Debt*, 21–22; Arthur W. Pepin, *The End of Debtors' Prison: Effective Court Policies for Successful Compliance with Legal Financial Obligations* (Williamsburg, VA: Conference of State Court Administrators, 2016), 11.

62. In re Hammermaster, 139 Wash. 2d 211, 224–225, 985 P.2d 924, 931–932 (1999).

63. Turner v. Rogers, 564 U.S. 431, 446 (2011) (holding that an indigent defendant in a civil contempt proceeding facing potential incarceration is not automatically entitled to counsel); *In for a Penny*, 43–50 (on the use of civil contempt). Private debt collection companies have taken advantage of this loophole to get civil courts to issue arrest warrants for civil debtors who miss court appearances. Turner, *A Pound of Flesh*, 5.

64. For a full exploration of this double-edged quality of decriminalization, see Alexandra Natapoff, "Misdemeanor Decriminalization," *Vanderbilt Law Review* 68, no. 4 (2015): 1058–1059, 1084. See also Ex parte Karlson, 160 Cal. 378, 380–381 (1911) (Cal. Penal Code § 1205 limitation on incarceration does not affect courts' authority to fine and incarcerate under their civil contempt powers).

65. Tex. Crim. Proc. Ann. Code § 45.046; Kendall Taggart and Alex Campbell, "In Texas It's a Crime to Be Poor," *BuzzFeed*, October 7, 2017, https://www.buzzfeed.com/kendalltaggart/in-texas-its-a-crime-to-be-poor?utm_term=.raVnGx9YK#.jk8Xzelmr [https://perma.cc/529Q-PBEN] (quoting Texas judge). On Ohio, see Strattman v. Studt, 253 N.E.2d 749, 754 (Ohio 1969) (incarcerating indigent defendant for failure to pay costs violated Ohio constitution); *In for a Penny*, 43–44 (describing incarcerations for failure to pay in Ohio); *Outskirts of Hope*, 6 (same); see also Logan and Wright, "Mercenary Criminal Justice," 1222 (Clinch County sheriff). I have described elsewhere how rule of law functions differently for serious cases than it does for misdemeanors. Alexandra Natapoff, "The Penal Pyramid," in *The New Criminal Justice Thinking*, ed. Sharon Dolovich and Alexandra Natapoff (New York: New York University Press, 2017).

66. Hall v. Florida, 134 S. Ct. 1986, 1992 (2014); Harmelin v. Michigan, 501 U.S. 957, 999 (1991) (Kennedy, J., concurring in part and concurring in the judgment).

67. Samuel H. Pillsbury, *Judging Evil: Rethinking the Law of Murder and Manslaughter* (New York: New York University Press, 1998).

68. Randall Kennedy, *Race, Crime and the Law* (New York: First Vintage Books, 1997); Jill Leovy, *Ghettoside: A True Story of Murder in America* (New York: Spiegel and Grau, 2015). But see Alexander Volokh, "Privatization and the Law and Economics of Political Advocacy," *Stanford Law Review* 60 (2008): 1217–1231 (describing pro-incarceration economic interests and political advocacy).

69. The officer's comment was contained in an August 9, 2016, email on file with author. I was interviewed for German Lopez, "The Tyranny of a Traffic Ticket: How Small Crimes Turn Fatal for Poor, Minority Americans," *VOX*, August 10, 2016, https://www.vox.com/2016/8/5/12364580/police-overcriminalization-net-widening [https://perma.cc/8UAD-GQQP]. On the impact of perceived bias in law enforcement, see Charles R. Epp, Steven Maynard-Moody, and Donald Haider-Markel, *Pulled Over: How Police Stops Define Race and Citizenship* (Chicago: University of Chicago Press, 2014); Tom R. Tyler, *Why People Obey the Law* (Princeton, NJ: Princeton University Press, 2006).

70. Terry v. Ohio, 392 U.S. 1, 13 (1968).

71. *Inmate Fees as a Source of Revenue, Review of Challenges, Report of the Special Commission to Study the Feasibility of Establishing Inmate Fees* (Boston: Executive Office of Public Safety and Security, July 1, 2011); Aaron C. Davis, "D.C. Council Weakens Bill to Decriminalize Marijuana, Keeps Smoking in Public a Crime," *Washington Post*, February 4, 2014.

72. Lauren-Brooke Eisen, "Paying for Your Time: How Charging Inmates Fees Behind Bars May Violate the Excessive Fines Clause," *Loyola Journal of Public Interest Law* 15 (2014): 319 (documenting support for the idea that criminals should contribute to the costs of the criminal system); Broyles v. State, 285 Ark. 457, 460–461 (1985).

73. Sharon Dolovich, "State Punishment and Private Prisons," *Duke Law Journal* 55, no. 3 (2005): 507, 512 (noting that cost-cutting motivates public as well as private prison officials). On the nature of criminal justice bureaucracies, see Rachel Barkow, "The Criminal Regulatory State," in Dolovich and Natapoff, *The New Criminal Justice Thinking*; Mona Lynch, "The Situated Actor and the Production of Punishment: Toward an Empirical Social Psychology of Criminal Procedure," in Dolovich and Natapoff, *The New Criminal Justice Thinking*.

74. Harris, *A Pound of Flesh* (on the impact of felony fines and fees); Brian A. Reaves, *Felony Defendants in Large Urban Counties, 2009—Statistics Tables* (Washington, DC: Bureau of Justice Statistics, December 2013), 26 (mean prison sentence in the United States is fifty-two months). For articulations of the uniquely punitive nature of long-term incarceration, see Keremet Reiter, *23/7: Pelican Bay Prison and the Rise of Long-Term Solitary Confinement* (New Haven, CT: Yale University Press, 2016); Sharon Dolovich, "Incarceration American-Style," *Harvard Law and Policy Review* 3 (2009): 237.

75. The Russian novelist Fyodor Dostoyevsky is widely credited with the saying "The degree of civilization in a society can be judged by entering its prisons."

CHAPTER 6: RACE

1. The racialization of crime also occurs through the juvenile justice system, which disproportionately targets and criminalizes African American youth. Tamar R.

Birckhead, "The Racialization of Juvenile Justice and the Role of the Defense Attorney," *Boston College Law Review* 58, no. 2 (2017): 379.

2. For explorations of the relationships between race, crime, and African American history, see James Forman Jr., *Locking Up Our Own: Crime and Punishment in Black America* (New York: Farrar, Straus and Giroux, 2017); Elizabeth Hinton, *From the War on Poverty to the War on Crime: The Making of Mass Incarceration in America* (Cambridge, MA: Harvard University Press, 2016); Michelle Alexander, *The New Jim Crow: Mass Incarceration in the Age of Colorblindness* (New York: New Press, 2012); Khalil Gibran Muhammad, *The Condemnation of Blackness: Race, Crime, and the Making of Modern Urban America* (Cambridge, MA: Harvard University Press, 2010); Randall Kennedy, *Race, Crime and the Law* (New York: Vintage Books, 1997).

On Native American incarceration and police violence, see Jon Marcus, "Bringing Native American Stories to a National Audience," *Neiman Reports*, February 11, 2016, http://niemanreports.org/articles/bringing-native-american-stories-to-a-national-audience [https://perma.cc/X7Y4-7HGP] (American Indian and Alaskan Natives represent 0.9 percent of the US population and 1.4 percent of local jail populations); Steven W. Perry, *Tribal Crime Data Collection Activities, 2015* (Washington, DC: Bureau of Justice Statistics, 2015); Tina Norris et al., *The American Indian and Alaska Native Population: 2010* (Washington, DC: US Census Bureau, 2012). These data do not include another 2,500 people incarcerated in jails maintained by Indian tribal authorities. Todd D. Minton, *Jails in Indian Country, 2015* (Washington, DC: Bureau of Justice Statistics, November 2016). On Hispanic and Latino incarceration rates and police encounters, see *Report to the United Nations Human Rights Committee Regarding Racial Disparities in the United States Criminal Justice System* (Washington, DC: Sentencing Project, August 2013), 1, 12; Thomas E. Perez to Hon. Joseph Maturo, December 19, 2011, US Department of Justice, Civil Rights Division (East Haven, Connecticut); Kate Willson, "Driving While Brown," *Investigate West*, February 16, 2017, http://invw.org/2017/02/16/driving-while-brown [https://perma.cc/5BKK-7J8H]. See also *Federal Civil Rights Engagement with Arab and Muslim American Communities Post 9/11* (Washington, DC: US Civil Rights Commission, September 2014), 41. The UN observations were made in *Concluding Observations on the Combined Seventh to Ninth Periodic Reports of United States of America* (Geneva, Committee on the Elimination of Racial Discrimination, United Nations, 2014), 10.

3. *Bailing on Baltimore: Voices from the Front Lines of the Justice System* (Washington, DC: Justice Policy Institute, September 2012), 22.

4. Robert Brame et al., "Demographic Patterns of Cumulative Arrest Prevalence by Ages 18 and 23," *Crime & Delinquency* 60, no. 3 (2014): 471–486; Robert Brame et al., "Cumulative Prevalence of Arrest from Ages 8 to 23 in a National Sample," *Pediatrics* 129, no.1 (2012): 21–27; Charles R. Epp et al., *Pulled Over: How Police Stops Define Race and Citizenship* (Chicago: University of Chicago Press, 2014), 2. See also Emma Pierson et al., "A Large-Scale Analysis of Racial Disparities in Police Stops Across the United States" (working paper, Stanford Open Policing Project, 2017) (finding that the bar for searching black and Hispanic drivers is lower than for searching white drivers).

5. *Investigation of the Ferguson Police Department* (Washington, DC: US Department of Justice, Civil Rights Division, 2015), 4.

6. *Investigation of the Baltimore City Police Department* (Washington, DC: US Department of Justice, Civil Rights Division, 2016), 37–38, 55–56. In other contexts, such overtly racial enforcement patterns have been declared unconstitutional. Yick Wo v. Hopkins, 118 U.S. 356 (1886) (declaring unconstitutional the practice of enforcing a San Francisco laundry ordinance only against Chinese laundry owners).

7. Scott Holmes, "Resisting Arrest and Racism—the Crime of 'Disrespect,'" *University of Missouri–Kansas City Law Review* 85 (2017): 625, 636–637 (Durham, North Carolina); spreadsheet from Nebraska Administrative Office of the Courts on file with author, "Defendant Characteristics by Race and Gender, Nebraska District and County Courts" (15,288 cases filed against black defendants out of 80,170 total cases documented); "Quickfacts," US Census Bureau, https://www.census.gov /quickfacts/NE [https://perma.cc/YU7A-DZJ8] (Nebraska population by race); Christy E. Lopez, "Disorderly (mis)Conduct: The Problem with 'Contempt of Cop' Arrests," *American Constitution Society Issue Brief* (2010): 7 (San Jose, California); Thomas E. Perez to Hon. Joseph Maturo, December 19; Willson, "Driving While Brown" (Oregon).

8. Michael Braun et al., "Racial Disparity in Enforcement of Ambiguously Defined Crimes: A Bayesian Analysis of Texas Organized Retail Theft Arrests" (Research Paper no. 18-3, SMU Cox School of Business, 2017), https://ssrn.com /abstract=2959076 [https://perma.cc/6Q4G-J7W9].

9. J. Kelly Lowenstein, "Crunch Time: Black People and Jaywalking in Champaign," *Chicago Tribune*, August 21, 2012; Topher Sanders et al., "Walking While Black: Jacksonville's Enforcement of Pedestrian Violations Raises Concerns That It's Another Example of Racial Profiling," *ProPublica and The Florida Times-Union*, November 16, 2017, https://features.propublica.org/walking-while-black/jacksonville -pedestrian-violations-racial-profiling [https://perma.cc/A7PK-MTFD] (five-year study of pedestrian stops); *Investigation of the Ferguson Police Department*, 4.

10. *The War on Marijuana in Black and White* (New York: American Civil Liberties Union, June 2013), 47, 48, 58.

11. Kathleen Kane-Willis et al., *Patchwork Policy: An Evaluation of Arrests and Tickets for Marijuana Misdemeanors in Illinois* (Chicago: Illinois Consortium on Drug Policy, May 2014); Steve Harrison, "For Small Amounts of Marijuana, Blacks Are Far More Likely Than Whites to Go to Jail in Charlotte," *Charlotte Observer*, February 12, 2016. See also Pierson et al., "A Large-Scale Analysis of Racial Disparities," 13 (finding that racial gaps in search rates persisted in Colorado and Washington after marijuana legalization).

12. William O. Douglas, "Vagrancy and Arrests on Suspicion," *Yale Law Journal* 70, no. 1 (1960): 13.

13. On violent felony arrest-offense correlations, see James Forman Jr., "Racial Critiques of Mass Incarceration: Beyond the New Jim Crow," *New York University Law Review* 87 (2012): 21, 47 (high black arrest rates for violent crimes like murder and robbery are better correlated with higher black offense rates than other crimes); Paul Butler, *Chokehold: Policing Black Men* (New York: New Press, 2017), 120–122 (explaining black violent crime and victimization statistics). On misdemeanor diver-

gences, see *The War on Marijuana*, 97, 105 (documenting divergence between arrest and offense rates); Lopez, "Disorderly (mis)Conduct," 5 (finding "no benign explanation for this disparate enforcement" of contempt-of-cop offenses). The Department of Justice specifically found that high black arrest rates in Ferguson were unjustified: "Our investigation indicates that this disproportionate burden on African Americans cannot be explained by any difference in the rate at which people of different races violate the law. Rather, our investigation has revealed that these disparities occur, at least in part, because of unlawful bias against and stereotypes about African Americans." *Investigation of the Ferguson Police Department*, 5. For discussions of historic and current policing disparities, see Muhammad, *Condemnation of Blackness*, 238–241 (reviewing scholarship on arrest disparities in the 1920s), and Jeffrey Fagan and Garth Davies, "Street Stops and Broken Windows: Terry, Race, and Disorder in New York City," *Fordham Urban Law Journal* 28 (2000): 457 (documenting current disparities).

14. *Investigation of the Baltimore City Police Department* (Washington, DC: US Department of Justice, Civil Rights Division, 2016), 56. Over half of all gambling arrests in the United States are of African Americans. "Crime in the United States 2015: Table 43, Arrests by Race and Ethnicity—Table 43A," FBI Uniform Crime Reporting, 2015, https://ucr.fbi.gov/crime-in-the-u.s/2015/crime-in-the-u.s.-2015/tables/table-43 [https://perma.cc/3NTE-H7UF].

15. Wilfred Chan, "#CrimingWhileWhite, #ICantBreathe Dominate Twitter Talk in Eric Garner Case," *CNN*, December 4, 2014, http://www.cnn.com/2014/12/04 /us/criming-while-white-hashtag/index.html [https://perma.cc/C4S8-USNZ]; Rachel Abrams, "Starbucks to Close 8,000 U.S. Stores for Racial-Bias Training After Arrests," *New York Times*, April 17, 2018.

16. Carlos Berdejó, "Criminalizing Race: Racial Disparities in Plea Bargaining," *Boston College Law Review* 59 (2018): 32–35 (Dane County, Wisconsin, study); Wayne McKenzie et al., *Prosecution and Racial Justice: Using Data to Advance Fairness in Criminal Prosecution* (New York: Vera Institute of Justice, March 2009), 7 (Charlotte, North Carolina, study); Brendan Cheney, "For Non-White New Yorkers, Marijuana Arrests More Often Lead to Conviction," *Politico*, May 9, 2017.

17. L. Song Richardson and Phillip Atiba Goff, "Implicit Racial Bias in Public Defender Triage," *Yale Law Journal* 122 (2013): 2635–2641; *Investigation of the Ferguson Police Department*, 62–63; Ed. A. Muñoz and Barbara McMorris, "Misdemeanor Sentencing Decisions: The Cost of Being Native American," *Justice Professional* 15, no. 3 (2002): 239–259; Ed. A. Muñoz et al., "Misdemeanor Sentencing Decisions: The Cumulative Disadvantage Effect of 'Gringo Justice,'" *Hispanic Journal of Behavioral Science* 20, no. 3 (1998): 298–319. See also Jon'a Meyer and Paul Jesilow, *"Doing Justice" in the People's Court: Sentencing by Municipal Court Judges* (Albany: State University of New York Press, 1997), 92–95 (finding no evidence of racial bias, but some evidence of language bias, in interviews with dozens of Southern California municipal court judges).

18. Marie Gottschalk, *Caught: The Prison State and the Lockdown of American Politics* (Princeton, NJ: Princeton University Press, 2015), 124 (describing similar accretion of racial disparities in felony system).

19. Pena-Rodriguez v. Colorado, 137 S. Ct. 855, 868 (2017) (internal quotation marks omitted).

20. McCleskey v. Kemp, 481 U.S. 279, 308–312 (1987).

21. Whren v. United States, 517 U.S. 806 (1996).

22. *McCleskey*, 481 U.S. at 292 ("To prevail under the Equal Protection Clause, McCleskey must prove that the decisionmakers in his case acted with discriminatory purpose"); *id.* at 298 ("'Discriminatory purpose' . . . implies more than intent as volition or intent as awareness of consequences. It implies that the decisionmaker . . . selected or reaffirmed a particular course of action at least in part 'because of,' not merely 'in spite of,' its adverse effects upon an identifiable group"); United States v. Armstrong, 517 U.S. 456, 465, 469–470 (1996) ("The requirements for a selective-prosecution claim draw on 'ordinary equal protection standards.' The claimant must demonstrate that the federal prosecutorial policy 'had a discriminatory effect and that it was motivated by a discriminatory purpose.'").

23. *McCleskey*, 481 U.S. at 315, 319 (affirming constitutionality of racial disparities in the application of the death penalty). Notwithstanding the high doctrinal bar, some lower courts have found intentional race-based constitutional violations in the context of racial profiling. Floyd v. City of New York, 959 F. Supp. 2d 540, 558–562 (S.D.N.Y. 2013); Melendres v. Arpaio, 989 F. Supp. 2d 822, 827 (D. Ariz. 2013). For a thorough survey of how criminal procedure forecloses constitutional challenges to the racial inequities of the criminal system, see David Cole, *No Equal Justice: Race and Class in the American Criminal Justice System* (New York: New Press, 1999). On the Supreme Court's treatment of race-based decision-making in noncriminal arenas, see Reva B. Siegel, "Foreword: Equality Divided," *Harvard Law Review* 127 (2013): 1, 6, 47–50, 63–66 and n.310, 93–94 (arguing that the Supreme Court has a robust suspicion of racial decision-making in the affirmative action context, which it has refused to extend to the criminal context); Kennedy, *Race, Crime and the Law*, 158–161 (arguing that the strong resistance to racial decision-making and the concern for the burdening of innocent parties in connection with affirmative action should be enforced in the criminal justice arena as well).

24. L. Song Richardson, "Arrest Efficiency and the Fourth Amendment," *Minnesota Law Review* 95, no. 6 (2011): 2039. See also Richardson and Goff, "Implicit Racial Bias in Public Defender Triage"; Eduardo Bonilla-Silva, *Racism Without Racists: Color-Blind Racism and the Persistence of Racial Inequality in America* (New York: Rowman & Littlefield, 2014), 26–27.

25. Mona Lynch, "The Situated Actor and the Production of Punishment: Toward an Empirical Social Psychology of Criminal Procedure," in *The New Criminal Justice Thinking*, ed. Sharon Dolovich and Alexandra Natapoff (New York: New York University Press 2017), 201 (on the nature of decision-making within various criminal justice institutions). On police arrest practices, see Michael Tonry, *Malign Neglect: Race, Crime and Punishment in America* (New York: Oxford University Press, 1995), 105–106 ("For a variety of reasons, it is easier to make arrests in socially disorganized neighborhoods."). On the effects of prosecutorial charging habits, see McKenzie et al., *Prosecution and Racial Justice*, 6–7; Berdejó, "Criminalizing Race," 4. On judicial bail determinations, see Crystal S. Yang, "Toward an Optimal Bail System," *New York University Law Review* 92 (2017): 1453–1467 (describing bail-setting practices and discrepancies among judges in Philadelphia and Miami-Dade County); Ian Ayres and

Joel Waldfogel, "A Market Test for Race Discrimination in Bail Setting," *Stanford Law Review* 46 (1994): 987.

26. "Dear Child—When Black Parents Have to Give 'The Talk,'" video posted to YouTube by "Jubilee Project," November 3, 2016, https://www.youtube.com/watch?v=Mkw1CetjWwI.

27. Butler, *Chokehold*, 62–63; Muhammad, *The Condemnation of Blackness*, 2–5, 272–273; Devon W. Carbado, "(E)racing the Fourth Amendment," *Michigan Law Review* 100 (2002): 946; David Dante Troutt, "The Race Industry, Brutality, and the Law of Mothers," in *Not Guilty: Twelve Black Men Speak Out on Law, Justice, and Life*, ed. Jabari Asim (New York: Harper Collins Publishers, 2001), 59. On the impact of arrest, see Eisha Jain, "Arrests as Regulation," *Stanford Law Review* 67 (2015): 809.

28. Sophia Epley, "Race, Socioeconomic Status and 5th Grade Students' Attitudes Toward Police Officers, Doctors, Firefighters and Teachers," California State Science Fair, 2017, http://cssf.usc.edu/Current/Projects/J0407.pdf [https://perma.cc/X64T-2NGJ] (full paper on file with author).

29. Craig B. Futterman et al., "Youth/Police Encounters on Chicago's South Side: Acknowledging the Realities," *University of Chicago Legal Forum* 2016, no. 5 (2016): 125, 145.

30. Victor M. Rios, *Punished: Policing the Lives of Black and Latino Boys* (New York: New York University Press, 2011), 44–45.

31. Epp et al., *Pulled Over*, 1, 2, 52. See also Amy E. Lerman and Vesla M. Weaver, *Arresting Citizenship: The Democratic Consequences of American Crime Control* (Chicago: University of Chicago Press, 2014), 23–24.

32. Hamed Aleaziz, "Black Lives, Black Voices," *San Francisco Chronicle*, July 29, 2016.

33. "End Broken Windows Policing," *Campaign Zero*, https://www.joincampaignzero.org/brokenwindows [https://perma.cc/ZSM9-82U4] (arguing for the elimination of offenses including "Consumption of Alcohol on Streets, Marijuana Possession, Disorderly Conduct, Trespassing, Loitering, Disturbing the Peace [including Loud Music], Spitting, Jaywalking, Bicycling on the Sidewalk"); Tierney Sneed, "From Ferguson to Staten Island, Questions About Broken Window Policing," *U.S. News & World Report*, August 14, 2014 (quoting Brooks); see also Mario L. Barnes, "Foreword: Criminal Justice for Those (Still) at the Margins—Addressing Hidden Forms of Bias and the Politics of Which Lives Matter," *UC Irvine Law Review* 5 (2015): 711, 715–717.

34. Devah Pager, *Marked: Race, Crime, and Finding Work in an Era of Mass Incarceration* (Chicago: University of Chicago Press, 2007), 67–71, 90–91.

35. Pager, *Marked*, 91.

36. Lerman and Weaver, *Arresting Citizenship*, 127 (quoting Ronnie) and 177–178 (quoting Cameron). The text provides only first names.

37. Brown v. Bd. of Ed., 347 U.S. 483, 494 (1954); *Over-Policed, yet Underserved: The People's Findings Regarding Police Misconduct in West Baltimore* (Baltimore: No Boundaries Coalition, 2016), 18.

38. Jill Leovy, *Ghettoside: A True Story of Murder in America* (New York: Spiegel and Grau, 2015) (on the disparate handling of homicide in different Los Angeles

neighborhoods); *Over-Policed, yet Underserved*, 10–11 (documenting disparate police resources given to black and white neighborhoods in Baltimore). See also Muhammad, *The Condemnation of Blackness*, 226–227 (tracing underpolicing and tolerance of crime in black neighborhoods back to the 1920s); Lerman and Weaver, *Arresting Citizenship*, 121–122 (quoting Carlos).

39. Forman, *Locking Up Our Own*, 11, 35; Kennedy, *Race, Crime and the Law*, 19.

40. Jeffrey Fagan and Daniel C. Richman, "Understanding Recent Spikes and Longer Trends in American Murders," *Columbia Law Review* 117 (2017): 1292–1296 (associating overpolicing with lower homicide clearance rates). See also Jeffrey Fagan and Tracey L. Meares, "Punishment, Deterrence and Social Control: The Paradox of Punishment in Minority Communities," *Ohio State Journal of Criminal Law* 6 (2008): 173–227 (describing how heavy policing and punishment in minority neighborhoods can exacerbate crime). On African American attitudes toward crime and law enforcement, see Emily Ekins, *Policing in America: Understanding Public Attitudes Toward the Police. Results from a National Survey* (Washington, DC: Cato Institute, 2016); Jamelle Bouie, "Actually, Blacks Do Care About Black Crime," *Slate*, December 1, 2014, http://www.slate.com/articles/news_and_politics/politics/2014/12/black_community_is_concerned_with_black_on_black_crime_suggesting_otherwise.html [https://perma.cc/69AH-SZAK]; Nancy La Vigne et al., *How Do People in High-Crime, Low-Income Communities View the Police?* (Washington, DC: Urban Institute, 2017) (study of six low-income, high-crime communities); Charles M. Blow, "A Kaffeeklatsch on Race," *New York Times*, February 16, 2015. See also David Garland, *Punishment and Modern Society: A Study in Social Theory* (Chicago: University of Chicago Press, 1990), 117 ("The criminal law provides protection as well as 'terror' for the working classes. . . . If penality serves a class purpose, it does so in a way which enlists support among the subordinate classes and which protects interests which are experienced as being universal rather than specific").

41. Alexandra Natapoff, "Underenforcement," *Fordham Law Review* 75 (2006): 1719, 1771–1774.

42. Compare Tracey L. Meares, "Policing: A Public Good Gone Bad," *Boston Review*, August 1, 2017 (conceptualizing policing as a public utility), with Gerald E. Frug, "City Services," *New York University Law Review* 73 (1998): 23, 36 (arguing for a less consumerist, more communal model of policing).

43. Christopher Uggen et al., *6 Million Lost Voters: State-Level Estimates of Felony Disenfranchisement, 2016* (Washington, DC: Sentencing Project, 2016), 3, 16; Lerman and Weaver, *Arresting Citizenship*, 10, 28, 201–217.

44. Muhammad, *The Condemnation of Blackness*, 2–5, 226, 233, 273–277. See also Alexandra Natapoff, "Speechless: The Silencing of Criminal Defendants," *New York University Law Review* 80, no. 5 (2005): 1452–1453, 1490 (on the ways that the criminal system excludes people of color from the public discourse on crime). On political uses of racial stereotypes, see "Full Text: Donald Trump Announces a Presidential Bid," *Washington Post*, June 16, 2015, https://www.washingtonpost.com/news/post-politics/wp/2015/06/16/full-text-donald-trump-announces-a-presidential-bid/?utm_term=.5dc4fe3b7ed5 [https://perma.cc/CP8E-Y34R]; Kath-

erine Beckett, *Making Crime Pay: Law and Order in Contemporary American Politics* (New York: Oxford University Press, 1997), 15, 106–107 (describing the complex relationship between elite political crime discourses on the one hand and popular perception on the other).

45. Fagan and Meares, "Punishment, Deterrence and Social Control."

46. Forman, *Locking Up Our Own*, 155 ("In the ghetto, you are . . . presumed guilty, or at least suspicious, and you must spend an extraordinary amount of energy—through careful attention to dress, behavior, and speech—to mark yourself as innocent. All with no guarantees that these efforts will work"); Herbert L. Packer, *The Limits of the Criminal Sanction* (Stanford, CA: Stanford University Press, 1968), 160–161 (describing how the "presumption of guilt" is integral to the crime-control model).

47. See Tracey Meares, "Policing and Procedural Justice: Shaping Citizens' Identities to Increase Democratic Participation," *Northwestern University Law Review* 111 (2017): 1530–1531 (arguing that criminal justice, like the education system, teaches people how to understand their own citizenship and that its "hidden curriculum" signals to some people that they are "anticitizens"); Ian F. Haney López, "Post-Racial Racism: Racial Stratification and Mass Incarceration in the Age of Obama," *California Law Review* 98 (2010) (describing mass incarceration as a mechanism of racial stratification that facilitates the strategic misallocation of resources away from African Americans).

48. *Bailing on Baltimore*, 22 (emphasis added).

49. Carol S. Steiker, "Punishment and Procedure: Punishment Theory and the Criminal-Civil Divide," *Georgetown Law Journal* 85 (1997): 806–809 (describing the special democracy and liberty protecting roles of criminal procedure). On the other hand, sometimes the democratic injury flows not from official rule breaking but the unfairness of the rules themselves. Paul Butler, "The System Is Working the Way It Is Supposed to: The Limits of Criminal Justice Reform," *Georgetown Law Journal* 104 (2016): 1425–1426.

50. On the intersection of race and wealth, see Forman, "Racial Critiques," 54; Lerman and Weaver, *Arresting Citizenship*, 118–120. On how the wealthy can obtain better treatment, see Shaila Dewan and Andrew W. Lehren, "After a Crime, the Price of a Second Chance," *New York Times*, December 12, 2016 (on the expense of participating in diversion programs); Alysia Santo et al., "Upgrade Your Jail Cell—for a Price," *Los Angeles Times* and the Marshall Project, March 9, 2017; Hadar Aviram, *Cheap on Crime: Recession-Era Politics and the Transformation of American Punishment* (Oakland: University of California Press, 2015), 144–147 (documenting rise of the private pay-to-stay jail phenomenon).

51. On the interconnected plights of vulnerable whites and blacks, see Nancy Isenberg, *White Trash: The 400-Year Untold History of Class in America* (New York: Viking, 2016), 2–3, 135–140; Forman, "Racial Critiques," 58–61; Gottschalk, *Caught*, 6, 138 ("As the racial order continues to invent new ways to target blacks, it has generated punitive policies and practices that migrate to other dispossessed groups"). On the status of black men within the criminal justice conversation, see Devon W. Carbado, "Men in Black," *Journal of Gender Race & Justice* 3 (2000): 427, 429 ("Heterosexual Black men occupy a privileged victim status in antiracist discourse"). See also Atwater v. Lago Vista, 532 U.S. 318 (2001).

CHAPTER 7: HISTORY

1. Lawrence M. Friedman and Robert V. Percival, *The Roots of Justice: Crime and Punishment in Alameda County, California, 1870–1910* (Chapel Hill: University of North Carolina Press, 1981), 4.

2. Julius Goebel Jr., *Felony and Misdemeanor: A Study in the History of Criminal Law* (1937), xxi, xliii–xliv, 114–115, 199–210; John H. Lindquist, *Misdemeanor Crime* (Thousand Oaks, CA: Sage Publications, 1988), 15; William Oldnall Russell, *Russell on Crime*, 3rd ed. (London: Stevens, 1845), 44–45; William Oldnall Russell, *Russell on Crime*, 12th ed. (London: Stevens, 1964), 4; William Blackstone, *Commentaries on the Laws of England* (Oxford: Clarendon Press, 1769; Chicago: University of Chicago Press, 1979), 4:5, 94–95, 141, facsimile of first edition; United States v. Watson, 423 U.S. 411, 438–440 (1976) (Marshall, J., dissenting) (listing serious misdemeanors at common law).

3. Douglas A. Blackmon, *Slavery by Another Name: The Re-Enslavement of Black Americans from the Civil War to World War II* (New York: Doubleday Broadway, 2008), 1–2, 301–302, 321–322. The term "neoslavery" is Blackmon's. Blackmon, *Slavery by Another Name*, 402. See also CPI Inflation Calculator, Bureau of Labor Statistics, https://www.bls.gov/data/inflation_calculator.htm [https://perma.cc/8XVD-QJ9Z] ($38.40 in 1913 equivalent to $975.64 in 2018).

4. Blackmon, *Slavery by Another Name*, 305; see also Mark Colvin, *Penitentiaries, Reformatories, and Chain Gangs: Social Theory and the History of Punishment in Nineteenth-Century America* (New York: Palgrave Macmillan, 1998), 243–245.

5. Eric Foner, *Reconstruction: America's Unfinished Revolution, 1863–1877* (New York: Harper & Row, 1988), 198; see also Colvin, *Penitentiaries*, 220; Blackmon, *Slavery by Another Name*, 7.

6. Foner, *Reconstruction*, 157, 205, 363, 372–373, 594; Colvin, *Penitentiaries*, 217; Blackmon, *Slavery by Another Name*, 377–381. See also Clyatt v. United States, 197 U.S. 207 (1905) (peonage is a federal crime); United States v. Reynolds, 235 U.S. 133 (1914) (forced convict labor constituted illegal peonage).

7. Chris Albin-Lackey, *Profiting from Probation: America's "Offender-Funded" Probation Industry* (New York: Human Rights Watch, February 2014), 60–61 (describing Harpersville arrangement); Order, Burdette v. Town of Harpersville, CV-2010-900183 (Shelby Cty. Cir. Ct., Ala., July 11, 2012), https://www.clearinghouse.net/chDocs/public/CJ-AL-0005-0001.pdf [https://perma.cc/6DBV-TF7N]; Alexes Harris, Heather Evans, and Katherine Beckett, "Drawing Blood from Stones: Legal Debt and Social Inequality in the Contemporary United States," *America Journal of Sociology* 115, no. 6 (May 2010): 1791.

8. Ava DuVernay, dir., *13th* (Los Angeles, CA: Kandoo Films, 2016); James Q. Whitman, *Harsh Justice: Criminal Punishment and the Widening Divide Between America and Europe* (New York: Oxford University Press, 2003), 173–177, 198.

9. Foner, *Reconstruction*, 200–201; Kelly Lytle Hernández, *City of Inmates: Conquest, Rebellion, and the Rise of Human Caging in Los Angeles, 1771–1965* (Chapel Hill: University of North Carolina Press, 2017), 29–44; see also Jennifer M. Chacón, "Unsettling History," *Harvard Law Review* 131 (2017): 1084–1088 (reviewing *City*

of Inmates); Katherine Beckett and Steve Herbert, *Banished: The New Social Control in Urban America* (New York: Oxford University Press, 2009), 12–14.

10. Blackstone, *Commentaries*, chap. 13, section 6 (emphasis added). See also Frances Fox Piven and Richard A. Cloward, *Regulating the Poor: The Functions of Public Welfare*, 2nd ed. (New York: Vintage Books, 1993), 10, 14 (on the sixteenth-century roots of vagrancy laws).

11. Papachristou v. City of Jacksonville, 405 U.S. 156, 158 (1972) (quoting Florida vagrancy statute); Caleb Foote, "Vagrancy-Type Law and Its Administration," *University of Pennsylvania Law Review* 104 (1956): 617–624 (describing banishment practices in Philadelphia).

12. Risa Goluboff, *Vagrant Nation: Police Power, Constitutional Change, and the Making of the 1960s* (New York: Oxford University Press, 2016), 2–3.

13. Goluboff, *Vagrant Nation*, 4.

14. Goluboff, *Vagrant Nation*, 5.

15. William O. Douglas, "Vagrancy and Arrests on Suspicion," *Yale Law Journal* 70 (1960): 13.

16. *Papachristou*, 405 U.S. at 171.

17. Coates v. Cincinnati, 402 U.S. 611 (1971) (striking down disorderly conduct statute); Kolender v. Lawson, 461 U.S. 352 (1983) (striking down loitering and identification statute); City of Chicago v. Morales, 527 U.S. 41, 53 (1999) (striking down gang loitering statute).

18. Goluboff, *Vagrant Nation*, 341.

19. On how *Terry* expands the scope of order-maintenance offenses, see Goluboff, *Vagrant Nation*, 341; David Thacher and Ben Hansen, "Policing After Papachristou: A Case Study of the Impact of Legal Change on the Police" (draft paper, presented at the Law and Society Association Annual Conference, Boston, Massachusetts, May 30, 2013): 8–9 (on file with author); Alexandra Natapoff, "A Stop Is Just a Stop: Terry's Formalism," *Ohio State Journal of Criminal Law* 15 (2017): 120–122. On Justice Douglas's dissent, see Terry v. Ohio, 392 U.S. 1, 38 (1968) (Douglas, J., dissenting); Paul Butler, "'A Long Step down the Totalitarian Path': Justice Douglas's Great Dissent in *Terry v. Ohio*," *Mississippi Law Journal* 79 (2009): 9.

20. Josh Bowers, "Grassroots Plea Bargaining," *Marquette Law Review* 91 (2007): 85–86.

21. Beckett and Herbert, *Banished*, 11, 15; see also *California's New Vagrancy Laws: The Growing Enactment and Enforcement of Anti-Homeless Laws in the Golden State* (Berkeley: BerkeleyLaw, University of California, Policy Advocacy Clinic, February 2015).

22. Thacher and Hansen, "Policing After Papachristou," 22–24 (on the increase of nonvagrancy order arrests); Trista Baurman et al., *No Safe Place: The Criminalization of Homelessness in U.S. Cities* (Washington, DC: National Law Center on Homelessness & Poverty, 2014), 21 (on homelessness bans); Beckett and Herbert, *Banished*, 41 (on loitering laws). See also Reva B. Siegel, "'The Rule of Love': Wife Beating as Prerogative and Privacy," *Yale Law Journal* 105 (1996): 2179 (describing the "preservation through transformation" of social norms and hierarchies notwithstanding changes in legal rules).

23. James Q. Wilson and George L. Kelling, "Broken Windows: The Police and Neighborhood Safety," *Atlantic Monthly*, March 1982; Cynthia Lum and Daniel S. Nagin, "Reinventing American Policing," in *Reinventing American Criminal Justice*, ed. Michael Tonry and Daniel Nagin (Chicago: University of Chicago Press, 2017), 359 ("In theory, [stop question and frisk (SQF)] is distinct from broken windows policing in that its focus is not on preventing disorder. However, SQF has been coupled with broken windows policing in both practice and critique."); Jeffrey Fagan and Garth Davies, "Street Stops and Broken Windows: Terry, Race, and Disorder in New York City," *Fordham Urban Law Journal* 28 (2000): 457.

24. *The Promise of Sanctuary Cities and the Need for Criminal Justice Reforms in an Era of Mass Deportation* (Cambridge, MA: Fair Punishment Project, Harvard Law School, May 4, 2017); Bernard E. Harcourt and Jens Ludwig, "Broken Windows: New Evidence from New York and a Five-City Experiment," *University of Chicago Law Review* 73 (2006): 272; Louis Nelson, "Trump Calls for Nationwide 'Stop-and-Frisk' Policy," *Politico*, September 21, 2016, https://www.politico .com/story/2016/09/donald-trump-stop-and-frisk-228486 [https://perma.cc/TW9P-FGJS].

25. Bernard E. Harcourt, *Illusion of Order: The False Promise of Broken Windows Policing* (Cambridge, MA: Harvard University Press, 2001), 1, 3–4; David Thacher, "Order Maintenance Policing," in *The Oxford Handbook of Police and Policing*, ed. Michael Reisig and Robert Kane (Oxford: Oxford University Press, 2014), 128–130; Preeti Chauhan et al., *Trends in Misdemeanor Arrests in New York* (report presented to the Citizens Crime Commission, New York, October 28, 2014) 18, 19, http://johnjay.jjay.cuny.edu/files/web_images/10_28_14_TOCFINAL.pdf [https:// perma.cc/L35B-2UKZ].

26. Harcourt, *Illusion*, 8–11, 59–61, 80–82; Fagan and Davies, "Street Stops," 457, 465–467; Robert J. Sampson and Stephen W. Raudenbush, "Systemic Social Observations of Public Spaces: A New Look at Disorder in Urban Neighborhoods," *American Journal of Sociology* 105 (1999): 603, 637–638; Robert J. Sampson and Stephen W. Raudenbush, *Disorder in Urban Neighborhoods—Does It Lead to Crime?* (Washington, DC: National Institute of Justice, February 2001), 4 ("The forces that generate disorder also generate crime. It is the structural characteristics of neighborhoods, as well as neighborhood cohesion and informal social control—not levels of disorder—that most affect crime").

27. E.g., Dorothy E. Roberts, "Foreword: Race, Vagueness, and the Social Meaning of Order-Maintenance Policing," *Journal of Criminal Law and Criminology* 89 (1999): 775; Fagan and Davies, "Street Stops"; see also Reed Collins, Note, "Strolling While Poor: How Broken Windows Policing Created a New Crime in Baltimore," *Georgetown Journal on Poverty Law and Policy* 14 (2007): 419.

28. Robert J. Sampson and Stephen W. Raudenbush, "Seeing Disorder: Neighborhood Stigma and the Social Construction of 'Broken Windows,'" *Social Psychology Quarterly* 67 (2004): 319, 329–332; see also Friedman and Percival, *The Roots of Justice*, 12 ("Order is a complex concept. . . . Generally speaking, rules of order control behavior that is not bad in itself; it is only a danger or nuisance if too many people do it at once, at the wrong time, or in the wrong place"); Jane Jacobs, *The Death and Life of Great American Cities*, reissue ed. (New York: Random House,

1961; New York: Vintage Books, 1992), 50, 150; Clyde Haberman, "NYC; Better Quality of Life Found Behind Wheel," *New York Times*, January 16, 1998.

29. David Garland, *The Culture of Control: Crime and Social Order in Contemporary Society* (Chicago: University of Chicago Press, 2001), 181 ("Today there is no such thing as victimless crime. . . . Every minor offense, every act of disorderly conduct—particularly if committed by poor people in public spaces—is now regarded as detrimental to the quality of life"); Harcourt, *Illusion*, 7.

30. I. Bennett Capers, "Crime, Surveillance, and Communities," *Fordham Urban Law Journal* 40 (2013): 959; Erin Murphy, "Paradigms of Restraint," *Duke Law Journal* 57 (2008): 1132; Harcourt, *Illusion*, 101.

31. Goluboff, *Vagrant Nation*, 5 ("Telling the history of vagrancy laws' demise . . . means telling a legal history of the 1960s writ large").

32. See Judith Resnik, "Courts and Economic and Social Rights / Courts as Economic and Social Rights," in *The Future of Economic and Social Rights*, ed. Katharine G. Young (Cambridge: Cambridge University Press, forthcoming) (conceptualizing courts and the right to court services as a form of social welfare entitlement like housing and education).

CHAPTER 8: JUSTICE

1. Darryl K. Brown, *Free Market Criminal Justice: How Democracy and Laissez Faire Undermine the Rule of Law* (New York: Oxford University Press, 2016); Dan Simon, *In Doubt: The Psychology of the Criminal Justice Process* (Cambridge, MA: Harvard University Press, 2012).

2. A sociologist, for example, might have begun elsewhere. David Garland, *Punishment and Modern Society: A Study in Social Theory* (Chicago: University of Chicago Press, 1990), 9–10 ("Quite simply, we need to know what punishment is in order to think what it can and should be").

3. Sharon Dolovich, "Legitimate Punishment in Liberal Democracy," *Buffalo Criminal Law Review* 7, no. 2 (2004): 310. See also Jonathan Simon, *Governing Through Crime: How the War on Crime Transformed American Democracy and Created a Culture of Fear* (New York: Oxford University Press, 2007), 14 ("All legal authority ultimately rests on the threat of lawful violence within the criminal law"); Carol S. Steiker, "Punishment and Procedure: Punishment Theory and the Criminal-Civil Divide," *Georgetown Law Journal* 85 (1997): 809 (describing "the need for a special procedural regime within which punishment should be imposed, both to limit the state's ability to harness the power of blame and to preserve blaming as a social practice").

4. Marbury v. Madison, 5 U.S. (1 Cranch) 137, 163 (1803); David A. Skeel Jr. and William J. Stuntz, "Christianity and the (Modest) Rule of Law," *University of Pennsylvania Journal of Constitutional Law* 8, no. 4 (2006): 809. For more critical views of rule of law, see Markus Dirk Dubber, *The Police Power: Patriarchy and the Foundations of American Government* (New York: Columbia University Press, 2005), xv, 56–57, 158–160 (arguing that the police power is historically and inherently in tension with rule of law); Ahmed A. White, "Capitalism, Social Marginality, and the Rule of Law's Uncertain Fate in Modern Society," *Arizona State Law Journal* 37 (2005): 759 (arguing that rule of law is incompatible with criminal law's social

control agenda). For Justice Scalia's comment, see Rogers v. Tennessee, 532 U.S. 451, 467–468 (2001) (Scalia, J., dissenting).

5. Harris v. United State, 404 U.S. 1232, 1233 (1971) (Douglas, J., sitting as circuit justice) (on the need for evidence); North Carolina v. Alford, 400 U.S. 25, 37–38 (1970) (relying on the existence of "strong factual basis" in upholding plea); Ronald J. Allen and Brian Leiter, "Naturalized Epistemology and the Law of Evidence," *Virginia Law Review* 87, no. 8 (2001): 1501, 1537.

6. Henry M. Hart Jr., "The Aims of the Criminal Law," *Law & Contemporary Problems* 23 (1958): 405 (identifying community condemnation as key to legitimate criminalization). See Larry Alexander, Kimberly Kessler Ferzan, and Stephen Morse, *Crime and Culpability: A Theory of Criminal Law* (Cambridge: Cambridge University Press, 2009) (proposing a "culpability-based criminal code"); Douglas Husak, "'Broad' Culpability and the Retributivist Dream," *Ohio State Journal of Criminal Law* 9 (2012): 449; Model Penal Code § 1.02(1)(a) ("The general purposes of the [MPC] are . . . to forbid and prevent conduct that unjustifiably and inexcusably inflicts or threatens substantial harm to individuals or public interests."); but see Bernard E. Harcourt, "The Collapse of the Harm Principle," *Journal of Criminal Law and Criminology* 90 (1999): 109. On what cannot legitimately be criminalized, see Robinson v. California, 370 U.S. 660, 666 (1962) (unconstitutional to criminalize the status of being ill or addicted to narcotics); Jonathan Swift, *Gulliver's Travels* (London: Benjamin Motte, 1726).

7. Stephanos Bibas, *The Machinery of Criminal Justice* (Oxford: Oxford University Press, 2012), xxix; Michael Walzer, *Spheres of Justice: A Defense of Pluralism and Equality* (New York: Basic Books, 1983), 269 (emphasis in original).

8. Dolovich, "Legitimate Punishment," 314; Nicola Lacey, *The Prisoners' Dilemma: Political Economy and Punishment in Contemporary Democracies* (Cambridge: Cambridge University Press, 2008), 7.

9. Amy Bach, *Ordinary Injustice: How America Holds Court* (New York: Metropolitan Books, 2009), 77–129 (chronicling the career of a scofflaw city court judge); Robert C. Boruchowitz et al., *Minor Crimes, Massive Waste: The Terrible Toll of America's Broken Misdemeanor Courts* (Washington, DC: National Association of Criminal Defense Lawyers, April 2009), 15 (quoting Chief Justice Hoefer Toal); Josh Bowers, "Grassroots Plea Bargaining," *Marquette Law Review* 91 (2007): 85–86 (describing Eddie Wise's cases).

10. Amanda Geller and Jeffrey Fagan, "Pot as Pretext: Marijuana, Race, and the New Disorder in New York City Street Policing," *Journal of Empirical Legal Studies* 7 (2010): 591; Eric J. Miller, "Role-Based Policing: Restraining Police Conduct 'Outside the Legitimate Investigative Sphere,'" *California Law Review* 94 (2006), 617; Debra Livingston, "Police Discretion and the Quality of Life in Public Places: Courts, Communities, and the New Policing," *Columbia Law Review* 97 (1997): 551.

11. The slippage between purported and actual function is another old problem. Stanley Cohen, *Visions of Social Control: Crime, Punishment and Classification* (Cambridge, UK: Polity Press, 1985), 114 ("Control and welfare systems are not different from any part of a complex civilization in which institutions go about doing what they have to do, while at the same time saying they are doing many other things"); Simon, *Governing Through Crime*, 4 ("We can expect people to deploy the

category of crime to legitimate interventions that have other motivations."); see also Tommie Shelby, *Dark Ghettos: Injustice, Dissent and Reform* (Cambridge, MA: Harvard University Press, 2016), 238–245 (arguing that the state loses its moral authority to condemn crime—although not its institutional authority to enforce it—when it engages in systemic injustice). On lynching's connection to the death penalty, see Carol S. Steiker and Jordan M. Steiker, *Courting Death: The Supreme Court and Capital Punishment* (Cambridge, MA: Harvard University Press, 2016), 17 ("One of the strongest predictors of a state's propensity to conduct executions today is its history of lynch mob activity more than a century ago."). On the "New Jim Crow," see Michelle Alexander, *The New Jim Crow: Mass Incarceration in the Age of Colorblindness* (New York: New Press, 2012); Loïc Wacquant, *Punishing the Poor: The Neoliberal Government of Social Insecurity* (Durham, NC: Duke University Press, 2009), 195–208.

12. Medina v. California, 505 U.S. 437, 443–445 (1992) (according more deference to the state's criminal procedural rules than to its civil rules); see also Rachel E. Barkow, "Institutional Design and the Policing of Prosecutors: Lessons from Administrative Law," *Stanford Law Review* 61, no. 4 (2009): 869 (arguing that prosecutors have unchecked power and should be regulated more like other administrative agencies).

13. David Garland, *The Culture of Control: Crime and Social Order in Contemporary Society* (Chicago: University of Chicago Press, 2001), 193, 194; Simon, *Governing Through Crime*, 4, 18–19.

14. On the myriad functions of the criminal system, see Garland, *Punishment and Modern Society*, 14–15, 23, 83, 111 (on punishment as a social institution including Émile Durkheim's theories of social solidarity and Marxist theories of labor control); Alexander, *The New Jim Crow*, 2 (racial control); Vesla M. Weaver, "Frontlash: Race and the Development of Punitive Crime Policy," *Studies in American Policy Development* 21, no. 2 (fall 2007): 230–265 (describing how elites in the 1960s and 1970s used the criminal system to push back against the civil rights movement); Bernard E. Harcourt, *Against Prediction: Profiling, Policing, and Punishing in an Actuarial Age* (Chicago: University of Chicago Press, 2006); Katherine Beckett, *Making Crime Pay: Law and Order in Contemporary American Politics* (New York: Oxford University Press, 1997); Wacquant, *Punishing the Poor*, 41, 197 ("Not crime, but the need to shore up an eroding caste cleavage, and to buttress the emergent regime of desocialized wage labor to which lower-class blacks are fated by virtue of their lack of marketable cultural capital, and which the most deprived amongst them resist by escaping into the illegal street economy, is the main impetus behind the stupendous expansion of America's penal state in the post-Keynesian age and its de facto policy of 'carceral affirmative action' toward lower-class African Americans.").

15. This group-based managerial approach is a central feature of what Malcolm Feeley and Jonathan Simon have termed more broadly "the new penology." Malcolm M. Feeley and Jonathan Simon, "The New Penology: Notes on the Emerging Strategy of Corrections and Its Implications," *Criminology* 30, no. 4 (1992): 467 ("[The underclass] is treated as a high-risk group that must be managed for the protection of the rest of society"); Malcolm Feeley and Jonathan Simon, "Actuarial Justice: The Emerging New Criminal Law," in *The Futures of Criminology*,

ed. David Nelken (London: Sage Publications, 1994), 192–193. See also Garland, *Culture of Control*, 128.

16. Juvenile justice and immigration enforcement are also large, quasi-criminal institutions that regulate vulnerable populations in similar ways. Robin Walker Sterling, "Fundamental Unfairness: In re Gault and the Road Not Taken," *Maryland Law Review* 72 (2013): 607 (tracing the racial and social control contours of the juvenile justice system); Jennifer M. Chacón, "Producing Liminal Legality," *Denver University Law Review* 92 (2015): 744 (noting that "the legal vulnerabilities produced by the interaction of civil and criminal legal mechanisms in heavily policed communities are not unique to noncitizens").

17. Caleb Foote, "Vagrancy-Type Law and Its Administration," *University of Pennsylvania Law Review* 104 (1956): 613–614. See also Lawrence M. Friedman and Robert V. Percival, *The Roots of Justice: Crime and Punishment in Alameda County, California, 1870–1910* (Chapel Hill: University of North Carolina Press, 1981), 133–134.

18. Malcolm M. Feeley, *The Process Is the Punishment: Handling Cases in a Lower Criminal Court* (1979; rpt. New York: Russell Sage Foundation, 1992), xxii, 9, 295; John Irwin, *The Jail: Managing the Underclass in American Society* (Berkeley: University of California Press, 1985), 2.

19. Issa Kohler-Hausmann, "Managerial Justice and Mass Misdemeanors," *Stanford Law Review* 66 (2014): 627; Katherine Beckett and Steve Herbert, *Banished: The New Social Control in Urban America* (New York: Oxford University Press, 2009), 57, 64; Charles R. Epp et al., *Pulled Over: How Police Stops Define Race and Citizenship* (Chicago: University of Chicago Press, 2014), 2–3, 134–136; Devon W. Carbado, "(E)racing the Fourth Amendment," *Michigan Law Review* 100, no. 5 (2002): 957.

20. Peter Edelman, *Not a Crime to Be Poor: The Criminalization of Poverty in America* (New York: New Press, 2017); Forrest Stuart, Amada Armenta, and Melissa Osborne, "Legal Control of Marginal Groups," *Annual Review of Law and Social Science* 11 (2015): 235; Garland, *Culture of Control*, 5 ("Institutions of crime control and criminal justice . . . form part of a network of governance and social ordering that, in modern societies, includes the legal system, the labour market, and welfare state institutions."); Wacquant, *Punishing the Poor*, 6; Lacey, *Prisoners' Dilemma*, 131–132.

21. Catherine Kim et al., *The School-to-Prison Pipeline: Structuring Legal Reform* (New York: New York University Press, 2010); Kimberlé Williams Crenshaw, Priscilla Ocen, and Jyoti Nanda, *Black Girls Matter: Pushed Out, Overpoliced and Underprotected* (New York: African American Policy Forum, 2015); Kaaryn S. Gustafson, *Cheating Welfare: Public Assistance and the Criminalization of Poverty* (New York: New York University Press, 2011), 51–68; Michele Goodwin, "Prosecuting the Womb," *George Washington Law Review* 76 (2008): 1676–1677; Armando Lara-Millán, "Public Emergency Room Overcrowding in the Era of Mass Imprisonment," *American Sociological Review* 79 (2014): 873; Alice Goffman, *On the Run: Fugitive Life in an American City* (Chicago: University of Chicago Press, 2014), 34–35.

22. Elizabeth Hinton, *From the War on Poverty to the War on Crime: The Making of Mass Incarceration in America* (Cambridge, MA: Harvard University Press, 2016) (tracing the roots of mass incarceration back to the welfare programs of Lyndon Johnson's War on Poverty).

23. On the demise of penal welfarism, see Wacquant, *Punishing the Poor*, 6, 41–43, 299–300; Garland, *Culture of Control*, 27, 75–76, 175; Simon, *Governing Through Crime*, 22–23; see also Francis A. Allen, "The Decline of the Rehabilitative Ideal: Penal Policy and Social Purpose," *Social Service Review* 56 (1981). On how law enforcement provides welfare services, see Forrest Stuart, *Down, Out, and Under Arrest: Policing and Everyday Life in Skid Row* (Chicago: University of Chicago Press, 2016), 4, 13, 81; Megan Comfort, *Doing Time Together: Love and Family in the Shadow of the Prison* (Chicago: University of Chicago Press, 2008), 17–18, 182–183 (on the social welfare function of the prison). I have described the welfarist role-swapping of various criminal justice actors in more detail in Alexandra Natapoff, "Gideon's Servants and the Criminalization of Poverty," *Ohio State Journal of Criminal Law* 12 (2015): 445, 448, 453–454.

24. Lacey, *Prisoners' Dilemma*, xv.

25. Abraham Lincoln, *The Gettysburg Address*, November 19, 1863 ("[W]e here highly resolve that . . . this government of the people, by the people, for the people, shall not perish from the earth"); Amartya Sen, *The Idea of Justice* (Cambridge, MA: Harvard University Press, 2009), 323–326; John Rawls, *Justice as Fairness: A Restatement* §§ 2.1, 7.3 (Cambridge, MA: Harvard University Press, 2001); Lacey, *Prisoners' Dilemma*, 9.

26. David Alan Sklansky, *Democracy and the Police* (Stanford: Stanford University Press, 2008), 109. See also David Alan Sklansky, "Police and Democracy," *Michigan Law Review* 103 (2005): 1699–1830 (tracing the move from pluralistic to more participatory notions of democracy in relation to theories of legitimate policing); Amy E. Lerman and Vesla M. Weaver, *Arresting Citizenship: The Democratic Consequences of American Crime Control* (Chicago: University of Chicago Press, 2014), 58–61.

27. Jan-Werner Müller, *What Is Populism?* (Philadelphia: University of Pennsylvania Press, 2016), 3 (describing "populism as an exclusionary form of identity politics [] that tends to pose a danger to democracy"); Brown, *Free Market Criminal Justice*, 3–4, 26–27, 39, 59 (describing how the democratic politics of crime can eclipse law and expertise); Beckett, *Making Crime Pay*, 11–12 (on the politics of crime); James Q. Whitman, *Harsh Justice: Criminal Punishment and the Widening Divide Between America and Europe* (New York: Oxford University Press, 2003), 15, 203 (on the punitiveness of US politics); Lacey, *Prisoners' Dilemma*, 8.

28. See, e.g., Bruce Western, *Punishment and Inequality in America* (New York: Russell Sage Foundation, 2006); David Cole, *No Equal Justice: Race and Class in the American Criminal Justice System* (New York: New Press, 1999); Wacquant, *Punishing the Poor*, 313 ("[T]he penalization of poverty splinters citizenship along class lines, saps civic trust at the bottom, and sows the degradation of republican tenets.").

29. Jack Balkin, "The Constitution of Status," *Yale Law Journal* 106 (1997): 2314. The point about criminal justice being inegalitarian is typically made with respect to mass incarceration. See, e.g., Hinton, *From the War on Poverty*, 1 ("Prisons, jails, and law enforcement institutions have functioned as a central engine of American inequality."); Wacquant, *Punishing the Poor*, 313 ("[T]he penalization of poverty . . . [is] profoundly injurious to democratic ideals."); Western, *Punishment and Inequality*, 67 ("[T]he penal system has emerged as a novel institution in a

uniquely American system of social inequality."); Ian F. Haney López, "Post-Racial Racism: Racial Stratification and Mass Incarceration in the Age of Obama," *California Law Review* 98 (2010): 1045–1060 (charting how mass incarceration creates and promotes structural racism).

30. See Sen, *Idea of Justice*, 296–297; Rawls, *Justice as Fairness*, §§ 7.3, 13.1; Lacey, *Prisoners' Dilemma*, 16.

31. See Alexes Harris, *A Pound of Flesh: Monetary Sanctions as Punishment for the Poor* (New York: Russell Sage Foundation, 2016) (making similar arguments in the felony context).

32. James Madison, *The Federalist Papers*, No. 10 (J. Cooke ed. 1961), 44–45 (quoted and discussed in Edward J. McCaffery, "Tax's Empire," *Georgetown Law Journal* 85 (1996): 122–124).

33. For a careful delineation of the judicial power to order taxes, see Missouri v. Jenkins, 495 U.S. 33, 51, 54–55 (1990) and also ibid. at 65 (Kennedy, J., concurring in part and dissenting in part) ("This reflects the Framers' understanding that taxation was not a proper area for judicial involvement. 'The judiciary . . . has no influence over either the sword or the purse, no direction either of the strength or of the wealth of the society, and can take no active resolution whatever.'"), quoting Alexander Hamilton, *The Federalist Papers*, No. 78 (J. Cooke ed. 1961), 523. On the tax power, see Cheek v. United States, 498 U.S. 192 (1991) (finding that Congress did not intend to criminalize common errors or misunderstandings but only willful violations of the tax code); National Federation of Independent Business v. Sebelius, 567 U.S. 519, 563–566 (2012) (broadly construing individual mandate to obtain health care as a "functional tax" within Congress's taxing power and describing "the essential feature of any tax: It produces at least some revenue for the Government"); Opinion, Michigan v. Cameron, Case No. 330876 (Mich. Ct. App., April 4, 2017) (holding that court fees constituted a tax). See also Carl Reynolds and Jeff Hall, *2011–2012 Policy Paper: Courts Are Not Revenue Centers* (Williamsburg, VA: Conference of State Court Administrators, 2012).

34. See Mark Tushnet, "Authoritarian Constitutionalism," *Cornell Law Review* 100 (2015): 448 ("[A] rough definition of authoritarianism [is] that all decisions can potentially be made by a single decision maker, whose decisions are both formally and practically unregulated by law,"); Lynne Henderson, "Authoritarianism and the Rule of Law," *Indiana Law Journal* 66, no. 2 (1991): 379–385 (surveying various formal and informal definitions of authoritarianism).

35. Rawls, *Justice as Fairness*, §§ 13.3, 32.4; Margaret Jane Radin, "Reconsidering the Rule of Law," *Boston University Law Review* 69, no. 4 (1989): 789 (quoting John Rawls, *A Theory of Justice* [Cambridge, MA: Harvard University Press, 1971], 241). In a slightly different vein, William Stuntz thought that criminal rule of law is eroding alongside, not because of, local democracy due to the inability of poor African American neighborhoods to influence crime policies controlled by forces outside their communities. William J. Stuntz, *The Collapse of American Criminal Justice* (Cambridge, MA: Harvard University Press, 2011), 7 ("As local democracy has faded, the rule of law has collapsed,").

36. William J. Stuntz, "The Pathological Politics of Criminal Law," *Michigan Law Review* 100 (2001): 578 (describing "lawlessness" of prosecutorial power);

Barry Friedman and Maria Ponomarenko, "Democratic Policing," *New York University Law Review* 90 (2015): 1835 ("Policing suffers from a failure of democratic accountability, of policy rationality, of transparency, and of oversight that would never be tolerated for any other agency of executive government."); Jerome H. Skolnick, *Justice Without Trial: Law Enforcement in Democratic Society*, 2nd ed. (1966; New York: John Wiley & Sons, 1975), 1–22 (describing long-standing, historical, inherent tension between rule of law and policing); Kohler-Hausmann, "Managerial Justice and Mass Misdemeanors," 619–620, 684 (on lack of formal constraints in New York's lower courts); Ian Weinstein, "The Adjudication of Minor Offenses in New York City," *Fordham Urban Law Journal* 31 (2004): 1158–1162, 1176 (on lawlessness in New York's lower courts). Malcolm Feeley described the lack of due process in New Haven criminal court but also argued that lower-court justice may be effectuated through means other than legal rules and formal adjudication. Feeley, *The Process Is the Punishment*, 7–10, 24–25, 29–31.

37. Or perhaps more precisely, it represents the worst excesses of unchecked local democracy. Müller, *What Is Populism?*, 8, 20–21 (describing populism as the destructive shadow of representative democracy); Whitman, *Harsh Justice*, 15, 203 (on penal populism); Lacey, *Prisoners' Dilemma*, 8, 16 (on popular support for exclusionary penal policies); Sklansky, "Policing and Democracy," 1707 (noting that under certain illiberal conceptions of democracy, "perhaps the last thing we should want is genuinely democratic policing; perhaps the whole point of constitutional criminal procedure is, and should be, precisely to remove politics from fundamental decisions about law enforcement.").

38. Patterson v. New York, 432 U.S. 197, 224 (1977) (Powell, J., dissenting).

CHAPTER 9: CHANGE

1. "The History of MADD," MADD, http://www.madd.org/about-us/history [https://perma.cc/M5PJ-VZBU]; Paul H. Robinson and Sarah M. Robinson, "Trigger Crimes and Social Progress: The Tragedy-Outrage-Reform Dynamic in America," Penn Law Legal Scholarship Repository, May 5, 2017, http://scholarship.law.upenn .edu/faculty_scholarship/1738 [https://perma.cc/ND4F-AGNK]; John D. McCarthy and Mark Wolfson, "Resource Mobilization by Local Social Movement Organizations: Agency, Strategy, and Organization in the Movement Against Drinking and Driving," *American Sociological Review* 61, no. 6 (December, 1996): 1070–1088; Welsh v. Wisconsin, 466 U.S. 740 (1984).

2. "Marijuana Legalization and Regulation," Drug Policy Alliance, http://www .drugpolicy.org/marijuana-legalization-and-regulation [https://perma.cc/C5DM-CZUT]; "States That Have Decriminalized," NORML.org, http://norml.org/aboutmarijuana /item/states-that-have-decriminalized [https://perma.cc/UA2V-DBUF]; Alex Kreit, "Marijuana Legalization," in *Reforming Criminal Justice*, ed. Erik Luna (Phoenix: Arizona State University, 2017), 1:115–137; Scott C. Martin, "A Brief History of Marijuana Law in America," *Time*, April 20, 2016.

3. Memorandum Opinion at 3, 99, ODonnell v. Harris Cty., Texas, No. 4:16-cv -01414, 2017 WL 1735456 (S.D.Tex., April 28, 2017) (memorandum and opinion setting out findings of fact and conclusions of law); An-Li Herring, "States and Cities

Take Steps to Reform 'Dishonest' Bail System," *NPR*, December 17, 2016; "Interactive Map: Actions Taken by the States on Fines, Fees, and Bail Practices," National Center for State Courts, https://public.tableau.com/profile/publish/FFBP2_0/Activities ByType#!/publish-confirm [https://perma.cc/5RUX-V9PD]; "50-State Criminal Justice Debt Reform Builder," Criminal Justice Policy Program at Harvard Law School, https://cjdebtreform.org [https://perma.cc/RQJ6-JG5V].

4. Saki Knafo, "A Black Police Officer's Fight Against the N.Y.P.D.," *New York Times Magazine*, February 18, 2016; Complaint, Raymond v. City of New York, No. 15-CV-6885 (S.D.N.Y., December 10, 2015).

5. Erica McWhorter and David LaBahn, "Confronting the Elephants in the Courtroom Through Prosecutor Led Diversion Efforts," *Albany Law Review* 79 (2016): 1222, 1227; Robert C. Boruchowitz et al., *Minor Crimes, Massive Waste: The Terrible Toll of America's Broken Misdemeanor Courts* (Washington, DC: National Association of Criminal Defense Lawyers, April 2009), 33 (quoting Judge Joseph Bellacosa).

6. Ben Hall, "Sheriff Calls Rutherford County's Probation System a 'Rat Wheel,'" *WTVF* (Murfreesboro, Tennessee), November 19, 2015, https://www.newschannel5 .com/news/newschannel-5-investigates/sheriff-calls-rutherford-countys-probation -system-a-rat-wheel [https://perma.cc/7QQX-U75S]; Michael Hardy, "In Fight over Bail's Fairness, a Sheriff Joins the Critics," *New York Times*, March 9, 2017 (quoting Sheriff Gonzalez).

7. "Top National State Court Leadership Associations Launch National Task Force on Fines, Fees and Bail Practices," National Center for State Courts, February 3, 2016, http://www.ncsc.org/Newsroom/News-Releases/2016/Task-Force-on-Fines -Fees-and-Bail-Practices.aspx [https://perma.cc/74RH-52MT]; Sen. Bob Hertzberg, "A Cycle of Incarceration: Prison, Debt and Bail," video posted to YouTube by "The White House," December 3, 2015, https://www.youtube.com/watch?v=ErcSHP12deE.

8. Ruth Wilson Gilmore, *Golden Gulag: Prisons, Surplus, Crisis, and Opposition in Globalizing California* (Berkeley: University of California Press, 2007), 27 ("Where scholarship and activism overlap is in the area of how to make decisions about what comes next."); David Garland, *Punishment and Modern Society: A Study in Social Theory* (Chicago: University of Chicago Press, 1990), 277–278 ("Theoretical work seeks to change the way we think about an issue and ultimately to change the practical ways we deal with it.... When theory does succeed as a form of action, it does so first of all by changing how people perceive things.").

9. Don Herzog, "Democracy, Law, Compliance," *Law & Social Inquiry* 42, no. 1 (winter 2017): 9 ("It's dumb to count 'I would have jaywalked but the law says I shouldn't so I didn't' and 'I would have murdered those schoolchildren but the law says I shouldn't so I didn't' the same way.").

10. Ewing v. California, 538 U.S. 11, 23–24 (2003).

11. John Rawls, *Justice as Fairness: A Restatement* (Cambridge, MA: Harvard University Press, 2001), 80–87; Amartya Sen, *The Idea of Justice* (Cambridge, MA: Harvard University Press, 2009), 54–55; Sharon Dolovich, "Legitimate Punishment in Liberal Democracy," *Buffalo Law Review* 7, no. 2 (2004): 315.

12. Bryan Stevenson, *Just Mercy: A Story of Justice and Redemption* (New York: Spiegel and Grau, 2014), 14.

13. Common, "Letter to the Free" (music by Lonnie Lynn [Common], Robert Glasper and Karriem Riggins, 2017), https://www.emmys.com/shows/13th [https://perma.cc/46GP-GTC2].

14. Jonathan Simon, "The Second Coming of Dignity," in *The New Criminal Justice Thinking*, ed. Sharon Dolovich and Alexandra Natapoff (New York: New York University Press, 2017); see also Jeffrey Fagan, "Dignity Is the New Legitimacy," in Dolovich and Natapoff, *The New Criminal Justice Thinking*.

15. William J. Stuntz, "The Uneasy Relationship Between Criminal Procedure and Criminal Justice," *Yale Law Journal* 107, no. 1 (1997): 1, 23; Reva B. Siegel, "'The Rule of Love': Wife Beating as Prerogative and Privacy," *Yale Law Journal* 105 (1996): 2179 (describing the "preservation through transformation" of social norms and hierarchy in law).

16. Stanley Cohen, *Visions of Social Control: Crime, Punishment and Classification* (Cambridge, UK: Polity Press, 1985), 41–42, 44, 38; James Austin and Barry Krisberg, "Wider, Stronger, and Different Nets: The Dialectics of Criminal Justice Reform," *Journal of Research in Crime and Delinquency* 8 (1981): 188. In his study of the origins of plea bargaining, George Fisher described how prosecutors created probation, a net widener, to increase their ability to obtain plea bargains—yet another net widener. George Fisher, "Plea Bargaining's Triumph," *Yale Law Journal* 109 (2000): 957–965.

17. Cynthia H. Orr et al., *America's Problem-Solving Courts: The Criminal Costs of Treatment and the Case for Reform* (Washington, DC: National Association of Criminal Defense Lawyers, 2009), 42 (quoting Morris B. Hoffman, "The Drug Court Scandal," *North Carolina Law Review* 78 [2000]: 1505); Eric J. Miller, "Embracing Addiction: Drug Courts and the False Promise of Judicial Interventionism," *Ohio State Law Journal* 65 (2004): 1561; Richard Boldt, "Problem-Solving Courts," in *Reforming Criminal Justice*, ed. Erik Luna (Phoenix: Arizona State University, 2017), 3:273–304.

18. For a full exploration of the entire phenomenon, see Alexandra Natapoff, "Misdemeanor Decriminalization," *Vanderbilt Law Review* 68 (2015).

19. Douglas NeJaime, "Winning Through Losing," *Iowa Law Review* 96 (2011): 992 (referring to the elimination of antisodomy statutes as "decriminalization"); see also Darryl Brown, "Democracy and Decriminalization," *Texas Law Review* 86 (2007): 225 (describing legislative decriminalization broadly as including "repealing or narrowing criminal statutes, reducing offense severity, and converting low-level crimes to civil infractions").

20. Griswold v. Connecticut, 381 U.S. 479 (1965). Misdemeanors have a long history of being used to regulate gender roles and intimate behavior. William N. Eskridge, "Law and the Construction of the Closet: American Regulation of Same-Sex Intimacy, 1880–1946," *Iowa Law Review* 82 (1997): 1007–1107. Even legalization does not always eliminate the broader societal impulse to punish intimate choices. Melissa Murray, "Loving's Legacy: Decriminalization and the Regulation of Sex and Sexuality," *Fordham Law Review* 86 (2018): 2694–2700.

21. Mass. Gen. Laws Ann. chap. 272, § 53(b); *National Indigent Defense Reform: The Solution Is Multifaceted* (Chicago: American Bar Association, Standing

Committee on Legal Aid and Indigent Defendants, American Bar Association, 2012), 9, 15–16.

22. See Chapter 6.

23. Samuel R. Wiseman, "Pretrial Detention and the Right to Be Monitored," *Yale Law Journal* 123 (2014) (proposing wider use of electronic monitoring). On the risks of widespread monitoring, see United States v. Jones, 565 U.S. 400, 955 (2012) (Sotomayor, J., concurring); see also Avlana K. Eisenberg, "Mass Monitoring," *Southern California Law Review* 90 (2017): 123 (surveying history and punitive significance of electronic monitoring).

24. Robert Weisberg and Joan Petersilia, "The Dangers of Pyrrhic Victories Against Mass Incarceration," *Daedalus* 139, no. 3 (2010): 132.

25. What Ruth Gilmore might call "nonreformist reform . . . changes that, at the end of the day, unravel rather than widen the net of social control through criminalization." Gilmore, *Golden Gulag*, 242.

26. Alysia Santo, "How Conservatives Learned to Love Free Lawyers for the Poor," Marshall Project, September 24, 2017, https://www.themarshallproject.org/2017/09/24/how-conservatives-learned-to-love-free-lawyers-for-the-poor [https://perma.cc/7VJJ-QVAC].

27. New State Ice Co. v. Liebmann, 285 U.S. 262, 311 (1932) (Brandeis, J., dissenting). In a similar vein, Professor Franklin Zimring has pointed out the centrality of local government in juvenile justice reform. Franklin E. Zimring, "Levels of Government, Branches of Government, and the Reform of Juvenile Justice," *Texas Tech Law Review* 46 (2013): 1–3 ("It is local government where retail [juvenile justice] policy is made.").

28. On the history and implications of cost-driven prison reform, see Hadar Aviram, *Cheap on Crime: Recession-Era Politics and the Transformation of American Punishment* (Oakland: University of California Press, 2015). See O'Donnell v. Harris Cty, Mem. Op. at 178 (quoting district attorney); Trista Baurman et al., *No Safe Place: The Criminalization of Homelessness in U.S. Cities* (Washington, DC: National Law Center on Homelessness & Poverty, 2014), 30 (on Albuquerque homelessness program); Robert C. Boruchowitz, *Diverting and Reclassifying Misdemeanors Could Save $1 Billion per Year: Reducing the Need for and Cost of Appointed Counsel* (Washington, DC: American Constitution Society, 2010), 3–4.

29. *Fines, Fees, and Bail: Payments in the Criminal Justice System That Disproportionately Impact the Poor* (Washington, DC: White House Council of Economic Advisors, 2015), 5; *Cited in Milwaukee: The Cost of Unpaid Municipal Citations* (Milwaukee, WI: Justice Initiatives Institute, June 2015), 2–3; see also *The Outskirts of Hope: How Ohio's Debtors' Prisons Are Ruining Lives and Costing Communities* (Cleveland, OH: American Civil Liberties Union, 2013), 13 (on how costs exceed collections).

30. Richard A. Bierschbach and Stephanos Bibas, "Rationing Criminal Justice," *Michigan Law Review* 116 (2017): 191 (explaining the "correctional free lunch"); Adam M. Gershowitz, "Consolidating Local Criminal Justice: Should Prosecutors Control the Jails?," *Wake Forest Law Review* 51 (2016): 693–697 (arguing that if prosecutors rather than sheriffs were in charge of jail budgets, they would impose lower misdemeanor sentences and incarcerate fewer offenders); Cynthia G. Lee et al.,

A Community Court Grows in Brooklyn: A Comprehensive Evaluation of the Red Hook Community Justice Center (Williamsburg, VA: National Center for State Courts, 2013), 5–8 (describing the use of alternative sanctions for misdemeanor offenders and corresponding lower incarceration rates). For efforts to parse out more broadly the costs and benefits of various criminal justice practices, see Crystal S. Yang, "Toward an Optimal Bail System," *New York University Law Review* 92 (2017); Darryl K. Brown, "Cost-Benefit Analysis in Criminal Law," *California Law Review* 92 (2004).

31. Atwater v. City of Lago Vista, 532 U.S. 318, 353 (2001).

32. Terry v. Ohio, 392 U.S. 1 (1968) (giving police authority to stop and detain based on reasonable suspicion of crime); City of Chicago v. Morales, 527 U.S. 41, 53 (1999) (gang loitering statute impermissibly infringed liberty interests); City of Houston v. Hill, 482 U.S. 451, 462–463 (1987) (ordinance making it unlawful to interrupt a police officer in his duties infringed free speech rights). Those decriminalized statutes include Philadelphia Code § 10-615; N.Y. Penal Law § 240.20; Mass. Gen. Laws Ann. chap. 272, § 53(b) (West 2014).

33. *Summary of State Speed Laws*, 11th ed. (Washington, DC: National Highway Traffic Safety Administration, US Department of Transportation, April 2011), v–ix; Jordan Blair Woods, "Decriminalization, Police Authority, and Routine Traffic Stops," *UCLA Law Review* 62 (2015): 698, 707; Spangenberg Project, *An Update on State Efforts in Misdemeanor Reclassification, Penalty Reduction and Alternative Sentencing* (Fairfax, VA: Center for Justice, Law, and Society at George Mason University, 2010).

34. William H. Rehnquist, "Is an Expanded Right of Privacy Consistent with Fair and Effective Law Enforcement? Or: Privacy, You've Come a Long Way, Baby," *Kansas Law Review* 23 (1974): 1, 5, 20–21 (quoted in Christopher Slobogin, "Rehnquist and Panvasive Searches," *Mississippi Law Journal* 82 [2013]: 312–313); Risa Goluboff, *Vagrant Nation: Police Power, Constitutional Change, and the Making of the 1960s* (New York: Oxford University Press, 2016), 329 (quoting Richard Nixon, "Remarks at the Opening Session of the National Conference on the Judiciary in Williamsburg, Virginia, March 11, 1971," American Presidency Project, http://www.presidency.ucsb.edu/ws/index.php?pid=3344 [https://perma.cc/W54Z-AVGU]). See also Darryl Brown, "Decriminalization, Regulation, Privatization: A Response to Professor Natapoff," *Vanderbilt Law Review En Banc* 69 (2016): 6 (on the need for regulation of low-level antisocial conduct).

35. Rachel A. Harmon, "Why Arrest?," *Michigan Law Review* 115 (2016): 359–360.

36. Cynthia Lum and Daniel S. Nagin, "Reinventing American Policing," in *Reinventing American Criminal Justice*, ed. Michael Tonry and Daniel Nagin (Chicago: University of Chicago Press, 2017), 20, 30–32; Jeffrey Fagan, "Race and the New Policing," in *Reforming Criminal Justice*, ed. Erik Luna (Phoenix: Arizona State University, 2017), 83–116; see also Amina Khan, "In New York, Major Crime Complaints Fell When Cops Took a Break from 'Proactive Policing,'" *L.A. Times*, September 26, 2017; Harmon, "Why Arrest?," 347.

37. *Citation in Lieu of Arrest: Examining Law Enforcement's Use of Citation Across the United States* (Alexandria, VA: International Association of Chiefs of Police, April 2016), 6–7; see also Harmon, "Why Arrest?," 334–335 (on the strengths

of citation). For state responses, see Md. Code Crim. Pro. § 4–101 (limiting arrest authority). See also *Atwater*, 532 U.S. at 355–360 (collecting statutory provisions authorizing and/or limiting police arrest power for all fifty states).

38. Knafo, "A Black Police Officer's Fight"; Complaint, Raymond v. City of New York, No. 15-CV-6885-LTS-HBP (S.D.N.Y., December 10, 2015); *Investigation of the Baltimore City Police Department* (Washington, DC: US Department of Justice, Civil Rights Division, 2016); *Investigation of the Ferguson Police Department* (Washington, DC: US Department of Justice, Civil Rights Division, 2015).

39. *Final Report of the President's Task Force on 21st Century Policing* (Washington, DC: Office of Community Oriented Policing Services, May 2015), 26.

40. Compare "Crime in the U.S. 2015, Table 29," FBI Uniform Crime Reporting, https://ucr.fbi.gov/crime-in-the-u.s/2015/crime-in-the-u.s.-2015/tables/table-29 [https://perma.cc/7LWS-T5HG] (10,797,088 arrests), with "Crime in the U.S. 2006, Table 29," FBI Uniform Crime Reporting, https://ucr.fbi.gov/crime-in-the-u.s/2006 [https://perma.cc/75AX-GWJ8] (14,380,370 arrests). See also Megan Stevenson and Sandra Mayson, "The Scale of Misdemeanor Justice," *Boston University Law Review* 98 (forthcoming 2018); Ryan J. Reilly, "Dubious 'Disorderly Conduct' Arrests Plummet as the Public Turns Cameras on Cops," *Huffington Post*, September 26, 2016, https://www.huffingtonpost.com/entry/contempt-of-cop-arrests-disorderly-conduct-charges_us_57e94d56e4b0e80b1ba32d57 [https://perma.cc/8M4R-Q9HA]; Associated Press, "California Crime Initiative Leads to Lowest Arrest Rate in State's History," *New York Times*, August 21, 2016 (California Proposition 47 led to nearly 30 percent reduction in felony arrest rates and nearly 10 percent increase in misdemeanor arrest rates); Al Baker, "Street Stops by New York City Police Have Plummeted," *New York Times*, May 30, 2017 (documenting drastic reduction in New York stop-and-frisk tactics since 2011).

41. Ronald Wright and Marc Miller, "The Screening/Bargaining Tradeoff," *Stanford Law Review* 55, no. 1 (2002): 29; Josh Bowers, "Legal Guilt, Normative Innocence, and the Equitable Decision Not to Prosecute," *Columbia Law Review* 110 (2010): 1655; Ronald F. Wright, "Reinventing American Prosecution Systems," *Crime and Justice* 46, no. 1 (2017): 409 (arguing that legislatures should give courts the power to review declination decisions).

42. Testimony of Wayne S. McKenzie, Director, Prosecution & Racial Justice Program, Vera Institute of Justice, "Racial Disparities in the Criminal Justice System," before the House Judiciary Committee on Crime, Terrorism and Homeland Security (October 29, 2009), https://judiciary.house.gov/_files/hearings/pdf/McKenzie091029.pdf [https://perma.cc/ZD9N-VP2Y]; Wayne McKenzie et al., *Prosecution and Racial Justice: Using Data to Advance Fairness in Criminal Prosecution* (New York: Vera Institute of Justice, 2009), 7 (on the Milwaukee and Charlotte studies).

43. Bowers, "Legal Guilt"; see also Bruce Frederick and Don Stemen, *The Anatomy of Discretion: An Analysis of Prosecutorial Decision Making—Technical Report* (Final Report to the National Institute of Justice, December 2012), 131–135.

44. Alec Karakatsanis, "Policing, Mass Imprisonment, and the Failure of American Lawyers," *Harvard Law Review Forum* 128 (2015): 255.

45. In re Humphrey, Case No. A152056, 2018 WL550512, Slip Op. at 46 (Cal. App. January 25, 2018); Sandra Benson Brantley to Alan M. Wilner, October 25,

2016, Counsel to the General Assembly, Office of the Maryland Attorney General, to the Standing Committee on Rules of Practice and Procedure, http://www.marylandattorneygeneral.gov/News%20Documents/Rules_Committee_Letter_on_Pretrial_Release.pdf [https://perma.cc/4RL4-6NS5]; Michael Dresser, "Maryland Court of Appeals: Defendants Can't Be Held in Jail Because They Can't Afford Bail," *Baltimore Sun*, February 8, 2017; Lisa Foderaro, "New Jersey Alters Its Bail System and Upends Legal Landscape," *New York Times*, February 6, 2017; Pretrial Integrity and Safety Act of 2017, S.B. 1593 (introduced by Sen. Kamala Harris [D-CA] and Sen. Rand Paul [R-KY]); Kamala D. Harris and Rand Paul, "To Shrink Jails, Let's Reform Bail," *New York Times*, July 20, 2017; Brian E. Frosh, Maryland Attorney General, to Hon. Alan M. Milner, October 25, 2016, Maryland Rule 4-21, http://www.marylandattorneygeneral.gov/News%20Documents/Rules_Committee_Letter_on_Pretrial_Release.pdf [https://perma.cc/4RL4-6NS5].

46. Constitutional law's existing limits are delineated in Bearden v. Georgia, 461 U.S. 660 (1983), and Tate v. Short, 401 U.S. 395 (1971), but there are more options. See Note, "State Bans on Debtors' Prisons and Criminal Justice Debt," *Harvard Law Review* 129 (2016); "State Bans on Debtors' Prisons and Criminal Justice Debt—Appendix," *Harvard Law Review Forum* 129 (2016); Strattman v. Studt, 20 Ohio St.2d 95, 102–103 (1969) (holding that incarceration for failure to pay court costs violated Ohio constitution); S.B. 1913, 2017 Leg., 85th Sess. (Texas 2017) (restricting the arrest and incarceration of indigent defendants who cannot pay fines or fees). For additional reforms, see Alicia Bannon et al., *Criminal Justice Debt: A Barrier to Reentry* (New York: Brennan Center for Justice, 2010); *In for a Penny: The Rise of America's New Debtors' Prisons* (New York: American Civil Liberties Union, 2010); *Profiting from Probation: America's "Offender-Funded" Probation Industry* (New York: Human Rights Watch, February 2014).

47. Boruchowitz, *Diverting*, 7–9.

48. "Our Mission," LEAD National Support Bureau, https://www.leadbureau.org [https://perma.cc/33WK-JWPU]. On the difficulty of eliminating the criminal mark, see James B. Jacobs, *The Eternal Criminal Record* (Cambridge, MA: Harvard University Press, 2015), 133–140; Rothgery v. Gillespie Cty., 554 U.S. 191 (2008).

49. Shaila Dewan and Andrew Lehren, "After a Crime, the Price of a Second Chance," *New York Times*, December 12, 2016.

50. McWhorter and LaBahn, "Confronting the Elephants in the Courtroom."

51. See, e.g., S.B. 1913, 2017 Leg., 85th Sess. (Texas 2017).

52. Beth A. Colgan, "Graduating Economic Sanctions According to Ability to Pay," *Iowa Law Review* 103 (2017): 53, 69–72 (documenting US experimentation with day fines in the 1980s); Sally T. Hillsman, "Fines and Day Fines," *Crime and Justice* 12 (1990): 49; Joe Pinsker, "Finland, Home of the $103,000 Speeding Ticket," *The Atlantic*, March 12, 2015; Suzanne Daley, "Speeding in Finland Can Cost a Fortune, if You Already Have One," *New York Times*, April 25, 2015.

53. See *Fines, Fees, and Bail*.

54. Jenny Roberts, "Expunging America's Rap Sheet in the Information Age," *Wisconsin Law Review* 2, no. 2 (2015): 321; Michael Pinard, "Criminal Records, Race, and Redemption," NYU *Journal of Legislation and Public Policy* 16, no. 4 (2013): 989–991; Kevin Lapp, "American Criminal Record Exceptionalism," *Ohio*

State Journal of Criminal Law 14 (2016): 318–322 (proposing that protective principles from the juvenile arena be extended to criminal records more broadly).

55. Jacobs, *Eternal Criminal Record*, 308; Jenny Roberts, "Judicial Responsibility for Justice in Criminal Courts" (public remarks, Hofstra University Maurice Deane School of Law, April 6, 2017).

56. Memorandum Opinion at 17, Robinson v. Purkey, No. 3:17-cv-1263, 2017 WL 4418134 (M.D.Tenn. October 5, 2017) (holding that suspending the driver's licenses of people who cannot afford to pay is irrational). See also Order, Fowler v. Johnson, Civil Case No. 17-11441 (E.D.Mich., December 14, 2017) (granting preliminary injunction against failure-to-pay license suspensions); Alex Bender, *Not Just a Ferguson Problem: How Traffic Courts Drive Inequality in California* (San Francisco: Lawyers Committee for Civil Rights et al., 2015).

57. "Council of State Governments Collateral Consequences Database," *Justice Center—the Council of State Governments*, https://niccc.csgjusticecenter.org/search [https://perma.cc/52VT-3DPB]; Ingrid V. Eagly, "Immigrant Protective Policies in Criminal Justice," *Texas Law Review* 95 (2016): 245.

58. Michelle Wilde Anderson, "Losing the War of Attrition: Mobility, Chronic Decline, and Infrastructure," *Yale Law Journal Forum* 127 (2017): 528 (describing urban fiscal crisis); Darrick Hamilton and Michael Linden, "Issue Brief: Hidden Rules of Race Are Embedded in the New Tax Law" (New York: Roosevelt Institute, May 2018), 6–7 (on the links between reduced state and local tax revenues and higher fees and fines); *Gideon's Broken Promise: America's Continuing Quest for Equal Justice: A Report on the American Bar Association's Hearings on the Right to Counsel in Criminal Proceedings* (Chicago: American Bar Association, Standing Committee on Legal Aid and Indigent Defendants, 2004), 7–14 (describing historic and chronic underfunding of the public defense bar).

59. Lorri Montgomery, "Top National State Court Leadership Associations Launch National Task Force on Fines, Fees and Bail Practices," National Center for State Courts, February 3, 2016, http://www.ncsc.org/Newsroom/News-Releases/2016/Task-Force-on-Fines-Fees-and-Bail-Practices.aspx [https://perma.cc/74RH-52MT]; *Missouri Municipal Courts: Best Practice Recommendations* (Williamsburg, VA: National Center for State Courts, 2015), 26, https://www.courts.mo.gov/file.jsp?id=95287 [https://perma.cc/9DMN-WURE]. See also "50-State Criminal Justice Debt Reform Builder"; Henry Ordower, J. Onésimo Sandoval, and Kenneth Warren, "Out of Ferguson: Misdemeanors, Municipal Courts, Tax Distribution, and Constitutional Limitations," *Howard Law Journal* 61 (2017): 113; "Developments in the Law: Policing: Chapter One: Policing and Profit," *Harvard Law Review* 128 (2015): 1723.

60. Md. Code Ann., Cts. and Jud. Proc. § 7-302(g) (West); Annie Gilbertson, "Prop 47: Tracking Lawmakers' Promise of Drug Treatment over Prison," 89.3 KPCC, March 17, 2016, http://www.scpr.org/news/2016/03/17/58455/prop-47-promised-drug-treatment-instead-of-prison [https://perma.cc/WD94-JDGD]; Robert Patrick, "Almost a Year After Ferguson, Missouri Passes Court Reforms," Governing, July 13, 2015, http://www.governing.com/topics/public-justice-safety/tns-missouri-court-reform-law.html [https://perma.cc/Y3YZ-Y7HW] (quoting Governor Nixon). Parts of the Missouri law were subsequently struck down as unconstitutional. On conflicts of interest, see Ward v. Monroeville, 409 U.S. 57 (1972); Carl Reynolds

et al., *2011–12 Policy Paper: Courts Are Not Revenue Centers* (Williamsburg, VA: Conference of State Court Administrators, 2012); *Missouri Municipal Courts*, 26–29.

61. See Amy Bach, *Ordinary Injustice: How America Holds Court* (New York: Holt, 2009), 35–36; US Const. amend. VI ("In all criminal prosecutions, the accused shall enjoy the right to a speedy and public trial").

62. *Missouri Municipal Courts.*

63. Penson v. Ohio, 488 U.S. 75, 84 (1988). On the lack of misdemeanor counsel around the country, see *Gideon's Broken Promise*; Boruchowitz et al., *Minor Crimes*; Diane DePietropaolo Price et al., *Summary Injustice: A Look at Constitutional Deficiencies in South Carolina's Summary Courts* (Washington, DC: National Association of Criminal Defense Lawyers, 2016), 19–20. On attorney caseloads and standards for misdemeanor defense, see *ABA Standards for Criminal Justice Providing Defense Services*, 3rd ed. (Washington, DC: American Bar Association, 1992), 72, n.13; Wilbur v. City of Mount Vernon, 989 F. Supp. 2d 1122, 1124 (W.D.Wash. 2013). See also Irene Oritseweyinmi Joe, "Rethinking Misdemeanor Neglect," *UCLA Law Review* 64 (2017) (arguing that public defender offices should redirect resources to prioritize misdemeanors).

64. Scott v. Illinois, 440 U.S. 367 (1979) (holding that misdemeanor defendants who are not actually incarcerated are not entitled to counsel); 18 U.S.C. § 3006A; N.Y. Crim. Pro. Law § 170.10(3) (providing counsel for misdemeanors).

65. Alexandra Natapoff, "Gideon Skepticism," *Washington and Lee Law Review* 70 (2013): 1049.

66. See Stephanos Bibas, *The Machinery of Criminal Justice* (Oxford: Oxford University Press, 2012).

67. Thirty-two states and the District of Columbia currently report aggregate caseload data to the Court Statistics Project. "About the Court Statistics Project," Court Statistics Project DataViewer (Williamsburg, VA: National Center for State Courts, 2017), http://www.courtstatistics.org [https://perma.cc/V363-VNWV].

68. Florida recently passed this kind of legislation. Amy Bach, "Missing: Criminal Justice Data," *New York Times*, March 21, 2018. More of this information will become available through the new Measures for Justice database (https://measuresforjustice .org [https://perma.cc/J6US-6LRF]).

69. Alec Karakatsanis, interview with author, June 7, 2017 (notes on file with author).

70. See Bob Edwards and John D. McCarthy, "Resources and Social Movement Mobilization," in *The Blackwell Companion to Social Movements*, ed. David A. Snow et al. (Oxford, UK: Blackwell Publishing, Ltd., 2004), 125–128 (categorizing social movement resources in order to better understand the impact of stratification on the possibilities for social mobilization); Douglas NeJaime, "The Legal Mobilization Dilemma," *Emory Law Journal* 61 (2012): 663 (surveying the benefits and challenges of various forms of social and legal mobilizations).

71. On reforming the crack-cocaine sentencing disparity, see David A. Sklansky, "Cocaine, Race, and Equal Protection," *Stanford Law Review* 47 (1995): 1283. On the often long and circuitous route to change, see Michael J. Klarman, "Brown, Racial Change, and the Civil Rights Movement," *Virginia Law Review* 80, no. 1 (1994): 7 (tracing how Brown v. Board of Education indirectly transformed US race

relations); William J. Stuntz, *The Collapse of American Criminal Justice* (Cambridge, MA: Harvard University Press, 2011), 6–7, 287 (arguing that more local democracy would empower communities to improve their criminal justice systems).

EPILOGUE

1. Not my former client's real name. This story originally appeared in Alexandra Natapoff, "The Penal Pyramid," in *The New Criminal Justice Thinking*, ed. Sharon Dolovich and Alexandra Natapoff (New York: New York University Press, 2017), 91–92.

INDEX

ALEXANDRA NATAPOFF is professor of law at the University of California, Irvine. A 2016 Guggenheim Fellow, she is also author of *Snitching: Criminal Informants and the Erosion of American Justice*, which won the 2010 American Bar Association Silver Gavel Award Honorable Mention for Books, and coeditor of *The New Criminal Justice Thinking*, which won a 2017 Choice Outstanding Academic Title Award. She lives in Irvine, California.

Photo courtesy of Loyola Law School, Los Angeles